PROFITABLE FOOTWEAR RETAILING

PROFITABLE FOOTWEAR RETAILING

William A. Rossi

FAIRCHILD PUBLICATIONS
NEW YORK

Designed by Juliana Barnes

Standard Book Number: 87005-630-1

Library of Congress Catalog Number: 87-83191

Printed in the United States of America

Table of Contents

Preface

*"A man who does not have
a picture of the whole in his
head cannot possibly arrange
the pieces." (Montaigne)*

You often hear shoe people say, "I love shoe business. It's fascinating because it's filled with excitement, constant change, fresh ideas, new challenges, creative and imaginative people." That's the good news. Then there are other shoe people with another view: "Shoe business is filled with problems and headaches—the worries, the long hours, the pressures, the mistakes, the disappointments. I don't know why I stay with it."

One's involvement with shoe business is often a love-hate relationship. It has its highs and lows, its periods of euphoria and depression, its victories and defeats, its spells of ego-pride and its times of humility. In short, shoe business is a mirror of life itself. It was never meant to be easy. Nothing worth having ever is.

As any experienced merchant knows, there is no magic formula for success in retailing, no magic button to press to open the doors to success. What experience teaches is that success in retailing involves the coordination of a lot of separate parts that comprise the whole in a business operation. Like a jigsaw puzzle, if all the pieces are put into the right places in the right way, the final picture comes out right. And that's the essence of this book—presenting the many separate pieces that make up the whole for a profitable shoe business.

The careers of most shoe people are usually focused on one specialized segment: manufacturing, sales, retailing, designing or styling, fitting, fashion, marketing, buying, etc. As both an observer and active participant in shoe business for over 40 years, my own career has perhaps been much more varied than most. Starting as an apprentice in my father's family shoe store in my early teens (he was also a custom shoemaker), my shoe business roots were planted early.

After a short spell as a practicing podiatrist and instructor, for the next 20 years I served as editor of two footwear industry publications, followed by another 20 years as a footwear industry consultant. This broad range of involvement gave me the opportunity to intimately observe and participate in the operations of almost every segment of the industry—shoe and leather manufacturing, retailing, fashion and styling, sales, advertising, marketing, fitting, foot health, research, etc. It also allowed for extensive travel, such as visiting and studying the footwear industries and retailing in some 24 different countries, including Russia and the East European nations.

I cite this background for a particular reason. This unique experience provided me with the opportunity to view footwear and shoe business from an advantageous, panoramic view. This has been invaluable in learning how all the operating parts work together to form the whole that we call the shoe industry and shoe business. While it's important for a career to be focused on one specialized area, this also has its shortcomings. For example, the shoe manufacturer knows every detail about production, but he may have little understanding of retailing. The same with the shoe retailer in reverse. The stylist or designer has intimate knowledge of fashion and fashion trends, but is likely to have little understanding of shoe fitting or retail operations. The podiatrist knows the foot but usually has little knowledge about shoes. The tanner is skilled in leathermaking but has very limited knowledge about shoe manufacturing or shoe selling.

And so it goes, specialization without versatility; great strength at the center, but weaknesses in the important areas around the center. It's like asking: Which star or planet is the center of the universe? For each star or planet, *it* is the center around which everything orbits. But to the astronomer with the advantage of the broader perspective, there is no center. There is only the whole, the universe, with each star or planet as only a part of the whole.

I have prepared this book with the same concept in mind. I have focused on one galaxy, shoe retailing, and have tried to give individual attention to each of the important stars that comprise the whole galaxy. This becomes the "universe" of shoe retailing. Thus, for a given store, if each star is in its right orbit and functioning properly, the galaxy of the store's various operations becomes an efficient unit, a profitable whole.

Over the many years both as an editor and consultant, I was often asked by shoe retailers, both beginners and experienced, to recommend a good book on shoe retailing. Surprisingly, there wasn't a single such book available in the United States—no "complete" book on shoe retailing published over the past 75 years. Many times in the past I had thought about writing such a book, but there always seemed to be other priorities that got in the way. A couple of years ago I gave the book top priority and wrote it.

I continue to be amazed at the expanding size of shoe retailing in our economy and the appreciable role it plays in the lives of consumers. Some numbers illustrate this. For example, in 1987, retail footwear sales surpassed $26 billion, and by 1995 should reach or exceed $40 billion. In 1987, 1.2 billion pairs of footwear were sold, and by 1995 the pairage will amount to 1.6 billion. That, obviously, is a huge amount of transactions at retail.

But even more startling are the figures of traffic that passes through retail footwear outlets. In 1987, an estimated 1.6 *billion* people visited retail shoe outlets. A billion of them made actual purchases, while the remainder consisted of "lookers," or friends and relatives accompanying the buying customers, or shoppers going from store to store seeking the right style or price, etc.

But 1.6 billion people is 6½ times the size of the total U.S. population. That's an enormous amount of traffic exposed to footwear and retail shoe outlets each year. It indicates the immense sales potential of footwear, plus related accessories, if retailers do full justice to these traffic prospects. But perhaps most retailers don't. Relative to traffic, shoe retailers fall short of their potentials—an estimated 40 percent short of the sales that *could* be made but aren't.

And that very theme is the objective of this book: recognizing the exciting opportunities of shoe business, and how to improve sales and profits and stimulate store growth and prosperity.

William A. Rossi
Marshfield, Massachusetts

1

Introduction: A Short History of American Shoe Retailing

Shoe retailing in America got off to an awkward, bumbling beginning. In fact, it wasn't until 174 years after the Pilgrims landed in 1620 that the first shoe store started. So over those first two centuries, how did people buy or get their footwear?

There were any of several ways. They could be made by a shoemaker (though the first two shoemakers, Thomas Beard and Isaac Rickman didn't arrive until 1629). It wasn't unusual for a family to buy leather, or use the crudely tanned hide from a horse or buck, to make their own shoes. Except for the colder months or Sunday church-going, most children and often adults went barefoot. The few more affluent Puritan families ordered fashionable shoes from London or Paris.

If a family lived in a rural area, as most did, they were visited about once a year by itinerant shoemakers who traveled on horseback or with a little wagon. The shoemaker would stay two or more days making shoes for the family (his wages were pegged by law at 12 pence a day). He also rendered other services like sharpening tools and pulling teeth.

In the Colonial days shoe prices were set by the inch. The larger the size the more the cost because the larger sizes required more leather and labor. Today, we still use essentially the same pricing system for juvenile shoes.

There were no ready-made shoes. In the shoemaking shops you haggled about price. It was a buyer-beware situation because many shoemakers lacked scruples. In fact, the first consumer action case on U.S. court record was in 1648, when shoemaker Goodman Meigs was sued by a group of townspeople for making defective shoes sold at full price. The court ruled that "he made and sold shoes of such fault material, and so loaded with evils of workmanship, the court is appalled." He was severely fined.

That lawsuit spawned America's first guild, The Shoemakers of Boston. Members were required to abide by a code of ethics to eliminate inferior workmanship and deceptive pricing.

Nothing much changed until 1750 when a Welshman, John Adams Dagyr, introduced the first "assembly line" shoemaking in his Lynn, Massachusetts shop. All shoes were still made entirely by hand. But with Dagyr's system, instead of each shoemaker making the shoe start to finish, each now did one specialized task or operation until the finished product emerged. This greatly speeded the process.

START OF RETAILING

As a result of Dagyr's system, a surplus of shoes in excess of those made to order became available. These were the first ready-made shoes and were called "unordered" or "sale" shoes. They were shown in the shop windows, sometimes with a boy outside hawking the shoes to passersby. These became the first factory outlet shops.

Other shops adopted the Dagyr system. There wasn't enough "bespoke" (custom) work to go around. Shoemakers found themselves with more idle time, which they put to use producing ready-made or "sale" shoes. They began selling their shoes to general merchants who traded or bartered in a wide variety of merchandise—grain and feed, flour and fish, harness, cloth, tools, etc., including shoes and boots. These were little more than trading posts. There still wasn't an exclusive shoe retailer.

With the ready-made shoes there wasn't the vaguest semblance of shoe sizes. The shoes came in two lengths, long and short, and two widths, fat and slim. From there, the wearer endured the breaking-in ordeal.

Even the book stores and bookbinders were making and selling some shoes. They used their leftover bookbinding leathers to make women's shoes.

The first "retailer" to offer a wide selection of ready-made shoes to the public was Thomas F. Pierce & Sons of Providence, Rhode Island, in 1767. Nevertheless, shoes were only one of many commodities in his establishment. It wasn't until the early 19th century that his place became a full-fledged shoe store and remained so thereafter until 1956, after 189 years.

In the South there were few shoemakers. A large plantation owner would offer the handsome wage of $1.50 a day and "import" a skilled shoemaker from the North. He made shoes for all the plantation personnel, sometimes also for those on neighboring plantations.

The less lucky plantations bought "sale" shoes from the North. Each slave broke off a stick, called a stoga, to the length of his or her foot. These were bundled and sent north for shoes to be made to the stick or stoga size. Later, when crude, cheap cigars were made and sold in small bundles, they were called "stogies" after the rough sticks—a name still in use today.

During the first half of the 1700s, shoemakers were paid piecework wages of 15 to 25 cents a pair, averaging $4 to $6 a week. Price haggling was common and it was a matter of buyer beware. Finally, under pressure from the Quakers, Pennsylvania fixed shoe prices by law: 6 shillings and 6 pence for a pair of well-made men's shoes, 5 shillings for women's, 4 for children's. The price system spread to other colonies.

By 1750, shoes sold for less than a shirt or pair of stockings. A good shoemaker could make two pairs over a 12-hour day. By 1776, shoemakers were earning 50 to 75 cents a day.

In 1776, when America officially became an independent nation, the U.S. population was 2.5 million, average annual per family income $634, family size averaged six persons, 45 percent of the population was 15 years and under, farm workers comprised 95 percent of the work force, and there were only four cities with populations of 10,000 or more.

The shoe "industry" was burgeoning and prospering. There were some 8,000 shoemaking shops. They now began to protest against footwear "imports" from England and France. So in 1789, one of the first acts of the new Congress was imposition of tariffs on footwear—the first American tariff on any product. A duty of 50 cents a pair was placed on boots, 7 cents on shoes. In 1794 this was raised to 15 percent of cost.

In 1789, the Society of Master Cordwainers was founded in Philadelphia to distinguish their members from the inferior craftsmen who produced inferior "sale" shoes. These lesser skilled workmen were known as "cobblers," an insulting term to a cordwainer (a name derived from the famed shoe and leather craftsmen of Cordova, Spain).

THE FIRST SHOE STORE

The brothers Quincy and Harvey Reed were young shoemakers in Weymouth, Massachusetts, about 12 miles outside of Boston. Like many shoemakers, they were making both custom and sale shoes. Twice weekly they loaded their sale shoes onto their small wagon and went to Boston, where they sold the shoes to passersby on the street.

Their business grew. In 1794 they rented a small shop in Broad Street and moved their shoes from the wagon into the store. The store was open only on Wednesdays and Saturdays because there wasn't enough business to support this new-fangled specialty store more days of the week. It was America's first store selling shoes exclusively at retail. The prices were $2 a pair for the best boots and shoes, $1.50 for others.

Over the next ten years the Reed's business thrived and was now open six days a week, 7 AM to 7 PM. Other shoe stores opened, not only in Boston but in New York, Philadelphia and Baltimore. American shoe retailing was officially launched nearly two centuries ago.

There was no such thing as fitting service. Shoes were hung from a wire or rope. The customer selected what he or she thought was a suitable size and tried them on. They bought when a reasonable fit was found. So the first shoe stores were mostly self-service.

There was a small elitist shoe trade catered to by a few master cordwainers. While wealthier gentlemen went to the shops for their custom boots or shoes, the craftsmen would go to the homes of the wealthy "by appointment" to measure the feet of the ladies for the making of their footwear. It wasn't unusual for these craftsmen to wear gloves so that their "bare hands" would not touch the foot or ankle of the ladies, a gesture considered an unthinkable intimacy.

The wholesaling of shoes exclusively began about the same time as shoe retailing. The wholesale shoe trade began as early as 1790 with shoes sold in lots "for cash or barter" by auction shoe houses. The Rich Brothers of Boston were the first to open an auction house, the equivalent of a wholesaler or jobber, selling shoes and boots exclusively.

Macah Faxon of North Bridgewater (now Brockton), Massachusetts, was the first to produce shoes solely for the wholesale trade, in 1811. His first large-lot sale was to the firm of Monroe and Nash, who then sold and shipped the shoes to the South. Faxon was also the first "manufacturer" to sell shoes to the growing number of shoe stores whose sole function was shoe retailing.

In 1820, Popple's Shoe Store opened in Newport, Rhode Island. It was to continue for 165 years until it closed its doors in 1985—the longest continuous run on record for any American shoe store. In 1832, Colburn's Shoe Store started in Belfast, Maine. Today it is still in operation, now the oldest extant shoe store in America.

By 1825, St. Louis and Chicago had begun their own small shoemaking enterprises. Massachusetts was producing 70 percent of the expanding nation's footwear and was developing a good export trade.

In the middle of the 19th century there were an estimated 1,100 retail shoe stores, and about 25 wholesalers dealing exclusively in boots and shoes. In 1825, the first shoe cartons and shoe boxes were produced. Up to then, footwear was shipped to retailers in barrels.

The big explosion came in the late 1850s with the world's first machine-made shoes. Two new American shoe machines were the catalyst: Howe's sewing machine for stitching uppers, and the McKay sewing machine for stitching soles to uppers.

For footwear, this was the beginning of the industrial revolution. Prior to then it took a skilled shoemaker almost a day to make a pair of boots or shoes. With the new machines, one person could turn out 10 pairs. There were mass protests by shoemakers against the machines that threatened their livelihood. This soon quelled as their wages shot up to $1.75 a day and over $300 a year. By 1870, shoe manufacturing was America's largest industry and largest employer.

The shoe "industry" began to mature enough to support its first trade publication. In 1857 the *Shoe and Leather Reporter* was founded to serve both the wholesale and retail trade. It was the country's second trade publication. It survived 94 years, until 1954.

The Civil War broke out and the machine shoe factories of the North mass-produced the needed shoes for the Union Army. Ulysses S. Grant, himself a tanner, was later to say that without the supply of shoes and boots the North may not have won the war. The South was severely handicapped because it had no machine shoe factories.

There were other important parts of the industrial revolution during this period. The first left and right shoes were introduced for the soldiers, a great aid on their long marches. Up to then, and throughout history, almost all footwear was made on "straight" lasts for the economic reason that they could be worn on either foot and thus required only one last instead of a pair to make them. Nevertheless, after the war the shoes went back to straight lasts. It wouldn't be until the end of the century that lefts and rights would be available on a mass basis. They were first known as "crooked shoes," and the first men to wear them were called "sports."

The first sneakers with rubber soles and cloth uppers were introduced in 1868 and were called "croquet shoes." They were expensive and worn only by the rich.

Retail shoe stores were now prospering, even though their markup or margin averaged only about 20 percent (margins were to gradually rise to 28 percent in 1890, 33 percent in 1925, 42 percent in 1950, and 50 percent in 1965). But the mass production of machine-made shoes substantially lowered prices and made shoes much more affordable.

"Fashion" began to enter shoe business with women's kidskin and calfskin boots in colors at around $1.75 a pair. High button boots (14 buttons per shoe) were introduced, and with it another innovation, the buttonhook, which became as essential as shoe horns in shoe stores.

RETAILING INNOVATIONS

The first shoe traveler, Joel C. Page, appeared in 1852. He worked for the shoe wholesaling house of James A. Estabrook, Boston. He was the first to sell shoes by traveling with samples to stores. His first retail customer was a store in Montpelier, Vermont. Prior to then, the shoe retailer went to the wholesale/jobbers or auction houses to look over the samples and place his order. The second shoe traveler was Edward Ray of Rochester, New York, in 1855.

By 1885, almost all manufacturers and wholesalers had traveling salesmen. In April of that year the first shoe travelers organization was formed, The Boot and Shoe Travelers League, in Boston, later to evolve into the National Shoe Travelers Association.

A year later the first shoe retailers organization was established—the Retail Boot & Shoe Dealers' National Association, in Philadelphia, 1886. In 1912, the current National Shoe Retailers Association was founded, also in Philadelphia.

New shoemaking technology was advancing at a rapid rate. Between 1865 and 1900 hundreds of new shoemaking machines, methods and components were invented and applied. It was the glory era of American shoemaking. In 1870, there were 7,570 tanneries in the U.S. (compared with about 100 today). The combined shoe and leather manufacturing industry was the country's largest, and by 1910 two of the ten biggest corporations were tanners.

Shoe retailing was also moving into its own age of innovation. In 1880, Edwin B. Simpson of New York developed and introduced the world's first system of standardized shoe sizes and measurements for men's, women's, children's and infants' footwear. It was a phenomenal breakthrough, and in 1886 was officially adopted by manufacturers and retailers alike. It was the first time that half sizes and several widths per size appeared. Up until then, shoe sizes were chaotic, lacking uniformity or system, each manufacturer and lastmaker free to use his own measurements.

But even with Simpson's new system to create clarity out of confusion, it still took another 20 years before it became universal in the industry.

Retailers became zealous about the new "scientific" shoe fitting, and eventually, in 1900, even quarter sizes were introduced, though these had a short life because of the inventory problems.

The "heart" sizes in women's shoes were 1 to 6, widths D and E, in contrast to today's heart sizes of 6 to 10, widths B and C.

The first fitting stool was introduced in 1887 by the Sellers Shoe Mfg. Co., Philadelphia. It was quickly adopted and became standard equipment in shoe stores.

In 1882, the *Boot & Shoe Recorder,* a leading magazine for shoe retailers, was started. It prospered until 1974, a reign of 92 years.

With competition intensifying, shoe manufacturers became more aware of marketing. In 1886, John H. Hanan was the first to stamp his name on the sole of every shoe he produced. In the same year his company ran the first shoe brand advertising in a national magazine. A year later Hanan & Son became the first retail shoe store chain.

A New York shoe manufacturer, Edwin C. Burt, was the first to offer his retailers free window and counter display cards, in 1870.

W. L. Douglas, a Brockton, Massachusetts, shoe manufacturer, innovated by stamping the retail price of the shoes on the soles. He also opened his own retail store chain which prospered right into the 1950s.

Shoe retailing was also spreading into other areas. In 1879, Lord & Taylor of New York was the first department store to have a full-fledged shoe department. A year later, John Wanamaker of Philadelphia opened a shoe department in his store—the first with electric lighting. In the same year it became the first store to run a full-page newspaper ad.

Montgomery-Ward, in 1878, was the first mail order house to show shoes in its nationally distributed "catalog"—a one-page sheet with pictures and prices.

Milligram's Women's Shoe Store, Rochester, New York, created a buzz when it became the first shoe store to run a newspaper ad using shoe art and illustrations.

In 1890, America's largest department store was A. T. Stewart & Co., New York, with over 1,700 employees and occupying a full block on Broadway at 9th Street. The average daily traffic was 15,000, but with peaks of 50,000. Its shoe department was open from 7 AM to 7 PM.

At the World's Fair in Chicago in 1893, inventor Whitcomb L. Judson introduced the first "hookless fastener" or zipper. It was originally designed for use on footwear to replace laces, buttons and buckles. His firm, the Hookless Fastener Co., became Talon, Inc., in 1937. The term "zipper" was first used by B. F. Goodrich in the 1930s when it introduced zippered galoshes to replace buckles.

Though zippers were originally designed for footwear, they never really took hold. But they became big in apparel and many other articles, and today 1.6 billion of them valued at $200 million are sold in the U.S. alone.

Just before the turn of the century the fitting of women's shoes by men was a delicate and touchy business. For a male salesperson to touch a woman's ankle or lower leg during the fitting process was just short of scandalous. Some of the larger stores advertised "special fitting booths with trained females to render fitting services to ladies."

In the 1960s, Mrs. Ellen Robbins, who at age 74 retired after working 47 years for the Marott Shoe Store in Broad Ripple, Indiana, vividly remembered selling high button boots to women in the early part of this century. In her recollections, published in the *Indianapolis Star,* she said, "We couldn't even raise the customer's skirt above the ankles. And if a salesman slipped and touched the woman's ankle, it was considered outrageous."

In 1869, the New England Shoe & Leather Association was founded, continuing until the early 1970s when it was merged with the National Shoe Manufacturers Association. Its 104-year history made it the oldest trade association in the country.

In 1905, the National Boot & Shoe Manufacturers Association was founded (later to undergo several name changes to become today's Footwear Industries of America). There had previously been several small, short-lived national shoe manufacturers groups.

The first National Shoe Fair took place in 1921 in New York. Prior to then there had been a few regional shoe shows, but this was the first on a national scale for retailers.

The greatest shoe show ever presented in America occurred in 1909, the First World's Shoe & Leather Fair, in Cambridge, Massachusetts, facing Boston's skyline. It was attended by 50,000 persons, equivalent to an attendance of 150,000 today. It was a spectacular, covering 83,000 square feet of exhibit space. Up until then, it was the world's largest exhibit ever presented by one industry, and was attended by a host of dignitaries—governors, congressmen, celebrities. At the time, the shoe industry was the country's third largest employer. Shoe production in 1909 was 286 million pairs, more than the 245 million of 1986. The event, which lasted five days, was open to the public for three days, then exclusively to retailers and buyers for two days.

In 1918, America's largest shoe store was R. H. Fyfe & Co., Detroit, with 73,000 square feet of space.

THE NEW AGE OF SHOE RETAILING

The 1920s ushered in a new age of shoe retailing. It was a radical and abrupt turnabout of every traditional retailing practice that had existed before. It introduced a series of major innovations: mass, popular-price fashion; shoe shows, the era of arch support and "corrective" shoes; the shoe chains; seasonal shoe and leather colors; rapid style turnover in lasts; the debut of the shoe designers; the upward movement of retail markons; the elevation of women's heels to new heights of 20/8 and 24/8; fashion shoe shows with live models and runways.

For the first time in history, fashion footwear for the general public burst onto the scene in 1921. Up until then, footwear fashion was elitist, expensive and only for the few. But suddenly in the 1919–1920 period two events had a cataclysmic effect: the passage of the Volstead Act (prohibition of liquor), and women's suffrage, for the first time giving women the vote.

Emancipated women moved into the Roaring Twenties and the Flapper Age with skirts that shot up scandalously from the ankle to knee length. This full view of the leg gave the foot new exposure and prominence. It demanded to be dressed up. And so entered footwear fashion for the masses. Both manufacturers and retailers were unprepared. There were no shoe designers, stylists or fashion coordinators. Nevertheless, the industry quickly adapted, and soon a huge flow of fashionable footwear at popular prices ($2 to $4 a pair) poured onto the market.

Shoe shows highlighting fashion made their bow. The first shoe show with a theatrical fashion presentation—live models on a runway—occurred in 1922 in Boston. Other shoe shows adopted the same.

But the sudden flood of fashion created problems for retailers. Markdowns became a major headache. Buying became more difficult with the rapid seasonal turnover of styles, plus the problem of selection in colors, patterns, heel heights, plus the timing of buys. More brand names flourished as manufacturers vied for a competitive edge.

In 1915, the Textile Color Card Association had been formed, and in 1919 the shoe and leather industry joined for the selection of seasonal colors for leathers and footwear. Up until then it had been chaos, with each manufacturer trying to push his own colors. Now there was some cohesion of colors throughout the industry.

The shoe chains became an influential force beginning in the early 1920s. W. L. Douglas now had several hundred stores. Regal Shoe Co. also numbered over 200 stores, with all shoes at one price. In 1922, the first Thom McAn store opened in New York. On opening day it had 141 customers who bought the one-price men's and boys' shoes at $4 ($2 under the competition), and offered an astounding 27 styles.

The 1920s, with its abrupt and radical new directions, was perhaps the most dramatic decade in the history of shoe retailing, before or since.

THE SUBSEQUENT YEARS

The grim depression years of the 1930s made all retailing a struggle for survival. So-called popular-price shoes sold for $3 and $4 a pair, and 94 percent of all footwear sold for under $8 a pair. Mostly all leather. By 1935 there were 16,000 shoe stores employing 55,000.

By 1939, retail footwear sales for the first time reached the $1 billion mark (as compared with nearly $30 billion today). Shoe stores (chains and independents) accounted for 68 percent of all footwear business, department stores another 25 percent. In shoe stores and other retail outlets the minimum wage was 40 cents an hour, and average weekly wages for a 48-hour week were $20 to $22.

The postwar years between 1946 and 1960 brought the next major upheaval in shoe retailing. With the rapid postwar economic expansion the mass exodus to the suburbs began, and an explosion of new births prevailed for almost 20 years. It was a totally new lifestyle for America with the entry of "casual" living that spawned the massive influence of casual clothing and footwear, a major new category.

The 1950s ushered in a new concept, the highway or free standing shoe stores, most of which had a short life. Retailing began its major restructuring with the burgeoning discount stores, the fast-expanding regional shopping centers and strip centers, the opening of suburban branches by the department stores, the rapid opening of shoe stores in the suburbs, the startup of self-service shoe stores, the spread of factory-owned shoe stores. It was a major relocation of retail shoe business. Downtown was no longer king.

It was also a severe shakeout period for the independents. Many mom-and-pop stores and other marginals were forced to close against the competition of the faster-moving newer retailers. Other independents sold out to the expanding factory-owned shoe store organizations. Rising costs forced markons to rise from 44–45 percent to 47 percent, and by the early 1960s to 50 percent.

By the 1970s the restructuring was still in process with the entry of off-price retailing, the closed malls, the factory outlet malls, membership buying clubs, super discount stores and other "unorthodox" retailers whose policy, for the most part, was low margins and prices, high volume and self-service. By the early 1980s, shoe stores (independents and chains) were accounting for only about 40 percent of total footwear business.

Footwear imports had begun seriously in the early 1960s, and by 1985 had captured almost 80 percent of the total U.S. footwear market. The number of domestic shoe manufacturers had declined from 1,000 in 1968 to about 225 in

1987—and of those, the top 100 accounted for 75 percent of the shipments. Some 60 percent of the imports were being brought in by domestic manufacturers, many of whom had become more distributors than manufacturers. The number of nationally advertising footwear brands had fallen sharply as many domestic lines disappeared.

SHOE RETAILING'S FUTURE

Where is shoe retailing likely to go during the remainder of this century? Nobody, of course, has an infallible crystal ball. But there are some strong probabilities. Among them:

Electronic retailing. The computer will be as essential to the shoe store as the cash register. Computers of various sophisticated levels to serve a host of functions.

Just-in-time buying by retailers with just-in-time delivery by resources. Buying much closer to selling season, with resources able to produce equally fast to meet delivery schedules.

Growth of retail footwear sales averaging an increase of $1.5 to $2 billion annually—and by the year 2000 reaching about $55 to $60 billion.

More diversification of merchandise lines in shoe stores and departments. More accessories lines. A natural considering that these stores and departments handle an annual traffic of around 1.5 billion.

A further shrinkage of independent shoe stores, with virtual elimination of the chronic marginals. An inevitable consequence of competition from a widening variety of outlets selling footwear. The strong and alert independents will continue to prosper and remain the toughest of all competition.

Shoe shows will continue to experience the same dilemmas and conflicts of timing and location.

Via computer screens, retailers will be hooked up to resources to obtain instant information on availability of wanted styles, colors, prices, closeouts, deliveries, and much other information. Orders and fill-ins will be placed the same way. And even screened "previews" of new shoes via computers.

"Standard" markons will rise to 60 percent or more to cover inexorable rises in costs and the need for more margin for reasonable profit.

Invasion of the mass merchandisers (chains, major discounters, etc.) into smaller towns of 6,000 to 10,000 as regional centers and sites become saturated (this trend has already begun.) Small-town independents, up to now safely isolated, will feel the competitive squeeze.

Department stores will continue to see a shrinkage in their share of footwear business—from 24 percent in the 1950s, to about 17 percent today, probably declining to 14 percent. They're being nibbled by too many outsiders and newcomers.

Consumers buying from home computer screens is unlikely to have much influence on footwear, a product which the consumer wants to touch and also needs to try on for size.

The demographics are important. Over the next 15 years the huge and dominant bulge in the population will be in the 45-years-and-up age group. This indicates more conservative tastes and lifestyles—likely reflected in more classic styling in clothes and footwear.

It will also mean more importance for national brands, more and better retailing services, and upgraded quality. The trend will continue toward better educated consumers with higher incomes—indicating consumers who are more selective and with more understanding of value.

Shoe retailing itself will intensify in competitiveness as retail outlets selling footwear become more diversified, giving the consumer a broader scope of choice.

As we've seen, shoe retailing in America started and grew more by accident than by plan. It was a long process of adaptation to changing lifestyles and a public's evolving needs and wants.

Perhaps its prime characteristic has been its many imaginative innovations in both technology and merchandising. This is what has given American shoe retailing its unpredictability, its excitement and creative force.

WHOLESALE AND RETAIL

Where did our words "wholesale" and "retail" come from?

Wholesale is from very early English. A wholesaler is one who buys merchandise in large or "whole" lots to sell in smaller lots to retailers.

The retailer buys from the wholesaler for resale to the consumer in even smaller lots.

The word "retail" comes from the French *tailleur,* meaning to cut into pieces. For example, a tailor cuts up a bolt of cloth to sell in small pieces, or to sew the small pieces together into a garment for resale to a consumer. He deals in small, cutup pieces of the whole.

Retailer is also linked to other words of ancient origin. For example, *detail,* a small part of the whole.

And *tally*—keeping score of the small parts of the whole.

Thus a *re-tailer* is one who repeatedly buys and resells in small lots of the whole.

SOME FIRSTS IN AMERICAN RETAILING

1) The first department store. Uncertain among three. Lord & Taylor began as a general merchandise store in 1826, evolved into a large specialty store. Macy's began as a specialty store in 1858, and became a department store in 1879. Wanamaker's, Philadelphia, started in 1876 and is believed to be the first "real" department store.

2) The first retail shoe chain: Hanan & Son, in 1885.

3) The first mail order house: Montgomery-Ward in 1872. It also issued the first mail "catalog," a one-page sheet.

4) The first self-service store was Piggly Wiggly, which started in Memphis, Tennessee, in 1916.

5) The first shopping center: Country Club Plaza, Kansas City, Missouri, 1925.

6) The first cash register was invented in 1879 by James Ritty, who went on to found the National Cash Register Co. in 1882.

7) The first "satisfaction guaranteed or money back" policy was advertised in 1843 by J. Sullivan Foster, Manchester, New Hampshire (though this innovation has sometimes been credited to John Wanamaker).

8) The first returned goods policy, introduced by Marshall Field & Co. in 1852.

9) The first "odd price" policy (prices ending in odd cents), initiated by R. H. Macy, New York, about 1860.

10) The first bargain table began with F. W. Woolworth in 1881. He placed all his "closeouts" on one table with a sign, "Anything on this table 5 cents." About the same time Macy's did the same with its chinaware.

11) The first bargain basement was started by Marshall Field & Co. in 1880, advertised as an "underprice basement."

12) The first resident buying office originated with Frederick Atkins, New York, in 1888.

13) The first automatic bargain basement began with Filene's, Boston, in 1909. Prices were reduced 25 percent after 12 selling days; another 25 percent at the end of 18 selling days, and another 25 percent at the end of 24 selling days, then given to charity after 30 selling days.

14) The first retail employees strike occurred in 1835 with the retail clerks of Philadelphia and was citywide. The clerks "requested" the merchants from the sunrise-to-sunset policy to a schedule of 6 AM to 6 PM. They won.

15) The first woman retail executive: Margaret Getchell was made store superintendent at Macy's in 1860.

16) The first retail personnel labor union was founded in 1888—the Clothing, Gents Furnishings and Shoe Clerks Union of Muskegon, Michigan. It was granted a charter by the AFL.

17) The first full-page retail newspaper ad: John Wanamaker, Philadelphia, in December, 1879.

18) The first air conditioning in a retail store: Filene's Basement, Boston, in 1902.

19) The first department store chain was launched by Hahn Department Stores in 1928, merging 27 separate stores with $100 million in sales in 13 states. The organization changed its name to Allied Stores in 1935.

THE GOOD OLD DAYS

Do you yearn for the good old days? Well, back in 1872, a Philadelphia department store had the following rules permanently posted on the bulletin board for its sales personnel, most of whom were men:

1) Employees each day will fill lamps, clean chimneys and trim wicks.
2) Each clerk will bring in a bucket of water and a scuttle of coal for the day's business.
3) Make your pens carefully. You may whittle nibs to your individual taste.
4) Men employees will be given an evening off each week for courting purposes, or two evenings if they go to church regularly.
5) After 13 hours of labor in the store, the employees should spend the remaining time reading the Bible or other good books.
6) Every employee should lay from each pay a goodly sum of his earnings for his declining years so that he will not become a burden on society.
7) The employee who has faithfully performed his labors and without fault for five years will be rewarded with an increase of five cents a day in his pay, providing profits from the business permit.

Store
Operations

2

The Twenty Most Common Mistakes of Shoe Retailers

Mistakes keep repeating themselves because we weren't listening the first time.

One doesn't really profit from experience; one merely learns to predict the next mistake.

Everybody makes mistakes, beginning with geniuses. But in the shoe business many smaller merchants especially tend to make more mistakes and make them more frequently. Most of them are sins of omission, and most tend to fall into a similar pattern.

That's the finding of retailing analysts who look for weaknesses in a business, then try to plug up the holes. None of this suggests that bigger merchants are smarter than smaller ones. But because the smaller ones are independents, they tend to operate the business in an "independent" style. That often means less discipline and looser controls.

Here, now, are the 20 most common mistakes made by such retailers.

1) Lax Expense Control. One of the main profit leaks in the average shoe business. The borrowing from store funds for personal uses. Or the failure to budget every expense segment of the business and rigidly hold to budget. For each 2 percent saved on expenses, 11 percent is added to net profit.

2) Slipshod Sizing Up. Most walks or lost sales are due to missed sizes. A lax size-up or fill-in policy—or none at all—not only dents sales but tarnishes store reputation ("they never have my size"). It also leads to broken lots, PMs and markdowns.

3) Inadequate Record-Keeping. The plaint of "one man can't do everything" is no excuse. Without a good record system you have no business being in business. It's like sailing a ship without a compass. You're at the whim of the winds which can often land you on the rocks.

4) Duplication in Buying. The wasteful overlapping of competitive lines or styles in an effort to be covered in everything. Result: no inventory depth and costly markdowns. Buying must be governed by the head, not the heart. Hunches are a sport for Las Vegas, not shoe business.

5) Excessive Markdowns. Smaller merchants show a higher rate of markdowns.

Chief causes: faulty buying, lax inventory control, slow turns, delayed clearances, lax pre-planning, mismanagement of buying budgets, etc. Many markdowns are the consequence of insufficient pre-buying homework. Smallness isn't the problem. Smartness is.

6) Faulty Inventory Control.   About 60 percent of the store's operating costs are in inventory. It seldom gets 60 percent of the store's concerted attention. The problems are well known: lack of a firm record and control system; lack of discipline in maintaining control. The results are also well known: broken stocks, lost sales, forced clearances, locked-in cash, reduced profits.

7) Faulty or Inconsistent Advertising.   In many instances it's the attitude: When business is poor I can't afford to advertise, and when it's good I don't need to. The failure to assign a minimum of 3 percent of sales to the ad budget. Also, a 6-months advance ad plan; a careful examination of the ad media used, plus frequent review of the quality of the advertising itself.

8) Failure to Use Cooperative Advertising.   Each year, millions of dollars in manufacturers' co-op ad money goes unused, wasted. Smart retailers consistently use cooperative advertising, often doubling their advertising at half the ordinary cost. Most smaller stores make little use of co-op advertising—which may be one reason they remain small.

9) Drab Window Displays.   "If you've seen one shoe window display you've seen most." That's an axiom among display specialists. A variety of common short-comings: little imagination, clouded windows, dust, flies, faded trimming or fixtures, infrequency of change, clutter, poor organization of merchandise, lack of descriptive placards, poor lighting, etc. Yet, windows account for 25 percent of average store traffic. Many stores lose much of this potential.

10) Drab Store Decor.   Almost typical of many shoe stores. Worn carpeting or flooring, frayed seating or fixtures, dull lighting, haphazard layout or traffic flow, cluttered space. The decor is the store's personality that reflects the merchandise, values, service. People prefer to shop in pleasant, attractive surroundings.

11) Waste of Interior Space.   Shoe stores waste inordinate amounts of space. For example, "air space" that can be used for hanging displays; lighted corner displays; converting posts or columns into display shelves; use of islands; wall space; small mobile displays that can be "rolled up" to the customer; etc. Most stores don't get full return on space paid for.

12) Weak Effort in Accessories.   The average modest-sized independent does less than 6 percent in accessories. Some larger stores do up to 20 percent of store volume in accessories. The only difference: one has a policy and program and tries harder. It's estimated that the average moderate-sized independent doing a volume of $300,000 forfeits $30,000 or more a year in accessories sales potential.

13) Extra-Pair Sales.   For women's shoes the minimum should be 15 percent, and for men's 10 percent. That's bare minimum. Most independents average below that because they have neither a policy nor a planned technique. Result: the average store forfeits about 15 percent of volume in missed multiple-pair sales.

14) Fragile Credit Status.   A good credit rating is the prime collateral of a business. Taking liberties with it is like playing Russian roulette. The chief cause is undisciplined cash flow management. When a business is habitually "in a bind," it really refers to a tightening noose around its neck.

15) Failure to Take Purchase Discounts.   Failure to take purchase discounts consistently can cost the store 25–40 percent of its net profits. This mistake is usually due either to a frequent shortage of cash or sheer bookkeeping negligence.

16) Walkouts.   For the average shoe store, three of every ten customers become walkouts. The reason for the walkouts are common: mostly missing sizes, but also limited style selection, poor or discourteous service, among others. Efficient stores keep a record of walks—how many and their cause. Most stores don't—and never know how much and why they're getting hurt. Cutting walks by only half can add 15 percent or more to store volume.

17) Store Image.   The average shoe store has little clear-cut identity other than it's a place where shoes are sold. A store should have a positive image, a distinct personality, that establishes its reputation *for* something. This can be price, fashion, service, extensive size or style selections, brands, unusual merchandise. This is further supported by advertising and promotions. Without a memorable personality, it's just another faceless shoe store.

18) Poor Time Management.   The average shoe store owner is locked into a work week of 60 to 70 hours. Those hours must be spread over many essential functions. But few stores efficiently schedule those hours. Result: a lot of essential tasks suffer from inadequate time or neglect with consequent penalties.

19) Pre-Planned Profits.   Stores pre-plan sales and assume they're automatically pre-planning profits. That's a mistake. Sales can meet budget, but profits can fall short of expectations. Average net profit, especially for smaller stores, shows a dismal record—between 2 and 4 percent; a very poor return against the heavy investment of time and effort. Net profit isn't the "surprise" of what's left over after costs and expenses. It should be pretargeted for a specific amount—then using a road map to get from here to there on a straight line.

20) Long-Term Goals.   Surveys show that the average shoe store has no long-term (3–7 years) goals. It has no pre-determined direction or destination or growth pace plan. It isn't sure what it wants to *be*. Growth by accident never succeeds as well as growth by plan. A store without a dream is a business without reason for existence.

Nobody's perfect. But running a business is like running a life—you try to make as few mistakes as possible. The root of the maladies is the same for many independents and smaller stores—a wide range of responsibilities in the hands of one or two people. Inevitably, some essentials get neglected or sacrificed.

Is there a remedy? Yes. It's a combination of better pre-planning, time management, pre-determined policies—and a rigid discipline to stick to plans. Case histories show that this strategy can eliminate half of the common mistakes, and minimize the negative effects of the other half.

3

Productivity and Operating Efficiency

Productivity is one answer to rising costs. That's why rabbit fur is cheaper than mink.

Shoe store productivity, along with retailing productivity in general, has just about the poorest record of all segments of the economy. In fact, it has shown little important change over the past half century. It's the main reason why store operating costs have risen steadily, and why profits often remain static. It's the chief reason why shoe retailers have required constantly higher markons (averaging a climb of almost one-half of one percent a year over the past 50 years) just to stay even. Perhaps the increasing use of computers will help to improve this situation. But computers are no panacea by themselves, so improved productivity in retailing must be achieved by other means.

"Productivity" isn't some complex concept that belongs solely to the economists and manufacturers. It applies to every kind of business, no matter the type or size. Productivity is simply a measure of operating efficiency, the results returned on investment made in every segment of the business—buying, inventory, salespeople, advertising, expenses, etc. Good productivity converts into more sales, lower costs and higher profit. Mediocre or poor productivity results in just the opposite. Ironically, few shoe stores make any direct and conscious attack on improving productivity.

A common mistake is the misconception that operating success and profit is the result of more sales. It isn't. You can frequently see financial statements of companies showing a substantial increase in sales and gross income but a decrease in net income. Volume alone isn't the answer to profit. It's like the merchant who was asked, "How's business?" He replied, "I'm so busy I haven't had time to go out and borrow the rent." Amusing but frequently true.

Thus the target isn't growth but *profitable* growth. There's a big difference. In a given year you can show a 20 percent volume growth but with a net income increase of only 7 percent. Somewhere you've short-changed yourself with the added business. Thus the key gauge is what you *do* with growth; or better still, what you make growth do for you profitwise. And your operating productivity is usually the answer to profit success, mediocrity or failure.

Each store should maintain an *Operating Efficiency Checklist,* and each year should check store performance against it. Avoid making a "general" attack on improving productivity. You don't cut down a forest. You cut down the forest tree by tree. The same with store productivity. You work on improving it segment by segment. The Operating Efficiency Checklist helps to keep you both honest and efficient by spotting your strengths and weaknesses. If you score well against this list, your net operating profit will consistently show healthy numbers. In short, net profit is the consequence of your Operating Efficiency Score.

SCORING GUIDANCE BEFORE THE TEST

At the end of this chapter is an Operating Efficiency Checklist to fill out and score your own operation. It consists of 27 operations items. However, to enable you to best evaluate your performance, let's first make a few brief comments about each of these items to serve as guidelines for your scoring.

Expense Control. National operating expense averages for shoe stores range between 38 and 45 percent, depending upon location and type of store (large or small, family or specialty, etc.). And also by operating efficiency. For example, a family or single-store operation may have expenses as low as 37 percent, while multiple-store operations may average 43 percent; downtown stores may average 39 percent while mall stores might go as high as 48 percent. Knowing the average for *your* kind of store is important, then rating your performance against that. Most stores have at least some expense fat that can be trimmed. And remember, for each two percentage points saved on expenses you add 33 percent to net profit.

Inventory Control. Don't appraise this just on current status but on your average annual performance. You've heard the saying: A shoe well bought is half sold. True. But it's the other half that can sometimes clobber you. Do you frequently overbuy or underbuy (and lose sales), or make poor buys or buy late? Are you lax on fillins and miss sales due to absent sizes in wanted styles? What's the age of your stock? Is it kept fresh with minimal drag from old merchandise? How would you rate your "stockmanship" performance?

Net Markon. It's more important than gross markon because it's a key indicator of operating efficiency and productivity level. Is it consistently on a healthy level, or is it on a yo-yo course year to year? You shouldn't have to hold your breath season to season or year to year to learn your net markon after costs and expenses are deducted. It should be reasonably predictable—that is, pre-targeted with good chance of hitting it—if most of the other parts of the operation are functioning efficiently. Your ability to be reasonably assured of your pre-planned net markon, and also to consistently deliver a good net markon, is the basis for scoring yourself on this item.

Markdowns and Clearances. This, of course, varies by type of store and merchandise—fast fashion versus basics, men's versus women's, etc. Know the markdown averages for *your* type of store and merchandise category, then rate yourself accordingly. Frequent above-average markdowns signal trouble, such as faulty buying, poor performing lines, buckling to competitive prices, etc. In 1985, for example, markdowns averaged from a low of 13.6 percent for men's stores to a high of 29.9 percent for women's stores, for an overall average of 19.6 percent. Each of these averages was above the norm and had a devastating effect on profits.

So beware of matching averages. You have to better them. And the better you consistently better them, the better your rating on this item.

Clearances need the same tight control. Clearances, of course, are inevitable. But how much is inevitable? Do you delay clearances? Do you unnecessarily clear some still-selling merchandise simply because it's the "clearance season"? Do you use special methods to clear merchandise beyond the customary seasonal clearance sales—such as the use of hashing in continuous clearance sections of the store? Are your clearance prices set to move the merchandise fast, or are you too cautious with only modest price cuts? Do you use special techniques to clear merchandise with minimal loss? These sum up to a "clearance policy" for your store. Do you have one? It's a measure of your operating efficiency.

Sales Per Square Foot. Again, this depends upon the type and size of store and the type of merchandise. Sales per square foot can range from lows of $106–$115 in a strip center store to highs of $185–$200 in a mall store; from $110–$115 in a small-volume store to $180 in a large-volume store; from $115 in men's stores to $185 in women's and children's stores. Or an overall average of about $150 for all stores combined. And some stores reach $300–$350 per square foot, though these are obviously the exception.

Nevertheless, sales per square foot is one of the clearest measures of store productivity and operating efficiency. You can't go by overall average for all stores. You have to gauge it by type of location, store and merchandise, then measure your own store's performance against it. But one thing is absolutely certain. Whatever your sales per square foot, in almost all instances it can be improved. When you rate yourself on this score, keep that in mind.

Average Sale Per Customer. This depends upon your price brackets, type of merchandise and clientele. Many stores fall short on maximizing customer sales potential. Too few multiple-pair sales, for example, are usually due to lack of store policy or training on multiple-pair selling, or lack of trying; or lack of trying to upgrade single-pair sales per customer. You know (or should know) the exact number of pairage units sold over a six-months period, as well as your total pairage dollar sales. This gives you an indication of average sale per customer. Studies show that 40 percent of customers are willing to buy or spend more, provided that they're encouraged to do so via the selling and merchandise. So when scoring yourself on this item, ask yourself if you're maximizing your sales productivity potential with all your customers, then judge your performance accordingly.

Stock Turns. This again varies by type of store and merchandise. For shoe business overall the average is about 2.2 turns. But beware of averages. You've probably heard about the man who drowned in a stream whose average depth was only three feet. He forgot that in some parts of the stream the depth was nine feet.

So beware of that 2.2 average. Men's stores may average 1.7, family stores 1.9, children's 2.1, women's 2.7, small stores 1.8, volume stores 2.7. And, of course, some stores consistently average 3 and 4 turns. The aim should be to find the overall average for *your* type of store and merchandise. If you match it, then you're average. But don't feel smug about it. Average simply means the best of the worst or the worst of the best. Your task is to *better* the average for your category. If you accomplish that, your productivity rises, as will your net profit, earning you a higher rating on this item.

Net Profit. If year to year it shows erratic ups and downs, it clearly signals something wrong throughout the operation. It can't be blamed on the "unexpected" or contingencies. These should be taken into account in the pre-planning and budgeting. Net profit should reasonably match pre-targeted goals, otherwise you haven't planned properly. A reasonably consistent and healthy net profit is probably the best indicator of good operating efficiency and overall productivity.

Credit Status. How do you stand with the local banks plus your resources? Your credit line is your business lifeline. Credit performance should not be based on anticipated sales and income. When the expected collides with the unexpected, credit often gets bruised. That's why credit-strong businesses are also strong on cash flow and cash reserves. Sound credit status is an important pillar of operating efficiency.

Records. Bare-bones records aren't enough. There are at least nine or ten basic ones, and more is even better. Records are the navigational compass of a business. Without them your business is at the mercy of the winds, shoals and rocks. Most retailers fall short on records and record-keeping, especially independents. How many do you keep? How well? Quantity and quality are the gauge for scoring on this item.

Financial Position. This isn't to be confused with credit rating. It focuses on cash flow and cash reserves, plus debt burden. This can be the Achilles heel of many retailers, being under-capitalized. The lack of liquidity is a roadblock to taking advantage of buying/selling opportunities, or purchase discounts. It locks the business into a small closet, restricting movement. It prevents doing many of the things needed for sound operation and improved productivity.

Accessories Sales. These should comprise a minimum of 15 percent of total store volume to earn a "good" rating, and 20 percent or better for an "excellent" rating. Accessories are perhaps the single most neglected area of sales potential in the average shoe store or department. Consider that a store with a volume of $350,000 will have an average store *traffic* of about 15,000 a year; the potentials for sales of accessories items is substantial. Your own performance rating should be judged by the figures cited above.

Local Market Research. You say or think you know your customers. Maybe. But do you know your trading area? Do you know its population? Do you know how many pairs of footwear, and the footwear dollars spent, are represented by your trading area? And a breakdown by men's, women's and children's? If not, how can you know what share of the footwear business you're getting, or your competitive position in the area? Do you know if you're trading area is growing or shrinking, and by what percentage a year? That will give you an indication of growth potential. A little local market research will give you the answers to those important questions. Your rating on this score will depend on whether you obtain and make use of such data relative to your business.

Advertising. Average spending by shoe stores is about 3 percent of sales. For a $350,000 volume store that's $10,500 a year. Are you spending that much? Are you getting a $10,500 (or better) return in sales? How do you know? Advertising is a common productivity leakage spot—low returns on money spent. What's the quality of your advertising? Does it have consistently good pull-power? Are you using the right and best media? Are you taking advantage of the cooperative ad dollars available to you? Don't take your advertising for granted. Its performance is an important productivity gauge for your return on investment.

Displays.   This means both window and interior. You spend money for displays and for the display space itself (equivalent to rent money). Have you figured what your displays, plus the display space, cost you (the numbers, based on square footage related to rent, may surprise you)? What return are you getting on the investment? How frequently are the displays changed? Productivity evaluation often isn't a matter of what you show, or even the display space allotted, but the quality and effectiveness of what and how you show.

Purchase Discounts.   These can amount to 25 percent to 40 percent of your net profits, depending upon how consistently they're utilized. Frequent lack of cash flow or shaky credit status can be an obstacle to taking advantage of purchase discounts. How do you fare on this score? Do you take these discounts regularly or spasmodically? Do you keep a record of your "earnings" from discounts?

Store Image.   Does your store have a strong identity in your trading area? Does it stand out as a particular *kind* of shoe store—or is it just another shoe store? Does it have a reputation for something particular, or is it just run-of-the-mill? Does your store have an attractive or unusual decor—the front, signs, windows, lighting, fixtures, layout, floor coverings, etc.? Do your ads help convey the store image? Store image bears influence on store traffic and sales. It's a good idea to get an objective evaluation of your store—all the things that contribute to image— from a qualified outsider such as a store designer.

Salaries.   Frequently it's a case of a liberally paid boss. Liberal salaries are fine if they're justified and affordable. Otherwise they dent and distort legitimate profits. It also works in reverse with the owner taking too small a salary on the assumption that he owns the business, anyway. Again, it's not unusual for the owner to "borrow" from the business for personal uses and not pay back. This also distorts the books. Owner salaries average in the wide range of 3 percent to 6 percent. Is yours within this range?

Performance of Salespeople.   A vital key to store productivity. Do you keep records on both dollar and unit sales performance of each salesperson? This enables you to measure sales productivity, and also to pinpoint the strong and weak performers with specific numbers. Are wages and earnings measured fairly against performance and productivity, plus bonuses and other incentive payouts? Do you use a sales training program? In-store sales meetings? Sales employee expenses average between 9 percent and 13 percent. But the important thing isn't what's paid out but whether the payouts are in fair proportion to sales performance and productivity.

Buying Acumen.   This is a judgment call. But it can be gauged by consistently good sales, low markdowns, good net markon and minimal mistakes. Your buying commits you to 55 percent or 60 percent of your total operation costs and investment. With that heavy share at stake there's little margin for errors that can jeopardize sales and profits. Nor is it all a matter of what you buy. Timing is very important, plus the buying of fillins and reorders or opportune closeouts, plus the selection of lines and resources. Keep in mind the axiom: a shoe well bought is half sold. Much of your overall store productivity hinges on your buying skills.

Promotions.   Are these planned in advance on a six-months basis? How imaginative are they? How effective? Do you get help on these (or ask for help) from your resources? Are you properly inventoried for your promotions? Do you run too many—or not enough? Do you keep records of results on each promotion to give you a basis for repeating the successful ones and avoid repeating the duds? Do you confuse seasonal clearances with promotions? You shouldn't. Good promotions are important to productivity because they increase sales and help reduce selling and overhead costs, hence boosting profits.

Walkouts. Do you keep a record of how many and also the reasons why? Are they excessive or minimal? Is the fault due to inventory shortcomings (sizes, selections, etc.), or the service or salespeople? Do you have a program to minimize walks? In the average shoe store or department, 30 percent of wanting-to-buy customers are walks for any of various reasons. This amounts to tens of thousands of dollars in lost sales annually. A mediocre record of walks—anything over 15 percent or 20 percent—indicates serious productivity leaks in other parts of the store's operations such as inventory control, salespeople's performance, among others.

Peak and Lull Hours and Days. On average, about 70 percent of the store's traffic and sales will be accounted for by only 30 percent of the store's hours and days. The low periods are the costly productivity gaps because they contribute little to sales, yet at the same time are taking the same toll on overhead costs as your busier periods. Do you keep a record on percentage of sales by the week's days and the days' hours? Once you have this information do you try to devise promotional ideas to stimulate traffic and sales during the slower periods? If you don't, then the productivity dike has a big hole of overhead costs draining profit potentials.

Forward Planning. To the average shoe retailer, forward planning means next season or a year ahead at best. To more alert merchants it means two or three years down the road. What's changing in your trading area—the demographics, size, competition, traffic, etc.? Are you making the necessary adjustments for your market in your lines and merchandise, in your clientele targets? You can't just float on the whim of the trade winds. You have to steer the ship. Forward planning is good productivity insurance for your foreseeable future.

Customer Relations. How does your store rate on customer loyalty and repeat business? Studies show that in an average trading area, each year about 17 percent of a store's customers "disappear"—move away, deaths, patronage shifted to competitive stores, dissatisfactions with service, etc. That means you need 17 percent new customers just to stay even, and at least 25 percent new ones to show growth. Do you have a program to retain customer loyalty? Do you use keep-in-touch techniques such as phone calls, direct mail or personal card mailings? Do you try to learn why customers become lost? Some customer drainage is inevitable. But much of it isn't. It's the latter kind that takes a toll on store productivity.

Services. Many stores presume to be "full service" stores. But when asked to name their customer services they often fade out after citing fitting and credit cards. Genuine full service means quantity, variety and quality. For example, fashion counseling, product counseling, free parking, extra services by salespeople (see the chapter, "Is Yours *Really* A Service Store?") Most stores offer fitting service. How is yours different or better? What is the quality of each of your services?

The difference between excellent and average service influences customer relations, repeat business and customer loyalty, hence sales and productivity.

Growth Pattern. Is your business growing at least 6 percent or 7 percent a year in dollars and 3 percent to 4 percent a year in units? Do you *plan* for growth with a program to achieve realistic targets? Has your location reached sales saturation level? Is it feasible to plan for an additional store to sustain growth? Are you satisfied with a status quo? With a good overall productivity program growth is assured, and with a good growth program productivity continues to improve. Each feeds on the other. Your future isn't what happens to you but what you *make* happen to you.

You're familiar with the 80–20 law. For example, at any given time of the year 80 percent of the sales are made with 20 percent of the stock; or 80 percent of the sales are made during 20 percent of the store hours; and so on. Have you ever considered what would happen to your sales and profits if you raised the 20 percent share to 40 percent or 50 percent? The end result would be spectacular. And that essentially is what productivity and operating efficiency is all about—doing more and better with what you have to work with. That's the essence of success, making the most of your assets. So that's the secret: getting up off your assets.

Now you're ready for the Store Operations Efficiency Test. If you score in the *Excellent* range you're a top performer and among an elite minority. If you're in the *Good* range you're competitive but can sharpen performance. If you score in the *Fair* range you're living dangerously and need to make a lot of improvements to shape up your weaknesses.

STORE OPERATIONS EFFICIENCY TEST

Scoring: 5–6 Points, Excellent; 3–4 Points, Good; 1–2 for Fair; Zero for Poor

Operations Item	Excellent	Good	Fair	Poor
Expense control	☐	☐	☐	☐
Inventory control	☐	☐	☐	☐
Net markon	☐	☐	☐	☐
Markdowns and clearances	☐	☐	☐	☐
Sales per sq. ft.	☐	☐	☐	☐
Average sale per customer	☐	☐	☐	☐
Stock turns	☐	☐	☐	☐
Net profit	☐	☐	☐	☐
Credit status	☐	☐	☐	☐
Records	☐	☐	☐	☐
Financial position	☐	☐	☐	☐
Accessories sales	☐	☐	☐	☐
Local market research	☐	☐	☐	☐
Advertising	☐	☐	☐	☐
Displays	☐	☐	☐	☐
Purchase discounts	☐	☐	☐	☐
Store image	☐	☐	☐	☐
Salaries	☐	☐	☐	☐
Performance of salespeople	☐	☐	☐	☐
Buying acumen	☐	☐	☐	☐
Promotions	☐	☐	☐	☐
Walkouts	☐	☐	☐	☐
Peak & lull hrs. & days	☐	☐	☐	☐
Forward planning	☐	☐	☐	☐
Customer relations	☐	☐	☐	☐
Services	☐	☐	☐	☐
Growth pattern	☐	☐	☐	☐
TOTALS	☐	☐	☐	☐

Ratings: Excellent—130–162
Good — 91–129
Fair — 65–90
Poor — 64 or less

4

Fifteen "Controls" Essential for Successful Operation

Don't complain how the ball drops
if you're the one who dropped it.

A good intention is like a
wheelbarrow—it's useless unless
pushed.

In 1986, the market research firm of Lowenthal & Horwath conducted a national survey of small business enterprises, including retailers. One of the two main questions asked was: "What is the greatest advantage of owning your own business?" The three top replies were:

Controlling your own business future—22%

Making your own decisions   —20

Being independent, your own boss   —17

Thus, for three of every five small business owners, the chief advantage and main incentive for owning a business is the satisfaction of being in control not only of the business but of one's own destiny and future. That is the epitome of personal freedom. Other surveys confirm this, revealing that the ambition of the majority of Americans is not to get rich but to own one's own business. And the prime motive: To be in control of both one's business and one's future.

That's a laudable goal. Independent retailers are among those who proudly achieve that goal. For many of them, however, once the goal is achieved it proves to also contain disadvantages. In the Lowenthal & Horwath survey a second, followup question was asked: "What is the greatest disadvantage of owning your own business?" The five top answers were as follows:

Getting capital, cash flow   —12%

Having your own assets at risk—12

Pressure, stress   —11

Responsibility, worry   — 9

Lack of personal time   — 9

But something else quite significant was revealed in the survey. The combination of disadvantages of owning one's own business often created problems that jeopardized the control the owner has over his business. He often finds that the business owns him more than he owns the business. The goal of "being in control" of both his business and destiny gradually slips from his fingers. Thus the irony: the control he has worked hard for is diminished because of lack of the controls essential to the business he owns.

Now a final finding from a Dun & Bradstreet survey analyzing the reasons why most businesses fail or run into serious difficulties. The prime reason: lack or loss of controls of the business. What kind of controls? Dun & Bradstreet lists the top 15 that get out of hand, as follows:

Inventory Control. Faulty handling of merchandise once bought; the sins of both inventory overload and underload; failure to reorder fast enough on good sellers, or to maintain disciplined policy of sizeups on steady sellers; too many broken lots in the inventory makeup.

Buying Control. Failure to design a sound buying budget and stick to it; overbuys and underbuys; faulty merchandise selection relative to local market, clientele; late buying with consequent late deliveries; duplication of lines; slow response to developing style trends; faulty selection of sizes.

Expense Control. Pre-budgeting expenses and maintaining disciplined control of expenses; failure to keep weekly or biweekly checks on expenses measured against budget; inclusion of non-business expenses with business expenses; loose forecasting of expenses; imbalanced ratio of some expenses relative to others.

Markdown Control. It isn't what you sell but what you don't sell that counts. Among the shortcomings: delayed clearances and closeouts; an excess of PMs in stock; top-heavy in aged stock; too little or too much discount on markdown prices; faulty pricing relative to local market or clientele; too much breadth, not enough depth in inventory; failure to analyze causes of markdowns by lines or items.

Merchandising Control. This relates to advertising, promotions, displays, etc.— all the elements that help move the merchandise. Here there are shortcomings in predetermining budgets for each; selection of ad media, plus frequency and consistency of the advertising; mediocre quality of displays; unimaginative promotions; infrequent display changes.

Sales Control. You project your buying and other budgets on the basis of your anticipated sales. Problems occur when the sales forecasts are too low or too high, creating inventory problems. Also, the mistake of budgeting or forecasting sales on the basis of dollars instead of units. Failure to stay attuned to local market and economic trends that can affect sales pro or con.

Services Control. This means primarily the salespeople and their training and performance. Failure to maintain and keep close check of sales performance; lax policies on returns, credits, sales training; vague policies on other services such as customer counseling on product, fashion, shoe care, etc. Service costs are built into the price of the shoe, and hence the customer deserves full return on what he or she is paying for.

Customer Control. Few retailers give specific consideration to this. Yet the average store will lose 15 percent to 20 percent of its customers a year. Where did the customers go? And why? Among the shortcomings: failure to keep customer records, plus failing to do a checkup on customers "missing" for a year or more; not knowing what share of the customers comprise your repeat business, and what share are transients or one-time buyers; absence or policies or practices focused on building customer loyalty.

Credit and Debt Control. One of your prime assets is your credit status with your resources and the banks. Laxity or weakness here leads to problems on both loans and cash flow needs for full availability of merchandise from resources. A halt or reduction of either puts you against the wall. High debt and low credit are not the consequence of lack of cash flow but the cause of it.

Records Control. Any business is essentially a numbers operation. The combination of how much and how well—quantity plus quality—is the main generator of the business machine. But it all starts with numbers. That means a variety of separate records related to separate segments of the business operation. Failure to maintain adequate records, according to Dun & Bradstreet, is one of the most common weaknesses of businesses—and a prime cause of business failures. In fact, says D&B, "The soundness of a business can be judged by the soundness of the records it keeps." Your resources and your bank are well aware of this. So should you.

Profit Control. Profit should never be a hold-your-breath proposition—waiting to see what's left over after all costs and expenses are accounted for. It should be pre-budgeted into the operation with the same preciseness as you try to budget your buying and expenses. And also checked monthly to see that it's on budget target. Many retailers fail to do this, and thus lose control of the prime objective they work so hard to reach.

Local Market Control. If you are in a local market you should have claim to a share of it. Equally important, you should know what your share is (see the chapter, "Figuring Footwear Sales In Your Market"). Lack of this information forces you to operate in the dark, never knowing your market status, or whether you are gaining or losing market share. You cannot be genuinely competitive unless you have a sound fix on your competitive position.

Prices Control. If your competition rather than yourself determines your prices, you are no longer in control of your own prices, margins and profits. Price is hitched to value. From the customers' standpoint, value includes such factors as the quality of the services, style selection, availability of sizes, store reliability, etc. If you provide these customer-want values, you are then in a better position to control your own prices.

Identity or Image Control. If yours is just another "faceless" store that sells shoes, you have little or no identity in your local market, and hence no control of who you are or what your store stands for. A store must have a distinct personality, a clear-cut image. This doesn't happen by accident but is *made* to happen by design. If it does, the store has a strong identity which you control because it is something you made, a personality unlike any other.

Self Control. This is as important as any of the other controls. Self control means operating a business by the head instead of by the gut; by the numbers instead of by intuition and emotion. It's a rein on excesses—buying, expenses and other areas where lack of self-control can create unnecessary problems.

When you can make legitimate claim to being in full control of those 15 vital business operation controls, you then can rightfully say you own your own business. And your record of success will be clear evidence of your claim of fully controlled ownership.

5

Cutting Down on Markdowns

*Many people don't put their best
foot forward until they get the other
one in hot water.*

*A genius is a man who takes the
lemons that fate hands him and
starts a lemonade stand with them.*

It used to be a simple process for shoe stores to figure their markdowns because most markdowns occurred during the semi-annual clearances sales. No more. Dramatic shifts in pricing and merchandising and discounting practices during the 1980s changed all that. For example, in the mid-1980s well over half of all footwear was sold below regular retail price, meaning below regular markon of 50 percent to 55 percent. If half were sold below regular price, are they to be considered markdowns?

Off-price retailers sell branded merchandise year round and have become a permanent fixture in footwear and apparel retailing. Is all of this discounted merchandise to be included in the "markdown" category?

Conventional shoe and other stores have greatly increased the number and frequency of their price promotions. Are sales of this price-discounted merchandise to be considered markdowns?

The issue of markdowns today can be quite confusing. For example, a 1986 survey by *Footwear News* showed the percentage of footwear purchases *below* regular prices for 1985 were as follows: men's athletic, 60 percent; men's dress shoes, 49 percent; men's casuals, 52 percent; men's work, 38 percent. For women's: dress shoes, 53 percent; casuals, 53 percent; athletic, 59 percent. Those figures include footwear averages for all types of retail outlets combined.

However, for the sake of both simplicity and sanity let's not include the complex situation of off-price retailing and the unnatural conditions of frequent discounted price promotions by conventional stores trying to remain competitive with the off-pricers. Let's stay with the traditional concept of markdowns—the end-of-season clearances along with the occasional special price promotions to unload heavy inventories or slow-moving merchandise.

National surveys taken by the National Shoe Retailers Association show markdowns in shoe stores averaging 19.6 percent, though there is a broad range from 34 percent to 13 percent, depending upon the type of store. Women's shoe stores, for example, average 30 percent in markdowns, children's 17.6 percent, and men's

13.6 percent. These, remember, do not include off-price and other discount-type outlets. (See Table "Markdown Averages by Type of Outlet" on page 32).

Figuring an average of 20 percent "normal" markdowns, this means, for example, that in 1987, 260 million pairs of footwear were sold via the markdown route, for a loss (the difference between regular markon price and average markdown price) of about $5.2 billion for retailers. Figuring an average markdown of 33 percent, that means that while 80 percent of the sales were made with full gross markon of about 50 percent, 20 percent were made with only a 17 percent gross markon, and hence a substantial net loss.

It's easy to retort, "Some markdowns are inevitable. Even the most efficient stores have them." Very true. But now a sticky question: What share of sales should "normally" be markdowns? Again, take a look at the table showing the wide range in percentage of markdowns by different types of stores. Why, for example, should stores with a volume of over $750,000 have a markdown level double that of stores in the $300,000 to $750,000 volume group? Why should single shoe stores have a markdown average of 57 percent greater than for retailers with over ten stores? Why should downtown stores have a 26 percent higher markdown rate than shoe stores in enclosed malls?

Some of these differences, of course, may be self-evident. For example, women's shoe stores show an average markdown rate of 29.9 percent versus a 13.6 percent average for men's stores, a 120 percent difference. Granted, women's footwear is far more volatile than men's and hence involve more markdown risk. But a 120 percent difference? So again the inevitable question: for women's stores, how much of that 29.9 percent average is excessive and due to mistakes or faults of one kind or another?

The message: Beware of averages. In the case of women's shoe stores, for instance, it means that while some of these stores are averaging an exorbitant 40 percent or more markdown level, other more efficient women's stores are averaging only a 20 percent or less level.

Retailers are constantly claiming they know their customers and local market. But if they know so much about their customers and market, how come their markdowns are so high? Never feel comfortable if you hover around the averages. The name of the game for *you* must always be: Beat the averages.

Almost all shoe retailers keep records of their markdowns. But few stores keep records of or analyze the causes of the markdowns. And right there is an important giant step toward reducing markdowns, and especially eliminating the excessive or unnecessary markdowns. As with any disease, the better the diagnosis the better the chance of a cure. Not all retailers have markdowns consistently for the same reasons. For some it may be faulty buys or lax inventory controls, while with others it may be faults in selling or promotions or timing.

HOW MUCH MARKDOWN?

How much markdown: 20 percent, 30 percent, 50 percent? The answer is simple. Whatever it takes to move the merchandise is the right amount of markdown. Not you but the customers judge that. So you have to test, plus using your own experience.

Sometimes successive markdowns are better than one big markdown, and with less loss. Say you have 200 pairs to clear. Original cost is $25 a pair ($50 retail). You decide on a smash clearance of 50 percent off, or $25. You recover your original investment of $5,000, minus the carrying and promotional costs loss.

Now take the same 200 pairs and use three successive markdowns, and the markdowns started earlier, as follows:

$$
\begin{array}{llll}
80 \text{ pairs cleared at } 25\% \text{ off—} & \$3,000 \\
70 \quad " \qquad " \qquad " \ 40\% \ " \ — & 2,100 \\
50 \quad " \qquad " \qquad " \ 50\% \ " \ — & \underline{1,250} \\
& \$6,800
\end{array}
$$

Your take is $1,850 or 37 percent better than the big one-shot way. This isn't always the best way, but if done on a selective basis the successive method can often be more productive.

It's important to distinguish between markdowns of regular stock to stimulate sales and markdowns to reduce inventory or clear closeouts. In the first instance make sure the markdown is at the end of the selling season, and in the second instance the merchandise remains at reduced price until liquidated.

Should markdowns be limited in number and timing each year? For example, June and January clearances? Or should they be used anytime when necessary to stimulate sales or clear inventory? Then there's the tricky question: When does a price promotion become a legitimate markdown sale, or vice versa?

Timing or frequency of markdowns can be argued as being a matter of necessity to reduce inventory, unload closeouts or stimulate sales. But an often unconsidered risk is involved when the markdown sales become frequent. This obviously reduces the share of merchandise sold at regular markon prices. The store also risks acquiring a mixed image of being partly a discount or off-price store and partly a regular-price store. No business can survive long with a mongrelized image. It must be either one breed or another.

One of the common sins of retailers is delay in taking markdowns. They fail to heed the rule that it's better to have a sellout (markdowns and clearances) than be left holding the bag. While they vacillate the losses continue to mount—in carrying charges, aging and harder-to-sell merchandise, etc. For example, if you have $20,000 tied up in slow-moving merchandise, it's costing you as follows:

$$
\begin{array}{lll}
12\% \text{ interest} & —\$2,400 \\
2\% \text{ carrying charges—} & 400 \\
3\% \text{ obsolescence} & — \ 1,600 \\
4\% \text{ storage} & — \ \underline{\ 800} \\
& \$5,200
\end{array}
$$

Every shoe in stock should be assigned a pre-determined shelf life. This policy, however, has to be mixed with judgment. If a shoe gives early signs that it's going to be a dog, unload it before dated deadline, even if it's at peak season. Realism pays better than optimism. If the shoe is moving better than anticipated, extend its deadline and reorder while it's hot. Also, there are some basic shoes or lines that sell year round and hence are not subject to, or much less subject to, pre-posted markdown deadlines.

Consistently keep records on the markdown performance by lines. This is usually overlooked by retailers. Your records will usually show that some of your lines consistently show higher markdown rates. If so, then seriously consider unloading or replacing the line or resource—no matter how nice a guy you think the sales rep is, or whether the resource management is "nice folks to do business with," or that you've had the line a long time. Your prime responsibility is to consistently produce a reasonable profit on your merchandise. The resource or vendor equally has the responsibility of contributing to your profit with his merchandise. If he fails in this responsibility it's solid grounds for divorce.

But a point of caution here. Sometimes it isn't the line or resource that is at fault. The shortcomings can often be your own—making wrong selections from his line, or lax promotional backup of your buys, or poor displays or faulty selling, etc. That's why records and analysis of *why* certain shoes or lines consistently have above-normal markdowns are so important. They help fix the blame where it belongs.

Markdowns don't have to take the usual me-too route. Reach for the unusual. For example, during the usual June or January clearance sales, promote a "Lemon Week" and serve free lemonade (or tea with lemon) with your shoe lemons. Or in your ads or windows show a picture of a giraffe with a sign: "We're breaking our neck to please you with savings." Or a sailboat: "We're under full sale."

Markdowns don't always have to be traditional clearance sale promotions. A permanent "special values corner" can be set up in a section of the store—well lighted, attractive, and with signs on racks or tables. It's more effective to group shoes by sizes (size hashing) than by styles. Customers buy by size. Have size groupings clearly marked. Add visual pizzazz to attract browsers.

Occasionally include a free giveaway with your markdown promotions. Your ad might read: "Our markdown sale 30 percent off, *plus* a *free* kit of shoe cleaners with each footwear purchase." The kit may cost you $2, but the markdown price plus the giveaway may double your clearance sales. And it would make your markdown sale stand out from the rest during the clearance season.

Stores keep records of how much the salespeople sell, but seldom on *what* they sell. Many salespeople sell the "easy" sellers and neglect others; or they have their personal favorites while they shun others. These attitudes or practices commonly contribute to markdowns. They can also convert what should be a good seller into a slow-mover. By keeping a check on each salesperson's sales records over a three–four-week period, much can be learned about negative attitudes of salespeople toward certain shoes in stock that you think should be selling better than they are.

This applies also to PMs, which many salespeople tend to avoid because they're harder or more time-consuming to sell. This can often be counteracted by doubling the commission payout on PMs. If PMs and slow-movers are headed for clearance, anyway, it's better to pay the salesperson 15 percent to 20 percent on the PMs than to take a loss of 40 percent to 50 percent on its markdown price later.

If you have two or more stores, group all markdowns from all the stores and run one huge markdown sale in *one* store. One spectacular has much more impact than smaller clearance sales dispersed among two or more stores.

Some retailers buy closeouts from their resources to include in their seasonal markdown sales. This provides opportunity for a larger clearance promotion with more impact. And it permits the retailer to get *full* markon on the closeouts which are being sold, legitimately, as markdowns.

A couple of points of caution. On what have been good sellers over a span of weeks or months, at some point think twice about placing the last reorder. The shoe may have run out of its peak sales span and may be ready to join the markdown ranks. Also, keep a close, advance watch on the closeout merchandise of your resources. Closeouts are a signal that the shoe isn't moving well. It may be a signal for you to move the same shoe, if you have it in stock, into the markdown category quickly.

Markdowns are the profit-eating monster of shoe business. You can't kill the dragon but you can dull the points of his teeth and render him much less harmful in chewing up your profits.

Markdown Averages By Type of Outlet

Type of Outlet	Aver. % Markdowns
All stores, average	19.6%
Under $300,000	21.3
$300,000–$750,000	17.4
Over $750,000	34.3
Single store	29.8
2–9 stores	19.6
10 or more stores	18.9
Downtown location	23.9
Strip center	23.1
Enclosed mall	18.9
Concept/specialty store	15.9
Traditional store	20.5
Leased department	19.9
Family shoe store	20.9
Men's store	13.6
Women's store	29.9
Children's store	17.6

Source: 1986 Shoe Store Operations Survey, National Shoe Retailers Association.

18 COMMON MARKDOWN CAUSES TO AVOID

1) Duplication of lines, styles, resources.
2) Wrong buys, overbuys, careless buy planning.
3) Excess of fringe sizes and widths.
4) Delay in spotting and delay in moving slow-sellers.
5) Late ordering, late deliveries for selling season.
6) Salespeople concentrating on easy-sellers, neglecting others.
7) Lack of records to plan by, buy by.
8) Unnecessary low/slow stock turns.
9) Inadequate promotional effort relative to size of buy.
10) Letting sales rep dominate your selections and size of buy.
11) Too many fringe or "window dressing" items.
12) Too many variations on one shoe (colors, heels, materials).
13) Too much breadth, not enough depth.
14) Insufficient incentives for moving PMs and slow-sellers before markdowns and clearances.
15) Inadequate inventory control.
16) Too little or too much markdown on the clearances.
17) Wrong pricing relative to the local market and clientele.
18) Allowing broken lots or size runs to occur on good-selling shoes.

6

Expense Control Is Success Insurance

If your outgo is greater than your income, your upkeep will be your downfall.

We would gladly pay as we go if we could only catch up from where we've been.

Men do not stumble over mountains but over molehills.

The retailer thinks he owns his business. But if he owes more than he owns, then what he owns is debt. That's a position where he's undercapitalized, lacks cash flow, can't take advantage of purchase discounts or opportune buys, slow-pays his bills, and has a shaky credit status.

Often what traps him in that uncomfortable corner is lack of expense control. It may well be the most vulnerable area of shoe business operation.

Expense control is essentially waste control. Experienced retailing accountants estimate that the average shoe store can shave at least two or three percentage points off its expenses with no loss in efficiency. When operating expenses exceed gross margin (not unusual), it's a trouble signal. Accountants say that for a safe and comfortable cushion there should be at least a six-point spread. If gross margin is 43 percent, expenses shouldn't exceed 37 percent; or the ratio can be 44–38 or 42–36.

Let's look at what expense of waste control can mean to a business. Let's say a store's expenses amount to 40 percent of sales, and the average sale is $35. Thus for every $35 sale, $14 is automatically shaved off the top for expenses.

Let's say our sample store does a $350,000 volume, or 10,000 sales or transactions averaging $35 each. But by disciplined control, expenses are cut from 40 percent to 38 percent. Now instead of $14 only $13.30 comes off the top of each $35 sale. The savings of 70 cents on each of 10,000 transactions amounts to $7,000. If the store's net profit is 7 percent ($24,500), then the saved $7,000 amounts to 28.6 percent of the store's net profit. And the store's net profit rises to $31,500 or 9 percent.

Retailers frequently speak of "the rising cost of doing business" and the need for higher markon (when was it ever different?). But seldom do they turn their sights with equal fervor on expense control, despite the obvious opportunities to raise net profit by 20 percent to 40 percent via this route.

Studies show that average shoe store expenses range from a low of 36 percent to a high of 48 percent. That's a 12-point spread. A 2 percent points reduction in expenses can amount to a 33 percent gain in net profit (see the supplementary table in this chapter). On the basis of this expense difference alone, that could mean a 200 percent difference in net profit between the high and low. Incredible? No, because that's what actually happens.

EXPENSES AND PRODUCTIVITY

Expense control is partly a surgical procedure of eliminating tumors and flab. But that's only part of it. Another vital part of expense and cost control is the process of *increasing operational efficiency,* an approach often given too little attention. If sales are increased without expense increase, the obvious result is more net profit.

For example, let's take two modest-size stores, each doing $300,000 volume. But one store averages $190 per square foot of selling space, the other $150. The first store, however, is doing its volume with much less space, with less overhead and other costs, and hence is realizing a better profit on the same volume. The difference, of course, is in the productivity level, resulting in lower expenses and costs.

Let's cite another example. Retailers are almost unanimous in saying that selling costs are the most difficult expense item to control. But let's say that a $300,000 volume store has selling costs of 14 percent or $42,000. Say its sales productivity was raised a modest 10 percent, boosting volume to $330,000. The selling cost is now reduced to 12.1 percent. A net profit of 7 percent on the additional $30,000 gives the store an extra $2,100, which amounts to 10 percent of its previous net of $21,000.

Thus selling cost is down 13.6 percent, net profit up 10 percent—just by a modest 10 percent increase in sales productivity via fewer walks, more multiple-pair sales, more upgraded sales, more accessories sales, etc. So even if dollar expenses remain the same, their percentage to sales declines.

Rent is usually the store's second highest expense item. Moreover, it's a fixed cost and less subject to cutback. Retailers sometimes complain that they're "working for the landlord." But that's a state of mind. For instance, say a store doing $300,000 is paying 7 percent of sales for rent, or $21,000. If volume is increased to $330,000, rent drops to 6.4 percent; with $350,000 it's 6 percent; and with $400,000 it's 5.3 percent. It's a matter of raising the bridge rather than lowering the mast.

The same applies to advertising, rated as a difficult cost control item and one of the leakiest of store costs or expenses. But here, too, productivity is often the answer. Two stores can have identical ad budgets, but one consistently gets a 30 percent better return on its advertising. So in reality it's spending a third less on its advertising via higher productivity (more selective use of media, better ad copy and art, etc.), thus reducing ad expense.

Expense control isn't a matter of pinch-penny arithmetic. The mathematics of profitable business favors increasing sales rather than oversqueezing costs. You can't reduce your costs more than 100 percent. But there are no laws to stop you from increasing your sales 1,000 percent.

The owner's salary is often arbitrary, ranging from too low to too high. What's a "right" salary? One good gauge is to ask, "What would my services be worth on the open market?" An honest answer is usually sobering.

One of the common sins, especially among smaller stores, is the owner's frequent "borrowing" against the store's income—and often with no putback. These are funds used to pay for a vacation, a new car, a loan to a brother-in-law, the kid's college tuition, etc. The owner "reasons" that it's cheaper to borrow from his own business than pay high interest on a loan from the bank. This borrowing becomes a hidden expense, buried under "miscellaneous." But it creates a distorted reading on operating expenses and net profit. It also affects the store's cash flow, its credit rating and other factors.

TAKING ACTION

Well, how should a store attack its expenses budget? Here are suggestions:

1) Set a realistic target—say two percentage points, such as from 40 percent to 38 percent as the cutback point.
2) List every expense category or item and set a year's (or six months') budget for each, based on realistically projected sales. Trim to the targeted amount. (Not every item or category will be subject to the same amount of change, but the overall averaging should come out on target).
3) Think in terms of *both* expense cutback and productivity increase, both of which lead to the same goal of operating cost reduction.
4) Budget expenses on a monthly basis, and check at the end of each month to see if all are on target. Make the necessary adjustments.
5) Keep records. Yes, it's the same old advice. But without records it can result in repeating the same old mistakes. Records give the answer to the retailer's age-old plaint, "Where did all the money go?"
6) Make sure that *everything* that's an operating expense gets properly listed and accounted for. And beware of that snakepit expense category called "miscellaneous."

Don't take any expense cost for granted. You'll be surprised at the leaks you can find. With persistent probing you may find that you can get lower insurance rates, or lower rates on credit card payments. Check your freight billings. It has been found that some 15 percent are being over-charged via errors (and similarly with utilities). If a minimum reorder is six pairs, don't do the dumb thing by placing two three-pair orders (quite common).

Shore up security against pilferage and shortages, bad checks, stolen credit cards, etc. Have a local lighting engineer check your store lighting setup. You may be able to save 25 percent to 40 percent or more and end up with even better lighting. Re-examine your advertising—the pull quality of the ads themselves, where and when you're spending your ad money. By upgrading ad performance you reduce ad costs. Make more use of cooperative advertising, a real saving.

Don't resign yourself to the "inevitability" of continually rising costs. The stores that show the most efficient expense control are consistently the best profit-makers, the most securely capitalized, and own the best credit ratings. It isn't that they have any special secrets. But they have learned this one secret: It isn't what you know, but what you *do* with what you know.

Save 2% On Expenses, Add 33% to Net Profit

In shoe business, a little can often mean a lot. Take expenses, for example. If you save only two percentage points on operating expenses, your net profit increases by 33 percent. Here's an example of how it works:

1) A store does an annual volume of $350,000.
2) Say its expenses are 40 percent or $140,000.
3) Say its net profit is 6 percent or $21,000.

Now . . .

4) The store reduces expenses to 38 percent or $133,000.
5) The saved expenses of $7,000 raises net profit to $28,000, an increase of 33.3 percent.
6) Thus a drop of only two percentage points in expenses adds a hefty 33.3 percent to net profit.

The National Shoe Retailers Association's survey studies on Shoe Store Operations show an operating expenses spread of about seven percentage points between the average family store (37 percent) and volume stores (44 percent); and almost 10 percentage points between the average downtown store (38.5 percent) and the average mall store (48 percent). Surely in those spreads is some fat that can be trimmed.

How many expense leaks are there in your operation? Take a close look, item by item. Beware, however, of cuts simply for the sake of cutting, such as your ad budget. Nevertheless, there's a little fat on all of us. Look for it, then dissolve it and watch your profit muscle grow.

7

Purchase Discounts and the Profit Connection

Most profits are wasted in dribbles, not flows. A bucket with a small hole in the bottom gets as empty as a bucket that's kicked over.

The Bottom Line is the holy grail of business. But the annual pilgrimage to it doesn't necessarily have to be via profits on sales. There are more roads than one leading to better profits.

One of these is purchase discounts. By consistently taking advantage of these discounts a store can increase its net profit by 20 percent to 50 percent. There are no tricks to it. It's done every year by alert merchants on the lookout for savings opportunities that convert into profits.

In an average year, shoe manufacturers and other volume shoe wholesalers make about $450 million available to shoe retailers in purchase discounts. Of that, over $100 million or an estimated 25 percent goes unused or unclaimed—wasted or lost by negligent retailers. Ironically, most of this loss is taken by those who need it most, the smaller retailers. An estimated 40 percent of them fail to make regular use of these discounts.

Now, almost every retailer gets into an occasional bind where he must temporarily forfeit his discounts. But those are, or should be, exceptional occurrences. In most instances, however, it's a matter of laxity or poor planning—lack of planning for cash flow or reserves, faulty inventory control, undisciplined expense control, inadequate record keeping, forgetful timing, buying from too many resources, etc. Such retailers are often in a position of being stock-heavy and cash-light.

Well, what are purchase discounts really for? For the retailer they are *not* to be used as price concessions to be passed on to the consumers. Discounts earned for prompt payment are hedges against the store's occasional buying errors, and also an icing on the store's profit cake. They are something earned and not a gift.

Nor are shoe manufacturers doing the retailer a favor by offering purchase discounts. It's more profitable for the manufacturer to give you a 3 percent "credit" for your prompt cash than for him to borrow at 10 percent or 12 percent to maintain his cash flow while waiting for the retailers' payments.

Purchase discounts can amount to up to 60 percent of the store's net profit. For example, of each $100 on net profit, $60 may be operating profit and $40 from discounts. Let's say a store regularly earns 3 percent discount on 30 days (net 31 days). Here's an example of what happens:

1) $150,000 a year for merchandise—@ 3 percent earns $4,500.
2) Sales @ 50 percent markon—$300,000.
3) Net operating profit of 7 percent or $21,000.
4) The 3 percent earned discounts ($4,500) equal 21.4 percent of net profit. Or—
5) Net profit is now $25,500 or 8.5 percent—up 21.4 percent.

The manufacturer's paid-out discounts are costed into the shoe's price. So whether you take those discounts or not, you're paying for them, anyway. And if you're not taking *your* discounts, you're paying for the other fellow's. So the discounts aren't "found" money but money owed to you in the first place.

Look at those savings in another way. If the $4,500 in earned discounts are placed in an interest-bearing account at 7 percent, your $4,500 grows to about $4,830 compounded at the end of the first year. At the same interest rate compounded over five years, your original $4,500 has grown to around $6,000. If you keep depositing $4,500 annually, then the accumulated deposits plus compounded interest over the five-year period will give you a nice nest-egg of about $28,000. In fact, some companies (not in the footwear industry) have now set up special "mutual funds" in which the retailers' discounts are automatically invested for long-term growth at maximum return.

Many years ago when the purchase discount idea got started, it was erratic and ethically suspect. Some retailers got it, some didn't. It was a matter of the squeaking wheels, or the big wheels, getting the advantages. Some retailers got more, some less (and some none), depending upon how shrewd a deal they could make or how much business volume clout they had. Fair-play legislation was finally imposed, and today purchase discount rates are standard for all, available to all.

There are other benefits from taking purchase discounts regularly. It helps develop an excellent credit rating with your resources and with your local bank. If allowed to develop as a reserve fund, it's a great asset when you need money for remodeling, a special buying opportunity, or other business uses. And that, incidentally, is why it's a good idea to keep your purchase discount "earnings" in a separate account or in a separate record. At the end of the year it lets you know exactly what you earned via discounts (and also what you failed to earn). It lets you know further what share of your final net profit was accounted for by those discount earnings.

But the main gain is where it counts most—at the bottom line in your own profit pocket. As you can see in the accompanying table, the cost of money—that is, the cost of not taking or the benefit of taking discounts—amounts to a lot more than generally realized.

Discount Rates Translated Into Annual Percentages of Money Earned or Lost

1%/10 days/net 30 days = 18% a year
2%/30 days/net 60 days = 24% a year
2%/10 days/net 30 days = 36% a year
3%/30 days/net 60 days = 36% a year
3%/10 days/net 30 days = 54% a year
5%/30 days/net 31 days = 60% a year

8

A Closer Look At Stock Turns

It's true you can't do business from an empty wagon. But you'll never make money unless you empty the wagon three or four times a year.

Retailers use the rate of stock turns as a barometer of sales performance. The average shoe store is conditioned to an average or standard 2-time stock turn rate as "normal." If you match it you're supposed to be okay, and if you beat it you're that much smarter.

Shoe business has traditionally been a low-turn business. For example, women's wear specialty stores average 4.8 turns; men's wear 2.6; appliance stores 5.5; department stores 3.4; but family shoe stores only 1.9.

However, many successful stores consistently do 2.5 or 3 turns. A good merchant creates turnover, makes it happen. A healthy turnover rate often reflects a store's efficiency in buying, inventory control, merchandising, sales flow, profitability, etc.

A healthy turnover rate also feeds on itself by generating a steady flow of fresh merchandise, traffic, sales, plus motivating the enthusiasm and energies of salespeople.

Nevertheless, beware those averages. Stock turn rates can be tricky and deceptive. High isn't always necessarily good, nor low always necessarily bad. Turnover depends upon the type, quantity and quality of the merchandise, plus the type of store operation. There's really no such thing as a "standard" turnover rate applying to all shoe stores or shoe departments.

However, unnecessarily slow turnover can cause a costly tieup of capital and cash flow that otherwise can be used to take discounts on bills, take advantage of hot-item buys, avoid borrowing at high interest rates, etc. (See Table 1 on page 42).

Slow turnover also results in costly carryover stock. Shoes cost money just by sitting on shelves. Static stock contributes nothing to sales or profits, but does add to expenses. (See Table 2 on page 42).

Many shoe stores carry stock too long. Let's compare women's dresses and women's shoes, as shown by the Retail Merchants Association data for department and specialty stores. On average, only 2 percent of women's dresses inventory is older than 6 months—as compared with 28 percent to 30 percent for women's shoes. Stock turns for women's dresses are three times that for women's shoes, and markdowns are half that for women's shoes. Yet both items involve styles, sizes and obsolescence.

Women's shoes in department stores require an investment of $2 to earn $1, but women's dresses require only $3 to earn $4. According to RMA, dollar return on investment for women's shoes is 47 percent, but for dresses 127 percent. Much of the difference lies in turnover rates and carrying costs.

Does all this mean that the "ideal" is a high turnover rate? Not at all. Some retailers boast of their 4- or 5-time turnover. But there's no special magic to it. Excessively high turnover is rife with risks and penalties. It usually indicates one or more of the following: 1) Operating with starved stocks.

        2) Inadequate style or size selection.

        3) Limited services.

        4) A high percentage of walks.

        5) Broken stocks and hashed inventory.

        6) Shlocky store image.

Such stores usually operate with the inventory philosophy of "live off the best, the devil take the rest." A supermarket can achieve a 10-time turn on slippers by carrying them only during the Christmas season, or kids' sneakers only in summer. A discount store operates with low markon and prices and high turnover—but with limited size and style selection, seasonal inventory, and no services.

Shoe stores, of course, can't operate that way. Inevitably, some stock gets carried over. Some sizes sell slower than others. Some types of merchandise (work boots, duty shoes, basic styles, etc.) have a limited turn. Some merchandise with limited seasonal appeal, such as slippers, must nevertheless be available year round.

Again, a store dealing exclusively in fast fashion will have an appreciably higher turn rate than one dealing in basic footwear and in-depth size inventory. However, the first store will have much higher markdowns.

Nevertheless, most shoe stores, often without realizing it, at any given time are living off the top third of their inventory while the rest of the inventory is a drag on the overall stock turn rate. (See Table 3 on page 43).

And right here is the key to improving stock turn rate with its many consequent benefits. Look again at Table 3 on page 43.) If the bottom third were lifted to an average 2-time turn, the overall store average would rise to 2.5 times, an improvement of 25 percent.

Few retailers maintain a watch or scoresheet on turnover by inventory *categories*—men's, women's, children's, basic versus fashion, seasonal merchandise, etc. This is where the real stock turn readings are found; and also the determination of where the action is and isn't. Before improvement can be made you have to know precisely where the vulnerable areas are. Here, now, are suggestions for improving your turnover performance:

1) Keep the fat off inventory at all times—but don't operate with a skin-and-bones inventory, either.
2) Avoid excess of fringe sizes and widths that become carryovers or markdowns and a drag on turns.
3) Avoid duplication of styles, lines.
4) Increase sales and traffic without increasing inventory.

5) Fill in or reorder quickly on good sellers to maximize turns.
6) Quickly assign slow sellers to PMs, markdowns or clearances.
7) Keep closer watch on carryovers and stock shelf life, which many stores fail to do.
8) Avoid deliveries much ahead of season, which adds to carrying costs.
9) Buy more frequently but in smaller lots.
10) Keep records of stock turns by inventory categories, lines or styles.

Remember that excessively high turn has its risks—but unnecessary low turn has its penalties. There's a happy medium, and it's almost sure to be better than your present level.

What's the best or ideal stock turn rate? It's the best one suited for *your* type of store—but which also delivers the best cash flow and profit, and moves each category of footwear at its maximum sales rate potential.

TABLE 1

Slow Turnover Ties Up Capital

Annual Sales Cost Value	Annual Stock Turns	Inventory	Capital Released
$100,000	1	$100,000	—
"	2	50,000	$50,000
"	3	33,333	66,667
"	4	25,000	75,000
"	5	20,000	80,000

TABLE 2

The Cost of Carrying Costs

Annual Sales Cost Value	Annual Stock Turns	Inventory	Carrying Costs	Reduction in Carrying Costs
$100,000	1	$100,000	$12,000	—
"	2	50,000	6,000	$6,000
"	3	33,333	3,960	8,040
"	4	25,000	3,000	9,000
"	5	20,000	2,400	9,600

TABLE **3**

How Turnover Averages Out

% Inventory	Months to Turn Stock	Turnover Rate
33.3%	4	3
33.3	6	2
33.3	12	1
100.0%	7.3 aver.	2 aver.

A CHART LESSON ON HOW TURNOVER AFFECTS PROFITS

With a $50,000 Inventory and 50% Markon:

    A) 1.8 turns = $180,000 in sales
    B) 2.0   "   =   200,000 "   "
    C) 3.0   "   =   300,000 "   "
    D) 4.0   "   =   400,000 "   "

If the store markon is distributed as follows:

    30% fixed costs
     7% controlled costs
     8% markdowns
     5% net profit
    50%

Then the operating results would look like this:

	Store A 1.8 Turns	Store B 2.0 Turns	Store C 3.0 Turns	Store D 4.0 Turns
Sales	$180,000	$200,000	$300,000	$400,000
Cost of sales	90,000	100,000	150,000	200,000
Gross profit	90,000	100,000	150,000	200,000
Fixed costs	54,000	54,000	54,000	54,000
Controlled costs	12,600	14,000	21,000	28,000
Markdowns	14,400	16,000	24,000	32,000
Net profit	9,000	16,000	51,000	86,000
Net profit with 3% cash discounts	11,700	19,000	55,000	92,000

Note: It is now easy to see how volume retail stores (such as discounters) can operate with lower markon and prices and still realize higher net profits than many conventional stores. The obvious answer, of course, is in higher turnover.

9

What Records Should You Maintain?

Hindsight is how we explain the mistakes that foresight could have avoided.

Planning is a map to determine where you are, where you've been, where you want to go, how you want to get there, when you want to arrive, and how you want to pay for the trip.

Several years ago the University of Pittsburgh made a study of retailers to determine the differences between the successful, the mediocre and the poor (or failure) performers. They found that the single most consistent difference was records. In 80 percent of cases successful stores kept good and proper records while most of the poor performers kept inadequate or erratic records. The most lax were found among smaller to medium size stores.

The common plaint of many retailers regarding records is, "I don't have the time for all that paperwork." Well, you've heard the saying, "How come there's no time to do it right the first time, but always time to do it right the second time?"

Don't brush off records as "paperwork." All business boils down to a numbers game. Success goes to those who keep the numbers to work with. Many of the rest flounder.

Keeping good records doesn't cost time but saves time. It also saves and makes money. It eliminates the guesswork, reduces mistakes and faulty decisions. Records not only tell you precisely where you've been and where you are, but also point you to where you're going. Your records are as important as your merchandise for making a profit.

Two perennial questions retailers ask are: how many records should I keep? Which records? Perhaps no two retailers keep identical records. However, there are certain *basic* records that should be kept by all shoe stores. These can be altered or further embellished as desired. Let's take a look at those basics and some of the sub-records they contain.

Operating Expenses. These include all the essentials: rent, insurance, utilities, advertising, freight, services (legal, accounting, etc.), remodeling, fixtures, etc. They should *not* be lumped under one heading of "expenses." Each operating expense category should be separately listed. This tells you exactly where your expense spending is going and keeps a rein on excesses.

Payroll. One single total isn't enough. It should be broken down by salaries, wages, overtime, bonuses, fringes (hospitalization, etc.), and other extras. Again, the sub-listings give you a clearer insight into the cost makeup of your payroll, which gives you a better means of control.

Cost of Merchandise. Separate records should be kept for units and dollars, and by separate resources. Further listings should be made for dates of all purchases, dates of payments due and payments made, purchases by category (men's, women's, children's, athletic, etc.), and purchase discounts taken. These data tell you not only how much (pairs and dollars) you bought, but from whom you bought, how much by categories, what you earned in discounts, and other important information.

Inventory Status. Your records should show beginning of month (BOM) and end of month (EOM) inventory status. This helps prevent unbalanced inventories. Records should also show fillins and reorders and cancellations. A record of age of merchandise is very important to keep markdowns and other losses to a minimum. Every box should be date-marked when delivered. Merchandise age can be listed, for example, 0–3 months, 3–6 months, 6–9 months, over 9 months. Age, of course, varies. A fashion shoe can be old after 3 months, while a men's work boot, a staple, can still be young after a year.

Inventory Performance. Many retailers fall short here. A family is a group of persons, but each is treated as an individual. So too with your inventory. A record should be kept of inventory performance by categories (men's, women's, children's, slippers, athletic, fashion, basic). This tells you not only how each category is performing, but also what each is contributing to volume and profits. Further, performance by lines should be recorded. This helps to separate the wheat from the chaff, the consistent winners from the consistent draggers and losers.

Sales. This is an obvious one for the records. But overall dollar sales are merely the beginning. Records should also be kept by unit sales; sales by merchandise category (men's, women's, children's, athletic, fashion, basic, etc.); sales by lines or brands; by stock number. A record should be kept of walks—how many and reasons why. You should know not only how many sales you're making but also how many you're losing—and why. And finally, a record of selling costs to give you a gauge against sales and to prevent excessive selling costs.

Markons or Margins. A record of sales both on initial markon and net markon. And again, not merely overall but by individual lines. This tells you which lines are delivering the best net markon. It also indicates your own buying/selling performance—whether you're buying the right shoes—or, if you are, whether you're doing them justice with your pricing and selling.

Markdowns. The records should show not only overall average but markdowns by merchandise categories, by lines or brands, even by stock number. Markdowns are the prime enemy of profits. You should know as much about your enemies as your friends.

Turns. Beware of averages—like an overall average of 2.1 turns for your store.

It's really a useless figure. It has no value unless separated by merchandise categories (men's, women's, children's, fashion, basic, etc.), and also by lines. Not all categories or lines should be expected to show the same turn rate. Each has its own "norm" rate. Keeping records on turns as suggested here helps you pinpoint inventory performance with more accuracy.

Accessories. A record should be kept of dollar sales overall (to give you the accessories share to overall store volume). But also a record of accessories sales by categories (handbags, hose, etc.).

Salespersons' Performance. Are you underpaying some salespeople and over-paying others? Only records of individual sales performance will tell you. Records should include total sales per individual; multiple-pair and accessories sales; percentage of sales per earnings cost; commissions and other extra earnings against basic wage. It isn't enough to know what you've paid the salespeople, but what you're paying them *for*.

Customer Records. This is one of the most neglected of all records, yet one of the most important. It's not only a record but an excellent marketing tool. It should contain name, address, phone, shoe size, dates and amounts of purchases. Customer records provide you with an active mailing list. Using an annual check, you can learn which and how many of your customers you haven't seen for a year—then to phone or write and ask why. In many instances you can regain otherwise lost customers. It informs you of your customer attrition rate—an important trend indicator for your business.

Cash Position. This would include records of debts due, debts paid, cash reserve, and other financial data. You should know your net and liquid position at the end of each month.

Profit. This lists overall gross, overall net, profit by merchandise categories, and also by separate lines. While most stores know their profit, many don't know where their profit is coming from.

Special Records. This is a miscellany that can include extras not contained among the basic records. For example, your six-months budgeted sales versus actual results—to keep you humble with a periodic measure of your forecasting ability. A record of pull performance of your ads—to guide you in what to repeat and what to delete. Credit or charge sales versus cash sales. Sales by color, materials, heel heights—an important guide for your new buys. The delivery performance record for each of your resources. Bad debt losses. Freight charges. Special sizes charges.

Keeping records requires discipline. However, the more you make it a habit the easier it becomes. Some records should be kept daily, others weekly, a few monthly. But at the end of the month *all* your records should be totaled and examined. This gives you a sound month-to-month progress report, an accurate fix on all operations.

Develop a simple file and record system. Your accountant can help to set it up.

If you don't have a computer, buy a simple, inexpensive one. Even an ordinary personal computer to start with. You can program it to fill most of your basic needs. It will put most of your records at your fingertips for instant feedback.

Later you can buy a more sophisticated computer if and when you need it. Computers for record keeping today are as essential to the store as the cash register.

The most important thing to remember is that a business usually lives or dies by its records. The stores that maintain good records usually live best and longest.

15 Basic Records

1) Expenses
2) Payroll
3) Cost of merchandise
4) Inventory status
5) Inventory performance
6) Sales
7) Markons or margins
8) Markdowns
9) Turns
10) Accessories
11) Salespersons' performance
12) Customer records
13) Cash position
14) Profit
15) Special records

10

Pre-Planning Your Profits

The world isn't interested in the
storms you encountered, but
whether you brought in the ship.

The justification of private profit is
private risk.

We get our word "profit" from the Latin *profectus,* which literally means to advance, move forward, gain. For example, we speak of profiting from experience, meaning we learn or gain something from it. In a monetary sense, of course, it means a gain on any investment or risk venture.

Profit is the prime motive for virtually everything we do. In business the employer makes his profit from selling or moving his merchandise. The employee profits from selling or hiring out his skills and services. Without the profit motive the world would stop in its tracks.

But despite our investment of time, money, skills or services, a profit is never guaranteed. The profit may be less than expected or planned or what we think is deserved; or there may be no profit at all, and sometimes even a loss or profit deficit.

In recent years, shoe retailers have fared poorly in profit-making. According to nationwide surveys conducted by the National Shoe Retailers Association, here is a sample of average net pretax net profits for shoe stores over the 1975–1987 period:

Year	% Net Profit	Year	% Net Profit
1975	6.3%	1983	1.2%
1976	5.3	1984	3.1
1977	4.5	1985	2.6
1980	6.2	1986	2.5
1981	5.9	1987*	2.6
1982	1.3		

*Estimated

Traditionally, average net profits for shoe stores has been in the 5.5 percent to 6 percent range. The 1980s saw sharp declines in net profits due to several factors: intense competition from the proliferation of off-price retailers, plus the greatly increased frequency of cut-price promotions by conventional retailers, plus a heavily over-stored condition in shoe retailing. During some of the years in the 1980s as many as one-third of shoe stores reported net losses, with another 18 percent reporting break-even or simply no profit.

Those are clearly disastrous numbers. Consider, for example, that the average shoe store doing $350,000 in volume averages 10,000 transactions with an average of $35 per sales ticket, plus serving a total traffic of about 14,000 (including walks, lookers, etc.). That retailer also spends about 60 hours a week at his business. Considering all the time and money investment involved, and measured against a net profit of, say, only 3 percent, the total net earnings of $10,500 is a tragically low reward or return. Yet, as the data averages show, it has not been unusual.

On first glance, profit-making is a simple process. The retailer buys merchandise for a particular price, sells it at a higher price, deducts his operating expenses, and presto, the remainder or difference is his profit. But every merchant knows it isn't that simple. What, then, so often makes it complicated or difficult? The reason can often be found in the traditional approach to profit-making. Consider two important elements involved in all profit-making:

1) Profits aren't made from merchandise but from *customers*. Therefore, all profit-making begins with attracting customers by a variety of factors that influence the customers to buy the merchandise.
2) Profits are made from merchandise *only* if profits are made from each operating segment of the store aside from the merchandise itself.

It's like a battle plan. The front-line troops are the merchandise. But the effectiveness of the troops is totally dependent upon the supply lines of weapons and ammunition, food and clothing, medical supplies and other vital equipment. The success of the troops is also dependent upon the battle plan designed by the military brass. Thus troops (merchandise) alone don't win battles. Their success depends upon all the supports of supplies and strategies behind them.

Profitable operation of a retail shoe business demands the same approach. Granted, the better the quality of the troops (merchandise), the better the chance of victory. But no matter how fresh, courageous and well-trained the troops, there can be no victory (profits) without those vital backup supports and strategies.

Simple and obvious? Yes. But the simple and obvious get ignored or violated every day by retailers. The proof is in those profit records—low profits, no profits, or profit deficits.

WHAT MAKES A PROFIT?

Everything, but *everything* in your store operations must turn a profit or contribute to the overall store profit. You're familiar with the mathematical law: the whole is the sum of its parts. So too with profit-making in a retail shoe business. Each part of the operation must be seen as an entity of its own and must be profitable on its own. When all those separate "profits" are combined, the sum of their parts adds up to the "whole" of the store's profits we call the bottom line. But to focus solely or mainly on the "whole" without giving equal attention to the parts creates leaks which drain the profit pond.

All kinds of profit "systems" have been devised, many with sophisticated arithmetic showing how to arrive at a handsome net profit. Inventory control or buying systems, for example. However, you can have the perfect inventory control system and even maintain it, yet still show little or no profit. The inventory itself may contain a lot of poor buys or slow-moving merchandise. Or the merchandise may be right but the advertising, selling and promotion weak. Or the operating expenses get out of hand. And so on. So the "perfect" inventory control system, while still perfect by itself, can prove impotent in producing a profit. The weaknesses within the operating parts can cause a failure of the operating whole.

What, specifically, do we mean by the "parts" involved in the profitability of the "whole"? Here are the main ones:

1) Buying Efficiency.   The selection, budget or amount, timing and profitable return on the lines carried and merchandise purchased.

2) Inventory Control.   The amount (over or under adequate supply on hand), and quality (age, salability, selection, availability of sizes).

3) Expense Control.   The maximum fulfillment of operational needs at minimal cost.

4) Marketing and Merchandising.   Assuring that the merchandise, services, displays, store decor and image are attuned to the local market and the targeted clientele.

5) Sales.   Maximum ratio of sales relative to store traffic and customers served.

6) Pricing.   Scaled to be competitive but without sacrifice of reasonable profit margins.

7) Advertising and Promotion.   The effectiveness of the strategies to attract traffic and sales.

8) Salespeople.   The performance quality of the front-line troops for maximum productivity of sales while keeping selling costs at the lowest level.

9) Customer Relations.   The process of satisfying and retaining customers once attracted to the store—via the merchandise, services, product performance, values, store atmosphere, etc.

10) Stock Turns.   Maintaining an above-average performance for your type of store and merchandise.

11) Markdowns.   Maintaining a below-average performance for your type of store and merchandise.

12) Location.   Situated for maximum convenience or accessibility for your targeted clientele to assure maximum traffic against the potential.

13) Store Image.   Having a clear-cut identity for a particular type of merchandise or prices or reputation, etc. Having a distinct personality of its own.

Each of these "parts" has its own contribution to make to overall profits. Each seeks to reach for the highest level of productivity. The strength of the whole (the bottom line) relies upon the strength of the individual parts. Liken it to a baseball team. If the team has strong pitching but weak hitting it can't be a pennant contender. If it has a strong outfield but weak infield the team performance will be mediocre. If it has a strong frontline team but a weak bench and bullpen, it's in a constantly precarious position.

Let's cite some specific examples with a shoe store. Let's start with traffic versus sales, because there's a difference.

1) A store's annual volume: $350,000.
2) Net profit 5 percent or $17,500.
3) Average sale: $35.
4) Store has 10,000 buying customers.
5) But store traffic is 40 percent more or 14,000 (including walks, just-looking browsers, etc.)
6) So net profit per *buying* customer is $1.75.
7) Net profit per *traffic* customer is $1.25.

The difference between buyers and traffic is 40 percent. Keep in mind that it costs as much to serve non-buying as buying customers. If half of the non-buying customers were converted into buying customers, sales would rise $70,000 or 20 percent, and net profit (at 5 percent) would increase by $3,500 or 20 percent. True, you can't sell everybody. But do you have to lose 40 percent of your interested-in-buying traffic? By converting more traffic into buyers, this part of the store operation improves profit contribution to the whole.

Another example:

1) Two stores, each doing an annual volume of $350,000.
2) Each spends 3 percent of sales or $10,500 on advertising.
3) Store A, due to better quality and timing of its advertising, plus better selection of media, gets 25 percent sales return from its advertising. Store B, with poorer quality and time of advertising, and less selective use of media, gets only a 10 percent return. The advertising of Store A is not only 150 percent more productive, but its advertising is costing less per customer-response and making a much larger contribution to the store's profits.

Still another example:

	Store A	Store B
Annual volume	$350,000	$450,000
Total space	2,500 sq. ft.	2,500 sq. ft.
Sales per square foot	$140	$180
Display space (windows, inside)	300 sq. ft.	300 sq. ft.
Display space $ sales contrib.	$42,000	$54,000

Thus Store B is getting a 28.6 percent greater return from its display space (12 percent of total store space). The question here: Do you know how much your displays and display space are contributing to total sales and net profits? Do you know whether the return-on-displays performance is excellent, good, fair or poor? You know your dollar investment in your displays and display space. You should also know the contribution of this operating "part" to the store's net profit "whole."

A final example:

1) A salesperson is paid $6 an hour, $48 per 8-hour day.
2) He or she serves an average of 15 customers a day.
3) 10 of these customers are sold at an average $35 per sale, total $350.
4) The store's selling cost for this salesperson is 13.7 percent.
5) But say he or she sells 14 of those 15 customers at $35 per—total $490.

6) The salesperson's selling cost is reduced to 9.8 percent, or 28.5 percent less.
7) Or, say the salesperson sells only 10 of the 15 customers per day—but upgrades the average sale from $35 to $50 for half of them.
8) The salesperson's average daily total is now $425 instead of $350.
9) And his or her selling cost is now reduced from 13.7 percent to 11.3 percent, or 17.5 percent less.

Same salesperson, same customers, but with an upgraded performance the salesperson is making an appreciably greater contribution to the store's net profit, plus reducing the store's selling costs.

By now you have a clear idea of how each of the store's operating "parts" contribute to the store's bottom line. You also recognize the importance of maximizing the performance effectiveness of *each* part in order to achieve maximum net profit. It's like the human body itself. If a few of its parts are malfunctioning or functioning below par, the whole health system diminishes despite the sound health of the other parts.

PRE-PLANNING A PROFIT

Profit should never be seen as a residue, or what remains after all costs and expenses are accounted for. Profit should be pre-planned in the same way as buying budgets, expenses, promotions and other operational factors are pre-planned. How much of a net profit should be budgeted? Absolute minimum should be 7 percent. Net profit doesn't reach a state of robust health until a level of 10 percent is achieved. At a 7 percent level on a $350,000 volume the net take is $24,500. But even that isn't all free and clear. Some of it has to be kept in reserve or spent for occasional remodeling, or new fixtures, or other outlays not accounted for on the regular expense list.

And again keep in mind that if our retailer/owner is working 60 hours a week, his 7 percent net profit of $24,500 amounts to $471 a week—or a return of less than $8 an hour. Measured against the owner's responsibilities and risks, that's hardly a handsome return on his investment, despite the fact that 7 percent net is appreciably above average.

What's a "fair" profit? Judging your own net profit performance by the averages may give you some emotional consolation if your net is a shade above average. But it's no credit to your performance as a good merchant. So what's a fair profit? The maximum percentage you can earn while at the same time remaining competitive and providing good values for your customers. "Fair" has no numbers attached to it. The ebb and flow of the marketplace almost invariably keeps "fair" in realistic perspective.

A sign of operating weakness is to allow the competition to determine your net profit. Nevertheless, this frequently happens in respect to prices and margins. A dramatic example is the average net profit of only 1.3 percent in 1982 and 1983 resulting from the competitive pressures of the off-price retailers and the continuing price promotions by conventional retailers as a defensive reaction. Yet, there were other conventional retailers who stayed outside of the cut-price battlefield and not only prospered but continued to operate with healthy margins and net profits.

What is overlooked is that it isn't the competition that governs margins and profits, but *customers*. Hence the obvious question: How does the retailer attract and retain customers with regular prices despite the siren's appeal of lower prices by the off-pricers or the abundance of price promotions? The retailer must answer the question with one of his own: What has equal or greater customer appeal beyond price?

The answers are found in such customer-attraction factors as excellence of services, complete selections of sizes and widths, imaginative promotions (other than price), breadth of merchandise selection, reputation for quality and value, strong store image, reputable brands, fashion freshness, convenience of location, among others. These are assets that the competition usually doesn't or can't offer. They cover their shortcomings with the hype of "bargains."

The final message is actually a summation:

Profit is not made from merchandise but from customers.

Profit is not a residue or "bottom line" but the consequence of the interplay of all the separate parts of the operation.

Profit is not an entity by itself but the sum of all the parts that make up the whole.

Each part of the operation must be viewed as a separate investment. You invest in merchandise. But you also invest in advertising, promotions, displays, sales and other personnel, etc. Each of these must deliver a tangible return on investment. Therefore, you are not invested in a "business" but in a variety of separate enterprises which together become "the business."

Profit reflects the performance quality of the management—the ultimate gauge of the management's level of ability as an administrator of operational skills. No matter how smart one may be as a buyer, or how clever as a seller, or how dedicated as a manager, or how aggressive as a merchant—the final truth of his or her skills and ability is found in the consistency and health of the net profits.

HOW CUSTOMER SERVICE COSTS AFFECT PROFITS

1) Store's annual volume: $350,000.
2) Selling cost 12 percent or $42,000.
3) Average sale, $35.
4) 10,000 buying customers at $35 per.
5) Service cost per buying customer: $4.20.
6) Needed average sales per day (305 days): $1,147.
7) Average daily buying customers needed: 33.
8) Daily sales service cost: $138.60 ($4.20 × 33).

BUT . . .

1) An additional 30 percent (3,000) customers are served but do not buy (walks, etc.)
2) Yet salesperson's time used at $6 per hour—an average of 15 minutes or $1.50 per non-buying customer.

3) Serving those non-buying customers amounts to $4,500 a year (3,000 × $1.50).
4) If the store's net profit is 6 percent or $21,000, then the $4,500 of "wasted" or non-productive service time amounts to 21.4% of the store's net profit.

A PROFIT EFFICIENCY RATING TEST

Profit is never the result of any one or few parts of the store operation, but of a variety of functions. Each part of the operation must be seen as a separate profit center or investment contributing to the whole.

Here is a self-scoring test involving most of the profit investment parts. A column is filled in for our Sample Store. You fill in the blank column for your store. Here's how the scoring or rating system works:

Excellent—5 points	Total score of 60–70—Excellent	
Good —4 "	" " " 45–59—Good	
Fair —3 "	" " " 30–40—Fair	
Poor —2 "	" " " under 30—Poor	

	Sample Store	Your Store
Buying efficiency	4	
Marketing/merchandising	3	
Expense control	4	
Inventory control	3	
Sales	3	
Displays	2	
Pricing/margins	4	
Advertising/promotion	3	
Salespeople (productivity)	3	
Location (traffic density)	3	
Customer relations (repeat business)	4	
Stock turns	2	
Markdowns	3	
Store image	2	
	43	

11

Sixteen Common Profit Leaks

Most of the money a business calls profit is simply money that hasn't been wasted.

In many instances in retailing, more profits are lost than made. Retailers become frustrated after pouring so much time and effort into their business tub, only to find a shallow pool of profit at year's end.

While various "reasons" can be cited for this extremely poor performance of recent years, especially off-pricing and the high frequency of cut-price promotions, something of major importance is overlooked. Just as profits are made, so too profits are often forfeited or wasted.

In retailing there are two ways to make a profit: selling merchandise, and preventing profit leaks from within the operation. The first is obvious. The second, however, is often overlooked without realizing that if the profit leaks are plugged, the retailer can at least *double* his profits.

Following are 16 of the most common leaks in shoe retailing:

1) Out of Stock.   This consists of frequently missed sizes in wanted styles, or broken lots in good-selling styles, leading to lost sales and profits. Studies by IBM have shown that a habitual out-of-stock condition can cost the store as much as 40 percent of sales and an equal share of profits. It's the old story: you can't do business from an empty wagon.

2) Purchase discounts.   Failure to take them consistently can result in a loss of 25 percent to 40 percent of net profits. The causes are well known: lack of cash flow, negligence of lack of discipline, failure to recognize the large share of net profits accounted for by purchase discounts. Do the arithmetic on purchase discounts of merchandise bought over the past year and the numbers will surprise you. It suggests another old adage: a dollar saved is a dollar earned.

3) Customer Turnover.   A store's failure to retain a high level of customer loyalty and repeat business is an important key to sales and profits. Yet, most retailers can't specify what share of their business is repeat, what share transient or one-time. Further, few stores check up on lost customers (those who haven't made a purchase in over a year)—where they disappeared to and why.

Whereas the foundation of every business is customers, customers are the root of all sales and profits. Self-evident? Then how come most stores don't know where the "lost" customers went, or why?

4) Low Productivity of Salespeople.   This means lackluster performance on multiple-pair sales, accessories, upgrading sales tickets, etc. The less productive the selling performance the higher the selling cost and the lower the profits.

A small part of the fault may be with the salespeople, but most of it belongs to management which is responsible for the training and performance of the salespeople. Shoe store surveys show selling costs ranging between 8 percent and 14 percent—an enormous spread which reflects the differences in productivity of salespeople and its obvious effect on profits.

5) Loose Expense Control.   It's the difference between lean muscles and fat. Almost every store carries some excess expense fat. Sharper probing can usually result in improved costs on such items as insurance, freight charges, interest and loan costs, advertising costs, etc. Then there's always that insidious category called "miscellaneous" expense, the costly catchbasin that is the hiding place for non-business or personal expenses charged to the business—the mole that bores into profits.

6) Walkouts.   Three of every ten customers for the average shoe store or department, resulting in tens of thousands of dollars in lost sales and a further bite out of profits. Cutting walks from 30 percent to 20 percent adds 30 percent to net profit; and cutting them down to 10 percent adds 65 percent to net profit. Yet this potential profit bonanza continues to be ignored by many stores. A concentrated effort to cut walks can close a big hole in the profit dike.

7) Ineffectual Ad Program.   Low or non-existent ad budgets, poor media selection, erratic advertising, poor or mediocre quality of the advertising, failure to make use of cooperate advertising. The weak quality of the advertising becomes a conduit of wasted dollars, while the low or erratic ad budgets represent a penny-wise-dollar-foolish policy. Also, failure to use cooperative advertising on a consistent and selective basis allows free ad dollars to go unutilized. Put them all together and the low-productivity ad program not only performs poorly on sales and traffic returns, but contributes to the diminished profit performance.

8) Markdowns.   The National Shoe Retailers Assn.'s Shoe Store Operations Survey shows markdowns average between 13.5 percent and 34.3 percent, an extraordinary 230 percent difference among categories of stores. Even the overall average of 19.6 percent for all stores combined is excessively high. Many of those stores could reduce their markdowns flab and add more muscle to their profits.

9) Inventory Control.   The difference between quality (salability) and quantity (salable stock intermixed with sludge). Or being overstocked or understocked. Or delayed clearances. Retailers tend to focus on the quantity status, the fear of inventory overload, which is a legitimate concern.

But understocked condition is equally threatening to sales and profits. And much of it can be traced to delayed clearances and a gradual pileup of PMs. So shoes, shoes everywhere, but only a few that sell.

10) Buying Bloopers.   Even the most astute of buyers make them. But with some retailers the poor or bad buys, the overbuys and underbuys, happen more frequently. The causes are various: faulty planning or budgeting, failure to keep abreast of trends, duplication of lines, over-caution, lack of caution or self-control, listening to too many well-intentioned voices.

Then there's the common sin of delayed reorders on good-sellers, or late buying with consequent late in-season deliveries, which often becomes slow-moving or clearance merchandise. Each of these bloopers takes its nibble out of profits.

11) Erratic Sizeups.   A common shortcoming with many retailers, especially smaller ones lacking a disciplined policy on sizeups. The excuses of "don't have the time" or "I forget" are clear signs of a disorganized operation. Missing sizes account for an estimated 40 percent of missed sales. The cause is one simple word: neglect. The cure is equally simple: a sizeup policy with disciplined backup. The result: fewer walks, more sales, improved profits.

12) Ineffectual Displays.   Display space (windows and interior) generally account for 20 percent of store space. Figure out the per-foot cost of store space and that 20 percent accounts for a surprising amount of rental dollars. Yet, when ineffectual displays don't return more than the dollars spent on them, the space is wasted and becomes a profit debit.

Studies show that window displays can account for as much as 25 percent of the store traffic. Many stores fall far short of that share of traffic pull. The failure to make full use of display potential inside the store (walls, corners, aisles, counters, "air" space, etc.) is another space cost waste with loss of potential sales and profits.

13) Weak Pricing and Markons.   Allowing the competition rather than yourself to set your prices, thus depressing your markons and profits. Failure to keep prices in realistic perspective by underestimating other important things customers want, like good style selection, size depth, excellence of fitting and other services, reliable brands, attractive store image. Price is what we pay. Value is what we get for what we pay. Price paranoia with accompanying neglect of the value story is among the store's profit enemies.

14) Sluggish or Low Stock Turns.   There are many retailers who stay too long with slow-moving lines out of misguided loyalty, or feeling they have a vested stake in them, or simply not realizing that the lines aren't delivering a good stock-turn performance. Such lines drag on the better-turn lines and are a drag on overall store profit.

Each year, every line in the store should be carefully examined for stock-turn performance to see if it's paying its way. If not, the line should be unloaded. The slow stock turns, however, aren't always the fault of the line but of merchandising shortcomings by the retailer. This, too, needs a fair judgment.

15) Inadequate Records. Records are the essential road maps to keep a business on course. The two common faults here are inadequate records and poorly maintained records. The plaint of some retailers that "I don't have the time for all that paperwork" is equivalent to saying one doesn't have the time to run a business properly.

All business is a numbers business. Every segment of the business, from inventory and expense control to buying budgets and sales performance, is guided and ruled by numbers, which determine the ultimate number on the bottom line.

16) Loose Management. Seat-of-the-pants management is frequently seen in retailing, especially among smaller retailers where one person is in charge of almost everything and is constantly bemoaning the lack of time to keep pace. More usually, however, the causes of time and other problems are loose organization, lack of policies and discipline, and inadequate planning. Profit always reflects the quality of the management, the utlimate gauge of managerial and operational skills.

Profit is never made from any one segment of a business, such as buying or selling. Each of the store's operating parts must contribute something to the overall store profits. The retailer doesn't run a "store." He runs a variety of separate operations—advertising, inventory, expenses, buying, selling, personnel management, marketing, budgeting, trend tracking, money management, etc. Each part must be a profit center by itself in order for the whole to deliver a healthy profit.

12

Realistic Growth Planning

Business is like a bicycle—when it isn't moving forward at a good clip, it wobbles.

What if Noah had waited until it started raining before he began to build the Ark?

There are two ways for a business to grow: by accident or by plan. Most retailers grow by accident—by plodding and trusting to luck that the fates will be kind to them. But accidents can lead to injuries. There can be over-growth, or too rapid growth, or growth in the wrong direction. Some men have grown rapidly to giant size of eight feet tall, only to die suddenly at an early age. Or grow in girth to 600 pounds. In both instances it's a matter of too much too soon—too bad.

Growth is often misunderstood by many retailers. Some stores, like some companies, grow big and fast, only to abruptly go bust. The biggest challenge is to stay solvent and profitable while growing. This takes planning—a *realistic* growth plan.

Let's see how some retailers view the future with blurred vision. A retailer looks at his dollar volume over the past five years. His first year amounted to a very modest $180,000, and his fifth year $350,000. That shows an impressive

"I understand he's a retired shoeman."

94.4 percent growth, an average annual growth of 18.8 percent. He does some fast arithmetic and figures that on the same 18.8 percent annual growth rate, the compounded result over the next five years will result in a volume of $830,000 at the end of his tenth year in business. Superb, he declares. With those numbers ahead, he reasons, it's now time to think expansion for his rosy future.

But a colder, clearer eye takes a look at his sales. The analyst finds that over the same five-year period his *unit pairage* growth has increased only 12.5 percent, averaging 3 percent a year. At the end of the fifth year sales amounted to 9,286 pairs, a total increase of 1,036 pairs over the five years, or an average annual increase of only 207 pairs. Figuring that his average customer bought two pairs a year from the store, that meant that he added 518 "new" customers, or an average of 104 a year.

Our zealous retailer had been self-deceived by the $170,000 or 94.4 percent volume growth. But he hadn't bothered to shake out the 7 percent average annual inflation growth over those five years. He also overlooked his unit pairage growth— the *real* measurement of growth—which had advanced at only a modest 3 percent annual pace. Nor had he considered the small growth in customers or transactions, plus his overhead and other cost increases. He saw only those fat volume dollars, so much of his growth was illusory. When the cold-eyed analyst pointed out these facts, our retailer and his grandiose expansion plans were deflated.

GROWTH BY PLAN

All growth is relative. A five-foot-tall pigmy is a giant among his four-foot-tall peers, but is a runt in a society of six-footers. In retail shoe business, growth must be gauged against and relate to customers and transactions, unit pair sales, trading area growth, inflation growth, etc. For a business to measure its growth only with its past figures is a mistake. The view must be broader, which keeps growth thinking in realistic perspective, and also imposes a healthy humbling and sobering effect.

Growth by plan is better than growth by accident. And growth at a healthy, steady pace is better than growth in erratic spurts that can be caused by sudden spurts of business (a currently hot line, a spectacular demand for boots, etc.) You start growing by plan by setting goals based on realistic projections plus a growth *program.* For example:

Say yours is a women's fashion store in the moderate price range, targeted mainly to women in the 25–55 age range. Do you know the number of women in your trading area in this age group? You should, because it's your bull's-eye market. Do you estimate the number of pairs bought annually by these women? (Multiply the number of women by five and you have the approximate number of pairs purchased.) Do you know the approximate dollars spent on footwear by these women? (Multiply the estimated pairage by the average price—say $35—and you have the total footwear dollars spent in your market category). With this simple information you can now measure *your* share of the women's fashion footwear business within that market both in dollars and pairs.

You now have some specifics to work with in planning or measuring your growth. Say you've estimated your local market share to be 8 percent. You can now make growth projections to bring you up to a 10 percent or 13 percent (or more) share in both dollars and pairs over the projected period. That's *realistic* growth planning because you've worked with actual numbers and not magnified hope or exaggerated expectations. The state of the local market is the main thing you grow on.

Again, make sure you have a sound idea of the growth potential of the trading area itself. Is its population growing steadily? Is it growing mostly with young parents with small children? Or an aging population? If so, then these are not favorable signs for your type of business. Also, is the area growing more with lower-income families? Or is the general population dwindling? Those, too, are not encouraging signs. But if the opposite is developing—expanding population with good increases in moderate income, young-to-middle-age families and socially active—then the signs are favorable to support growth for your store. Therefore, know the customer base in your trading area, present and outlook.

The competition is also very important to know. How many retail outlets in your trading area are selling your category of footwear? Is the area over-stored? How many are direct competitors with your lines? Don't count only shoe stores, but all outlets selling your category of footwear—department and discount stores, clothing stores, off-price apparel stores, warehouse and factory outlets, etc.

This information is important not only to give you a gauge of what share of this business you're getting (and what the competition is getting), but also if there is enough overall business in your category to support the number of outlets in your trading area. That's essential for projecting your own growth potentials.

Again, some retailers open in a new trading area and do a brisk business, showing rapid growth over the first two-three years. They begin to get magnified visions of expansion and accelerating prosperity. But caution is required. Whenever a given location or trading area shows vigorous activity, be sure that competition will quickly move in to get a share of the action. This can abruptly slow growth and present a tougher challenge to sales and profits.

Other important elements are involved in growth planning. These include capital reserves and cash flow, credit status with resources and local banks, backup with qualified personnel. Trying to move too fast can mean trouble. It's like an armored tank battalion. It moves rapidly into enemy territory. Suddenly it finds itself far ahead of its vital supply lines—ammo, fuel, food, etc. It's success is now in jeopardy. The same applies to a growing store. It must make sure that its "supplies"— capital, credit, personnel, etc.—are keeping pace with sales growth. You can buy and grow "on credit" up to a point. But if the store suddenly runs into unexpected problems (a recession, prolonged bad weather, the principal with serious health problems, etc.), it finds itself over-extended. Lacking capital reserves, serious inventory problems appear that detour the whole growth course.

Some retailers are unprepared to make the transitions that occur with growth. For example, in the beginning the store owner spends much or most of his time on the selling floor in constant personal contact with the customers. But with rapid growth he finds more and more of his time and energies absorbed by administration— the buying, attending shows and probing markets, managing personnel, planning displays and promotions and advertising, keeping records, handling finances, etc. He gradually "loses touch" with the direct action on the floor as he assumes the boss role. Unless he has taken on an effective and trustworthy floor manager plus other personnel, he can find himself with problems. Thus his transition from floor boss to desk boss must be carefully directed to avoid the pitfalls.

IMPORTANCE OF RECORDS

There can be no sound basis for growth planning without records. The keeping of complete records should be ingrained as a habit from the beginning. Good records provide not only the pace of growth but also the direction. Two vital records are unit pairage sales and traffic (customers and transactions). Two others are capital and profit stability, which should remain consistent with sales growth. Otherwise you can find yourself ensnared in that common growth trap: over-extension and under-capitalization.

Well, what's healthy growth? There are no hard, fixed rules. However, there are some guidelines. For a sample store doing an annual volume of $350,000, a 10 percent annual growth in *pairage* is both realistic and healthy. That would mean, for example, an increase of about 1,000 pairs. At an average price of $35 per pair it would add $35,000 to volume. Using pairage as a gauge, the following are guidelines:

> Excellent—8% to 10% (or more)
> Good   —6% to 8%
> Fair   —3% to 5%
> Poor   —Under 3%

In the case of the family shoe store, growth by categories—men's, women's, children's, etc.—should be carefully observed. This may reveal, for example, that the women's business is growing at a 9 percent rate, men's at 6 percent, and children's 3 percent. If this pattern is fairly consistent over three or four years, then it provides a reasonably reliable course of direction that the business is taking. Under those circumstances the store may wish to consider closing out the children's business and concentrating on men's and women's. Or, in reverse, it may indicate that the store should be more aggressive in its children's business to create a better growth rate.

Such judgments should be based on the makeup of the local trading area and the competition. If there are two or three children's stores doing a strong job in the area, it might be advisable for the family store to relinquish its children's business. The family store, of course, is in a more difficult competitive position by trying to compete with specialty stores with more in-depth strength in their specialized merchandise categories. While the family store has the advantage of appeal to a broad range of customers, it at the same time faces the marketing problem of trying to be all things to all customers with limited inventory depth in its various product categories.

However, if there is to be a growth plan of any kind it is absolutely essential that there also be a merchandising and marketing plan to achieve the projected goals. There is a lot of empty space between the dream and the reality, the aspiration and the realization. So the three rules:

1) Have a direction and a destination.

2) Have a realistic pace of projected growth.
3) Have a merchandising program designed to take you to your goals at the projected pace.

Dun & Bradstreet records show that some 80 percent of all business difficulties or failures are due to lack of a realistic growth plan and being prepared for the unexpected. It usually isn't the competition that beats a business but the operation of the business itself.

ANALYSIS OF A SAMPLE SHOE STORE
GROWTH PATTERN

End of Year	$ Volume Growth	Unit Pairs Growth	Average Wholesale Price Pr.	Average Retail Price Pr.
1st yr.	$240,000	9,630	$12.50	$25.00
2nd yr.	264,000	9,600	13.75	27.50
3rd yr.	290,400	9,665	15.00	30.00
4th yr.	319,440	9,830	16.25	32.50
5th yr.	351,380	10,040	17.50	35.00
Change: 1st to 5th yr.	$111,380 (46.4%)	410 (4.0%)	$ 5.00 (40.0%)	$10.00 (40.0%)
Aver. annual increase	$ 24,835 (11.6%)	102 (1.0 %)	$ 1.25 (10.0%)	$ 2.50 (10.0%)

Comment: Dollar volume shows a 46 percent increase over the five-year span, an average annual growth of 11.6 percent. That looks respectable until it's compared with the puny 4 percent increase in pairage sales. So dollar volume grew 11 times faster than unit sales. The difference in dollars and pairage growth, of course, is due to the increase in wholesale and retail prices. Thus, despite the increased dollars, this has been virtually a no-growth store in units, customers and transactions.

13

Forty Ideas for Combatting Competition

The law of survival of the fittest
gives the fittest the right to decide
who is fit.

Use what talents you have. The
woods would be very silent if no
birds sang except those who sang best.

The words "competitor" and "competition" have various shades of meaning. Every shoe merchant interprets them in his own way, depending upon who the competition is. The attitude toward the competition usually takes one of three forms: tough but respected, feared or hated, unethical or unfair.

No matter what form it takes, competition is a reality of business life. And because you must live with it, it's vital to learn how to best cope with it in any of its forms. The worst sin is to view the competition as the enemy. To the contrary, your competition is often your best asset because he keeps you on your toes, forces you to operate at your peak performance. Any horse can win a race if it's the only one running.

All business competition boils down to one prime objective: competing for customers. Some retailers spend so much time worrying about the competition, or constantly watching for his next moves, that they can't give full focus to their own business. So keep in mind golfer Sam Snead's sage remark, "Forget the competition. Always play against par."

The world is filled with two kinds of people: actors and reactors. Actors are those who initiate action. Reactors are those who wait for others to act, then they react. We know the actors as leaders, the reactors as followers. If you're going to be a strong, effective competitor, your role must be that of actor, not reactor.

Successfully combatting competition, therefore, isn't a matter of trying to outwit or beat the other guy at his game, such as matching his low prices, but of having your own game plan focused on attracting and holding customers. It's not a process of being *against* the opposition, but being *for* your own program. If your strategies are right then the competition is forced to become the reactor with you in the lead role as actor.

Here, now, are 40 suggestions or ideas for attracting and holding customers and thereby successfully combatting competition.

1) Don't mimic the competition. It rarely works. If two men ride the same horse, one inevitably must ride behind. If two of you run similar operations, each mimicing the other, it reduces your market because both must share the same customer pool. You then don't have two apples. You share two halves of one apple. So the first law: be your own man, your own store.

2) Specialize. Carve out your own particular market niche. The category of customers, the merchandise appealing to those customers, the advertising, the prices, the store image, etc.—each precisely attuned to your market. There is no such thing as a "mass market." No store can be all things to all customers. Your competitive position strengthens as a one-of-a-kind store that fills its specialized role better than the competition around its rim.

3) Maximize your exposure via your advertising, displays, P. R., image, promotions, etc. Make your store as visible as possible in the eye and mind of the customers and prospects. Remember, in the average trading area, each year about 18 percent of its population disappears (moves aways, deaths, etc.), while usually about the same share of newcomers move in. So you need at least 25 percent of *new* business each year to show modest growth. That means that high store exposure is vital to holding regular customers, attracting new ones, and maintaining competitive position.

4) Constantly test your ads not only against the competition's but for their response performance. Don't be satisfied with "running" ads. Many ads run but go nowhere. So test your ads for pull-power and effectiveness. Compare yours to the competition's only to make sure yours are different. The idea is to set yourself apart from the competition. Advertising is your personality in print. Let yours be distinctive and not a close cousin of the competition.

5) Give special attention to your windows because they, too, contribute to the distinctive character of your store, setting it apart from the competition. This means the visual presentation of the merchandise, the lighting, the frequency of change, the excitement and pull-power. Studies show that 25 percent of all store traffic and sales come from windows. If competition is the process of bidding for traffic and customers, then your windows should be given high priority as a competitive weapon.

6) Don't try to fight price with price. It's a futile, losing proposition. Frequent cut-price promotions soon identifies your store as a cut-price store, which hurts your regular-price sales. If the competition is touting low or cut prices, find other promotions of equal attraction to offset them. Examples: hot new styles, a free size checkup for children, special category promotions (work boots, walking shoes, comfort casuals, duty shoes, etc.). Some fresh "imagenuity" often has more pull-power than the tired song of low prices.

7) Go the extra mile with service. Not just good service (which the customer expects, anyway), but outstanding, memorable service. A race horse who runs a few seconds faster is worth twice as much. Think of every customer service you can render. As a package they'll impress customers. Further, promote your services as you would your merchandise. If you provide and pay for services, they're worth advertising. And they are another competitive advantage.

8) Keep customer records, something overlooked by most stores. These records have various productive uses, such as providing a mailing list, keeping tabs on "lost" customers, giving extra clout for special promotions, announcing new merchandise, clearing closeouts, etc. Let each customer *know* you're keeping their record, and why (to render more precise service such as size, style preferences, etc.) This strengthens customer relations and customer allegiance. It further personalizes the sale. Print up personal business cards for the salespeople to hand to their customers. This gives the customer a point of reference instead of a nameless, faceless salesperson.

9) Make it a store policy to keep in personal touch with customers outside the store. If the customer hasn't visited the store in a year (the customer's record will show this), have the salespeople use lull time to send a "we've missed you" postcard, or make a phone call. Send a quarterly mailer to your customers—a chatty, informative piece about footwear, new things in the store, some special closeouts available, a brief fashion trend report. No hard sell. Let your customers know they're on your "preferred customers" list. It's flattering, strengthens their ties to your store.

10) Don't complain to your customers or others about the competition. It doesn't set well and it reveals weakness on your part. Play up your own strengths and the competition's weaknesses will become more glaring by unspoken comparison. Play the role of actor, not reactor. The customers aren't interested in the faults or shortcomings or your competitors, but only what you can do for them.

11) Instill your salespeople with a competitive spirit—"our team against theirs." In a competitive situation team spirit is a powerful motivator. Competitive team spirit shouldn't be focused primarily on selling more but rather on excellence of service, on better store housekeeping, on suggested "how to do it better" ideas. The main objective: how to attract, satisfy and hold more customers. Salespeople take pride in the store's success. But they need the motivation and leadership of management to stir the enthusiasm of the team spirit. High morale among the store's personnel is a powerful weapon on the store's competitive arsenal.

12) Make your store an exciting place to visit and shop. The decor, the lighting, the merchandise, the service. Use special bins or corners for closeouts and PMs, attractively lighted, unusual signs. Avoid dust and clutter. Change displays frequently to maintain a freshness about the merchandise. Studies show that many customers shop for pleasure, adventure and entertainment as well as for merchandise.

13) Run unusual, imaginative promotions. Don't do the usual in the semi-annual markdown sales. It just gets lost in the crowd. Pre-plan six major promotions for the year, and only a couple of them on price. Occasionally offer giveaways. For example, if you're selling men's shoes, offer a free shine kit with each shoe purchase— and show the retail price if the kit were bought separately.

14) Run a semi-annual contest, with good prizes. For example, a free bike to the winner in a kids' contest. A modest paid-vacation trip for two adults. Or a selection of four free pairs of shoes with a pre-specified value. Contests can be a springboard for free publicity in the local press, especially in smaller communities.

15) Use public relations. This is seldom utilized by shoe retailers. Don't wait for store news to happen, such as a 20th anniversary. *Make* news happen. For example, send the local media short pieces on walking, how to buy shoes, unusual

facts about shoes, tips on fitting, shoe fashion news, highlights of shoe industry history, etc. Make the material informative, newsy. Scores of such topics are available with a little research. And, of course, store news: a new remodeling job, a salesperson getting a certificate on completing a shoe fitting course, a report on returning from a recent fashion show in New York. This material gets used, especially in newspapers in smaller communities. It adds up to more store exposure, free advertising.

16) Push your brands. Usually yours will be different from the competition's. It's another factor that sets your store apart, identifies your store with well-known names and helps upgrade store image.

17) Give particular attention to lighting windows and interiors. Call in a local lighting engineer. He can make helpful suggestions at little cost. It can make the difference between a dull store and a pleasant, vibrant one. Lighting also influences sales, such as effective lighting for displays. Lighting affects the look of the footwear colors, too. And it influences customer moods. It's another facet of making the store a pleasant and exciting place to shop in.

18) Stay abreast of modern equipment, especially computers that can give you a competitive edge in inventory control, expense control, buying, etc. This gives you more operating mobility, quicker turnarounds. Today's computers are moderately priced and can perform numerous store functions to improve store efficiency.

19) Attend as many shoe shows as you can. Keep apace of what's happening with lines, new merchandise, new services, style trends. Talk shop with other retailers to pick up fresh ideas and industry information. Do the same with shoe travelers at the booths or rooms. Go to shows prepared with an itinerary, questions and specific things to look for. Attend special talks or seminar sessions. Shows can be very informative and educational if you know what to look for. And what you learn can be a competitive advantage.

20) Seek the assistance of your resources on special promotions. After all, *their* brands or merchandise are involved, and your competition is *their* competition. Aside from cooperative ad money sometimes they'll give special support to an unusual store promotion. Also, get all the guidance help you can from the sales representatives. And don't hesitate to occasionally pick up the phone and make a call to the company president or sales manager to get information on trends, what's selling and what isn't, or promotional plans. Exchange your own local information feedback with them. They appreciate such calls.

21) Occasionally buy, on a *selective* basis, closeouts that can be used for special price or other promotions. Let your resources know that you want to be informed early about the availability of closeouts. When you buy them, buy enough to do justice to a full promotion. This is one effective way to occasionally run a price promotion without lower margins—and usually with a nice profit. An occasional big-bang promotion can humble the competition.

22) Offer to give talks to local groups—PTA, Kiwanis, Rotary, women's clubs, sports groups. Tailor your talk to the type of audience. Make it informative, provocative, lively. Where possible, use slides. If you learn to do this well, you'll be invited to give more of them. Very important, send a *condensation* of each talk to the local press. This adds to store exposure, helps develop a "footwear expert" image.

The competition rarely thinks of this or does it.

23) Work with fashion people in the local media such as the newspaper or TV. Make your acquaintance with them. Offer to furnish the fashion editor of the local newspaper with fashion trend information on footwear, or photos (your resources can help with both). Offer to do the same for the local TV station when it plans to run a fashion show—and also offer to provide shoes for the models. And the same for a local women's club if it's planning a fashion show. In each instance, of course, your store and shoes gets publicity and announced credits. It also further enhances your store's fashion image. If these succeed, you'll get repeat requests. And this valuable exposure and publicity costs little or nothing.

24) Consider out-sizes—extra large or small, extra wide or narrow. These hard-to-find sizes can win you new customers who become repeat customers. And the word gets around. If you offer these sizes in basic or classic styles, your markdown risks are minimal. Multiple-pair purchases are common with these customers because they have so little opportunity of getting these sizes. And make sure you advertise them. Because few stores offer out-sizes, it gives you a competitive advantage.

25) Tout your fitting service. Run an occasional ad giving exposure to your salespeople as expert fitters. At the same time, talk about your broad selection of sizes, widths and lasts. But make sure your salespeople are well-trained in fitting so that their performance and service lives up to the promise of the ads.

26) Send "thank you" notes (or a postcard) to each customer after they've made a purchase. Customers like to be remembered. They're also pleased to know that you've taken time to express appreciation of their business. It's another special touch in personalized customer relations. This doesn't take extra time. It can be done by the salespeople during lull periods.

27) If you don't have a customer's size or wanted style, offer to special-order it instead of the common brushoff, "Sorry, we don't have it in your size." If a wanted style is missing, show the customer catalogs from your resources and let him or her make a selection for a special order. This may result in a sale otherwise lost. But even if no sale is made, the customer is impressed with the store's eagerness to please and help—and will likely patronize your store again.

28) Use demographics to a) determine the size and makeup of your local market; b) to estimate the competition's share of the local market; c) to determine your own share of the local market. (See "Using Demographics As A Sales Planning Tool" on page 116). Very few retailers do this and hence, marketwise, are really working in the dark. Demographics data enables you to pinpoint your competitive position, which is one of the most basic rules for successfully combatting competition.

29) Don't be intimidated by the competition—by its size, its brashness or tub-thumping. It isn't the size of the dog in the fight, but the size of the fight in the dog. Smaller stores can often out-maneuver and out-smart larger ones. Larger stores are more cumbersome, less flexible. So it isn't how big but how smart.

30) Use brainstorming with your sales and other personnel. Shoe business, like most, is an idea business as well as a merchandise business. The perennial challenge: how to do it better. Brainstorming sessions often spawn fresh and exciting ideas. Salespeople have good ideas but they won't come forth unless encouraged by management. Give rewards for good ideas that are used and succeed. Salespeople

are as proud and gratified of seeing their ideas work as management is. It's another facet of the "team spirit" in combatting the competition.

31) Make sales training a store policy and practice. Weekly or bi-weekly meetings for an hour before the store opens. One topic each time. For example, how to increase multiple-pair sales, improving customer service, shoe fitting, discussing new merchandise just come in, moving PMs, product knowledge, etc. Don't make it a "lecture." Involve everybody. Use props, demonstrations. Such meetings help build morale and enthusiasm of the personnel because they feel they're learning and advancing. Most of all, it gives the store a much more effective sales staff and another competitive advantage.

32) Broaden your accessories assortment. The majority of shoe stores seldom go beyond the usual handbags, hose and shoe cleaners. But there is an extensive range of other accessories related to feet and shoes that not only can add to sales and profits, but help to build store traffic and excitement. (See "Triple Your Accessories Power" on page 149).

33) Be a sponsor. For example, sponsor a local walking club and help program walking tours, walking contests, etc. This is excellent for local PR exposure and helps increase walking shoe sales for your store. The same can be done for other special groups such as nurses, Little League, hikers, etc.

34) Take customer surveys. These can be done simply (postcard) and at nominal cost. They accomplish two important things. They provide important feedback information, and they show your customers that you care about improving your service for them. Few stores do this, so yours will be a standout by doing it.

35) Pre-plan and set goals. Don't become smothered by day-to-day details. And don't think that "forward planning" is next week. It's six or twelve or more months down the road. Smaller retailers particularly fault on this.

36) Learn what the competition *isn't* doing, then do it. Most retailers apply this in reverse, over-concentrating on what the competition *is* doing, then trying to match it. If the competition offers only mediocre service, make yours superior. If the competition runs an occasional big ad, run smaller ads but with much more frequency. Let his weaknesses or gaps become your strengths.

37) Build a strong store image. This is one of your best competitive weapons. A store image is its public personality and identity. But don't allow that image to grow by accident. Decide what you want it to be, based on your market targets, then tailor everything in your operation to fit to that image. The worst sin is to have no image at all, to be just another faceless shoe store on the block. "Image" is the composite of all the segments of your operation—the merchandise, service, advertising, prices, store appearances, etc.

38) If you're in the fashion business, train your salespeople to become fashion counselors, then promote this unique service to the hilt. This training can be done via weekly or biweekly meetings (one hour before store opening); by bringing in guest speakers (someone from a local clothing store, a knowledgeable sales representative, the local newspaper fashion editor); by having the salespeople closely follow fashion trends via the fashion magazines and trade papers. Such a staff trained to give your customers helpful fashion guidance can put you a big stride ahead of the competition.

39) Give priority to profit rather than volume. If the competition does $500,000

volume with a 4 percent net, his net take is $20,000. If you do a more modest volume of $350,000 at 7 percent, your net take is $24,500. Yes, it's nice to have both high volume and high net profit. But make sure your priorities are in proper order, with net profit first. It's a clear sign of a successful competitor.

40) Avoid duplication of lines. It's a common weakness in combatting competition by trying to match everything the competition carries. The result is not only inventory overload and waste, but a flabby me-too operation. Be selective in your lines, policing them to see that each is delivering a solid turn rate and profit return—and let the competition worry about his own.

All business competition boils down to three things: customer traffic, sales and net profits. Everything begins with the first: customers. Without the customers you have no sales, no profits, no store, no reason for being in business. Therefore, everything you can do to attract customers, and also to hold them as repeat customers, achieves the objective of being a successful competitor.

Retailers constantly talk or think about increasing sales, overlooking the reality that sales are the consequence of customers. Yet, ironically, customers are often taken for granted. This is evidenced in various ways: mediocre service, weak store image, inadequate selection of styles or sizes, lax effort at customer relations, impersonal service, poor market appraisal, drab stores and displays, etc. In short, glaring shortcomings in the very factors responsible for attracting and holding customers.

The 40 suggestions or ideas listed in this chapter are focused on that vital foundation of customer development. Not merely traffic. Traffic is something that passes through. Customers stick—provided the right things are done to bring them in and hold their allegiance. No one or several of the suggestions made here is any magic answer to winning customers. But if all or most are applied, there is very high chance that the mission of being a successful competitor will be realized.

BLESS YOUR COMPETITORS

A competitor is one who spends his days, and often his nights, figuring ways to give his customers better service and values—and forcing you to do the same.

A competitor doesn't bother with "hard sell" or "soft sell." He recognizes only two kinds: smart sell and dumb sell.

A competitor often does more for us than a friend. A friend is too kind to point out our weaknesses. A competitor will advertise them.

A competitor is our best business analyst. If the quality of our performance lets down, we'll see him prospering at our expense.

A competitor's ability should never be underestimated. The business graveyard is full of those who figured the competition was stupid or lazy or short-sighted.

A competitor makes life worth living because he forces us to remain in peak condition.

A competitor is hard to live with but harder to live without. Competition is the *Great Realist* because it reduces us all to deserved size.

So blessed are our competitors, for they shall always keep us alert and in constant search for improvement.

CORRECTING MISTAKES

A big-game hunter in Africa was on his way back to camp one evening when a huge lion walked out of the jungle not 20 feet away. As the lion was about to spring, the hunter fired his last cartridge—and missed. The lion sprang too far and landed 15 feet beyond the hunter, who then ran for camp and made it safely.

The next day the hunter went behind the camp to practice up on his shooting at close range. He heard a strange noise in the brush and investigated. It was the lion—practicing short leaps.

The moral: It's smart to correct your mistakes. But the competition is out there doing the same. Remembering that, it keeps you humble.

THE EGG WAR

A long-established grocery store was suddenly faced with aggressive competition from a brash young newcomer. Eggs were selling for $1.50 a dozen in the established store. The young newcomer advertised his eggs at the slashed price of $1.20, and his eggs sold at a fast clip.

The next day the established store also advertised eggs at $1.20. The young grocer immediately cut his price to $1. The established store again met his price. And so went the price battle until eggs were down to 50 cents a dozen, with both stores doing a brisk egg business.

Finally, the young man came into the other store and said to the owner, "Okay, you win. I can't afford to cut my egg prices any more. But one question: how have you managed to meet my prices and take such a loss?"

"No problem," replied the other. "I've been buying your eggs."

CAUGHT IN THE MIDDLE

Two shoe stores were situated side by side on the same block and had been friendly competitors for years. An aggressive new shoe retailer opened his store beside the other two, determined to drive both out of business. He ran blaring ads, "Lowest Prices in Town," and his store front carried a large sign saying the same.

The second store on the opposite side of the trio panicked and posted a large sign over the store front, "We'll Match the Lowest Prices in Town."

"The third store, situated in the middle, was caught in a muddle. It then posted its own large sign over the front: "Main Entrance."

Inventory

14

The Art of Stockmanship

The biggest problem in the world could have been solved when it was small.

The sooner you fall behind, the more time you'll have to catch up.

Most retailers use some kind of "system" for inventory control. But while a system helps, it's no assurance that the inventory is under control.

Regardless of all the systems, inventory control can never be scientific—though neither can it be a crude skill. I prefer the term "stockmanship" or the art of profitable inflow and outflow of merchandise.

Inventory is usually controlled by factors *outside* of the "system." For example, you can control buying but not inventory. Once the buy becomes inventory it controls the store. Thus, what we often call inventory problems are more realistically buying or selling or merchandising problems.

The real key to effective inventory management isn't so much in the inventory itself but in (1) the factors that create the inventory, and (2) the factors that move the inventory. If those two factors are well managed and balanced, you then have good control of inventory.

Among the common trouble symptoms of faulty inventory management are:

1) Excessive markdowns.
2) Slow movement of merchandise.
3) Excessive walks due to out-of-stock condition.
4) Low turn rate.
5) Low net profit.

They indicate any or a combination of three things: buying the wrong merchandise, buying too much, or buying too little. However, inventory problems go beyond the matter of buying, as we'll soon see.

Even the most experienced and astute of horse bettors picks some losers. Nevertheless he consistently goes home with a profit. That's all that's expected of good shoe buying.

Then there are the overbuys. Some retailers are like a kid in a candy store. They can't resist having a taste of everything until they end up with a bellyache.

And finally there are the overcautious who always underbuy, figuring they can always reorder. But when they reorder on the hot shoes the deliveries are late. These are the stores usually in an out-of-stock condition who have a high level of walks, broken lots and missed sales.

VERTICAL AND HORIZONTAL BUYING

Ironically, most or many stores don't have a clear-cut policy on inventory structure. There are two kinds of buying: *Vertical and Horizontal,* and each determines inventory makeup. Vertical Buying (or inventory) is concentrated in selective merchandise featuring depth rather than breadth—fewer styles but broad size selection. Concept stores typify this kind of operation.

Horizontal Buying (or inventory) features breadth rather than depth—broad style selection but limited size selection. This isn't necessarily negative. It often applies to the *first* buy, such as in three colors. But once one of those colors takes off, it's quickly sized in depth. So what starts as a horizontal buy ends up as a vertical buy. The system requires much discipline and agility to reorder quickly where the action is.

Before you can determine a policy or system of inventory control, you should first know whether you are a dominantly vertical or horizontal operation. That determines the makeup of your inventory and what measure of control you have over it.

Buying closeouts from resources can be both good and bad. When the buy is right and sells well, its low cost turns a nice profit. But sometimes the low cost is the devil's temptation. If the shoe turns out to be a dog, you eat the "bargain" and intensify the inventory control problem. Before buying closeouts, remember that you *already* have closeouts in your own stock.

Avoid buying from too many resources. You've heard that time and again, but it's still a common sin whose penalty is inventory trouble. After a while, suppliers tend to accumulate like a ship's barnacles. Among the cost penalties: more bookkeeping costs, handling costs, time in seeing many salesmen, operating with a little of this and that, duplicating brands and price lines, more markdowns, slower turns, etc. Because you're buying small amounts from each resource, you're treated as a fringe account with low priorities.

Almost any store can eliminate 10 to 15 percent of its suppliers and benefit with better inventory control, fewer losses and more gains. Good stockmanship demands a more selective choice of resources and lines, and more depth in each.

There is a rigid rule in supermarkets: every item must earn its shelf space. The same should apply to lines in a shoe store. At least annually every line should be appraised on the basis of its profitability as related to markdowns, turns, sales, etc. Draggy, low-profit lines should be culled. Failure to do this is a common cause of inventory clutter and messed-up inventory control.

Date-mark each shoe box when it comes into the store, to indicate shelf life. Carrying charges on aging merchandise can cost up to 20 percent a year—a loss of $1,000 for each $5,000 of older merchandise. Also, a shoe sold one year after it's placed in stock has lost at least 5 to 10 percent of its price return value, even if sold at full price, due to inflation alone.

INVENTORY OUTFLOW

Inventory outflow determines the level of inventory accumulation. This is where you do or should have control. Failure to take markdowns and clearances often and fast enough is a common cause of buildup of inventory sludge and loss of inventory control. Shoes should have a predetermined shelf life unless, of course, the shoe is still moving strongly and profitably.

When a resource drops a shoe from his line, immediately do the same with the same shoe in your store. The resource's dropped shoe is a clear signal that it's over the hill.

The periodically advertised clearance sale or PMs aren't the only way of unloading. You can have a small section of the store—bins, special shelving, etc.—for continuous clearances. For example, use hashing (colors, styles, sizes) as one method. Or a special display of "Lucky Sizes" ("if your size is here, you'll find a lucky buy").

Retailers usually worry about excessive inventory as a control problem. They should also think about "shortage control." The out-of-stock condition immediately signals an inventory management problem. An IBM study showed that the average store loses 35 percent of its sales potential because of out of stock (colors, sizes, styles, etc.). Thus only 65 percent of customer wants are satisfied. Some of this, of course, can't be helped. But much of it can when it's the result of laxity in reorders on fast-moving merchandise, or size fillins, or over-cautious initial buys, etc.

Ironically, most out-of-stock conditions occur with the best-sellers. While they may account for only 10 percent of your inventory, they may account for 30 percent or more of your volume. If you're out of stock on a slow-mover, you lose one sale. If out of stock on a fast-mover, you lose four or five sales. So heed the rule: size up before you lock up.

On average 4 of 10 styles in your inventory are hot. Four others eventually sell out by or soon after the end of season. And two are duds. The big profit is made on the first four—large volume and high turn at full price on only a few models. If you don't run at full speed with those four—meaning fast and full reorders and quick fillins—you've missed the golden opportunity and head for inventory problems. Good stockmanship is knowing when to run and when to rest.

Timing is important for inventory management. Peak your stocks ahead of your sales peaks. Late stock peaking—waiting for sales to peak before bigger buys—not only costs you in lost sales but more markdowns as a Johnny-come-lately. Over-caution here also indicates that you lack confidence in your own buying convictions and a knowledge of your local market.

Deliveries are another inventory control problem. Some arrive too soon, others too late. Know *exactly* when you need and want the merchandise delivered, which gives you better control over the state of your inventory. If a resource consistently violates the requested delivery timing, unload him. Why should his problem become yours?

Don't over-protect your fringe merchandise—sizes, styles, colors, etc. Yes, you carry some slow-moving merchandise for the convenience of some of your customers. But on these, raise your markons and prices to cover the low turnover and cost of shelf space. This selective pricing makes sense.

Your cash flow position is vital to inventory management. Limited cash flow restricts your open-to-buy opportunities. Also, each borrowed dollar takes 12–13 cents out of your profits. Limited cash flow retards sufficient inflow of fresh merchandise, creates an overload of aging merchandise, and further drills holes in your stock. The same can happen with a seriously damaged credit rating. Thus you can't talk inventory control without also taking into account cash flow and credit rating position.

Take as many purchase discounts as frequently as you can. Many retailers don't realize that their available discounts can amount to as much as 40 percent of their net profits. And, significantly, they lower the cost of your inventory, an important part of inventory control.

Records and record-keeping are a vital core of inventory management. Absolutely avoid the "eyeball control" method. You and your inventory will end up with cataracts. Keep a six-months record of performance of your inventory. This can be viewed as a "reliability test," because it tests the credibility of your budgeting, buying, selling, markdowns and all other factors which determine the state of your inventory.

Keep a record of your walks or lost sales. They can indicate serious holes in your stock. Walks are an invitation to your customers to buy from your competitors. With only one missed sale in five, the retailer earns less than half his potential profit.

Keep a record of stock turns by merchandise categories. They're a good indicator of the quality of your inventory. If on an original purchase of 100 pairs, 75 sell in three months and the remaining 25 over the next three months, the turnover rate is five. But if the remaining 25 pairs are unsold for the next nine months, the turnover shrinks to two.

Keep a record of salepeople's performance—who is moving what and how much. At root, they are the *real* controllers of your inventory.

Keep a record of advertising performance. Advertising moves merchandise, hence is linked to inventory management.

Keep a record of your markdowns. They're warning signs of the quality and customer-appeal value of your inventory.

The rate of sales or outflow is a sound barometer of inventory productivity. Inventory is simply an inert mass of expensive merchandise that comes alive only via sales. Thus a Selling Plan is as much an influence on inventory management as a Buying Plan. When you buy a shoe don't ask, "Will it sell?" Instead, ask "How will I sell it?"—meaning that a selling strategy is an inseparable part of the buying strategy.

Good stockmanship is more than a numbers game. It's more than checking the BOM (beginning of month) and EOM (end of month) figures. It's more than an inventory control "system." Buying is only the beginning phase of stockmanship. Outflow is equally important. When the pace of outflow matches the pace of inflow, no stagnant pools form. The water flows steady, fresh and clean, the stream never too deep or too shallow. Same thing with an inventory.

MERCHANDISE YOUR INVENTORY

Over half your operating costs is invested in inventory. Yet few retailers do full justice to the merchandising potentials of their inventory. Yes, they sell shoes but seldom sell their inventory—and especially the *benefits* of their inventory to the customers. Here are some suggestions of how to merchandise and inventory:

Size and Width Selection.   Many stores will advertise a shoe, then in small print say "available in sizes 6 to 10, B to D." But if they analyze their inventory they'd find that their sizes in a given category, say women's, would range from 5 to 11, and widths AA to EE. And rarely do these retailers add that even larger or smaller sizes can be specially ordered on selected styles.

That broad size-width selection is something to sell *by itself,* unrelated to any particular shoe. This selection can be linked to fit. For example, "A full selection of sizes and widths for almost every foot—with assurance of perfect fit." This attracts the many women who deliberately avoid visiting shoe stores or departments because of repeated disappointments with size selection.

Style Selection.   How many different styles or stock numbers in your inventory? Most retailers can't answer that question. So count them. It's the basis for another ad: "Over 100 different styles in stock to please every eye, taste and want."

Also sell the fashion freshness of your inventory. Your ad might read: "A steady flow of new fashions are delivered to our store every month. Always something new to see."

Brands.   Same question: How many brands do you carry? Most retailers would have to back up and count. So count them. Then again, in an ad, list all the brands you carry. It will usually comprise an impressive list. For the customer it indicates a store with a broad range of brands backed up with a broad range of styles and sizes. That combination packs a lot of customer appeal.

Why force the customers to play guessing games about the merchandise you have for sale? They know you sell shoes, and they have a general idea of your price range. But there's still a lot they *don't* know but *want* to know about your merchandise. So tell them.

15

Out of Stock Can Cost 40 Percent of Sales

Good intentions, like good eggs,
soon spoil if not hatched.

If the first button on a man's vest
is buttoned wrong, all the rest will
be crooked.

The law of supply and demand is the most basic law of business. Yet many retailers constantly flaunt and break this law by operating with supply-and-demand imbalances. They become guilty of, or victim of, out-of-stock condition.

Ironically, surveys show that the top priority concern of retailers is inventory control. Yet, strangely, most of the emphasis here is usually to control or prevent inventory overload, and too often short shrift is given to inventory underload. True, while inventory overload is a legitimate worry, inventory underload or out-of-stock condition deserves equal attention because of its direct effect on sales; or, more precisely, its cause of lost sales.

Retailers know, of course, that missing stock results in lost sales. But how much loss? A few years ago IBM conducted a national study and found some shocking figures. Said their report: "Most stores lose at least 22 percent of their dollar demand on planned customer purchases because of out-of-stock position or because merchandise is not available in desired sizes or colors or styles. When the store is unable to satisfy these customer preferences or needs, the lost dollar sales against demand runs to 40 percent. In other words, only 60 percent of the sales demand represented by people who walk into the store intending to buy, is satisfied."

Other surveys confirm this. For example, it's well established that for the average shoe store or department, three out of ten customers walk out unsold. However, something of related importance here is often overlooked. When a customer experiences an out-of-stock condition a couple of times in a given store, it converts into more than a lost sale. The customer usually becomes *permanently* lost because of the attitude, "They never seem to have what I need or want in stock." And worse, this often becomes a negative word-of-mouth message that moves among the customers' friends.

The worry among retailers about excessive inventories causes some or many to move in the opposite direction of operating with skeletal or minimal inventories. It's the attitude: "Better to lose the sale than be stuck with the merchandise."

But the opposite maxim is also true: "You can't do business from an empty wagon."

This places the retailer between a rock and a hard place. With concern about both too much and too little inventory, the dilemma becomes: What is the just-right inventory? Here we may find the secret door to the answer. The answer isn't necessarily a matter of inventory quantity but inventory *quality*.

You're familiar with the 80–20 law. Among its many applications is the stark reality that at any given season or time of year, 80 percent of your sales will be done with 20 percent of your merchandise. And right there is the key: always having a full inventory of that vital 20 percent at the right time.

Misreading that vital fact of life about supply and demand commonly creates problems for the retailer. He looks at his *overall* inventory and concludes that he's heavily stocked and hence can't or shouldn't take on more inventory. As precaution, he cuts back on *all* his buying. This is common, for example, in department stores where the merchandise manager will decree a 20 percent cutback of buying in all the merchandise departments under his jurisdiction—even though one or two of the departments are showing brisk sales. Thus the winners are sacrificed along with the losers.

This applies as well in a shoe store—often the same indiscriminate cutback on all buying, including reorders even on good-selling shoes. This is a classic case of throwing out the baby with the bath water.

PREVENTING OUT-OF-STOCK

Buying and selling are inseparable Siamese twins. Back to our 80–20 law. The obvious key to getting the full effect of this law is to maximize the 20 percent at the right time while minimizing the 80 percent. That greatly reduces or eliminates the out-of-stock condition. You're equipped with full supply to meet peak demand of particular merchandise at any given time. It's that 20 percent that will account for 80 percent of your sales and profits during any given period. How is this achieved?

First and most obvious is your what's-selling records. This means *daily* records. Not in your head but visible numbers on paper. You classify those sales by amounts and pace sold—1, 2, 3—by stock number and style. And you reorder at the same pace so that supply matches demand and sales and prevents the out-of-stock condition where the peak action is.

Second, you enlist the views of your salespeople, beyond what your own merchandise records show. The salespeople are closely in touch with the customers' attitudes, preferences and comments. They know not only which shoes are in top demand but also *why*. The customers are telling them why they are asking for and buying certain styles or colors. This information will give you a sharper sense of the intensity of the demand for given shoes, which in turn will indicate how long that demand will be sustained. This is vital information for gauging your reorders—whether to step up the reorders, or whether and when to begin tapering off. So keep asking for feedback from your salespeople.

Third is the initial buying selections. This is where stock condition actually begins. If you've made wrong or poor buys in advance, then your 80–20 formula shrinks to a 90–10 formula. That means that only 10 percent of your inventory at any given time is providing most of the sales action. And 10 percent isn't enough to deliver the needed sales and profits, much less support that temporarily semi-active 90 percent of stock.

Therefore, keeping very closely attuned to fashion trends and hot items is vital to making the right buying selections that will comprise that essential 20 percent of top-action sales. That means maintaining an excellent communications system to provide this trend information via (1) attending and smart-shopping shoe shows; (2) getting as much trend information as possible directly from your resources and sales reps (pick up the phone and talk directly to the company president or sales manager); (3) observing trends in the trade press, plus the fashion magazines; (4) observing the windows and ads of fashion-leader stores in your area; (5) keeping a close tab on walkouts—especially *why* they are walking. This is a good indicator of the gaps that need filling.

In short, utilize every avenue of trend information available that can help you with buying decisions focused on comprising that healthy 20 percent of inventory where the out-of-stock condition must be prevented from happening.

A portion of your stock will likely be in basic categories not subject to seasonal demand and which moves steadily year round. For example, women's duty shoes, or work boots, or walking shoes, etc. These should *never* be in an out-of-stock condition in sizes or style selection. These are bread-and-butter lines with minimal markdown risk and hence should be fully stocked throughout the year. Obvious as this may be, out of stock is not unusual in these categories, due mainly to careless neglect.

Not all out-of-stock situations must necessarily become lost sales. Experienced salespeople know how to switch the customer from the requested not-in-stock shoe to a similar in-stock shoe. But many other salespeople take the lazy or loser route by saying to the customer, "Sorry, we don't have that shoe in stock" or "We don't carry anything like that."

That not only loses the sale but often the customer, as well, who resents the brusque brushoff treatment. If an attempt is made to show something else, the customer at least appreciates the courtesy and service and is likely to return for another visit. It's important for salespeople to be trained in the switching process not only as an effort to make the sale, but also as an expression of store courtesy and service.

The out-of-stock condition is usually caused by any combination of any of the following seven reasons:

1) Faulty Buying.   If the buys aren't precisely what's in demand, then the inevitable consequence is an out-of-stock condition of supply failing to meet demand.

2) Lack of Records.   If the buys have been right but poor what's-selling records are kept, then there's little sound basis for a reorder program to keep supply apace of demand.

3) Lack of Policy.   If the store operates with an erratic reorder system—erratic in timing or amounts—then the out-of-stock condition becomes habit.

4) Procrastination.   Delay in reordering of good-selling shoes disqualifies the retailer as a competent merchant.

5) Indecision.   Whether or not to reorder, and if yes, how much. Indecision indicates not only uncertainty but lack of confidence. These are judgment and risk calls. But that's the core of all business and buying decisions. However, the combination of records and "gut feeling" provides a sound basis for eliminating indecision.

6) Staying Tuned In. This means tuned in to trends via all helpful channels available. Nobody is smart enough to do it all by himself.

7) Lost Sales. Failure to keep closely attuned to *why* sales are being lost—the mating of customer demand with available supply. This information can substantially cut out-of-stock position.

If those seven shortcomings are eliminated or at least minimized, much of the out-of-stock condition can disappear. This obviously results in increased sales, more repeat business, better profits, plus higher morale among salespeople.

SIZEUPS

The retailer's frustration is to have a needed size missing in the wanted and available style. This becomes even more frustrating when the customer feels strongly about a particular shoe or style and refuses to switch to another style where the needed size is available. The obvious result is a lost sale, and sometimes even a permanently lost customer, equally frustrated, who moves the word-of-mouth message around: "That store never has the needed sizes in stock."

Out-of-size differs from out-of-stock. The latter often relates to current good-sellers. But out-of-size condition can apply as well to basic shoes that sell year round at slower but reasonably steady pace. The out-of-size situation should be rigidly avoided on any shoe that is not on a closeout course.

Yet, ironically, an estimated 50 percent of lost sales are due to missing sizes in wanted shoes. Most of this is unforgivable because it's almost always due to laxity of policy or system or discipline of timing on size fillins.

With all the talk of retailers about the importance of inventory control, it's often overlooked that a disciplined policy on sizeups is a vital part of inventory control. Without good size selection on steady sellers you have something little better than a hashed inventory available to customers on a catch-as-catch-can basis— meaning that if you happen to have the needed size, then both you and the customer are lucky. But it's rare that a business ever survives by luck alone.

The key to an effective sizeup system is simply a combination of records and discipline to maintain the policy. Many retailers, especially smaller ones, say, "I just don't have the time. I size up when I can or when I think of it." That's ironic because the same retailer is spending much of his or her time trying to drum up traffic to make sales—only to see a lot of those sales lost because of missing sizes he or she didn't have time to take care of.

How often should you size up? Some stores do it daily, others semi-weekly. It should never be less than weekly. The timing depends in part upon the store's sales volume and merchandise turnover. You should also always take into account late or incomplete deliveries of reordered sizes, which is another reason for increasing the frequency of sizeups. Sizeups should be accelerated during peak selling periods.

Many good sizeup systems are available, often from your own resources. Or it's no problem to devise your own. But no system will work unless you have disciplined follow-through. By all means avoid the habit of waiting for the sales reps to visit and do your sizing up for you on their respective lines. They can sometimes overload on sizes. But most of all, the span between their visits is much too great to leave the needed sizes unfilled.

Many of the problems involving inventory control, walkouts, lost sales and lost customers are unnecessary and avoidable. The problems boil down simply to lack of efficient and disciplined stock management. It's ridiculous to spend so much effort, time and money building traffic you hope will lead to sales, only to undercut it all by out-of-stock condition on wanted merchandise or missing sizes.

Again, it's not so much a matter of quantity as quality—the old shoe business axiom of having the right shoe at the right time in the right size at the right price. That's really the bottom line of good inventory control. If you abide by the rules of preventing out-of-stock and missing sizes, you'll be happily surprised with a 20 percent or better increase in sales, along with more customer allegiance and repeat business.

16

Determining the Profitability
of Your Lines

*Golf is a lot like business. You drive
hard to get to the green, then wind
up in the hole.*

*Small deeds done are better than
great deeds planned.*

Any retailer can tell you his gross and net profit. Yet few, ironically, can tell you precisely where the profit comes from.

I refer particularly to the profitability of each line carried by the store. This is often a big missing link in profit analysis in most retail shoe operations. It can cost the store thousands of dollars in missed profits each year.

It isn't enough that a line sells well and delivers a good turnover rate. More important is: what kind of bottom-line profit does it deliver? Line A can out-perform Line B in sales, yet deliver only half the profitability. So the big question: which lines are contributing the most and which the least to the store's overall profits?

Every line must contribute a pre-established share to the cost of doing business and contribute also a share to overall profit. To determine your break-even point and the minimum profit contribution a line should make, you first need to establish a simple Store Operation Data plan (see Table 1 on page 86).

You can then use a calculating system to check performance comparison by individual lines. There are various ways to do this. The "system" shown in Table 2 on page 87 is simply one of them.

Now, there are a number of basic elements involved in the profitability of any line. Some belong to the line itself, while others relate to how the line is handled by the store. These elements are as follows:

1) Markdowns
2) Net markon
3) Stock turns
4) Product category
5) Sales mobility
6) Sizes and widths
7) Reorder accessibility
8) Deliveries

84 Profitable Footwear Retailing

Let's take a brief look at each.

Markdowns.   A shoe or line may start with a sprint but drag or collapse midway in the race; or its performance may fall far short of expectations when it was bought; or a store may hold it for too long before clearance. These and other reasons lead to markdowns—some due to the store, some to the line or shoe. However, appraisal should not be based on a one-time or one-season performance, but rather consistency of performance.

High versus low markdown average is not, by itself, a reliable barometer. A line may show high markdowns (say 15 to 20 percent) but at the same time high sales. The important element is the consistency or average net profit the line returns year in and out.

Conversely, a more conservative line can consistently have low markdowns but also slower or lower sales. Here, too, the judgment must be based on its net profitability—or its contributed share to the store total net profit. What to avoid is consistently low profit-makers.

Net Markon.   This is the important bottom-line figure, the real return on investment. It is, of course, influenced by markdowns or excessive shelf life. Retailers know their initial markon (say 50 percent), but often they don't know the line's average net markon or how consistently it is maintained. Net markon and net profit are married and sleep in the same bed.

Stock Turns.   This can be deceptive. For example, a high turn rate can be achieved with a skeletal inventory of sizes and styles. But it can result in many lost sales and disenchanted or lost customers. Again, fashion shoes turn faster than basic or conservative shoes. But they also show differences in markdowns and net markon. The focus must be on the net profit delivered by the line, and its contributed share to overall store profit.

Product Category.   When judging line performance, beware of averages. For example, if the store averages 2.2 stock turns for its total inventory, it's a grave mistake to use this as a benchmark for stock turns of each line. The same applies to markdowns or net markon.

Each product category—men's, women's, children's, fashion, basic, canvas, slippers, utility boots, etc.—has its own "normal" pace. Thus each must be appraised separately in regards to markdowns, turns and net markon. So again the important bottom line question: what did each category—or more precisely which lines in each category—consistently deliver the best net profit? And what share of that profit represented against the store total?

Sales Mobility.   Some lines blow hot and cold. For a line to earn its keep in the store, it should show a reasonably steady sales flow matched by a healthy profit margin, net. The line can be fast fashion or slow basic. But its contribution to store profit, based on anticipated and realized pace of sales, should be reasonably predictable.

Sizes and Widths.   Here there are two obvious excesses: habitual shortages of needed sizes, and an overload of fringe sizes. Neither is the fault of the line but the fault of the store. But either or both can impose penalties on a line's profit showing.

Reorder Accessibility.   A good instock service by the resources—if properly utilized by the retailer—can increase the profitability of a line. Conversely, lack or absence of such accessibility can jeopardize profitability. For example, if early and full payment must be made on the order, borrowing costs may be involved, thus requiring higher markon to compensate. Or if there is little or no reorder service, then there is more risk of markdowns from broken size runs. Thus a profitable line is not necessarily reflected by the line itself but also by the services related to it.

Deliveries.   No matter how salably hot a line is, it's a frozen fish if you receive the shoes late or only in fractions of what you order. Many retailers fall into this trap—eager to buy the hot line just because it's making heat waves. They find themselves paying the profit penalty by dealing with crumbs instead of loaves.

A shoe store or department is essentially a "community" of lines. For it to be a viable community, every member must contribute its share. But if the average store is analyzed line by line for profitability, almost always will be found some freeloaders, some indigent, some part-time performers—and perhaps only half that are carrying most of the weight for the whole.

Retailers, like most groups, tend to be creatures of habit. If they've carried a particular line for years, even though the line is a mediocre profit performer, they'll continue to stay with it. One reason is sheer lethargy or the failure to examine the line with a hard, close look for profit performance. Another is that they feel they have a built-in "investment" in the line—which may be like having an investment in a dry-hole oil well. Still another is the fear of losing the line to a competitor; or the reluctance to offend or disappoint the line's salesman whom they've known for years.

None of these, of course, justifies retaining a line that is not a consistently healthy profit-maker for the store. And no retailer can know this until he keeps records of his inventory line by line. If he does keep such a check he's sure to find some surprises. And if he remedies the "surprises" his overall profit will show a definite upbeat.

TABLE 1

Store Operating Data

(sample store, $200,000 volume)

Divide Operating Expenses (say 36%)	—	$72,000
by Average Monthly Inventory	—	$80,000
to find Break-Even Point	—	$.90
Divide Break-Even Point		
by 12 (months)	—	$.075
This is store's Profit Key	—	7.5%
(Each dollar invested in inventory must earn the Profit Key just to pay operating expenses).		
Divide 12 (mos.) by the Annual Turnover Ratio	—	2.5
to find Average Time all Inventory		
remains On Hand	—	4.8 mos.

Multiply this Time	—	4.8
by the Profit Key	—	7.5%
to find Cost of Business on Inventory	—	36%
From the Average Gross Margin	—	43%
subtract Cost on Inventory	—	36%
to find pre-tax Profit	—	7%
Multiply pre-tax Profit	—	7%
by Dollar Sales for last year	—	$200,000
to find pre-tax Dollar Profit	—	$14,000

TABLE 2

Appraising Profitability of Line

(sample store, $200,000 volume)

		Line A	Line B
Divide Dollar Sales	—	$40,000	$48,000
by Average Monthly Inventory	—	$12,000	$20,000
to find Turnover Ratio	—	3.33	2.4
Divide 12 (months)	—	12	12
by Turnover Ratio	—	3.33	2.4
to find Time Key	—	3.6 mos.	5 mos.
(Time Key is aver. no. of mos. a pair of this line remains on stock shelf).			
Multiply Time Key	—	3.6	5
by Profit Key (store overall aver.)	—	7%	7%
to find Cost of Handling Line (as percentage of sales)	—	25.2%	35%
Subtract Cost of Handling	—	25.2%	35%
from Gross Margin	—	40%	37%
to find Profit on Line	—	14.8%	5%
Multiply by Dollar Sales	—	$40,000	$48,000
to find pre-tax Profit	—	$ 5,920	$ 2,400
Divide net pre-tax Profit	—	$ 5,920	$ 2,400
by aver. overall Store Profit (7%)	—	$14,000	$14,000
to find Percent of Profit contributed by the Line	—	42.3%	17.1%

17

The Costly Duplication of Lines

*Experience is something you don't
get until just after you need it.*

*Experience is a comb that Nature
gives to a man after he's bald.*

Duplication of lines is one of the most common and costly mistakes of shoe retailers, and a prime sign of management weakness. It's estimated that at least one-third of independent shoe stores carry too many lines, or duplicate lines; that is, duplication by prices or type classification or styles or items. There are several "usual" reasons why it happens:

The owner or buyer may be vulnerable to salesmen. "I like the guy and want to give him some business." Perhaps you've heard the story of the building inspector making a routine check of a grocery store. Piled high in the rear of the store were many 100-pound bags of salt. "You must sell a lot of salt," said the inspector. Replied the grocer, "Very little, in fact. But the salesman I buy it from—boy, can *he* sell salt."

Then there are those retailers who feel they must be "covered" in everything so they won't lose sales. Also, many retailers easily succumb to buying "hot" items until there are more items than lines and a mish-mashed inventory.

Succumbing to such temptations costs plenty. The greater the duplication of lines the more time you must spend with salesmen; the greater your handling and bookkeeping costs; the more drag on your turnover; the less your cash flow; the weaker your open-to-buy position; the foggier your store image, the more dent in your profits.

Duplication of lines or items usually leads to costly markdowns. Ironically, retailers are always talking about what's selling. But profit and loss stems more from what's *not* selling.

To avoid being caught in this bear trap you should start pre-planning your lines in the same way you pre-plan your six-months budget. This is called Classification Management—analyzing and buying by type and price (men's, women's, children's, boots, casuals, slippers, athletic, etc.). Then a further breakdown of *each* classification. For example, men's dress shoes. You start each time with the question: Is this line (or shoe) absolutely necessary? If there is close similarity with one or more other lines or shoes (style, price, type, etc.), then one or more *must* go.

The first rule of good inventory control is discipline. It's not a case of how many lines do I need, but how many can I do *without?* One of the most common areas of line duplication today is in sneakers and athletic-sports footwear because of so many prominent brands. It's a costly snare for many retailers because there is enormous price and style duplication. Falling victim to having a little of this and that is poor inventory control and expensive waste.

Duplication is the enemy of inventory depth. With surplus lines you can thin-spread yourself into trouble. More lost sales are due to lack of sizes than lack of styles or lines. At any given time 80 percent of your sales will be done with 20 percent of your inventory. That 20 percent should always have depth. But the more surplus of lines or items, the less concentration you can give to that vital, profit-making 20 percent.

Which lines will you keep, which will you let go? Records will enable you to sift the wheat from the chaff. You should keep a careful check on *performance by lines* (a surprising number of stores fail to do this). If you don't, some lines can be a drag on profits and turnover without you realizing it. If one line represents 5 percent of your inventory investment, it should deliver *at least* 5 percent of your sales. Does it? Only your records will tell.

Which are your best lines? Not only those with the most consistent sales but the fewest markdowns, the most consistent sustained markon. And finally, the best line is always the bottom line—the profit performance.

Do you complain about delivery service from your resources? By doing business with fewer resources, you'll be surprised how your deliveries will improve. As you do more volume with fewer resources, you get rated as a "good account." This translates into better deliveries, better sales service, more liberal credit, etc.

Many shoe retailers are under-capitalized, sometimes constantly. They are always in need of cash flow to maintain credit, avoid costly borrowing, hold a healthy open-to-buy. Because line or item duplication is waste, it is their worst enemy. By eliminating the excess (and chances are you can cut at least 10 percent), you can concentrate on fewer lines with equal selections, more depth, stronger store image—with improvement in sales and profits.

There's a saying: When two people consistently agree, one of them becomes unnecessary. The same applies to the lines in a store.

Buying
and Budgeting

18

Pre-Planning a Calendar of Operations

The past is valuable as a guidepost but dangerous if used as a hitching post.

Most shoe stores or departments usually function with a six-months calendar consisting chiefly or solely of a buying budget or inventory plan (initial buy, open-to-buy, end-of-month figures, etc.)

This is fine as a buying-inventory calendar. But it's *not* a full-fledged calendar of operations. A calendar of operations involves the pre-planning of *all* the major segments of store operation: expenses, displays, advertising, profits, promotions, pricing, markdowns, etc. It makes no sense to carefully plan the buying and inventory control and not as carefully pre-plan for the expenses and merchandise movement factors that are responsible for the fate of what has been bought.

What should be included in a full-fledged, six-months calendar of operations? Where does it all start? What is the logical sequence of the programing? Here is a suggested outline or framework:

Economic Planning.   What's the general business outlook in your locality for the next six months? This obviously bears much influence on your market and consumer spending—which in turn will influence your buying, sales, profits, loans, inventory, etc. So your first move is to discuss the six-months *local* general business outlook with your bank, the local Chamber of Commerce, or other qualified local business forecasters. All sound forward planning starts here.

Sales and Growth Planning.   Before you buy you should have an idea of how much you expect to sell. And this should be calculated in *units* (the true gauge of growth.) You can't just pluck a random "increase" out of the hat (as many stores do) based on last year's figures. You must have *reasons* for the projections—the economic outlook, a planned ad campaign, special promotions, a store remodeling, new or expanded lines, etc. Good sales planning is vital to sound buying budgets and expense controls.

Profit Planning.   This one isn't easy because so many variables can influence the outcome. However, if all the separate pieces of the calendar are well-planned, then a more realistic and accurate profit estimate can be made.

Expense Planning.   Yes, you've neatly listed all the items and their respective percentage shares based on last year. But did last year's budgeted expenses match the actual? How much were they off mark? And why? Budgeting expenses is one thing, but disciplined control of the budget is another. A monthly expense control on the calendar helps assure a more realistic outcome.

Buying and Inventory.   Only now are you ready—with the prior calendar items pre-planned—to determine your buying budget and inventory makeup. You can't plan your buying until *first* you have a sound estimate of what you will sell and what it will cost to operate. This is a common mistake—placing the buying plan at the top of the list when it should be in a lower or subsequent position.

In-store Meetings.   You've now made your buys and the new merchandise is coming in. Here's where the pre-planned calendar of operations really goes into high gear. It starts with the store personnel, especially the salespeople. It's important that they know *why* you bought what you did—every item. If your reasons and convictions are conveyed to them, they can sell the merchandise more intelligently, and with the same enthusiasm and conviction. Further, they should be informed about your plans for displays, prices, advertising, promotions, etc. All this contributes to more effective movement of the merchandise. Such in-store meetings should be assigned places on the calendar.

Promotions.   You know what you've bought. You're in debt for the merchandise until you move it. This is where the *creative* part of the business goes into action— pre-planning a calendar of promotions for each category of the new inventory, or certain items. But this is where many stores become "me-too" operations—failing to create fresh ways to move merchandise.

You can buy an excellent annual booklet, *Chase's Calendar of Annual Events* (Apple Tree Press, 2322 Mallery St., Flint, Mich. 48504), or obtain a similar booklet from your local Chamber of Commerce. This is a calendar of special days, weeks and months, many of which can be springboards for special and unusual tie-in promotions. One or two big promotions over a six-months period aren't enough. Continuing promotions, each with a different theme, give the store a live, action image.

Clearances and Markdowns.   Do yours get the same tired "Fall Clearance Sale" treatment? Pre-planning gives you time to use more creative and effective clearance or markdown promotions. Also, occasionally try a different timing than the usual January–June periods when everyone else is doing the same thing.

Slow-selling Periods.   All stores have slow-selling hours during the day, and slow-selling days during the week (in most shoe stores or departments, 65 percent of the day's business is done in 20 percent of the hours, and 70 percent of the week's business is done in 30 percent of the days). How can you attract more sales during those slow periods? Some stores do it by creative techniques. Pre-planning such efforts by calendar can help grow sales in these arid periods.

Displays.   Every display, interior or window, should center around an idea or focus on a theme. These don't come off the top of the head but require advance planning time. Each idea for each display should be on a six-months calendar.

Advertising.   Here's an obviously important item on the calendar—the ad budget, the media, the copy and art, the timing, etc. Yet, many stores go little further than pre-planning an ad budget. From there it's all played by ear, with consequent waste. Also important, investigate your co-op ad opportunities. These can cut your ad spending appreciably without affecting the size of your ad program. Many retailers default on this, at a loss to them. Put more pre-planning time and effort into your advertising and you'll double its effectiveness and cut its cost.

Publicity. Few stores think of pre-planned publicity for their calendar. This can supplement your advertising, and often is even more productive—as well as being free. What things can you say about your store of local news interest? Perhaps a remodeling job, or some award by one of your employees, or a fashion report, etc. Make it newsy, non-commercial. Try to issue at least three local press releases over the six-month period.

Shows, Seminars, Buying Trips, Etc. These are part of the store's operation and should be scheduled on the calendar.

There's a saying, "A shoe well bought is half sold." This can be parodied: "A season well planned has already half succeeded." Your "efficiency rating" as a retailer isn't governed solely or largely by how smart a buyer you are or the condition of your inventory. Planning the buy is only one part of a six-months operational calendar. Forward planning by calendar means that *all* the spaces must be accounted for in advance. That's what calendars are for—to alert you not only to the present but to the future.

19

Twenty-one Ways to Profitably Shop a Shoe Show

When things go right, I made the decisions. When they go wrong, I look for partners.

The future usually has in store exactly what's placed in store for the future.

How to shop a shoe show? You've heard or read it time and again. And perhaps if you're like a lot of other shoe retailers you say things like:

"You've seen one, you've seen 'em all."

"I do all my buying at the store, so who needs the shows?"

"I can't take the time away from the store."

"Showtime travel costs have gotten too expensive."

It's tragic. Not for the shows but for so many retailers. Consider some reasons:

Over half of your store investment is tied up in your buys, your inventory. One hundred percent of your sales, plus 100 percent of your profits, depend on the quantity and quality of your buys. Most of your markdowns and other merchandise losses are the consequence of your buys. Many of the inventory control problems of retailers are simply the result of what's bought.

You're probably familiar with the saying, "A shoe well bought is half sold." Yet perhaps as much as 25 percent to 30 percent of all footwear is faultily bought—in sizes, styles, colors, category mix, amounts, timing, etc.

These costly consequences could be greatly diminished if retailers did more justice to the shoe shows which cost companies and their sales representatives millions of dollars annually for the benefit of retailers. Yet, surveys by the National Shoe Travelers Association and National Shoe Retailers Association find that only 22 percent of retailers attend a national show; 46 percent attend one or two regional shows annually (usually the same show); 38 percent attend three to four shows; 4 percent more than four shows; and 12 percent none at all.

However, the significant fact is *how* the average retailer attends the shows. Two-thirds of retailers spend only one day (usually a Sunday) at a regional show. And often even that isn't a full or "serious" day.

Said one retailer, "It's a kind of token visit to clear my conscience. I do most of my buying back at the store, anyway. So I spend a few hours at the show looking around a little, saying a few hellos."

When it comes to shoe shows, perhaps most retailers need to "take the cure." What can and should they do to make the shows more productive for their business? How can they more profitably shop a show? Here are 21 suggestions:

1) Plan to spend at least two days at the show. A mere half or one day, especially when coffee breaks, lunch and socializing are deducted, is mere token time. You can't afford the time? What you really can't afford is the loss of guidance information at the show to help you with your buying decisions. And your brief show visit isn't resolved by telling the sales rep, "See me at the store."

2) Come prepared with a shopping/buying plan. Do your homework first.

3) Bring one or more key store personnel with you. Yes, it's an added expense, but it pays handsomely. They can help with the buying plans or decisions. When they're in on the buying they can sell with more conviction. It's also a strong boost for morale.

4) Make appointments in advance with your resources—sales reps—usually for the second or third day. This assures exclusive attention without interruptions. Also, make sure you see the *whole* program—the new promotional plans, the advertising schedule, new display materials, merchandising aids, etc.

5) Bring sales records and apply them to your buying plans—both initial buys and open-to-buy. Be guided by the numbers, not the gut.

6) Have a firm budget related to each merchandise category, based on your sales records. That's vital to keeping your inventory in good balance. That prevents borrowing from Peter to pay Paul and disrupting stock balance that hurts sales.

7) Have a clear-cut delivery schedule for each buy in each category and make your buys accordingly. Keep notes on requested delivery dates. It's a check on how well your resources keep delivery promises.

8) Make other business dates in advance—people you want to see at the show: company brass, new resource people, other retailers, etc. Set up

meetings for breakfast, lunch or elsewhere. This will save time and also put time to productive use.

9) Start early. Early starts help get things accomplished at the least-busy show periods.

10) Study the show directory. Find a corner for a half hour and make notes on who you want to see—lines, people, booth or room numbers. List them by priority. This economizes time.

11) Have an itinerary. A top priority list, a secondary or followup list, a final cleanup or miscellany list. Avoid random wandering.

12) Have a time-table and stick to it. If you're going to do justice to your itinerary, then it must reasonably abide by a time schedule.

13) Shop new lines. You've set up appointments with your priority resources for the second or third day. Let the first day (usually the busiest) be a shopping day—new or competitive lines, hot items, etc. This can be informative for trends, possible new resources, fresh ideas.

14) Look for fresh promotional and merchandising ideas that can be applied to your own business—often from sources remote from your own lines. Take notes.

15) Visit the non-shoe exhibits: accessories, services, store fixtures and materials, etc. This should be a must on your itinerary. This tour can often reveal some profitable plums.

16) Attend the show events—fashion shows, seminars, speakers, consulting services, etc. A NSRA survey found that only 26 percent of retailers attend show seminars; 25 percent hear luncheon or other speakers; 16 percent use consulting services; 14 percent attend fashion shows. That's a very poor record. As a result, retailers miss out on a lot of trend and other helpful information.

Twenty-one Ways to Profitably Shop a Shoe Show 97

17) Talk shop with other retailers. Seek out fellow shoemen for an exchange of information on trends, fresh ideas, buying tips, etc.

18) Keep a record of what you see and hear. Take notes. Use a camera for things you want to photograph (as a courtesy, always ask permission first). This retains a lot of what you'd ordinarily forget.

19) Pick up literature, free samples. These are available at many of the exhibits. Carry a briefcase to contain it. When you study the material back home, it can reveal some helpful discoveries.

20) Seek out the top brass of your own resources. They attend the national shows, but also some of the larger regionals. Talk with them. Don't focus on just the gripes and complaints. Sprinkle some praise, too. The important thing is to establish a personal relationship so that you're more than an account number.

21) Avoid time-killing, socializing at the bar or cocktail lounge, stretched-out lunches, etc. Daytime is work time. Save the fun for the evenings.

A comment about national shows. Less than a fifth of shoe retailers attend one or more national shows a year. The three main reasons: the expense, the unaffordable time required, and the fact that these are "looking" rather than buying shows for most retailers (only about 16 percent of retailers make actual buys at national shows).

But national shows offer advantages for small and medium retailers. They provide important advance fashion and market trend information which retailers can apply to their later buying at the followup regional shows. The retailer gets a national perspective of trends rather than the more insulated, local view. He can talk to the top brass of his resources.

Surveys show that 52 percent of retailers buy mostly or entirely at the store rather than at the shows. However, the shows serve an invaluable and indispensable function for the retailers. Yet, ironically, perhaps three-fourths of all retailers fail to make full productive use of their time at shoe shows. In fact, an estimated 50 percent to 60 percent of their showtime is wasted, ineffectual time spent.

With better planning and application of their showtime, the whole buying and seasonal program of the average retailer can be appreciably upgraded. That helps to achieve the retailer's natural objectives: better inventory control, fewer markdowns, more sales, more profit.

Advertising and Promotion

20

Getting More for Your Advertising Dollars

Doing business without advertising is like winking at a girl in the dark. You know what you're doing but nobody else does.

Cutting your advertising to save money is like stopping your watch to save time.

Take two stores, each doing a volume of $350,000. Each spends 3 percent of its sales on advertising. But one store gets double the productive return for its ad dollars. The advertising cost for that store is less than half that of the other.

Thus it isn't so much a matter of how much is spent, but rather the return on what's spent. Contrary to what most people think, the primary purpose of advertising isn't to increase traffic and sales but to lower selling costs. When advertising increases sales, this reduces selling and operating costs. It's the lowering of these costs that results in the increased profit.

Each year, shoe retailers spend an estimated $800 million on advertising. A good share of that falls short of return potentials—the equivalent of getting 50 cents on the dollar.

Today, perhaps more than ever, effective advertising is vital. Each year the average trading area loses about 18 percent of its former customers, who in turn are replaced by about the same share of newcomers. Also, the radius of the trading area continues to expand, meaning that customers are more mobile in their shopping. Thus stores must strengthen their advertising to retain the loyalty of present customers and also attract the newcomers.

So now the obvious big question: how do you get a better return for your ad dollars? You begin by applying a list of "musts" as follows:

1) An adequate ad budget.
2) Bull's-eye targeting your markets.
3) Selection of productive media.
4) The quality of the advertising itself.
5) Consistency of advertising.

6) Use of innovation and imagination.

7) Cooperation of store personnel.

8) Keeping records of ad performance.

Productive advertising, therefore, is much more than a matter of "running ads" or spending for advertising. It's a carefully planned package, each piece contributing to make a productive whole. Let's take a brief look at each.

THE RULES, THE MEDIA

The Ad Budget.   The minimum should be 3 percent of sales. But Dun & Bradstreet studies show that nearly a third of shoe retailers spend under 2 percent, and some nothing. Fewer than one-fifth spend the "standard" 3 percent. But almost half spend 4 percent or more—and these are usually the more successful stores.

Many of the low-ad-budget stores live by the philosophy, "When business is good I don't need to advertise, and when it's poor I can't afford to." That's playing Russian roulette. Your luck is bound to run out.

Other stores advertise spasmodically. No program or consistency. That's wasted money. Still others include a lot of "miscellany" into the ad budget, such as costs for attending shoe shows, a vacation with the wife, a car for the son at college. That's the same as burglarizing your own store.

Thus the prime law: establish a minimum 3 percent ad budget and make sure all of it gets spent on legitimate advertising.

The Ad Schedule.   About 90 percent of your ad budget should be pre-planned on a six-months schedule. You thus know how much you'll spend each month, how and where it will be spent, and for what purpose. The remaining 10 percent is for contingencies such as a non-scheduled promotion, or a followup on a hot seller, etc.

Ads should be pre-scheduled for specific events: Christmas, Father's Day, Mother's Day, new spring and fall merchandise, clearances, special promotions, etc. When you make a special buy, plan for special advertising to make it pay off. The key element in all effective advertising is pre-planning and consistency. If you waffle or vacillate on this, your ad program is standing on one leg.

Target Your Markets.   Much retail advertising uses buckshot instead of a rifle aimed for a bull's-eye. This scattershot approach hits a little and misses a lot. The result is much waste.

Ask yourself: with my categories of merchandise and kind of store, what kind of customers am I trying to reach? The market targets (or customers) may be classified on the basis of age, income level, occupations (white or blue collar), basic or fashion, etc.

With a clear idea of your customers or prospects as related to your kind of store (location, merchandise, prices, etc.), you then seek the kind of media most likely to be exposed to them.

Selection of Media.   Our accompanying table shows how the ad dollars of shoe retailers are distributed among the various prime advertising media.

Selection of media is one of the most important steps in the ad program. It's also often the area of greatest waste of ad dollars due to careless selection. For example, using only one medium such as the local newspaper without supplementing with other media opportunities. Or, if a selection of several media is available, the use of one that doesn't necessarily offer the best results at lowest cost.

Probe the audience makeup of each ad medium. Don't be razzle-dazzled by media claiming to reach a "mass audience." Ask for an audience break-down by age, income level, education, residence sectors, etc. Such a profile will answer your question: are these my kind of customers?

Newspapers.　These are still the main channel for shoe advertising. However, the main newspaper in town isn't necessarily your only choice. In addition, lesser papers may sometimes be available, such as direct mail tabloids or shopping news giveaways. They're very inexpensive. But if you buy space in them, make sure you're on the front page. Many readers of these glance only at the front page and throw the paper away. But your ad gets read or seen.

If you see other ads that are eye-catching or unusual but apply to other merchandise, don't hesitate to adapt the idea for your own merchandise or store with the necessary variations.

Now, some specifics about the newspaper ads themselves.

Maneuver for best position relative to your merchandise. Sports or business pages for men's shoes; women's or homemaker or food pages for women's or children's shoes; etc. Go for the bull's-eyes.

What size ad? Big ads cost a lot more but aren't necessarily the most productive. By using smaller ads more frequently—usually beside news or other editorial material—you can often get better readership at less cost.

What you say and how it's presented will largely determine the response to the advertising. This means ad headlines, copy, art, layout. Advertising experts frequently say "most shoe advertising looks the same." So use imagination and innovation to make your ads fresh and unusual. Create a clear identity for your ads. Remember, your advertising represents the public's image of your store and merchandise.

Avoid clutter in the ad. Sell one idea at a time.

Avoid cliches in your headlines or copy. For example: Step Into Spring; Footnotes to Fashion; Put Your Best Foot Forward. Cliches get shopworn and draw yawns.

Design the ad so that it convincingly answers the viewer's or listener's perennial question: what's in it for me? An ad should motivate interest that converts into desire to buy.

Ads should provide basic information: store logo, name, address, phone, hours, credit services, parking, etc.

Occasionally run an institutional ad. For example, feature your salespeople with photos and names. If yours is a service store say something about the salespeople's special skills and experience as fitters, fashion counselors, experts. Many customers are as interested in the quality of the service as the merchandise. Also, such ads increase pride and morale in the salespeople.

Other "service" ads can be equally effective. For instance, with the start of the new season run a "Fashion Trend Report" ad. No direct selling of your merchandise. Just an informative report. Readers will assume that your merchandise fits into the trend information. And they'll be impressed and grateful for the fashion guidance information. Such ads build store image.

The same can be done with your back-to-school ads, focusing on information about children's foot health, foot growth, fitting, the importance of proper shoes, etc. Again, no direct selling of merchandise. But what you establish is customer confidence in the store via a "public service."

Radio. This is getting an increasing share of retail shoe ad dollars. Some 99 percent of homes and cars have radios. High school and college students give radio listening much higher priority than TV or newspapers.

But be selective about the use of radio. If you're trying to reach mature-age customers you don't advertise on a rock-and-roll station. Conversely, if you're after a youth audience you don't advertise on a station highlighting classical music.

Direct Mail. This can be very effective if properly used—but a waste if not. It's most effective when you use it for your own customer (or prospect) list. And *how* you use it—the physical format of the mailing pieces, what you say and how it's said—are vital. Nevertheless, most direct mail gets read. It's an important supplement to your other advertising.

Yellow Pages. These are most effective if your store specializes in something unusual. For example, extra-large or small sizes and widths, or shoes for hard-to-fit feet. Otherwise, Yellow Pages have only minimal value.

Cooperative Advertising. Here's another place where advertising opportunities are lost by many shoe retailers. Shoe manufacturers offer millions of *free* dollars for cooperative advertising—usually about 50 percent of the retailer's ad cost on the brand—yet less than half of it is used. And most of it is used by larger retailers. An estimated 60 to 70 percent of smaller retailers, mostly independents, make little or no use of it. Now *that's* waste. So the message is clear: use more of those co-op ad dollars.

Keep Records. All your ads should be kept on file, with a comment on their performance or results. Repeat the successful ones.

Salespeople. Keep them informed of all your ads in advance. It's not unusual for a customer to come into the store and ask for the shoe advertised in yesterday's newspaper, and for the salesperson to say, "What shoe was that?" Also, ask your salespeople and other store personnel for their views on the ads you're running, or their ideas for new ads. They often can contribute good ideas and are flattered by being asked.

As you've now seen, advertising consists of a package of several elements, each contributing something to making the ad program productive by reducing selling and operating costs while building traffic, sales, profits and store image.

There are the cynics who say, "Half of all advertising is waste." The answer to that is, "Which half?" While it's true that much ad spending is wasted, the waste isn't in the principle of advertising but in the wasteful use of advertising. But if you follow the basic principles outlined in this chapter, you can minimize the waste and maximize the profitable results.

How Ad Budgets Are Spent by Shoe Retailers

	Independents	Chains	Dept. Stores
Newspapers	42%	34%	38%
Local radio	30	29	22
Local TV	14	20	18
Direct mail	14	17	22
	100%	100%	100%

Source: Dun & Bradstreet

Sample Schedule for a $9,000 Ad Budget
(Family store, $300,000 volume)

Jan.	Feb.	Mar.	Apr.	May	June
$900	$ 400	$900	$800	$700	$ 900
Semi-Annual Sale		Spring Shoes		Mother's Day	Father's Day Semi-Annual Sale

July	Aug.	Sept.	Oct.	Nov.	Dec.
$600	$1,000	$800	$500	$500	$1,000
	Back To School	Fall Shoes			Xmas

ADVERTISING LESSON

The codfish lays ten thousand eggs,
The homely hen lays one.
The codfish never cackles
To tell you what she's done.
And so we scorn the codfish,
While the humble hen we prize.
Which only goes to show you
That it pays to advertise.

21

Cooperative Advertising— Free Money Going to Waste

It may be true that half of all advertising is waste. But which half?

The only business that can afford not to advertise is the U.S. mint.

It's incredible. There are scores and scores of shoe manufacturers out there holding millions of dollars in their hands, urging and begging retailers to take it and spend it. And thousands of shoe retailers looking at that money and not reaching out to take a dime of it. Millions of *free* dollars going to waste.

We're speaking of cooperative advertising money available to retailers—and an estimated two-thirds of it unused. It's one of the mysteries of shoe business because those unused cooperative advertising dollars can represent up to 25 percent or more of a store's advertising costs and over 10 percent of its net profits.

Most shoe retailers are familiar with cooperative advertising, also known as advertising or promotional allowance. Many shoe manufacturers, especially brand houses, offer a cooperative advertising program in which the manufacturer will pay about 50 percent of the store's ad costs up to a value of 3 percent of the store's merchandise purchased from the manufacturer. For example, if over the course of a year a store buys $25,000 in merchandise from a resource, the manufacturer will pay up to $750 (3 percent) of the local advertising done by the retailer and involving the manufacturer's brand name.

Let's say a store's volume is $350,000 and its total ad budget is 3 percent or $10,500. Let's say its $175,000 of annual merchandise purchases are bought from several brand manufacturers, all of whom offer a co-op ad program. If the retailer utilized all of those promotional allowances it would amount to $5,250. That would be 50 percent of the store's total ad spending—and, of course, a saving of $5,250 on ad expense.

Let's say the same store's net profit is 7 percent or $24,500. Thus the ad allowances of $5,250 would amount to 21 percent of the store's net profit.

A *New York Times* study shows that of the $7 billion in co-op advertising money available to retailers, one-third goes unused. And most of the used money is accounted for by the larger retailers. This means that an estimated 60 to 70 percent of smaller retailers, the independents, make little or no use of those free ad dollars. Yet many of those smaller retailers are using *their own* money to advertise.

And a good share of those ad dollars are promoting manufacturers' brands—the same brands that have free ad dollars to share with the retailer.

Shoe manufacturers are spending an estimated $20 millions in co-op advertising, or about 15 percent of their total ad spending. However, they have millions more "in escrow" for co-op advertising that is never tapped by eligible retailers.

According to studies by the Federal Trade Commission and the Small Business Bureau, many large retailers have been getting as much as 35 percent of their total advertising expenditures paid for by the manufacturers. But among shoe retailers doing a volume of $250,000 or less, fewer than 10 percent make use of these promotional allowances.

A fairly recent shoe industry study reveals the following:

- 34 percent of shoe retailers have less than 20 percent of their advertising paid for by promotional allowances.
- with 59 percent, less than 40 percent of their advertising is shared by promotional allowances. And only 28 percent utilize promotional allowances in more than 50 percent of their advertising.

The study brought home one significant fact. The bigger and more successful the store, the greater use it makes of promotional allowances. It is mostly the smaller stores who *exclude themselves* from use of these free funds.

The chief reason smaller retailers fail to make sufficient use of promotional allowances is *negligence*. Many such retailers offer excuses: "I don't have time for the paperwork involved" . . . "I don't do enough advertising to make it worthwhile" . . . "I can't put up with the hassles." But these are excuses, not reasons.

If a retailer has sufficient confidence in a branded line to stock and sell it, he should carry the same conviction into his advertising. Consider this. The manufacturer's cost for promotional allowances is built into the cost of the shoes you're buying from him. If the larger stores are utilizing the promotional allowances but you aren't—then *you* are paying for part of your competitors' advertising.

Promotional allowances are a form of purchase discounts. A retailer will be quick to take his regular purchase discounts, but will ignore the same discounts in the form of promotional allowances. This is an obvious paradox, but thousands of shoe retailers are doing just that.

In the past there were numerous abuses of cooperative advertising by both manufacturers and retailers. But most of these abuses have largely disappeared since the FTC imposed stringent ruling (backed by the Supreme Court in 1968) concerning cooperative advertising agreements. Today, both retailers and manufacturers are much better protected and the arrangements more equitable.

Some retailers, especially in smaller stores in metropolitan areas, have bypassed cooperative advertising because they can't afford the high space rates in local media (74 percent of all promotional allowances go into newspapers). However, other such retailers have found an answer by pooling part of their ad budgets. For example, a manufacturer may have five non-competitive accounts spread over a metropolitan area. Using promotional allowances with their own money, the five stores will run a single large ad involving the manufacturer's brand, naming all five stores in their different locations. The big ad is effective; all the stores benefit;

and the cost, aided by the co-op ad money, doesn't strain the budget of any one store.

Cooperative advertising is no longer a kind of "tribute" or "contribution" by the manufacturer. It represents a sound advertising or promotional partnership between the manufacturers and retailer designed to work to the advantage of both.

Shoe travelers are supposed to inform the retailers about their companies' co-op ad program, but many fail to do this. The retailer should make it a point to ask and get all details—especially when considering taking on a new line.

Cooperative advertising is no panacea. But it holds tangible benefits for retailers—and the most important are lower advertising costs and an increase in net profit as a result of reduced advertising expense.

You're familiar with the fable of the man who searched the world in vain for a four-leaf clover, only to return home and find clusters of them in his own back yard. The moral of the fable can be applied to promotional allowances in your own search for lower expenses and improved net profit.

GETTING THE MOST FROM YOUR COOPERATIVE ADVERTISING

Here are some important guidelines to observe to help make your cooperative advertising most productive for you:

1) Don't run any co-op ads unless the timing, pricing and merchandising are right for you.

2) Don't be afraid to make special co-op ad requests from the manufacturer—time extensions, new ad materials, media exceptions, layout variations, etc. Many manufacturers will furnish in-store promotional materials, prizes, special promotional plans and allowances and other incentives to help make a full-blown promotion of a single ad. Be sure you know everything that's available from the manufacturer.

3) Maintain good contact with the ad department of your resources. If they know you're interested they'll give you the best service from the programs they work hard to provide for their customers.

4) Don't include estimated co-op ad contributions as part of your regular ad budget. Plan as if no co-op were available and use those "found" funds to increase your impact in the market. Look at it as a bonus, an extra.

5) Let your local media sales reps know you wish to use co-op whenever possible. They have access to information you may not see, and they can make the job of collecting co-op ad reimbursements much easier.

6) Keep good records. A file of current co-op plans by your resources is imperative. Also keep an accurate record of co-op plans presented and funds received and the amount of co-op receivables—reimbursements applied for but not yet received.

7) Finally, when you receive co-op reimbursements, put the money back into the ad budget. Don't mix it in with other revenues or the value will be lost in terms of additional advertising effectiveness.

22

How to Build and Use a Mailing List

If you're tired of waiting for your ship to come in, try swimming out to it.

A lot of people love their jobs. It's the work they hate.

Most shoe stores and departments advertise. About 80 percent of it, surveys show, is newspaper advertising. But one of the most overlooked yet productive advertising media is direct mail. It has become a multibillion-dollar industry, which is evidence of its value. It deserves much more attention by shoe retailers.

Perhaps your first reaction is, "Nobody reads junk mail. It's a waste." You'd be dead wrong. Studies show that 9 of every 10 persons open and read this mail, and over 50 percent say they *like* to receive it. Moreover, if it's from a local store with a familiar name, it gets an even better reception.

Stores talk a lot about "customer communications." But how does *your* store communicate? By way of newspaper advertising? That's impersonal, and it's competing with scores or hundreds of other ads.

Or perhaps you "communicate" when the customers are in the store. That's too late. The function of communications is to talk to customers and prospects when they're *not* in the store, giving them incentives or reasons to come in and buy.

And that's precisely the function of direct mail—customer communications. When you write a letter or send a message directly to one's home, that's communicating. It's personal marketing by mail.

However, under no circumstances is direct mail designed to replace your newspaper, radio or other advertising. Rather, it supplements them. It adds another weapon to your marketing arsenal.

Direct mail has certain advantages. If properly prepared and executed it's often the least costly and most effective of all forms of advertising. It starts with one important asset: no waste circulation or audience. It shoots with bullets, not buckshot. Its aim is on the bull's-eye, not a broad target.

Compare it, for example, with newspaper advertising. Say the local newspaper has a circulation of 75,000 and a readership of 125,000. Let's say your product is women's fashion shoes. The newspaper's readership might consist of 40 percent men, 8 percent teenagers, 8 percent elderly, plus another 10 percent not in your price range or not particularly interested in fashion footwear. Thus the readership for *your* product and message is only 35 percent of the 75,000—but you are paying for *all* 75,000.

By contrast, if your mailing goes to a list of your customers or selected local prospects, you have almost no waste circulation. What you pay for is what you get—100 percent readership.

THE MAILING LIST

The key to productive results for direct mail is a good mailing list. It all begins here. By far, the best mailing list is your own customers. If you don't keep an updated mailing list, you're running your business with a built-in handicap. There are various ways to develop such a list. Here's one simple and effective technique.

At the cash or checkout counter, have a large ledger book. Behind it is a placard that reads: "Sign your name and address and receive free shoe laces twice a year." Over 90 percent of your customers will sign—and on the actual signing give them the first pair of laces. You'll be sending out at least two mailings a year, so the laces will be included (which, incidentally, greatly enhances the reading of your mailed message).

If the customer is accompanied by a friend or relative, also get their names on the list. Keep in mind that the average shoe store or department doing a volume of $350,000 a year will have a store traffic of about 15,000 each year. That's a big mailing list potential.

Another way is to keep customer card records. These would include name and address, plus size, style purchased, etc. When the customer is told that these records enable the store to provide better service on future visits, he or she will almost always cooperate.

If you're a family store you can keep the mailing lists filed by groups: men, women and parents (or small children). This will enable you to pin-point your mailings with even more precision and economy.

You can, of course, buy local lists classified by such specialized classifications as area, occupation, sex, age, incomes, hobbies, etc. These, however, can be relatively expensive. But you can get around this.

For example, you can cull good lists of names from town voting lists or city directories. Roster lists can be purchased from the local PTA (for children's shoes) at very low cost. These lists give names of parents and children, including addresses, age of children, etc.

With a little ingenuity, time and effort you can find a number of ways to build low-cost mailing lists to supplement your own. A point of caution: avoid addressing mail to "Occupant" or "Resident." Direct mail is most effective when personally addressed.

Keep your lists updated and active. This can be done by occasionally using a direct mail piece with the imprint "Form 3547 Requested" on the address side of the mailing. You then automatically receive all undeliverable mail and notices of changes of address. This is well worth the small charge per returned piece. It weeds out inactive names and further cuts mailing costs.

GETTING RESULTS

Next to a good mailing list the most important thing is making it pay off with sales results. This is determined largely by the content of the mailing piece itself—what it sells, what's said and how it is presented, the physical appearance, etc. You have only a few seconds to capture the attention of the reader. Here are some tips:

1) Make your opener short, catchy, a lure to read on. Avoid being cute.
2) Avoid innocuous salutations like "To all our good customers."
3) Make your point quickly, concisely.
4) Keep the message personal, friendly, sincere, informal, low-key. Don't let the words scream.
5) Keep the sentences short, crisp, informative, motivating.

What do you sell via direct mail? Just about anything you sell in your store. For example, a special closeout sale (but *not* a cold notice of "our semi-annual post-season sale"); or an advance notice of new merchandise just in the store. In both such instances let these customers know they're being notified *before* newspaper ads appear because as "preferred customers" they're being given first choice. It's both true and flattering. And, of course, the mailing must go out before the ads appear.

The same can be done with special selling periods like back-to-school, Mother's or Father's Day. Or pre-Christmas. For example, many shoe stores or departments think chiefly of slippers for Christmas. Instead, present a complete suggestion list of gift merchandise available in your store—hose, shine kits, pedicure sets, handbags, fleece-lined boots, electric foot massagers, packaged shoe cleaners for all shoe colors and materials, weather boots, and yes, even shoes (or gift certificates). Show small sketches or photos, give prices. Tell them they can save shopping time buying several unusual and practical gifts in your store.

Or you can try eye-catching ideas. For example, instead of the usual discount coupon or notice, have a $10 bill photographed and blown up to larger size. This becomes a coupon. Your message: when brought into the store the bill is really $10 (or $5) off regular price to buy certain specified merchandise within the next two weeks. The outsize bill has more visual "value appeal" than an ordinary coupon.

Another idea: send out a quarterly "footwear fashion report" to the mailing list. These, if well done, are practical, helpful, well-read. If accompanied by small sketches illustrating the text, so much the better. And, of course, a tie-in with merchandise in your stock. You provide an information service—and it sells merchandise, plus building store image and loyalty.

Another effective mailing instrument is the "newsletter" format—a single 8½ × 11 page printed front and back; or an 8 × 5 folded leaflet. Both can be designed as self-mailers. The newsletter should have a newspaper-like masthead such as "The Bootery Bulletin." It should be issued on a scheduled two or three or four times a year.

The newsletter contains several different stories presented in a newspaper page format, each story with a catchy title; for example, "Children's Feet Grow, But Shoes Don't;" or "Heels Coming Down to Comfort Levels." Keep the writing light, conversational, with occasional touches of humor—but always informative. There are countless stories with interesting or helpful information about shoes or feet you can present. Such informative newsletters are extremely well read and are great image-builders for your store.

Now, what about costs? You should have a postal permit. Bulk mailing costs are relatively inexpensive considering that you're not paying for waste circulation. Your bulk mailing permit will be an annual, one-time charge. You can keep pace with Post Office regulations by subscribing to a *free* quarterly publication, *Memo to Mailers* (P.O.B. 1, Linwood, N.J. 08221). You're eligible for special rates if each mailing is 200 or more pieces.

How often should mail pieces be sent out? This is a very flexible matter. If you're going to do justice to direct mail, it shouldn't be used less than four times a year. Beyond that, it's a matter of store judgment—the ad budget, the number or types of promotions on your calendar, etc. Remember, you don't have to think in terms of costly "mass" mailings, but rather as smaller, more frequent ones to specialized groups of your customers or prospects.

Don't overlook the role of cooperative advertising. If you're promoting or advertising a particular brand, you can often get the manufacturer's financial support on the mailing cost. Cooperative advertising isn't necessarily restricted to newspapers, TV or radio.

Like any other form of advertising, direct mail is no panacea by itself. But it does deserve a place among the other media or forms. And it's a great medium to keep your store's name before your local trading area public to establish stronger store identity and image. Without direct mail, you're not using all your promotional potential.

23

How to Get Free Publicity

There are no hard times for good ideas.

It's one thing to itch for something, and another to scratch for it.

One of the most effective and least expensive ways to get exposure for your store and merchandise is via publicity and public relations. Unlike advertising, most of it is free.

Now, your first thought may be, "But our store seldom has anything of news value to interest the press." Wrong. All around you are things of news or other interest to the press and public. You've just overlooked them.

There are two kinds of publicity material: the "happenings" or events that are news; and the things or ideas that are created to *make* news. Most publicity and public relations consists of the latter.

The first rule is to make sure the publicity material is newsworthy. So before you prepare any publicity, ask yourself: "Will the editors and public find this interesting? Is it unusual? Will they learn something from it?"

Avoid anything in the publicity piece that reads or sounds like advertising for your store. It will end up in the editor's wastebasket. Keep it objective, newsy, informative, entertaining.

The preparation of the press release is very important. The more professional looking the better. Have it typed double-spaced on your letterhead. Make the writing concise, factual, to the point.

Develop a local press list. Addresses of local newspapers, TV and radio stations—plus the names of the editors or news program directors. It's important to direct a press release to a particular person.

Where possible, get to know these people personally—a managing or news editor, fashion editor, women's page editor, etc. Avoid being pushy. Be selective in the press releases you issue. It gets better results.

Never offer to pay for a legitimate press release. That's offensive, like bribery, and will turn editors against future material you submit.

WHAT MAKES NEWS?

Well, what makes "news"? Examples: moving to a new location; a remodeling or expansion project; an anniversary (10th or 20th); a new opening; new lines, such as starting a new children's department; promotions of personnel; the store owner or manager elected to an office in a trade association; attending (or receiving a diploma from) a technical seminar on, say, shoe fitting. These things show store progress and growth.

Where feasible, include a good 8 × 10 photo with the press release. For example, before-and-after photos of a store remodeling; or the owner receiving an award or certificate from a seminar or some special event.

Then there is the "created" publicity, which differs from the usual news happenings. This has almost limitless possibilities—human interest or educational information related to footwear and feet, with subtle tie-ins with your store and merchandise. Examples:

1) All people have "mismated" feet (based on survey findings). No two feet of a pair are exactly alike in size, shape or proportion. Tie this in with the importance of skilled shoe fitting.

2) The average person walks 150,000 miles over a lifetime (six times around the circumference of the globe). Relate this to wear and tear on feet and shoes and the importance of good shoes, good fit and good comfort.

3) The average person imposes a cumulative weight of 250,000 *tons* on their feet and shoes over a lifetime. Relate to wear and tear on feet and shoes and the shoe "engineering" required to take this abuse.

4) The average male buys about 210 pairs of shoes over a lifetime, the average female 520 pairs.

5) The average baby's foot grows at an average annual rate of 3/4ths of an inch over the first three years (8 full shoe sizes). At age 2½ the child's foot will be almost exactly one-half of its full length at adulthood. Relate to the importance of preventing outgrown shoes during the infant years.

6) Each year an estimated 200,000 new shoe "styles" (patterns, lasts, color and materials combinations, etc.) are introduced. Relate to the creative talent of the shoe designers, and also the broad style selection offered to the public.

There are many such human interest or educational items like this available. A little research can dig out the information. Then a little imagination to develop the information into an interesting press release.

Repeated appearance of such stories in the local press builds exposure for your store. And it's not unusual for the media to follow up with an interview that leads to a feature story.

There's also a lot of human interest historical material available about footwear. A little library or other research will furnish the information. Some examples:

1) We think pointed-toe shoes belong to "modern" fashion. They date back 3,000 years to ancient Egypt.

2) High heels aren't modern. They date back 450 years. Their history makes a fascinating story.

3) In Colonial America shoes were priced by the inch. The larger the size the more the cost (because of the extra materials and labor).

There are some collections of historical footwear held by private individuals or shoe companies. If you can borrow a few such shoes they'd make an interesting window display, with small card captions. It would also make an interesting feature story, along with photos, for the local newspaper. And would attract traffic.

The footwear trade publications are often good sources for ideas and information for press release material. Your local public never sees these, so you can develop them further with a little library research for local use.

Your own sales or other store personnel can sometimes be the makings of a press release. For example, it may surprise you that the average shoe salesperson processes about 9,000 trial shoe fittings a year (10 customers a day times an average of three fittings per customer). So over five years a shoe salesperson goes through nearly 50,000 fittings. Now that's a lot of shoe fitting experience—and the basis of an interesting news story.

Fashion makes excellent news material. Issue a quarterly footwear fashion report to the local newspaper (with photos, if possible—your resources can furnish these), plus local radio and TV stations. Contact whoever is in charge of fashion news. Tell the story of the trends for the incoming season—styles, colors, heels, materials, etc. Don't talk about *your* shoes. Let it be more general. You'll get the credit as the news source. Information like this helps build a fashion store image.

Tie in with national events or special "weeks"—National Foot Health Week, National Nurses' Week, National Baby Week, National Boy Scout Week, etc. (The U.S. Chamber of Commerce has a full calendar of such special-event weeks. Also Chases' Calendar of Annual Events, P.O.B. 1012, Flint, Michigan 48501).

Sponsor local events or activities: local walking clubs, or a Little League team, or a local scout troop. These will cost a modest investment, but they're productive in building local good will—and sales.

Establish or sponsor an annual award—a modest scholarship, a humanitarian award, a senior citizens award, etc. Give a plaque or prize. These always get press notice. The public service is good public relations.

Give talks on footwear to local groups, most of whom are hungry for speakers. Kiwanis, Rotary, women's clubs, parent-teachers, etc. Lots of interesting topics related to footwear (see our earlier suggestions) can be both informative and entertaining. Use slides where possible. The same topic can be used for different audiences.

If you're in a smaller community, suggest a monthly column on footwear for your local newspaper. Free. But avoid advertising plugs for your store (your column by-line is your advertising). The topics can vary: shoe fitting, fashion trends, something historical, shoe facts (wear, comfort, leathers).

Run unusual contests. The smallest women's foot (Cinderella contest); or the largest men's foot (Paul Bunyan contest). The winners get three free pairs of shoes. Such contests attract press attention, and often a story and photos about the winners.

Publicity and public relations programs usually are more productive in suburban areas or smaller towns where news is more localized.

Yes, it also helps if you're a local advertiser (newspaper, radio, TV). In some instances this gives your material better reception. But if your press releases and other publicity material are well prepared and interesting, it will get fair treatment even if you're not an advertiser. The media always needs such material.

All publicity and public relations boils down to one word: exposure. The same, of course, applies to advertising.

Creating productive publicity is a simple formula: a little research combined with a little imagination produces the ideas and material which converts into effective publicity. The publicity in turn builds store image and helps create traffic and sales.

Marketing and Merchandising

24

Using Demographics As a Sales Planning Tool

Today the consumer market moves fast. Don't aim for where it was.

Business is never so healthy as when, like a chicken, it must do a certain amount of scratching for what it gets.

You're familiar with the word "demographics." It's from two Greek words: *demos,* meaning people, and *graphos,* meaning to write or record. Modern demographics is the science of dealing with vital statistics, distribution and makeup of the population. It has become tremendously important as a marketing tool in forecasting trends for business, markets, products, consumer buying habits, among numerous other applications.

Applied on a national scope, demographics can be quite extensive and complicated. But its applications can be focused on a single market and product like footwear. And it can be even more simplified when focused on a single business like a retail shoe store. In fact, many retailers use some demographic data often without realizing it. But it can work much more effectively if it's applied with a little more knowledge and purpose.

You deal in merchandise. But before you can deal with merchandise you must first deal with people because they are the customers to whom you sell your merchandise. While the number of customers (traffic) is important, equally important is the demographic makeup of those customers by age groups, incomes, sex, lifestyles, buying habits, etc. When you speak of your "market" you are really speaking of the demographics which comprise the content and behavior of that market.

Demographics can provide a road map of *what's ahead* for your market and business. The demographics are what shape the very future of your business. All business is a numbers business. But the merchandise numbers and the dollars and sales numbers all begin with the people (customers) numbers. And even people numbers don't tell the whole story. We must also know something about the factors that influence the *behavior* of the various classifications of customers because this affects what and where people buy. That's where demographics come in as a sales and growth forecasting tool. We want to show you how to use it to your advantage.

Many retailers think they're keeping pace with trends by observing current changes; and they think they're "thinking ahead" when they project their planning a year in advance. That's short-sighted thinking. Demographics are designed for thinking and planning on a longer term—five or ten years ahead. So if you're seriously planning for growth in the right direction, you must apply demographics in the right way.

The boom enjoyed by the juvenile shoe business during the 1946–1966 period was all pre-written in the demographics, and those who pre-read the signs were better prepared and prospered most. The explosive reign of the youth and hippie culture of the 1965–1975 period and its enormous impact on footwear (remember "monster" shoes, high platforms, bump toes, macho boots, granny styles, grubby sneakers, etc.?) was forecasted by the demographics. The massive exodus of the population from the cities to the suburbs after World War II was foreseen in the demographics. That one trend alone created an upheaval in shoe retailing with the sharp decline in downtown shoe business and the sprawling growth of shopping centers and malls—today over 27,000 of them accounting for nearly three-fifths of all retail footwear sales.

We could cite several dozen such major trends and changes that have had major impact on shoe retailing as a consequence of demographic changes. The stores that heeded the demographics prospered, while many of those who "played it by ear" on a year-to-year basis saw their sales sag and their businesses flounder or even fail. They weren't prepared for the future. They ignored the demographics that flashed the advance signals.

Well, what are the specific factors within the demographics that you want or need to know for forward-planning the direction of your business? Let's look at the main elements and some of the ways they will affect your business currently and in the years ahead.

POPULATION TRENDS

Any knowledgeable retailer knows there's no longer any such thing as a "mass market." Markets have now become segmented and specialized, and this will continue to intensify with further refinements. A market is shaped primarily by six key factors: age grouping, income level, sex, educational level, geographical area, lifestyle. A seventh, ethnic mix, is a further but supplementary influence.

That combination will govern almost everything about the makeup of your business: the merchandise, prices, advertising, type of store and service, your buying and selling, the brands, etc. The claim of "knowing my market" has no validity unless one has a firm grip on the market demographics.

Well, what difference does this information make, anyhow? Let's start with the population numbers and trends, then apply them to shoe business. Here's a 20-year projection of the population by age groups:

Population Trends, 1986–2007 (in millions)

Age Group	1986	% of Popul.	1992	% of Popul.	1997	% of Popul.	2007	% of Popul.	% Change 1986–2007
4 & under	19	8.0%	19	7.5%	18	6.9%	18	6.4%	−5.2%
5–12	27	11.1	30	11.7	31	11.8	29	10.4	7.4
13–19	25	10.3	23	9.1	25	9.5	27	9.6	8.0
20–30	47	19.3	43	16.9	39	14.9	41	14.6	−12.8
31–40	38	15.5	43	16.9	43	16.4	37	13.2	−2.5
41–50	26	10.7	33	13.0	39	14.9	43	15.4	65.4
51–60	22	9.1	22	8.7	25	9.5	37	13.2	68.2
61–70	20	8.2	20	7.9	19	7.3	23	8.2	15.0
71–80	13	5.3	14	5.5	15	5.7	15	5.4	15.4
Over 80	6	2.5	7	2.8	8	3.1	10	3.6	66.7
Totals:	243	100.0%	254	100.0%	262	100.0%	280	100.0%	15.2 (aver.)

A look at the table instantly tells us where the shoe business action is and isn't going to be. While the population overall will show a 15.2 percent increase between the years 1986 and 2007, there are enormous variations from the overall average among the different age groups. Some of the signposts revealed by the figures:

Infants' shoe business (tots 4 years and under) will remain flat over the next 20 years.

Juvenile shoe business (ages 5 to 12) will show only a slight gain.

Teens and sub-teens footwear will also show very little gain.

The young adult market (ages 20–30) will take a fall of nearly 13 percent in sales. This will be a progressive decline in five-year spans. This reduction is significant because this age group has long been one of the most active of shoe-buying customers and with the highest per capita consumption level.

The young-mature group (ages 31–40) will show a small decline. This again is significant because, like the 21–30 age segment, these customers are in the fashion forefront and traditionally are active shoe buyers and consumers.

However, the combined 20–30 and 31–40 age groups, while contributing no gain in sales in the important fashion core of shoe business, will nevertheless pack much fashion-trend influence even though their share of the total population will shrink from one-third to 28 percent. So while their footwear buying will be substantial, unit sales to these two groups will remain flat or show a slight decline.

The middle-mature group (ages 41–60) will show spectacular expansion ahead— a whopping 67 percent rise over the next two decades. Their share of the population will increase from 20 percent in 1960 to almost 29 percent in 2007, when they will then outnumber the 20–40 age group. It's these middle-agers who will be at the peak of their earning and spending power and will comprise a powerful influence on a broad range of products, services and markets, including footwear. Perhaps their major influence on footwear retailing will be on more conservative styling, the expectation of top service, their preference for quality and national brands, their ability and willingness to pay better prices, and their keen awareness of value relative to price.

The senior group (61 and over) will show a robust 15 percent growth over the next 20 years. Their numbers will rise from 39 million in 1986 to 48 million in 2007, an obviously substantial market that offers some handsome opportunities. In this group, women outnumbered men by 28 percent in 1986, and will outnumber men by 33 percent in 2007. The large majority of people in this group are healthy, socially and physically active, financially secure. They'll comprise a substantial specialty market whose prime considerations in footwear will be good fit, good quality, good service, branded merchandise—and stores that cater to their footwear wants. This is becoming a major market for casual footwear, meaning comfort with attractive styling.

The total population, 1986 to 2007, will rise by 37 million. That will increase the footwear market by 200 million pairs and over $10 billion. But the important thing to recognize here is *where* the growth will be—in the mature-age segments of the population, while the younger age groups, those under 30, will show virtually no growth or will be in decline. Those trends are important guideposts for planning your own market targets.

Each age group comprises a specific market for shoe retailers. Each has its own "culture" and lifestyle which converts not only into the kinds of footwear and apparel they buy, but the preferred *stores* in which they buy. In short, they identify both the merchandise and the stores with *their* lifestyles, tastes, wants and needs. Just as a particular age group selects your store or some other, it's equally important for you to specify a particular group as *your* market and tailor everything about your business accordingly. The age of specialization in shoe retailing will continue to accelerate. Store identity or image will become more important than ever.

OTHER DEMOGRAPHIC INFLUENCES

Age groups, important as they are in market planning, are by no means the only influence in demographics. Among other important influences affecting shoe business are:

Ethnic groups.   These consist mainly of Hispanics, Asians and foreign blacks. They comprise the large majority of the one million immigrants a year, and their birth rates are substantially above those of native Americans. Hispanics alone will account for 25 percent to 30 percent of the total population growth, and all of the newcomer ethnic groups together will account for an estimated 45 percent of the U.S. population expansion.

The significance to retail shoe business is that these ethnic groups tend to have different foot sizes and shapes than the average native American, and their style preferences also tend to differ. For example, the Asian foot tends to be smaller, with men's sizes sometimes as small as 5 or 6, and women's as small as 4 or 5—sizes that would have to be considered by retailers in a trading area with a concentration of Asians. The native Hispanic foot tends to run to wider widths, and the foot of the foreign black leans toward larger and wider sizes. These ethnic groups will develop into new markets requiring some important changes for shoe retailers serving them.

Education. Educational levels continue to rise substantially with more high school and college graduates. Usually the more educated the customer the higher the income. It also influences buying habits as to what and where customers buy. Better educated customers are more selective about values and services and are smarter buyers. This bears influence not only on the retailer's footwear inventory makeup, but also the presentation of the merchandise via his ads, promotions and displays. Store image also plays an important role with these customers. Attracting and holding these customers will require upgraded merchandising strategies by the retailer.

Working Women. In the late 1980s, nearly half of the total labor force consisted of women. Between 1987 and the mid-1990s, 15 million more people will join the work force, and 80 percent of them will be women, plus minorities and immigrants. By 1995, 80 percent of the women in the 25–44 age group will hold jobs, and half of all married couples will be dual-income couples with incomes averaging $50,000.

Working women, as shown by surveys, spend about 30 percent more on footwear than non-working women—more pairs and higher prices paid. With less shopping time to spare, working women are strong impulse buyers. For the shoe retailer this means that ads and window displays will have to be upgraded to be as eye-catching as possible for quick response. Television shopping will also have increasing attraction for these busy women. These signals point to more transient and fewer repeat-business shoppers. That, in turn, means that retailers will have to step up their ad and promotional budgets to maintain a steady flow of transients.

Families. These continue to shrink in size as married couples opt for fewer (or no) children, or couples delay marriages with a resulting substantial increase in singles. In 1967, the average household size was 2.7 persons; by 1997, 2.3—in contrast to the average of 4.5 in 1910.

This poses a serious challenge for the future of the traditional family shoe store because of a much smaller market available to such stores. Thus we may see a steady phasing out of the family shoe store, not only because of the diminished size of families, but also because the split inventory makeup (men's, women's and children's) of the family store limits its selection of styles and sizes that can be offered in all three categories. The family shoe store does not appear to have a bright future.

Specialization. The developing demographics point increasingly to the dominance of specialization in retailing, whether men's, women's or children's footwear, or by price categories, or fast fashion or basic footwear, or catering to particular age or lifestyle market groups, etc. The emphasis will be on inventory depth rather than spread-thin breadth (as with the family store where inventory is dispersed over several categories). In short, the strong trend over the next decade or two will be to select one particular market, then serve its needs and wants to the maximum.

The future belongs to the concept stores. Typical examples are the athletic footwear stores (Foot Locker, Athlete's Foot, etc.) that have thrived through the

1970s and 1980s. Analyzing the population trends by age groups, the mature-age segments with their particular lifestyles and preferences in apparel and footwear, will comprise still newer opportunities for specialized concept stores serving these particular needs and wants.

Mass migrations. Where are the major population shifts occurring? Population density is important to any trading area and any retailer. Rural population will continue to decline. Farms and farm workers will continue to diminish in number; in the late 1980s about 2.5 million farm workers, and about 1.5 million by the mid-1990s. A similar trend has developed among other outdoor workers such as laborers, construction workers, forestry, and even among industrial workers.

This indicates lessening demand for work and outdoor boots. Here a smaller but more specialized market will be catered to by concept stores such as the Red Wing stores with maximum style breadth with full size depth.

Metropolitan areas will continue to expand, mainly suburbia and exurbia. Metropolitan areas now account for nearly three-fourths of the population, and this share will increase further. Small-town retailers will be further squeezed by two primary factors: more of their customers traveling longer distances by car to buy in shopping centers; and also with more national chains opening stores in smaller communities in an effort to find new locations for expansion. Shopping centers and malls accounted for 52 percent of all retail footwear sales in 1977, and this will rise to 60 percent by 1997.

The new megamalls such as the massive enterprise in Edmonton, Canada, with 817 stores on 110 acres, will comprise another new direction in retailing. Several even larger megamalls are developing in the U.S. This signals a further challenge to the future of downtown locations for shoe business. Stores move to where the people are concentrated, and vice versa.

For the established shoe retailer planning for the growth and future of his or her business, or the person planning to start up in shoe business, the thinking can't be in terms of "consumers" but in terms of *customers*. Consumers have no identity. They are statistics. But customers are personalities with particular behavioral characteristics that can be fitted into certain shoe-buying classifications, each classification with its own shoe-buying needs, preferences, buying habits. Each classification comprises a particular market. This splintering of markets will intensify in the years ahead and has already ushered in the age of specialization in shoe retailing.

In a commercial or marketing sense, demographics is the science of classifying markets by customer makeup and buying behavior. Because shoe retailing itself is becoming more of a "scientific" operation (computerized inventory control, budgeting, buying, etc., is only one example), the application of demographics becomes increasingly important for the retailer to clarify his or her market niche and serve it to the maximum efficiency to assure a prosperous future.

The idea of sales or growth planning without the application of demographic principles is unrealistic in today's intensely competitive markets. The foundation of every business is customers. It is thus essential to know precisely who and where they are, and their buying behavioral patterns. That's the business of demographics and why it is so vital to your own business planning.

25

Figuring Footwear Sales
in Your Market

*Nature gave man two ends—one
to sit on and one to think with.
Your success or failure depends on
which end you use most.*

You're asked, "How's business?" You reply "good" or "fair" or "slow." But your answer has no meaning or value. You're measuring your current business only against last year's figures. Common as that is, it's a faulty and deceptive gauge.

Much better questions are: How are you doing against the competition? What share of the local footwear market are you getting? Are you growing at the same pace as the local market and the competition?

Only a tiny minority of shoe retailers could give you answers to those questions. Yet those answers are the *only* reliable way to measure your competitive position in your trading area. And the *only* reliable way to ascertain whether your business is growing, standing still or shrinking.

For example, if your business shows a 7 percent gain in unit sales you feel you've moved ahead. But if footwear unit sales in your trading area have advanced by 10 percent, then your "gain" is actually a relative slippage.

This brings us to demographics. That's a fancy word meaning the application of selective statistics to marketing. It has many valuable uses in business operations.

Let's apply it to your business. Say you operate a family shoe store in a trading area with a population of 50,000. What's your competitive position with other footwear outlets in the area? Some simple facts and figures will give you the answer.

The average per capita footwear consumption (men's, women's and children's combined) is about 4.0 pairs. Current average retail price is $30. These basic figures immediately reveal the following:

1) Those 50,000 people are buying a total of 200,000 pairs of footwear.

2) They're spending a total of $6,000,000 a year on footwear.

Now, let's say your own store's footwear volume is $300,000. You instantly know that *your* share of that dollar volume in your trading area amounts to 5.0 percent. And also the same 5.0 percent share in pairage volume (if your prices are average).

If there are 18 retail outlets selling footwear in the area, the average footwear sales per outlet would be $333,333. That would give your own store an "average" rating. But if there are only 15 stores, then the average is $400,000 per outlet—which places you below average in size.

Now, however, you know two important things: (1) your percentage share of the total footwear business (pairs and dollars) in your trading area; (2) your volume size relative to the average in the area.

But the basic figures also give you a gauge to measure your growth progress. The population of the average community usually grows year to year. You apply those expanding population figures to do the same calculations—4.0 pairs per capita times the going average retail price. This gives you the trading area's growth figures in pairs and dollars. You then measure your own store's figures against those totals and you get a *true* picture of your own store's sales growth.

This same procedure can be used to get a fix on any particular category of footwear—men's, women's, children's, athletic/sneakers, etc. You simply use different per capita consumption and average retail price per pair figures. For example, these figures for 1987 would be approximately as follows:

Category	Aver. Prs. Per Capita	Aver. Retail Price
Men's	2.0	$40
Women's	5.5	30
Children's	2.3	25
Athletic/sneakers	1.2	18

Say you want to know your local market share in men's shoes only. Your sources (we'll cite them shortly) inform you that on average about 38 percent of the population consists of adult males 15 years and up. So your total trading area population of 50,000 has 19,000 adult males.

Multiply that by two pairs (average men's per capita shoe consumption) and you have 38,000 pairs. At an average of $40 per pair, a total of $1,420,000 in men's volume for the area.

Say your own men's volume amounts to 1,300 pairs and $60,000. You'd instantly know that your share of the local men's market is 3.4 percent of the pairs and 4.2 percent of the dollars.

The same process can be applied to women's or children's or athletic/sneakers, etc.

But, you may ask, don't per capita footwear consumption figures change over time or by regions? A bit, but not so much as to make a major difference in your calculations. In a moment we'll show how to keep tuned to any such changes.

What changes more often are average retail footwear prices. But these too are available from industry sources, as we'll show.

Well, where do you get the base figures for your calculations? It's really no problem. Here are guidelines:

Trading Area Population. First, specify your area. Its population will then be quickly available from the town offices or even the local newspaper. Not only total population but breakdown by sex and age groups. Ordinary census almanacs also publish such figures.

In an average trading area the population will be divided approximately as follows:

	% Share	Sample 50,000 Trading Area
Juveniles	22%	11,000
Adult males (15 up)	38	19,000
Adult females (15 up)	40	20,000

Per Capita Footwear Consumption. The figures we've already given are currently workable. You can check them about every other year (changes are usually minor) via such industry sources as National Shoe Retailers Association, or Footwear Industries of America. Figures are also published periodically in the trade papers.

Average Retail Price Per Pair. Again, this is available from Footwear Industries of America, or National Shoe Retailers Association. The U.S. Census Bureau also publishes average *factory* value per pair (men's, women's, children's, etc.). That price is simply doubled to get the average retail price.

That's all the base information you need to make your calculations. You can further adjust the data to suit your own special needs or wants.

For example, if you sell in the higher price brackets your market would be much narrowed. If you sell only women's high-fashion shoes in the $60–$80 range, then perhaps only about 15 percent of the women in your trading area would comprise your prospects.

If the trading area is 50,000, and the total adult females are 20,000 (40 percent), then your direct prospects (15 percent) would number 3,000. That number could support one or two stores of your kind, but not more.

The system itself is very flexible. As long as you know the simple calculation process you can shuffle the base data to make it deliver much of the demographic information you need or want.

Now, once you've learned your share or competitive position in the local market, what do you do with this information?

Say you've found that you have a 6 percent share of the market. Ask yourself: Is that good, fair or poor? How would you judge? Such a question is rarely faced by the average retailer—but constantly sought by larger or more sophisticated companies.

A 6 percent share of a $10 million local market would give you a hefty $600,000 operation. That's major league size. But the same share of a $3 million market would shrink you to $180,000, which is very modest.

However, don't judge by dollar volume only. Pairage or unit share is more important not only as a size measure but as a gauge of growth. Obviously, you can have a 5 percent unit share but a 10 percent dollar share because of your higher price points. Also, you can show growth in dollars (as prices rise) but remain static in units. Units are the real reliable gauge of growth.

Again, your store figures are showing that you are growing, and by how much. But do you know whether you are keeping pace with your competition, and also the growth pace of the trading area?

The simple calculation plan presented here will give you a reliable comparison which you can check year to year. It's a compass to give you a navigational fix on your competitive position. What's more, if you have some good estimates on the volume done by your competitors, you can make the same calculations for *their* competitive position in the local trading area.

Demographics is a modern marketing tool that is increasingly being put to use by alert retailers. It helps to give you a more objective (versus the more usual subjective or seat-of-the-pants) overview of your business, competitive position and growth progress.

Local Market Analysis for Footwear Sales

Trading area population	—	50,000
Aver. prs. per capita	—	4.0
Total prs. purchased	—	200,000
Aver. retail price per pr.	—	$30.00
Total footwear spending	—	$6,000,000
Your store's share:		
Pairs:	—	?
Dollars:	—	?

Local Market Analysis by Specific Category
(example: men's footwear)

Trading area population	—	50,000
Adult males (15 up—38%)	—	19,000
Aver. per capita prs.	—	2.0
Total pairs bought	—	38,000
Aver. price per pair, retail	—	$42
Total men's footwear spending	—	$1,596,000
Your store's share:		
Pairs:	—	?
Dollars:	—	?

26

Tracking Sales Peaks
and Valleys

*Big shots are only little shots who
keep shooting.*

Any retailer can give you a seat-of-the-pants answer to the question, "What are your busiest and slowest days?" He can tell you that Saturday is much busier than Tuesday, Friday busier than Monday.

But ask him for the specifics: How much of your average week's business is done on Wednesdays or Saturdays or evenings? The average retailer can't give you precise answers because he keeps no such count. By weeks, usually yes. By days, usually no.

The same applies to store hours. He knows by experience that certain hours are busier than others. But the average store can't give you specifics.

Now, when you run a business from "inside your head" instead of from records, you tread on thin ice. You can find yourself spending too much time and money when and where you least need it, and not enough when and where you most need it.

For example, you can have too many salespeople, plus utility and other costs, during lull periods, and not enough during busy periods. By staggering the salespeople (plus opening and closing hours) in accord with store activity, you can use your salespeople more productively, lower your selling costs, and upgrade customer service.

Yet, as obvious as that is, many retailers make wasteful use of time and money. For example, how many unnecessary "walks" occur because customers must wait to be served during busy periods? How many extra-pair sales are lost because of lack of time or personnel to push for added sales during busy periods?

It is no problem to establish a traffic/sales flow pattern in your store. The two sample tables shown here illustrate how it's done (the arrangement of store days or hours can be adjusted to suit your own operation). It's simply a matter of a little discipline on keeping a daily score sheet.

Two months or about eight weeks of such scorekeeping is sufficient to establish the traffic/sales pattern for your store. If you wish to refine or embellish it, you can do it for each quarter or each selling season. Each season may, for some stores, show a different traffic/sales pattern.

Some stores who use this method usually note the day-to-day weather because this can affect the traffic/sales pattern. For example, a blizzard or heat wave, etc.

A weather forecast of extreme cold or heavy snow might bring a rush of weather boot business over one or two days. Prolonged heat can keep shoppers at home. Such notations on your calendar help explain erratic or unusual traffic/sales figures. The same applies to special sales or promotions.

PUTTING IT TO WORK

If you've already established a traffic/sales pattern for your store, one practical application, as we've already noted briefly, is more efficient and productive use of your salespeople, plus upgrading customer service, plus lowering selling costs.

However, one of the most effective applications is finding ways to bring in more traffic and sales on the slow days and hours. In our table, for instance, our sample store is doing only 6.5 percent of the week's business on Monday, 8.3 percent on Tuesdays, or 14.8 percent for both days. The fixed costs or expenses continue, and often personnel costs as well.

You now put your ideas cap on. How can you increase traffic and sales during Mondays and Tuesdays (or any other consistently slow day)? You could, for instance:
• Hold a special price promotion for Monday and Tuesday only.
• Offer attractive giveaways with footwear purchases on those days.
• Conduct a big-prize contest (held over one or two months)—but only those who make purchases on Mondays or Tuesdays are eligible.
• Promote 10 percent or 15 percent discounts to senior citizens on purchases made on Mondays or Tuesdays.

You can have more than one traffic builder working at the same time. Be sure to keep a sales record on those ordinarily slow days to see what additional business you've picked up. Whatever extra business you've gained has automatically *reduced* your fixed overhead and personnel costs. And, of course, added to your volume and profit.

Apply the same principle to your daily store hours. In our sample store, for instance, the chart shows that only 12 percent of the day's or week's business is done during the morning hours. Could the store be opened at 10 AM instead of 9 AM with little or no loss in sales? And would the minimal sales loss be more than compensated by savings in some of the overhead and selling costs?

Or try it in reverse by applying methods that can increase morning sales. For example, a 10 percent discount on all purchases made before 11 or 11:30 AM. Or, each week run an "Early Bird Catches the Worm" sale—8 AM to 11 AM. Each week a different footwear category—athletic shoes, casuals, dress shoes, boots, slippers, sneakers, etc.

The question arises: By drawing more traffic to slow days or slow hours, isn't it a case of borrowing from Peter to pay Paul? And no net gain? No. That's the same argument used by opponents of Sunday openings—that the Sunday business is simply borrowed from the rest of the week, with no net gain. But it hasn't worked out that way. The Sunday shoppers are often those who don't have time to buy during the week, or who delay purchases. Further, they're often more leisurely shoppers who browse more, buy more, spend more because they're not in a rush.

Thus, much of the traffic drawn by special promotions or attractions on slow days or hours is *new* traffic. And new customers become word-of-mouth customers.

Those slow hours can also be assigned for special tasks by store management or personnel. The early morning is an excellent time for in-store sales meetings. Or for phoning or writing postcards to customers on your mailing list—informing them about new stock in the store, or special buys on closeouts, etc. Or checking customer files (how many of your customers on file haven't been in for more than a year—and why?)

We often say, "Where did the time go?" But what we should ask are questions like, "What did we do with the time while it was going?" "We spent time—but what did we get in return for what we spent?" "I'm consuming time—but is time also consuming me and my business?"

Time is one of your most important expenses because it's something with costs attached, such as your overhead costs. The only way you can pay for it and profit from it is by making it productive. So take a count on when you're getting the most and the least return on that time cost. Then zero in on those "least" areas with traffic-building exercises that will put muscle on them.

Percentage of Week's Sales by Days

Day	1st Week	2nd Week	3rd Week	4th Week	Aver. Wkly. %, 4 Weeks
Monday	8%	7%	5%	6%	6.5%
Tuesday	9	9	7	8	8.3
Wednesday	11	12	13	11	11.8
Thursday	15	14	16	15	15.1
Friday	18	19	20	22	19.8
Saturday	23	21	22	20	21.6
Sunday	16	18	17	18	16.9
Total Week	100%	100%	100%	100%	100.0%

Percentage of Day's Sales by Hours

Hours	Mon.	Tues.	Wed.	Thurs.	Fri.	Sat.	Sun.	Aver. % for Week
9:00–11:30 AM	17%	15%	12%	12%	10%	18%	—	12.0%
11:30 AM–2 PM	38	42	32	35	34	43	42	38.1
2:00–5:30 PM	45	43	40	39	37	37	58	42.8
5:30–9:00 PM	—	—	16	14	19	—	—	7.1
Total Day	100%	100%	100%	100%	100%	100%	100%	100.0%

27

Faster, More Profitable Clearances

When you're up to your tail in alligators, your job is to drain the swamp.

A man who knows he's made a mistake and doesn't correct it, is making another mistake.

Clearances are an inevitable, built-in part of shoe business. Each year, an estimated 150 million pairs of footwear go the clearance (30–50 percent off regular price) route, amounting to about $3 billion in retail sales. That's aside from footwear sold in off-price, cancellation and discount stores, and factory outlets.

Now, when clearance is mentioned, the average shoeman automatically thinks "clearance sale"—usually the customary January or mid-June clearance periods. While perhaps there's no escaping those clearance periods, they're becoming tougher to show productive results. At those times all the shoe stores in the trading area, along with apparel and other stores, are also running clearance sales.

The consumers, inundated by clearance sale lures from all sides, spread their limited spending dollars among the many. The effectiveness of the clearance sale is thus largely dissipated.

There has to be better ways. Or additional ways to unload clearances at minimum loss. It's important to recognize that clearances aren't limited to the semi-annual sales. They can be run at any time as needed or wanted.

First, ask yourself: What instruments or strategies are involved in moving clearance merchandise? The answer: advertising, displays (windows and interior), salespeople, direct mail, unusual promotions. Thus clearances amount to a lot more than simply an advertised announcement that you're having a sale. A clearance is an event involving coordination of several actions to create a multiple impact— each separate action to have its own maximum effect.

Your task is to separate yourself from the crowd to attract maximum traffic and sales. Let's look at some of the possibilities.

ADVERTISING

Most of all, let your clearance advertising be imaginative, different. Avoid the hum-drum "semi-annual clearance sale—25 percent to 40 percent off regular prices."

That will get you a ho-hum response.

Try, for example, something like "We bought too many. Our mistake is your bargain—25 percent to 50 percent off regular price." That's straightforward, honest, the human touch.

Or try eye-catching ads. For example, a giraffe stretching its neck, and your headline, "We're breaking our necks to please you with savings." Or a picture of a boat with billowing sails: "We're under full sale." In short, avoid the me-too look and words.

Supplement your newspaper advertising with frequent radio (or even TV if feasible) spots. You can deliver an effective message in 15 seconds.

Direct mail to a customer list is another route (you're missing a lot if you don't maintain and use a mailing list). Avoid the usual postcard "announcing" your semi-annual sale. Local consumers receive many of these. So let your card say it freshly, look different, provide motivating information.

If you keep customer records (you'd be in the smart minority), have your salespeople take turns on the phone calling *many* customers to tell them (a mere 30 seconds per call) about your sale. That's a personal touch that most customers like.

You can carry it a step further. On those phone calls or postcards you can call it a "private sale." Held a week *before* the advertised sale. This enables your regular customers to get first choice, to cherry-pick among the clearance merchandise. This "privileged customer" treatment usually gets excellent response.

Incidentally, that phone or postcard idea can work year-round, a great mover of PMs. That's provided you keep customer records, including sizes, date of purchases, etc. When some of your merchandise is shifted to PM or clearance status, notify customers what's available in *their* sizes. Again the personal touch that's appreciated and gets response.

YEAR-ROUND CLEARANCES

At any given time of the year, about 80 percent of the business is done with about 20 percent of the inventory—the old 80–20 law. That inactive stock has built-in storage and carryover penalty costs. In short, there's no time of the year that the average shoe store or department doesn't have clearance merchandise on hand.

PMs and other clearance merchandise are moved to some degree by the salespeople. But this can be supplemented, or even improved upon, by using *non*-advertised, year-round clearance "sections" in the store. For example:

An attractive rack or bin section or area with a large sign saying "Lucky Sizes"—signifying that if the customer finds his or her size here, they're in luck. The sign also cites that prices are 30 percent to 40 percent off. The display is well lighted, the shoes arranged by sizes regardless of styles, colors, brands, etc. It's great browsing territory. It also moves second-pair sales after the customer has made a regular-price buy.

The same idea with a different theme can be called the Lemon Tree—a small, artificial tree with firm plexiglass leaves or branches to hold shoes, with additional shoes piled around the base. A large sign may say something like, "Our Lemons

Make Juicy Bargains—25 percent to 50 percent off." Again, well lighted. And ideal for bargain browsing.

Consider a permanent "hash" section—again a rack or bin display. Shoes can be hashed by sizes or colors or style categories, etc. Customers prefer this rather than a mish-mash of everything. For example, a hash of all blue shoes: "We've got the blues—you've got the bargains." You can keep changing the displays and signs, depending upon the hashed merchandise available.

None of these year-round clearance sections is advertised. They're a permanent part of the store.

The two-for-one sale is hardly new. But it has variations. The first pair from new stock at regular price, the second pair selected from clearance merchandise at half price. If for these special sales you use a higher markon (say 60 percent) on the new shoes, your loss on the clearance shoes is less.

The Sidewalk Sale (usually several days or a week) also isn't new. But it can be given fresh treatments. Surround it with a festive look and feeling—colorful balloons and streamers, a recorder giving off soft but lively music, one or two salespeople in colorful "native" costumes. A free pair of shoes given away each hour to a lucky ticket holder. Back it up with advertising and publicity.

Run a Free Giveaway Week. Clearance shoes at 25 percent to 30 percent off—*plus* a good giveaway free with each shoe purchase at regular or clearance price. The giveaway has to be something worthwhile to attract—a shoe shine kit, closet shoe rack or hanging shoe bag, hose, small pedicure kit, handheld foot massager, etc. If the cost per unit to you is $3 or less, then it's the same as clearing only the shoes at 40 percent or 50 percent with no giveaways. The big difference: the giveaways attract traffic and spur sales.

SALESPEOPLE

Many salespeople don't fully understand or appreciate the economics of clearance merchandise. For example, the percentage (or dollars) of the inventory that becomes markdowns. Or what causes them. Or their role in them. Also, they should know that the faster clearance merchandise is moved out, the faster the new, easier-to-sell merchandise moves in, to their advantage.

Keep them informed in advance about the clearance ads you're running, and precisely what you're trying to clear. If you have permanent "clearance sections," get them to encourage customers to browse—such as when customers are waiting during busy periods; or after the first purchase of regular merchandise has been made. Ask them for their input of ideas for moving clearance stock better or faster. If they're invited to be part of the act, they'll work harder at it.

Salespeople can also be part of the problem of markdowns. Many salespeople (even store owners themselves) tend to push certain favorites or easy-to-sell shoes and neglect less favored shoes. The less favored shoes become slow-movers and eventually clearances. Management should carefully monitor this.

When new shoes come in, hold a meeting to explain *why* each was bought, and perhaps a key selling feature or two about each. When you give the shoe a reason for being, you give the salespeople a reason for selling, and the customer a reason for buying. Not all shoes sell themselves.

Clearance sales can also work in reverse. When traffic is attracted by the clearance prices, many of these customers are prospects for buying new or advance merchandise. If the customer is buying a clearance shoe in early July or late January, some will be receptive to seeing or trying on early fall or spring *new* shoes in advance of season. This is a function of the salespeople—provided they are so trained and that such merchandise is available in the store. The result can be more double-header sales, a combination of old and new merchandise.

TIMING AND PRICING

Procrastination as to when to clear out merchandise is the constant dilemma (and often the enemy) of many shoe retailers. Self-imposed discipline is vital. It's like having a tooth pulled. It can be painful, but the relief when it's over can be euphoric.

Put an alarm clock on every new shoe when it comes into the store. Give it a pre-determined life or shelf span. When the time is up and the alarm goes off, move the shoe quickly to clearance. If the shoe is still selling well (and you've reordered), reset the alarm for another timing.

Procrastination worsens your clearance problem. With fast style turnover today, many jobbers will offer very little for merchandise more than 4 or 5 months old. And consumers will ignore your clearance offerings if over-delayed because they've already bought the same styles elsewhere at clearance prices months earlier.

How long should a clearance sale last? There's no firm rule. It can be a week or a month, depending upon how much merchandise you have to clear, and how well the merchandise is moving during the sale period.

What is the most effective discount on clearances—25 percent, 40 percent, 50 percent? Again, there's no firm answer. The more you want to get rid of it the deeper the discount should be.

There's a lot more to clearances than a "clearance sale." The techniques are limited only by your imagination. Today, with discounting and offpricing so common-place, you have to be more creative and aggressive to move your clearances. But move them you must. You can't make money on frozen assets. So don't just sit on your assets.

HASHING MOVES MERCHANDISE FASTER

How can markdowns, PMs, closeouts and broken lots be moved more profitably without going the usual clearance sale route?

By selective use of merchandise hashing—by sizes, colors, style categories. This isn't new, but it works. Yet, ironically, most stores fail to use it on a continuing basis. If done properly it can help move clearance merchandise faster, but without the usual advertising cost, and often saving up to half the usual price discounts.

The principle of hashing is simply to combine all clearance merchandise on the basis of a single theme or category and to present it as a permanent display, such as a rack or bin or table. This display area is well lighted and with signs indicating the nature of the merchandise.

For example, gathering all your odd-size clearance merchandise together, regardless of styles: the extra-large or extra-small, or extra-wide or extra-narrow sizes. Even some regular sizes can be included. Then a sign: "Lucky Sizes, Lucky You—30 percent Off."

This is especially appealing to customers who wear unusual sizes. Say you've sold such a customer a pair of shoes at regular price. The customer is grateful for having been fitted to his or her hard-to-find size. If the customer is then invited to visit the hashed-sizes display, not only will there be further selection, but the customer is attracted by the lower closeout prices. It's not unusual for such a customer to buy one or more of these closeout pairs in these hard-to-find sizes. Your hashed merchandise sold at 30 percent off is better than 50 percent or more off via the usual clearance route—and better still than ending up as distressed, giveaway merchandise.

Hashing can also work in other ways operating on the same principle, such as shoes grouped together by color. For example, all your clearance blue shoes—with a sign perhaps reading, "Once In a Blue Moon." Or by style categories such as boots or sandals or slippers. Or by heels, such as high heels. The hashed groupings should be changed periodically, say every month or every other month, to give them freshness and a new theme.

There are distinct advantages to hashing:

1) They encourage customer browsing—especially with customers who visit the store several times a year to see "what's new."
2) They often result in multiple-pair or followup sales after a regular price pair has been purchased.
3) They can sometimes convert a just-looking customer into a buying customer.
4) They move PMs faster, especially where salespeople are reluctant to search out single pairs from stock.

Because of the larger selection of special-category merchandise in the hashed section, hashing makes a little look like a lot and moves this merchandise faster and more profitably.

28

Pricing for Profit

"There is hardly anything in the world that someone can't make a little worse and sell a little cheaper. The people who consider price alone are this man's lawful prey." (John Ruskin)

Someone has said, "Pricing has never been a science. It's an art. You have to apply talent and instincts to make it work profitably." Quite true. There's no neat mathematical formula, no hard-fixed rules. Too many variables are involved.

All pricing has three objectives: to cover costs, to attract customers and move merchandise, and to return a good profit. But the fact that many businesses often show disappointing profits indicates that pricing policies and practices are often misjudged, misplanned and misused.

Setting a price seems so simple. Costs (merchandise and operating costs) provide the base. Add your margin to cover them, minus discounts and plus freight, minus markdowns and clearances, then add another margin for profit, and presto! out comes the logical price.

But any merchant knows it isn't that simple. Enter the variables that challenge the "logical" pricing formula designed for profit. These include pesky things like unexpected high markdowns, poor buys, slow sales, unanticipated expenses, stiff competition, etc. They bruise and buffet the "logical" prices and the expected profit.

This certainly doesn't mean that the retailer can't price profitably because he's always at the mercy of the fates. The most reliable weapon he has for profitable pricing is his records. With these he can reasonably forecast sales (6 or 12 months), estimate buys and merchandise cost, estimate total markdowns, etc. He can then apply his margins to match his estimates and return a targeted profit. If he maintains good performance records, his budget planning has good chance of matching actual results.

Most retailers follow some fixed pattern of applying margins. For example, 42 percent to 45 percent on basic children's shoes; 45 percent on men's basics or 50 percent on men's fashion; 55 percent on women's fashion, 50 percent on basics; or 38 percent to 45 percent on sneakers; etc. These variable margins, of course, are keyed to markdowns by category.

But now enter the ogres. One is competitive pricing. The special sales or promotions of competitors; or the pressures of the off-pricers; or the need to stimulate sluggish sales. What happens to the "key" margins of the traditional retailer?

He usually does one of two things: tries to match the competition's lower prices (and shrinking his profits), or doing nothing and losing sales.

He seldom takes the third alternative—aggressive steps to justify his key markons and initial prices. For example, strongly promoting the excellence of his services, or his large selection of sizes, his broad merchandise selections, etc. He is making an attractive counter-offer to customers. And if he does it well enough and often enough, he and not his competition becomes the tough competition to beat.

Retailers are often so mesmerized by key or "standard" markons that they become freeze-stuck to them. No price or margin should be carved in stone. Markons should be flexible.

Value pricing is a good example. It's based not on a cost-plus-margin formula but *worth*-plus-margin. It's market-value pricing—what it's worth to the consumer. Essentially customers aren't asking "what's the price?" but rather "what's it worth to me?" A simple example is hula hoops. At their peak of popularity and demand they sold for $2 each. When the fad faded they sold at 10 cents each—and still turned a profit.

Many retailers fail to make justifiable use of value pricing. True, they may use a 60 percent markon for a volatile fashion shoe against 45 percent for a basic. But the markon differential is based on anticipated markdowns, not on value pricing.

If a fashion shoe is hot and in strong demand it would warrant, say, a 60 percent to 65 percent initial markon (or sustained markon) against a usual 50 percent to 52 percent. And it would be a fair value or price because it is consumer demand and not the retailer that is determining the fairness of the price. Price is what is paid. Value is what is received for what is paid. If the consumer is willing to pay the higher price for something very much wanted, then that's the fair value and the fair price.

Another example of the variables of pricing is in special buys—closeouts, group buys, special discounts, etc. Here markons can range from 60 percent to 100 percent and still be price competitive. It's simply another example of value pricing.

Some retailers are reluctant to impose maximum pricing. They're so glued to "standard" markons that they think more is "price gouging" or violating "honest values." That's naive. They forget that it works in reverse. When a shoe doesn't sell and is forced into a sharp markdown and a loss, do we say that the consumer is price-gouging the retailer? The consumer is simply taking advantage of market conditions. It should also work in reverse as part of the value pricing syndrome.

There's a distinct difference between higher prices and value pricing. Higher prices aren't always justified. But value pricing is. Moreover, value pricing is done on a selective basis. The trouble is, most retailers don't use it often enough.

Many retailers fail to price-test their market on selected shoes. Would a particular shoe sell just as well with 60 percent markon as with 50 percent? The answer can't be taken for granted. Early-season market testing with higher markon on certain shoes (quite aside from markdown considerations) can bring some pleasant surprises. If not, the shoe can, without fanfare, be quickly reduced to "key" markon. The message here is: stay flexible. You are still letting the market decide your prices. But at least test the market.

Flexible pricing also works in reverse with *below*-market prices—but still with a sharp eye on profit return. A classic example is the advertised "loss leader" item used in supermarkets. The objective is to attract traffic that will also buy other merchandise at regular (and sometimes higher) prices. Thus the bait of loss leaders results in more overall volume and profit.

Another example is the off-price stores, discounters, etc. They are no less profit-oriented than traditional retailers. They simply take the reverse approach to profits via low-margin prices. They buy at lower prices (because of volume buys), have lower overhead, high turnover and high sales volume. They simply prove the point that there is nothing sacred about prices or margins if the ultimate mission of profit is achieved.

In their concern about the burgeoning growth of off-price retailing today, traditional retailers tend to overlook the fact that even without off-price retailers, normally about 30 percent to 35 percent of all footwear is sold below "regular" or full prices via seasonal sales, clearances, PMs, special price promotions, cancellation stores, factory outlets, etc. In some recent years this has been as high as 50 percent to 55 percent of all footwear sales because of off-price retailing and the rash of price promotions by conventional stores either to remain competitive or to stimulate lagging sales.

OTHER PRICING INFLUENCES

The volatility of prices and pricing is again seen in relation to the type of store and also store location. A high-fashion store catering to a high-income clientele not only deals in higher grade merchandise but imposes a higher markon of 60 percent or 65 percent or more. It has little to do with markdown allowances. The clientele's priority isn't price but avant garde fashion, store prestige, designer labels, service, etc. Thus the cost-price or margin ratio is quite different than that used by other stores.

Timing is an important factor in pricing. Taking the markdown at the right time. Or holding to the original price if the shoe is still selling well even though the season is over. Some retailers nevertheless use faulty timing. For example, delaying the markdown, or unnecessarily marking down on well-selling shoes just because the season is finished. Time-pricing is a combination of good judgment and intuition, neither of which can be found in a rule book.

In years past, price lining was a much more common practice. In recent years, with prices more volatile because of inflation, price lining has lost some of its former importance. While we still think of low-, medium-, and high-price stores, the price ranges within these groups has broadened. And gone completely, of course, is the one-price store.

Nevertheless, many stores still try to operate within narrow fixed price brackets which they call their "price points." But in many cases this can be more habit than reality. Thus the retailer locks himself into limited price brackets, restricted margins and profits. He should periodically re-test his market with up-priced or better-grade merchandise to supplement his lines, again a matter of staying flexible. He might be surprised with increased sales and new customers.

The objective of all pricing, of course, is to achieve a good net profit. But what's a "good" or "healthy" profit? Beware the law of averages. For shoe stores the average net might be 5 percent. But that includes the losers as well as winners. But why measure your performance against the losers?

So begin by having a realistic profit policy. Set three net profit targets. For example, 5 percent as bare minimum; 7 percent to 8 percent as good; above 8 percent as healthy. Set your sights for the top, but don't settle for anything below the middle.

The most important rule is this. Don't trust profits to the fates. Don't abide by the common philosophy that profit is what's left over after all costs and expenses are accounted for. With that attitude you're in a crap shoot.

Certainly profit isn't necessarily derived only from high prices or high margins. Other factors are involved: good volume, smart buying, active turnover, controlled expenses, minimal markdowns, etc. Moreover, your prices and margins are always tempered by competition and the response of the market itself. But if you're so strongly governed by the competition, you've lost control and no longer own your own business.

What's the "best" price? It's the one that gives value satisfaction to the customer, generates a healthy sales flow, and above all, returns a respectable profit. A slide rule or calculator works—up to a point. But a healthy dose of judgment and instincts is equally important. That's the "art" of pricing for profit.

Markon Related To Required Sales

Original Cost	% of Price Cut	Selling Price	Markon	Gross Profit on 100 Pairs	Added Vol. Needed to Match Gross Profit at 50% Markon
$15	——	$30.00	50%	$1500	——
15	15%	27.00	44	1200	20% or 25 extra prs.
15	20	24.00	37	900	60% or 70 extra prs.
15	25	22.50	33	750	100% or 100 extra prs.

TAKING A LACING

For a couple of years a wealthy Wall Street broker on his way to work regularly dropped a half dollar into the box of a corner shoelace peddler—but without ever taking any shoelaces. One day the peddler tapped the arm of the broker after he deposited his usual half dollar.

"I know," smiled the broker. "You're going to ask me why I always drop in fifty cents but never take the shoelaces."

"No," said the peddler. "I just wanted you to know that due to inflation, next week the price of shoelaces goes up to seventy-five cents."

29

Display Space Everywhere— Much of It Wasted

You can't make them buy. But you can make them want it, and then you can't keep them from buying.

You commonly speak of the "selling floor." But does *your* floor really sell? You measure store performance on the basis of sales per square foot. But dead space common in shoe stores contributes nothing to sales per square foot.

Studies show that 80 percent of all merchandise is bought by sight. Thus shoe business is essentially *show* business—showing the merchandise. If a picture is worth 1,000 words, then actual merchandise that can be seen and touched is worth 1,000 pictures.

Consider that a store doing $350,000 volume has an annual store traffic of over 15,000 people. That's equal to a good-size town. Yet, most shoe stores sell much below the sales potential of their traffic. The reason: failure to make full use of impulse sales displays.

What's meant by dead or unused store space? Walls, floors, posts or columns, aisles, doors, checkout counters, even "air space."

For example, take those posts or columns in your store. You paint them to remove their eye-sore effect. But they can be converted into eye-catching displays. For instance, build tiers or circular shelves on the posts. Paint the shelves different colors or cover them with place mats. Use overhead spotlights. On each shelf, two or three shoes—or slippers or handbags, etc. The merchandise can be seen from any angle. So presto! a nuisance column becomes an attractive display. You've added sell power.

We mentioned "air space." Every store has it—usually wasted. Hang merchandise on wires or strings from the ceiling so that it "floats" at about eye level or a bit higher. And spotlighted. Such displays can be shown in small "clusters"—slippers or boots or handbags, etc. Very effective because the mild air currents keep the merchandise in slow motion.

If your store has a wide aisle or empty corner, use a circular turntable display unit about four feet high with hooks or shelves. Again, well lighted and attractively decorated. But *specialize* the merchandise on it—casuals, sandals, women's duty shoes, work boots, etc. And easy-to-read placards. Such displays occupy very little space, and much merchandise can be shown because of the tiers and turntable arrangement.

All displays should have signs or descriptive placards both to attract and inform, never just merchandise standing alone. The display should *say* something. Also, use different lighting effects for different displays to eliminate monotony.

Walls can hold small, projecting shelves or can be indented with wall frames. These are excellent for accessories displays that result in impulse sales. One store uses a small wall shelf, well lighted, for a variety of shoe care items. The sign reads, "Cared-for shoes look younger, live longer."

Have you thought of a "Pedocosmetics Bar"? Consumers are spending tens of millions of dollars annually for cosmetic foot-care products—soaps, lotions, powders, nail polishes, pedicure sets, foot deodorants, sprays, coolants, decorative foot jewelry and decals, electric foot massagers and whirlpool foot basins, etc. Shoe stores are getting very little of this bonus business—though they're naturals for such products. A special display section and a good selection of such items could prove a bonanza.

A "Gift Bar" is another great interior display idea. Birthdays and anniversaries happen every day. A gaily decorated gift bar could show slippers, shoe shine kits, hose, shoe closet racks, shoe bags, pedicure sets, handbags and various other items.

AND MORE IDEAS

A mobile display is another money-maker. A simple tea wagon appropriately decorated, and with its own overhead lamp or light. You've made the first sale. Now you go to a corner of the store where the tea wagons are "parked." Each wagon carries special wares—an attractive display of hose or handbags or slippers or accessory items, etc. Wheeled right in front of the seated customer. You've been to fancy restaurants where, at the end of the meal, the waiter wheels up the pastry wagon. You and your friends exclaim "Aaaah" and "Oooh"—and no one can resist. The same idea with *your* wagon. Often irresistible.

What about display fixtures? Aren't they costly? No. A little imagination plus a few pennies does the job in most instances. How? You simply put to work all those props you have around your attic or cellar, or can borrow from friends or neighbors, or can scavenge in second-hand stores.

Examples: pieces of old furniture—chairs, benches, small tables, chests, picture frames, mirrors, etc. An antique-looking chair, polished or painted, can hold a dozen shoes on the back, arms, seat, legs. The list of no-cost materials for building displays is as long as your imagination: logs, lamps, bricks, ladders, aluminum foil, scrap carpeting or fabric, place mats, old barrels, pillows, painted corrugated paper, andirons, brass rods, flags, travel posters, etc.

Be creative. Perhaps you have bin displays for closeouts. Instead, use a size hashing idea. You have accumulated closeouts or distress merchandise in fringe sizes (bigs, smalls, narrows, wides). Put them all on a brightly lighted table with a big sign: Lucky Sizes—meaning someone's hard-to-find size may be there at a bargain price. It attracts. It sells.

Avoid the old glass cases. They're costly. They take up too much room, give off too much glare, and the merchandise is hard to see. They tell the customer: "Look but don't touch." So the customer doesn't look, touch—or buy.

Interesting in-store displays can take countless forms to suit the type, size and space of the store. But they all have one mission: impulse sales. Good, imaginative displays can add 15 to 25 percent to your sales. They help make the most of store traffic. Supermarkets and modern drug stores are prime examples of successful use of open displays, "impulse islands" and other forms of merchandise exposure. Such displays also provide "entertainment" for waiting or browsing customers—and often convert into extra sales.

Seeing is more than believing. Seeing is buying. So let the customers see and touch—and buy.

WHY WINDOW DISPLAYS SHOULD BE CHANGED FREQUENTLY

1) Many of the same people pass your window every day.
2) Windows are the most conspicuous part of your store—your face and image. Keep it looking young, fresh, alive.
3) People like to see new and different things.
4) Everything in the store worth showing should have its chance in the window. Frequent window changes permit this.
5) Merchandise left in the window too long becomes faded and soiled. A shopworn look discourages lookers.
6) A window has only a few seconds to stop a passerby, so it must always look new and exciting to be a "stopper."
7) Frequent changes get people into the *habit* of looking at your windows to see what's new.
8) Frequent window changes assure inside-window cleanliness, gleam and freshness—and reflects the merchandise inside the store.
9) Most important, frequent window changes attract more lookers, which in turn attracts more people inside—which results in more sales.

30

Double Your Handbag and Hose Sales

"I must do something" will always solve more problems than "something must be done."

Many people have the right aim in business but never get around to pulling the trigger.

In the average shoe store, accessories account for less than 7 percent of total sales. And of this share, approximately 80 percent consists of handbag and hose sales.

Shoe store surveys conducted by Adelphi Associates and commissioned by *Footwear News* show a sub-par performance in these accessories by the large majority. Average share of total store volume in women's shoe stores shows accessories accounting for only 10 percent—and 90 percent of this consists of handbag sales. For men's shoe stores accessories amount to a mere 5 percent, over half of which consists of hose sales.

The potential for handbag and hose sales in shoe stores is much greater than what is being realized. In 1987, total handbag and hose sales in shoe stores amounted to an estimated $365 million. But those sales could and should be *at least double* that amount. Why doesn't it happen? Most of the missed sales are forfeited to other types of outlets due mainly to lack of merchandising effort.

Let's see how you can help remedy this situation for your own store.

HANDBAGS

Approximately 90 million handbags a year are sold for a total of around $1.2 billion. Handbags are the single most important accessory carried by women's shoe stores (and also some family stores). About 82 percent of the women's shoe stores sell handbags, and shoe outlets overall account for about one-fifth of handbag sales, or around $225 million.

Handbags represent an average of about 10 percent of store volume in the women's shoe stores where they're sold. This could easily be increased 50 percent by more aggressive and imaginative merchandising. Some stores achieve 18 to 20 percent of store volume in handbag sales. The ratio is generally (and conservatively) figured at 1½ handbags for every 10 pairs of shoes. If the clientele is younger, the handbag sales ratio rises to 2–2½. Some stores, however, average 3–3½ handbags per 10 pairs of shoes.

Markon is about 50 percent, the same as shoes, but markdowns average 75 percent less than shoes. This means the *net* markon for handbags is much better than for shoes. Handbags average about 65 percent of shoe prices.

The key to a successful handbag program is no different than for shoes—buying the right merchandise attuned to current fashion trends; and the right merchandise for *your* clientele (age, lifestyle, income, etc.). Also very important is a broad selection to demonstrate that you're serious about your handbag business. A good selection often attracts customers to buy handbags only. Some of these customers become impulse buyers of footwear to coordinate with the bags—a reversal of the usual pattern. Average inventory handbag investment for the store amounts to about 5 percent of the women's shoe volume.

Many shoe stores fall short on promoting their handbags with the same aggressive effort as with their footwear. They assume that the handbag sale begins after the shoe-buying customer is in the store. The stores that do a more successful job with their handbag program promote this merchandise to attract customers into the store *exclusively* to buy handbags. It's a reversal of the usual procedure, and it works. It not only sells more handbags but it creates more impulse footwear sales to these customers. Further, it enhances the store's fashion image.

Handbags can be advertised in either of two ways, or both: as solely handbag ads, or tied in with shoe ads. Not occasionally but frequently in order to impress customers and prospects that you are seriously into the handbag business. Such ads should, of course, include information—sketches of styles, materials, prices, etc. It should also be part of your direct mail program—handbag literature included with your footwear literature. If you've invested in a handbag inventory, you should also invest in its promotion.

Timing for promotions is very important. While handbags sell year round, a third of them are sold during the November–December holiday season, and another third during the March–June period which includes Mother's Day. Often overlooked, however, is the promotion of handbags with your footwear for college and high school girls during the back-to-school period.

Handbags are also ideal gifts for birthdays, anniversaries and other special events—which is another reason why year-round exposure is important. If your store uses a gift certificate program for footwear, it should also include one for handbags. This can occasionally be mentioned in your ads, direct mailings, displays. It can often spark a suggestion for persons undecided what kind of gift to give.

As with shoes, women own several handbags for different end-use needs. They're very much an impulse purchase bought for both utility and fashion. Unlike shoes, they don't wear out. So eye-catching appeal is a powerful buying motivation.

Studies show that two-thirds of women prefer to buy their shoes where handbags are available; three-fourths say they usually coordinate bags with shoes, and nearly half buy shoes and bags at the same time, though not necessarily in the same place. Thus the shoe store is the ideal atmosphere for handbag buying. And this is accelerating because of the burgeoning growth of working women.

The centerpiece of all handbag merchandising and sales is in the effectiveness of the displays. Handbags are strong *visual* merchandise, which accounts for their high impulse sales.

Displays should not be limited to just one place or "department." Different handbag displays should be visible in different parts of the store—walls, tables, racks, counters, showcases, turntables—with or without shoes. If you have an awkward post or two in the store, use circular shelving on it with handbag displays. Use aisle space for either stationary or turntable displays. Most handbags should be accessible for customer touch or examining. The more exposure the better the sales.

No matter where or what kind of display, make it easily accessible, well-lighted, attractive, provocative. An effective way is to group handbags by styles or materials or prices. Encourage browsing. Handbags have impulse power.

Use small, informative signs with each display. While handbags usually speak for themselves, a few guiding words can increase interest. Also make sure the displays are changed often to keep a fresh, contemporary look.

And use your windows. Many stores fail to highlight handbags in windows. Handbag exposure does two things: it helps sell specific styles (always highlight the newest and most exciting bags), and it lets customers know you have a good handbag selection. Let your window signs say that.

Selling handbags requires some special knowledge and training. In larger stores one person will sell handbags only, but in smaller stores the salesperson must do double duty with shoes and handbags. Customers will usually have more confidence in women salespeople because of their familiarity with handbags and the customer's needs.

But whether male or female, sales training is very important. This means a knowledge of the types of handbags, current styles, materials, construction or design, end-use detailing, etc. For example, the handbag manufacturer spends as much time and money on the interior construction as on the exterior design (an average handbag may have ten or more different materials and 37 different parts). Thus the bag can't merely be held up to show its style.

Many of the selling features are inside, and hence the bag must be opened and "explained." This obviously requires stock knowledge. If, for instance, the salesperson has to struggle with a tricky handle lock, the sale can be obstructed or killed. Materials and detailing and fashion also have to be understood to be effectively sold. Many stores overlook the importance of these realities for their salespeople.

To avoid confusion, not more than three bags should be shown at the same time. Almost every women's shoe sale should be quickly followed up with a suggested coordinated bag, or at least a suggestion to browse the handbag displays.

There are specific features to sell: style, color, materials, texture, construction and design, end-use needs, contemporary fashion. The greater the salesperson's handbag knowledge, the greater the customer's confidence in the product and the salesperson, and the better the sale moves.

Handbag fashions have the same turnover cycles as shoe fashions. A large handbag manufacturer may introduce as many as 100 handbags per season. Like shoes, handbags have their own style classifications with names like clutch, tote, duffle, drawstring, swagger, Bermuda, envelope or portfolio, evening, attaché or vanity, box, shoulder, sachel, pouch, vagabond. Each is used for a special occasion or purpose or costume. The salesperson should have a reasonable knowledge of these to sell effectively.

About 61 percent of all handbags are leather, 15 percent man-mades, 15 percent canvas and denim, and 9 percent fabrics or straw. Salespeople should be able to distinguish and specify the materials.

Few matching bags (such as a lizard bag with lizard shoes) are sold today except in the high-price lines. Most are blends and coordinates (go-with but not matching) in colors and materials; but also more noncoordinates are bought for the appeal of the handbag itself, especially by younger customers.

The complexities of handbag buying by the retailer can be as challenging as buying the right shoes. Working with reliable resources or their sales representatives will provide helpful guidance. Attending the handbag shows, or the handbag exhibits at shoe shows, is also important if you're serious about expanding your handbag business. Further helpful assistance for buying, selling and merchandising handbags can be obtained through literature available from The Handbag Association, 350 Fifth Avenue, New York, New York.

If a shoe store does a $350,000 total volume, and 10 percent consists of handbag sales, the latter amounts to $35,000. If the handbag share is raised to 15 percent—a realistic target—it adds another $17,500 to sales and an additional $1,700 to net profit. It also increases store traffic, contributes to additional footwear sales, enhances the store's fashion and service image. Certainly those are strong motives to build your handbag program.

HANDBAG STYLES

Like footwear, handbags come in countless designs and vary with contemporary fashions. But also like footwear, there are certain perennial or *basic* styles from which all handbag fashions are developed. Here are the ten basic styles.

ATTACHÉ OR VANITY
- often framed or with center zipper divider
- opens into two equal halves

BOX
- rigid shell, often lid-opening

CHANEL
- distinguished by chain handles
- frequently quilted

CLUTCH
- adaptable round-the-clock depending on material
- disappearing handle or no handle at all

POUCH
- generally soft, roomy and easy to carry

SATCHEL
- large and spacious
- wide, flat bottom
- luggage type handle

SHOULDER STRAP
- casual, ideal traveler
- generally has adjustable strap

SWAGGER
- outside pockets surrounding an interior frame or center zippered pocket

TOTE
- open-top sometimes tab-closed

VAGABOND
- enlarged envelope with flap opening

HOSE

Hose is the second biggest accessory item in women's shoe stores, and the first in men's shoe stores and some family stores. In women's stores, hose accounts for an average of 4 percent of total sales. And only half of women's shoe stores carry this merchandise.

Many shoe stores carry hose more as a convenience item rather than as an important and aggressively merchandised part of their inventory. In fact, surveys have shown that many consumers don't even realize that hose can be purchased in shoe stores. That's ironic considering the built-in advantage shoe stores should have to sell hose. Footwear and hose are as natural go-togethers as cup and saucer. Thus the average shoe-buying customer is both in a mood and environment to think of and buy hose in a shoe store.

Hose is a huge market, much larger than most shoe retailers realize. In 1987, for example, nearly four billion pairs of hose were sold—almost four times the number of pairs of footwear. The breakdown is as follows:

	Pairs (mils.)	Per Capita Pairs
Infants'/children's	336	10
Girls'/boys'	662	17
Women's	1,984	20
Men's	828	9
Total:	3,810	16

Let's take a shoe store doing $350,000 overall volume with 10,000 shoebuying customers (average $35 per sale), half of whom average two footwear purchases a year from the store. Those 5,000 customers (assuming a mixture of men, women and children) would consume 80,000 pairs of hose a year (average 16 pairs per capita). If the store sold an average of only two pairs of hose per customer—less than 13 percent of the average per capita consumption—hose sales would amount to a handsome 10,000 pairs and delivering a nice additional profit.

Hose is big business. In 1987, total hose sales amounted to $3.5 billion, or $14.25 per capita. A more detailed look (in billions of dollars):

Women's	—$1.9
Men's	— 1.1
Boys'/girls'	— .3
Infants'/children's—	.2
	$3.5

Yet shoe stores account for only about 4 percent of that, or about $140 million. Obviously a poor showing when measured against potential.

Hose is safe and profitable merchandise. Average stock turns in women's hose is three times, initial markon 50 to 55 percent, markdowns 7.6 percent, and gross margin 45.6 percent. In department stores the hosiery section averages around $160 per square foot. Except for a few special seasonal items, there is only small variations in month-to-month sales.

Displays are the primary factor in upgrading exposure and sales. Like handbags, many store areas can be used for hose displays—walls, counters, tables, aisles, racks, turntables. Each display should focus on a particular category: pantyhose, knee-highs, socks, unusual fashion patterns. New or exciting fashions should be in the forefront as eye-catchers. Each display should be well lighted and with informative signs. More use of hosiery on leg forms adds effectiveness.

In the average women's or family store, hosiery seldom gets window display exposure. As a result, most customers don't "discover" hosiery until they get inside. Footwear and legwear are natural mates and should be shown as such in windows. Counter and wall cards facing the seated or browsing customers serve as reminders and can lead to impulse purchases.

Hosiery clubs can be successful and profitable when properly promoted. They work in the same way as shoe clubs—the club member getting free merchandise or a commission based on the number of customers or sales she brings in with friends and relatives. Another promotional strategy consists of one free pair with every six pairs purchased, or 30 percent discount with the purchase of a dozen pairs.

Hosiery advertising should frequently be included with your shoe ads. The same applies to direct mailings.

In men's shoe stores hose is the main accessory, accounting for 52 percent of all accessories sales. Men's hose averages a 51 percent markon, with 3.3 turns, and only 8 percent markdowns. Nevertheless, most men's shoe stores present their hose more as a convenience rather than something aggressively merchandised. For example, a dull hose counter, and that's it. It's no wonder that only 10 percent of men's hose is sold in shoe stores.

More than one display should be highlighted and "specialized"—calf-length hose, short socks, sports and athhletic hose, support hose, etc., each with its own sign-told story. And the displays themselves bright, attractive, informative, to encourage browsing.

On average, in shoe stores one pair of men's socks is sold for every five pairs of shoes. That's a dismal score considering the potential, with the average man buying nine pairs of socks yearly. Hence the ratio should be at least one pair of socks for each two pairs of shoes, or even one to one. It should be firm store policy that every sale of men's shoes or boots should be followed up by the salesperson showing and suggesting socks—and *never* with that sale-killing phrase, "Will there be something else?"

Seldom do we see dramatic or interesting sock displays in shoe store windows. The use of prominent men's socks brands in displays can add effectiveness. The major brands, incidentally, usually provide a variety of good point-of-purchase display materials, plus selling-help materials. In the windows, specialty socks should be shown with different men's footwear categories: dress socks with dress shoes; athletic socks with athletic shoes; work socks with work or outdoor boots; etc.

Don't overlook the juvenile hose markets where per capita consumption for infants and children is 10 pairs, and for boys and girls, 17 pairs, for total annual expenditures of about a half billion dollars. The back-to-school period is a big season for hose, especially with the teen and college-age groups, and hence should be included with your back-to-school shoe promotions.

While the hose industry is only about one-seventh the size of the footwear industry in retail dollar volume, the branded hose producers spend more than double the advertising dollars spent by the entire footwear industry. In 1987, hose advertising amounted to $100 million. That means that your branded hose lines are receiving substantial backup promotional support.

With a good hose selection supported by your own aggressive promotion and merchandising, you can at least double your hose sales involving only a modest investment and low risk. If shoe stores are accounting for only about 4 percent of hose sales, it's evident that there's a lot of sales potential to grow with.

31

Triple Your Accessories Power

Willingness without action is like clouds without rain—lots of potential but no results.

If accessories aren't accounting for at least 20 percent of your shoe store volume, you're being ripped off—by yourself.

Surveys of shoe store accessories sales show a sub-par performance by the large majority. For example, 41 percent of independent women's shoe stores do less than 10 percent of total store volume in accessories; another 45 percent show 10 to 19 percent, and only 14 percent do 20 percent or better. The women's shoe chains have an even poorer record, with 80 percent doing under 10 percent with accessories, and 20 percent in the 10 to 19 percent share range.

Surveys commissioned by *Footwear News* and conducted by Adelphi Associates also show a sub-par performance in accessories by the large majority of shoe stores and shoe departments. Average share of store volume in women's shoe stores shows accessories accounting for only 10 percent, and for men's stores 5 percent, with the combination averaging about 7 percent, far below potential.

Over half of men's independents and 40 percent of men's shoe chains do no accessories business at all, while 35 percent of the independents and 50 percent of the chains do less than 10 percent. Thus 90 percent of the men's shoe stores average under 10 percent in accessories sales.

Again, according to National Shoe Retailers Association studies, shoe stores that show a good sales performance in accessories average a 20 percent higher overall store volume than the average shoe store. That 20 percent volume difference is largely accounted for by the additional accessories business.

If a shoe store is doing a total volume of $350,000 with 10 percent in accessories, its accessories share is only $35,000 (likely almost all of it in handbags and hose). But if accessories sales rise to 20 percent, a realistic share, it amounts to $70,000, a 100 percent increase. Where can that additional $35,000 be found? The opportunities are abundant, found all around you.

Perhaps I hear you saying, "But I'm in the shoe business not the accessories business." Wrong. To start with, shoes themselves are an accessory. Second, consider your store traffic. A store with a volume of $350,000 and an average of $35 per sale, has 10,000 transactions of buying customers. Figuring another 25 percent for walkouts and the total is 12,500. Add another 20 percent who come in as relatives or friends of the customers, and the total store traffic is about 15,000—equal to the population of a good-size town.

And all of it is a *captive audience* on your premises at the time of shoe buying when they're highly receptive to a wide range of accessories related to the foot and shoe. Yet, ironically, most of it is allowed to go to waste.

Beyond the usual handbags and hose is a wide range of other accessories that are naturals for shoe stores. Most are non-seasonal, year-round sellers. Most aren't subject to the usual markdowns or the customary inventory control problems. Most require relatively low investment with minimal risk and excellent markon and profit return.

WHAT KIND OF ACCESSORIES?

Well, other than the usual handbags and hose, what kind of "other" accessories? First, think in terms of *categories*. For example, foot care. This can include the Scholl-type items for minor foot problems—the pads, balms, lotions, etc. But it goes beyond: electric whirlpool foot baths, insole and heel cushions, deodorizers, pedicure sets, callus buffers, foot coolants, skin toners, and various others.

Shoe care items might include closet shoe racks and valets, shoe tote bags (for those who walk or jog to work, then switch shoes—or change from boots to shoes), scented sachet bags for shoes not in use, shoe and boot trees, shoe stretchers, shoe shine kits or electric shoe buffers, shoe mittens (for traveling), waterproof applications (for campers), saddle soap, clip-on shoe ornaments, shoe dyeing kits, shoe scrapers (for outside the door), a variety of shoe cleaners and polishes.

Then there is the "pedocosmetic" group which contains items like foot and leg decals (can be washed off after use), toe rings (chic with sandals), ankle bracelets, foot jewelry (highlighting the instep, back of heel), foot fragrances, toenail polish kits.

There are special footwear items: foot and leg warmers, slippersox, rubber garden boots, folding travel slippers, mitten socks to wear with sandals.

Millions of people jog or walk as a physical fitness activity. You sell them jogging or walking shoes. But why stop there? These customers are excellent prospects for items like pedometers, electric foot vibrators and massagers, foot exercisers for at-home use, among other related items.

There's an almost unlimited selection of novelty items, many excellent as gifts. Examples: shoe-shaped music boxes, boot-shaped vases or doorstops, foot mops, foot-shaped doormats, shoe-shaped bookends, slip-on "funny feet," protective heel covers for car driving, 18-inch bone shoe horns.

Mention leather and people instantly think of shoes and shoe stores (over 70 percent of all leather goes into footwear). So the shoe store is a natural place for small leather goods—waistbelts, cinchbelts, key cases, change purses, wallets, etc.

Then there are books. Yes, books. Many books are now published about foot care, footwear, walking, running. Hundreds of thousands of copies are sold—everywhere except in shoe stores. Ridiculous when you consider the "captive audience" for such books in shoe stores and departments. So have a turntable rack with a selection of titles—in either hard cover or paperback editions.

Many of these accessories are far from small-change items but carry substantial tickets up to $50. For example, pedometers, electric shoe buffers, electric foot massagers and vibrators, electric whirlpool foot baths, foot jewelry items, shoe music boxes. A nice profit with a 50 percent (or better) markon, and minimal markdowns.

GETTING THE EXPOSURE

How do you get the accessories message to the customers and prospects? There are several routes.

Start with interior displays for maximum exposure. The first rule: don't lump all accessories together. Let each group be a *specialized* display. For example, one group focusing on foot care, another on shoe care, or special footwear, or novelty and gift items, or leather goods, or cosmetic items.

Each display should be attractive, well-lighted, and be identified with its own sign. For example, Pedocosmetics Bar, or Shoe Care Bar, or Foot Care Bar, or For Walkers and Joggers. Give each its own location, such as in a corner, or against a wall, or free-standing in a wide aisle. All should be easily accessible and have its own attraction power.

"No! I'm not interested in a merger!"

Each time you change your windows, leave a small section for a display of a particular accessories group, and let small signs tell a "story" about them, emphasizing customer benefits.

Do the same with your newspaper ads. Let the prospective customers know that you're offering more than footwear, but also many interesting and service-related items associated with the foot and shoe. Get across the idea that you're providing a "full pedic service."

Once you have a good selection of accessories, prepare a small folder, about 3 x 7 inches, that can be used as a mailer or purchase stuffer, or both. Use it for a picture-and-text presentation of the items, including prices. Cite that many are excellent gift items as well as for self-use. The folders can be productive mailers (supplemented by newspaper ads) to stimulate gift-purchase traffic during the holidays—Christmas, Mother's Day, Father's Day, etc.

The salespeople are vital to the whole program. A couple of in-store sales meetings should be held to get across the following:

1) The store is in the merchandise business and not exclusively the shoe business. You're a pedic service store, not merely a shoe store. Accessories should be regarded not as an after-thought or an "extra" sale but as a basic sale like shoes themselves.
2) *Every* customer should be seen as an accessories buying prospect.
3) A quota target should be set for each salesperson—say a minimum of 15 percent accessories sales to footwear sales.

4) A how-to program on selling *each category* of accessories should be developed. Brainstorming will stimulate ideas from the salespeople themselves.

Work out an incentive program, with commissions on accessories, and bonuses or other extras for surpassing quotas.

Train salespeople to listen for clues that lead to accessories sales. If the customer mentions a "closetful of shoes," it's a lead-in for a closet shoe rack or valet or shoe trees. If the customer mentions foot perspiration or odors, it suggests foot and shoe deodorants, or sachet bags. If the customer complains of tired or sore feet, it's a clue to suggest a whirlpool foot bath, or electric foot massager. During the course of the shoe sale, virtually every customer will make one or more comments that can be linked to a related accessory item.

Use the show-and-suggest system. Don't merely suggest an accessory. Show it while citing its customer-benefits value.

Salespeople should be alert to gift-sale opportunities—holidays, birthdays, anniversaries—that can be suggested to customers.

Encourage the customers to browse. If you've done a good job with the displays, accessories can be great impulse purchase items.

Where can such accessory items be found, or how do you get ideas for them? Browse around the gift shops or boutiques, or the sporting goods stores. Attend a giftwares show. Visit the notions counters of department stores or large discount stores, or stores selling leather goods. Visit your local library to scan the back pages of the giftwares and fashion accessories magazines, or the women's magazines, and also men's. These show many items offered through mail order and can spark ideas for you. Check the local wholesale book distributors for titles of foot and shoe books you can carry. If you do the research you'll find many accessory items suitable for your store.

Finally, the question: If I develop a substantial accessories program, won't this detract from the store's shoe image or even the shoe business? No. To the contrary, it will add impetus to shoe business by increasing traffic and creating more inventory excitement and selection. In the earlier years, supermarkets' inventory consisted almost entirely of food-related items. Today, more than 25 percent consists of non-food items. This hasn't hurt their food-store image or lessened food sales.

Remember, you're not in the shoe business but in the *pedic service* business. That should place a fresh perspective on your merchandise function.

ACCESSORY ITEM IDEAS

Shoe care. Polishes and cleaners, suede brushes, closet shoe racks and valets, shoe tote bags, scented sachet bags, shoe and boot trees, shoe stretchers, shoe shine kits, electric shoe buffers, shoe mittens, waterproofing applications, saddle soap, clip-on shoe ornaments, shoe dyeing kits, shoe scrapers.

Foot care. Selection of Scholl-type items for minor foot problems, insole and heel cushions, electric whirlpool foot baths, deodorizers, pedicure sets, foot refreshers, foot soaps and skin lotions, foot coolants, applications for athlete's foot, foot perspiration and other minor skin ills, foot powders.

Foot cosmetics. Foot and leg decals, toe rings, foot jewelry, ankle bracelets, foot fragrances, toenail polishes (colors).

Special footwear. Slippersox, foot and leg warmers, garden boots, folding travel slippers, mitten sox (for sandals).

Novelties and gifts. Shoe-shaped music boxes, boot-type vases and doorstops, foot mops, foot-shaped door mats, boot-shaped piggy banks, shoe-shaped bookends, shoe decals, novelty laces, "funny feet," protective heel covers, long and fancy shoe horns.

Foot fitness. Pedometers, electric foot massagers and vibrators, foot exercisers.

Leathergoods. Waistbelts and cinchbelts, key cases, change purses, wallets.

Other accessories. Scarves, gloves and mittens, umbrellas.

Foot and shoe books.

32

Making Effective Use
of Point-of-Purchase Materials

You don't have to be bigger, just smarter.
A dwarf on a giant's shoulder sees the
farther of the two.

There's an old merchandising axiom: the more you show the more you sell. Point-of-purchase is the show business of shoe business.

POP is the silent salesman of your store. But its productive value depends on *how* it's used. Today, POP is a multibillion-dollar industry. Surveys by the Point-of-Purchase Advertising Institute and others show the following:

- 82 percent of shoppers are aware of POP materials in stores.
- 52 percent say POP materials often aid them in their buying decisions.
- 33 percent say they actually make purchases because of POP materials.

The purpose of POP materials—signs, displays, tags, poster cards, etc.—is to inform customers and stimulate sales. It connects merchandise with customers. It motivates with three progressive steps: Awareness, Decision, Purchase. It generates impulse buying.

To be effective, POP materials must be the right combination of the following elements: size, words, graphics, colors, and merchandise. Together they must create a strong attraction and attention-getter for the customer, the first step toward a decision to inquire, look and buy.

Most POP materials are essentially display materials. They can be located almost anywhere that catches the customer's eye—windows, counters, checkout desk, walls, corners, aisles, air space, near the front door, even beside the fitting stool. But it should be done without clutter or POP overkill. On the other hand, many stores allow much of this potential POP space to go to waste.

The average store doing an annual volume of $350,000 has 10,000 sales averaging $35 each. But counting walks, customers coming in with relatives or friends, etc., such a store has an annual *traffic* of about 15,000. That's a lot of looking power—customers for potential additional sales via POP materials.

A POP display can be anything from a small, simple counter sign to an elaborate display with merchandise. Whichever form, it should have a motivational message built into it. For example, a small sign with only a brand name has no motivational effect, no special message or other effect to move the customer in a buying direction.

The display piece should be something unusual—the message, the shape or materials, the idea, the merchandise. Animated displays are usually more effective than "still life" displays, though this shouldn't be overdone. Electric signs are also effective though expensive. The expense is cut considerably if the sign is adaptable and can be changed to carry new messages.

Window signs should be small and (very important) *informative*. Just a few words, sometimes with a small graphic. And related to adjoining merchandise. Keep in mind an important rule: give the product a reason for being and you give the customer a reason for buying.

Most stores hire window trimmers, but they usually handle the inside displays themselves. Two things often go wrong here: they don't give those inside POP displays enough attention, and they change them too infrequently. So the POP displays acquire a tired, stale look that loses impact.

The average customer will visit your store about three times a year. When they come in for new merchandise they don't want to see old, I've-seen-it-all-before signs and trimmings. So don't let your "silent salesmen" fall asleep on the job. Change your POP materials frequently, keyed to a new season or special holidays, new messages, new merchandise.

When possible, POP signs or materials should be tied in with related merchandise on display. A sign that reads, "Ask to see our new summer sandals" hits a dead end. Nobody asks. But if the sign is part of a small sandal display and says, "An advance look at our new summer sandals"—that moves the customer to look, decide and buy.

SOURCES OF POP MATERIALS

This brings us to POP materials (usually free) furnished by resources. Manufacturers spend large sums to supply dealers with such materials. Yet much of it goes to waste. Surveys show that the average shoe store receives 20 to 30 such POP pieces a year, and some stores as many as 100. But the average store uses only 20 to 30 percent of them. Just because they're free is little assurance that they're used.

Dealer complaints are common. Many of these POP materials are simply brand name signs without message or sell value. Retailers gripe that many of these materials are too general, designed for the average store, except that no store considers itself "average." Often the materials are unrelated to a particular season. Or sometimes they arrive at the peak of season instead of amply before. Some materials cite price, which they shouldn't. Some are flimsy and don't stand up, while others are too complicated to assemble.

But then there's the good side. Some of these materials are excellent, prepared at considerable expense by professionals. To save your resources expense and yourself time, ask them to send you an advance listing or catalog of the forthcoming new POP materials. This will give you an opportunity to screen and select what you want. If you have any complaints about past POP materials, let your resources know. It will help both of you.

Sometimes a resource will provide special POP materials for specific seasons or holidays (Christmas, Mother's or Father's Day, back-to-school, etc.) Also consider developing your own with cardboard or light plywood, perhaps with the help of a relative or salesperson who has some modest artistic ability. What you need is an idea to start with, and you build from there at very little cost.

Hang tags are another POP item often overlooked. Surveys reveal that on apparel items customers prefer and buy labeled merchandise 9 to 1 over non-tagged. Hang tags should provide helpful information about the product, such as a particular feature, or shoe care, or materials content. Tags not only inform and build customer confidence, but provide the salespeople with helpful selling information. Studies show that tagged merchandise increases the selling efficiency of salespeople as much as 50 percent.

Another overlooked POP instrument is the salespeople. They're right on the POP firing line where customers make their buying decisions. Small, 8 x 11 sign boards are excellent for what's called "graphic selling." For example, if you sell children's shoes, the use of an illustrated board showing proper fit (toe-room allowance, heel-to-ball, heel fit, etc.) permits you to sell in a graphic way. It also impresses the customer with your professional skill. There are many variations of this, depending upon the type of merchandise. Make sure that the board has a transparent cover to prevent soiling from repeated use.

STIMULATING ADDITIONAL PURCHASES

Another idea that's used successfully is a small, knee-high stand beside the fitting stool. It holds 4 or 5 shoes in a forward-slanting position, much like a window display fixture. As the salesperson goes through the trial fittings, the customer will reject two or three but will express interest in others. The rejected shoes can be returned to the boxes or put aside, but those in which the customer shows interest are placed on the small display stand facing him or her.

This accomplishes two important things. First, it eliminates the confusing clutter of shoes on the floor or chair. Second, it allows the customer concentrated focus on the shoes he or she has shown interest in, *in addition* to the pair already purchased. This often results in multiple-pair sales with the customer saying on impulse, "I think I'll also take that other pair"—pointing to one of the shoes on the stand. This technique is reported to increase multiple-pair sales by as much as 25 to 30 percent.

Accessories are ideal items for POP materials. Let each category have its own small card message and sell-appeal. For example, cushion insole inserts might have a small sign saying, "For your pillow-walking comfort." For shoe cleaners or polishes, "Easy to keep your shoes bright and new-looking."

POP materials can generate more movement of special merchandise—slippers, weather boots, work or outdoor boots, aerobic shoes, etc. Slippers, for example, usually remain buried until the Christmas selling season. But people wear them year-round, or buy them as gifts. Again, a small display with three or four slipper styles on a stand, with a POP sign: "The perfect at-home relaxers for you or a loved one."

If you have an in-store clearance section or bin or rack (PMs, closeouts), use a small, well-lighted area with POP signs: "Lucky Sizes—50% off." Or, "The Winner's Circle—Savings Up to 60%" Give the POP a lottery feeling, an adventure. Customers respond to this.

Use customer service signs that relate to things like shoe care, fashion guidance, comfort and foot care. These inform customers that you're not only selling shoes but provide customer services that go with the shoes.

At the checkout counter use a "reminder" sign: Have You Forgotten?—then list items like hose, shoe cleaners, laces, foot care items, etc.

Where can you get ideas for good POP materials?

Visit display houses or showrooms. They have an abundance of interesting POP ideas and merchandise. The houses don't have to be shoe store specialists.

Visit other stores and departments—shoes and apparel especially, though other types of merchandise often have POP ideas that can be adapted for your own use.

If you use an advertising agency, work with them to develop POP materials. After all, creating ideas is their business.

If the Yellow Pages can do the walking, your POP materials can do the talking. Those "silent salesmen" can influence a lot of extra business. When you generate more visual customer awareness of your merchandise and services, you arouse more customer response. That's precisely the function of effective point-of-purchase merchandising.

APPRAISING THE WORTH OF YOUR POP MATERIALS

1. Does it fit in with the "personality" of your store?
2. Is it the right size for the available space?
3. Are the materials sturdy and stand up to handling?
4. Are they easy to assemble, with simple instructions?
5. Are the colors appropriate with store decor or location?
6. Do they catch the customer's eye and attention?
7. Do they convey information, a message?
8. Do they contain graphics?
9. Do they show related merchandise?
10. Are they changed frequently?
11. Are they placed in the most effective locations?
12. Is there too much clutter of POP materials?
13. Do they motivate the customer to follow up and buy?
14. Do they make the customer want to inquire, browse?
15. Are they easy to see and read?

33

Merchandising Your Fitting Services

*Your job isn't to supply demand but
to create demand.*

Does the shoe fit or give you fits? It's a common question among consumers when they talk to each other about shoes. That's ironic because most shoe stores or departments provide a fitting service. So what's really in question is the availability of sizes and widths, the qualifications of the so-called fitters, and the quality of the service.

Perhaps your store's fitting service is above average; or you like to think so or you want it to be. What do you do about it? If yours is such an above-average store then you probably depend mostly on word-of-mouth to develop a local reputation for your fitting service. But that takes a lot of time and patience. Moreover, the fitting service you consider above average may not be as superior as you think it is. It may be more illusion than reality.

Anyhow, if excellence of fitting service is your objective, achieving it can provide some splendid opportunities to make your store stand out above the crowd. It will separate you from being "just another shoe store." It can also help you to escape from the price-cutting wars that severely wound margins and profits. Customers will be eager to pay regular prices at your store because of its fine reputation for excellence of fitting service.

Your obvious first task, however, is to establish the foundations for creating such a reputation, and then to do promotional justice to merchandising that service. Good fitting service isn't good enough. Many stores offer that. Excellence is a level above good, and it's what you should strive for. Here, now, is a simple blueprint for achieving these goals.

Availability of Sizes. This is where it all begins—the right inventory of sizes and widths to fulfill the promise of excellence of fitting service. Right at the beginning you have to make an important inventory decision: lots of style breadth with limited size depth, or more modest style selection but with full depth in sizes and widths. If yours is a large-volume store perhaps you can have both. But for the average or moderate store it's usually a choice of one or the other. That doesn't mean that *all* your styles require full size/width depth, but most of them should, otherwise you're fudging on your promise or claim of excellence of fitting service.

With a full size/width depth in most of your shoes, you now have something very important to promote, to set you apart from the crowd. This helps establish that invaluable word-of-mouth advertising: "I can always get my size in that store."

Size depth means more than sizes labeled N, M, or W. Those labels have little reliability. An M width, for example, can mean anything from a B to D, and hence has no size validity. Also, an M (or N or W) width can vary greatly among manufacturers or brands or styles. So if you're going to do justice to excellence of fitting service, then as many of your shoes as possible should be available not only in half sizes but in the traditional A-B-C-D-etc. widths system.

A few of your shoes should also be carried in out-sizes—extra large or small, or extra wide or narrow. These would be in basic styles not subject to seasonal markdowns. This adds extra leverage to your store's reputation for full ranges of sizes and widths and a further basis for excellence of fitting service.

Lasts. The bet is 100 to 1 you don't know how many different lasts (not styles) you carry in stock. But you should know. You can get this information from each of your resources in regard to each of their styles you have in stock. The total will astound you. But most important, you can promotionally *exploit* that information by letting your customers know (via ads, displays, signs) that, for example, you stock "over 100 different lasts to assure a correct shoe shape for every foot."

The right last, of course, is every bit as important as the right size and width for correct fit. Yet shoe stores rarely, if ever, promote their selection of lasts and relate it to shoe fit and fitting service. If you do it, it raises you another plateau above the crowd and further enhances your store's reputation for excellence of fitting service.

Fashion and Fit. Does specialization in high-standard fitting service mean that most of your stock must be in the "orthopedic" or dull-style categories? Not at all. True, your stock can't be dominated by sexy fashion shoes like strippy sandals with 24/8 heels. But today fashion wears many costumes—casuals, flats, medium heels, sports, smart patterns in pumps, ties, boots, etc. Thus excellence of fit can be assured if you have a good range and depth of sizes and widths and if the fashions are not extreme. This gives your merchandise a much broader appeal and avoids the "orthopedic" image.

Salespeople and Fitters. No matter how broad and deep your size/width selection, it all hits a dead end unless your salespeople are skilled and qualified as fitters. This means a combination of training and experience. The qualified ones aren't easy to find. But you can train your own to the level of excellence. An ideal book, *Professional Shoe Fitting,* is available from the National Shoe Retailers Association. It includes an extensive set of test questions. On completing the test program the individual receives a certificate confirming him or her as a "Professional Shoe Fitter." If the individual is interested in developing still more technical skill, such a course is available through the Prescription Footwear Association (an affiliate of the National Shoe Retailers Association).

The important thing here is that your salespeople/fitters with this training background and certificates can be given promotional exposure as further evidence of the store's claim and promise of expert fitting service. This stimulates pride and motivation for the salesperson/fitter as well as contributing additionally to the store's mission of excellence of fitting service.

Training and learning should be a continuing process. This can be done with periodic (monthly or semi-monthly) in-store, one-hour training sessions, each on some particular aspect of fitting or fitting service. As the skills are sharpened the quality of the fitting service steadily improves. It also permits the personnel to think and perform in line with the store's own policies on customer fitting services.

Personal business cards for the salespeople/fitters to hand out to customers is an added touch to the store's professionalism in fitting service. The card with the salesperson's name might read simply, "Professional Shoe Fitter." Or, if certified by passing a special training course, adding the word "certified." This adds credibility to the qualifications of the personnel.

Fitting Techniques. The store should have a policy on shoe fitting techniques followed by all the salespeople so that there is a uniformity of procedure. This should include measuring *both* feet with the customer standing. Disregard the claim or assumption that the foot can be measured with the customer seated because the amount of foot stretch on weightbearing is "built into" the measuring device. There is *no* "standard" amount of foot stretch. Hence, because all feet stretch in length and width in different amounts, the only accurate way to ascertain foot size is with the customer standing.

The same applies to measuring both feet. Surveys show that no two feet of a pair are exactly alike in size, shape or stretch. And while one foot is always larger than the other, there is no telling in advance which foot is larger. So measuring both feet is the only reliable route. And, of course, the shoe size selected is for the larger foot.

A small minority of stores use more sophisticated foot-measuring devices beyond the Brannock or size stick. There are several electronic devices that are both unusual and precise. If used, the customer should be *told* that the device is electronic and the most advanced for foot measuring. This adds to the store's image as a fitting specialist.

Most salespeople test for shoe fit at only two points: overall length and ball width. But your store, as a fitting specialist, can make the 10-point check test, adding the following: heel to inner ball, heel to outer ball (so that the ball joints fit precisely into the shoe's ball pockets), tip of little toe, heel, toplines, under the arch or waist, throat and throatline, across the top of the vamp.

It's important to let the customer *know* that the 10-point fitting test is being done. The salesperson can use a small, illustrated card *showing* the 10-point test sites, and informing the customer why the testing is done at these sites. The whole procedure takes little more than 30 seconds. But the customer is impressed by the thoroughness and care taken to assure proper fit. It's good shoemanship mixed with good showmanship.

Even before the size-measuring procedure, the customer's stocking feet, with shoes off, should be given a quick examination (20–30 seconds). To a skilled hand or expert eye this will reveal some important things that will bear influence on the selection of shoes, size and fit. For example, are the toes straight or crooked or curled back? Is the arch high, medium low or flat? Is the foot seriously pronated? Is the foot long-narrow, stocky-muscular, short-broad, fleshy? Is the heel extra small or large? Is the second toe longer than the big toe?

Children's Fitting. This is the single most important kind of shoe fitting because it involves foot growth and the constant risk of outgrown shoes. Most parents are highly aware of this and thus want special care given to the fitting of their children's shoes in the hands of skilled fitters.

If you're selling infants' and children's shoes, the use of a small, raised platform for fit and step testing can be very effective for its visual and practical value. It allows the child to take a few steps along the platform at almost eye level of the parent and fitter. It's a prop that contributes to the professionalism of the fitting procedure.

Before the measuring procedure the child's old shoe should be examined to see if it's outgrown. If it is, the parent should be cautioned. It's a good idea to have the customer reach inside the old shoe with fingertip touching the roof of the toe box. This touch test usually makes a deep impression on the customer or parent. The fitter should also make note of other wear features on the old shoe, such as runover counters or heels (a sign of pronation), runover outside forepart (a sign of too narrow fit, or pronation), turned-up toe (sign of overlong fit), etc. These are helpful clues for the fitting of the new shoe.

Adjustments and Modifications.   Some customers have hard-to-fit feet. As fitting specialists, your salespeople/fitters should be reasonably skilled in making the necessary adjustments or modifications for these special-needs requirements. This doesn't mean that you have to get involved in orthopedic work in fitting very difficult feet, but only those with moderate, everyday problems.

For example, it's not unusual for some people to have one foot one or two sizes larger than the other. If the fit is made to the larger foot, the loose fit of the smaller foot must be resolved. This can usually be done by using a slipsole (insole) insert, or a thick cushion insole, as may be required. If the foot has a low or "flat" instep resulting in an unsightly butting together of the lacerow edge on an oxford, a piece of foam padding can be pasted to the underside of the tongue to fill the cavity.

Some customers wear an orthotic or arch support insert. This causes a misfit when worn with a conventional shoe. But if worn with a shoe made on an "in-depth last," this provides the needed extra inner space to accommodate the arch support without affecting the fit.

There is a variety of such minor but common problems affecting shoe fit. The shoe and its salespeople should be trained to handle them with simple adjustments. This contributes further to the store's fitting expertise.

MERCHANDISING THE FITTING SERVICES

Let's assume you have all the essentials for high-standard fitting services. This valuable commodity must now be exploited with merchandising and promotion. You're not appealing to a "mass market" (nor, in fact, are any of the other shoe stores). Yours is a specialized store with two clear-cut messages to deliver:

1) That your store specializes in excellence of shoe fitting.
2) That your fitting services are superior to any that can be found in the local area.

Advertising, of course, is one obvious route. But *what* will you advertise? Focus on the things that consumers relate to exceptional shoe fitting care. Promote your broad range of sizes and widths, plus your extensive selection of lasts. If you carry out-sizes, highlight them and specify the sizes; feature them as extra-long or extra-smalls, or extra-wides or narrows.

Also via advertising publicize your salespeople/fitters—with their pictures and a few words about their experience, training, skills. If they have certificates from shoe fitting courses, emphasize it. If you have regular in-store training sessions, talk about your store's program of "continuing advancement in the skills of professional shoe fitting."

Promote these same assets via other media of exposure. Examples:

Windows.   Post one or more placards (window floor, wall or stand) citing your range of sizes and widths, outsizes, skilled fitters.

Interiors.   Do the same with wall and counter signs.

Direct Mail.   If you maintain a mailing list, prepare a special leaflet or folder that talks about (and illustrates) all your fitting services. The same folder can be used as a handout (or with the wrapup) with each sale.

Reminder Postcards.   Many stores selling children's shoes send out periodic (usually every three or four months) size checkup notices to parents. In your case, add a personalized, hand-written sentence or two. For example, "Mary is now age 3 when her feet are growing at the fastest rate of her lifetime." Or, "On Johnny's last visit his shoes were outgrown. We suggest an early checkup this time."

Customer Files.   Maintain a customer card file for both adults and children, showing date of purchase, size and width, plus other information. *Show* this to the customer each time. The customer is impressed that his or her foot and shoe record is kept on file. It helps keep a personal attachment to the store and encourages customer loyalty. If the customer has an unusual size, these same records can be used as a source for mailings when new merchandise or special closeouts become available in those hard-to-find sizes. Customer response is usually good.

It works as well with children. Periodically check the card files. Select those where purchases have been made over a year, say January to January, and check the difference in size. On the next postcard size checkup reminder card, write: "Dear Mrs. Jones: You'll be interested to know that over the past year your Johnny's foot has grown more than one inch or three full sizes." This not only helps to personalize the customer-store relationship, but becomes a "conversation piece" for the family. It further alerts the parents to the importance of vigilance about outgrown shoes.

Counseling Service.   Run an occasional ad such as: "Do you frequently have shoe fitting problems like hard-to-find sizes or a hard-to-fit foot? Our shoe fitting experts are highly qualified to provide helpful counseling for such problems." This doesn't mean that your store can resolve all the problems, but you can often order hard-to-find sizes, or make recommendations.

But counseling should be a regular service offered to all customers. For example, advice about shoe care such as avoiding runover heels, or using shoe trees to keep shoe shape in closets. Or advice to parents about children's shoes. No doctor stuff. But customers do appreciate the store's concern and guidance related to the shoe's fit, comfort, wear performance, etc.

Surveys.   If you sell children's shoes, try to arrange with the principals of one or two local public schools (both elementary and upper grades) for a shoe fit checkup exam. If you can get the cooperation of the school physician or nurse, so much the better. Your stated objective: to test to see how many of the children are wearing outgrown shoes (surveys show an average of 40 percent) that could affect the health of the growing foot. You may want to enlist the assistance or cooperation of a local podiatrist in conducting the survey.

The findings become excellent grist for local publicity, with your store cited as the sponsor of the survey as a public service (no commercial plugs). It becomes a feature story for the local newspaper, plus local radio or even local TV news. In addition, as a parent and school service—approved by the school physician or nurse— a form notice can be sent (you pay for the postage) to the parents of all children found to be wearing outgrown shoes.

Newspaper Column.   If you are in a smaller community, arrange with the editor of the local newspaper to write a monthly column: "All About Shoes." Each column focuses on a particular topic, most of which relate to shoe fit, buying new shoes, outgrown shoes, hard-to-fit feet, etc. No commercial plugs for your store. Your byline and store affiliation is enough. This becomes a community service, with favorable ruboff for your store.

Local Doctors.   You *don't* have to carry or sell "orthopedic" shoes or be a shoe therapist to win patient referrals from local doctors. Occasionally visit or write to the doctors, telling them that you specialize in high-standing fitting services and reputable brands. Cite your availability of a wide range of sizes and widths and lasts, plus the qualifications of your fitting personnel. Many patients with foot problems or hard-to-fit feet ask their doctors to recommend a reliable local shoe store.

Local Contests.   Run an occasional local contest: the man or woman with the largest or smallest foot, for example. The prize for the winners: three pairs of shoes. The free publicity in the local newspaper, especially in smaller communities, pays back handsomely.

Every shoe store needs a strong identity, a clear-cut image that creates a personality unlike any other. For one it may be fast fashion, price for another, expert fitting service for still another. If your store has chosen the latter, then it isn't enough merely to "offer" this service. The service itself should be raised to the highest possible level of excellence, and then it should be merchandised to its maximum promotional potential.

Stores specializing in expert fitting service have usually tended to be conservative in their promotional efforts. That's a mistake because a very large share of consumers are seeking precisely such a service. If there is a large market seeking your kind of store, you should do everything promotionally possible to let the market know who, what and where you are.

THE PEAK OF COMFORT

A few years ago, Nordstrom's store in Seattle received the following letter from a grateful woman customer:

Gentlemen:
I received the shoes you sent me and they are fine. For ten years my feet have hurt me. The last couple of years my feet have been so tender and sore that I couldn't even sleep with my husband.

After wearing your Nordstrom's shoes for only a month, I find that now I can sleep with anyone.

34

Store Image: Your Personality for Success

*A store has a captive audience only
so long as it captivates.*

There are numerous things that distinguish successful from mediocre shoe stores. But without question the single most important distinction is store image.

Successful stores have a strong, positive, clear-cut image. The less successful or mediocre ones don't. If you doubt it, test it for yourself in your own city, town or trading area.

A clear, positive image is one of the store's richest assets. It doesn't happen by accident but is something developed with a pre-planned direction. It converts into traffic, sales and growth.

Store image is your identity in the local marketplace. It's the picture of your business seen and understood by the local public—your personality, your reputation. It's the message you're sending as to who and what you are, what you stand for, your "reason for being" as a business. Like a fingerprint, it's a one-of-a-kind.

All successful stores fit to that pattern, while most other stores don't and fall into a "me too" category.

Now, answer three questions for yourself:

1) Do you know clearly what your store stands for and what its image is now—not from your view but from the view of your customers and customer prospects?
2) Do you have a clear idea of what you *want* your image to be—how you want your customers to view your store?
3) Do you know precisely what you must do to create the wanted image—and do you work with specifics to achieve that result?

It's not enough that your store provides "honest values" at "moderate prices" with "good service." Thousands of shoe stores fit to that pattern. They're me-too stores that lose identity in the fog of a nebulous, fuzzy image, lacking a personality of their own.

Well, what specifically establishes an image, a strong and positive identity, for a store? A strong-image store is almost always known for *one* particular feature, perhaps two. It is *never* known for a mixture of everything—the idea of trying to be everything to everybody in hope of hitting that non-existent target called the "mass market."

Let's look now at some examples of specific image features on which successful stores build a positive and clear identity.

Prices. A fixed price bracket—high, low or medium. Or discount or off-list prices. Prices are the constant keystone.

Fast Fashion. Up-to-the-minute fashion, usually at moderate prices. Shoe chains are adept at this.

Prestige Labels. High fashion at high prices offering top-name brands and catering to a snob clientele.

Age Appeal. Stores catering to a particular age group—a youth market, a comfort-oriented older clientele, etc.

Size Selection. Offering a very large selection of sizes and widths, including out-sizes, usually accompanied by skilled fitting service, and sometimes mail order service.

Large Brand Selection. Offering a very broad choice of national brands either at regular or off-list prices.

Customer Service. Not the usual me-too services, but exploiting a package of wanted services delivered in above-average quality or quantity—skilled fitting, parking, fashion counseling, size selections, credit, accessories, mail order, quality personnel, etc.

Concept Stores. Athletic footwear, comfort footwear, work or outdoor boots, one-brand stores, children's stores, etc. The focus as specialists on a single product category.

Hard-to-fit Feet. The hard-to-fit sizes, lasts, comfort features, special styles, skilled fitters, etc.

Those are examples. What they have in common is a given category of merchandise in particular price ranges surrounded by related services. It's not a little of this or that, but rather a concentrated focus on some one or two identifying features.

WHAT TO DO WITH WHAT YOU ARE

Now, the second vital step is what you *do* with the pre-determined merchandise, prices and services targeted to a particular clientele or market.

Here enters the arsenal of "exposures"—your advertising, displays, store decor, promotions, mailings, location, personnel.

It's very important that each of these must have its own distinctive image, and that each dovetails into the image of your merchandise, prices and services. This maximizes the impact or appeal to the targeted market or clientele. In short, there must be consistency of identity throughout.

For example, the advertising of a high-fashion, high-price store must have a "class" look in logo, layout, copy, art. The same with the store decor, the displays and windows, the packaging, the sales personnel, the services, the location, etc. They all come together to form a single mosaic of identity.

It is the dynamics of the merchandising, those vital elements of exposure, that give thrust and momentum to the store image. This implants a strong identity impression on the customers of your targeted market.

Thus if you develop a strong store image impact, you actually have to analyze your store or business piece by piece, asking, "Does each segment of the business contribute something to the desired total image?"

Assuming you first know clearly what your market is or what you want it to be, you then design each piece of your operation to appeal to that market. Then you and those customers are speaking the same language. You are working with common interests glued together by a common image.

Store image is simply the effort of a business to make a pronounced and lasting impression on the customers and prospects. As with everything, there's a right and wrong way, an effective and ineffective way to do it.

Positive store image moves you out of the me-too category and sets you apart. That's what gets you noticed and remembered, which in turn is what gets you traffic, sales, repeat business and growth.

Does it pay off? Back to our beginning statement: All successful stores have a strong image, while the mediocre ones don't.

Selling

35

Sales Forecasting and Budget Planning

The man who doesn't know where he's going can look forward to a long, exhausting trip.

Don't wait for your ship to come in unless you've sent one out.

Sales forecasting and budget planning are inseparable. A budget plan is Expected Outgo, and sales forecasting is Anticipated Income. The balance or difference, of course, is Projected Profit.

Simple and logical, yes? No. What fouls up the neat figures is an ogre called The Unexpected and his ugly brother, Slipshod Planning.

For example, the Shoe Store Operations Survey (National Shoe Retailers Association) revealed that retailers pre-tax profits were a skimpy 1.3 percent in 1982 and 1.2 percent in 1983. What went wrong? The unwelcome entry of The Unexpected that tripped up budgets and forecasts.

Traditionally, virtually all budgets and forecasts are based on "last year's figures." While necessary, they can also be vulnerable (as evidenced by those disappointing profits).

For example, budgeting costs and expenses, item by item, by adding a little for inflation. That leaves no room for improvements such as reducing costs or increasing productivity.

Sales forecasting is often a seat-of-the-pants process. The retailer simply tags on a increase of 5, 10 or 15 percent, depending upon his level of optimism or "intuition." Seldom are more hard-nosed data used for such forecasts. Proof? Again look at those low profit figures for 1982–1983.

In many instances Budget Planning is done *before* Sales Forecasting. It should be the reverse. What you spend depends upon what you take in. Thus the importance of a reasonably accurate Sales Forecast is obvious. It is the key to Projected Profit.

Further, too many retailers fail to maintain a monthly check on the performance of the actual versus the plan—for the Budget (costs and expenses), Forecasted Sales, and Projected Profit. This check not only tells you what happened, but it's an excellent and constant test of your budgeting, forecasting and planning skills.

Over a period of months it can tell you whether you're an optimist, pessimist or realist. And the difference will determine the difference in your year-end profit figures.

SALES FORECASTING

Sales Forecasting should focus not only on how much you expect to sell (units and dollars) but *what* you will sell by categories. For example, for a family store, men's, women's and children's shoes, sneakers and joggers, boots and slippers, accessories, etc. The total is simply the sum of its parts. The better your forecasts by categories, the better your chances of hitting both the overall forecast and your profit target.

While "last year's figures" are a starting point, beware of overdependence on them. Keep a close eye on sales trends by categories. For example, are boot sales still strong or declining in your area? Are your sneaker and jogger sales showing softer demand? What's the outlook for higher heels?

The Unexpected should be built into your forecasts. Boot sales can suffer from a mild winter—or prosper from a cold and snowy one. Check the long-range weather forecasts. Not precise, but an indicator.

The Unexpected clobbered many retailers in 1982 and 1983, as shown by the profit figures. For example, the sudden entry of the off-price retailers, plus the heavy use of price promotions by all stores. Few were prepared for this kind of price war. As a result, in those two years over half of all footwear was sold below regular price.

Markdowns can be another Unexpected surprise to upset the Sales Forecast. One or several "dogs" show up; or suddenly a prolonged period of sluggish business appears. These should be built into a Sales Forecast. If they happen, your forecast remains intact. If they don't, it becomes an added gain beyond the forecast.

The Sales Forecast should take into account the condition of your inventory. If you're moving into the new season or year with a heavy load of carryover merchandise, you can do either of two things: (1) sharply lower your sales sights because the sludge of old merchandise will be a drag on sales, or, (2) take the penalties of a thorough clearance and start afresh. Projected sales increases require the right merchandise to meet expectations.

Retailers commonly forecast gains of 5, 10 or 20 percent. Often it's more with hope than factual justification. So ask yourself: how are my numbers justified? Such factors as a recent store remodeling or enlargement, or new lines of merchandise, a new location, etc., can be reason for expected better sales. But if you plan for a 10 percent increase just because you're a year older, chances are you'll be disappointed.

Keep in mind a rule: sales aren't what happen to you but what you *make* happen to you. A Sales Forecast must be hinged to a Sales Plan.

This means a program of pre-planned promotions; or an expanded ad program; or upgraded window and interior displays; or sharpened productive performance by your salespeople; or plans to increase traffic. In short, the forecast must be backed by planned actions to achieve the mission.

It also means exploiting all your sales opportunities (a common shortcoming with many retailers). For instance, say you have a hot shoe doing a 6-time turn in season and even beyond. Do you ride that shoe to the hilt with frequent and full reorders, and with sustained promotion?

Do you assume that your hot shoe is available for instant delivery from your resource, only to learn that it's sold out and there's a long wait for deliveries? Never take the availability of hot shoes for granted. Keep in touch with your resources. Each year a ton of sales is lost because of an out-of-stock condition at both the retail and resource levels. Exploiting your hot shoes to the fullest is vital to your sales forecasts.

Be an alert opportunist. Take advantage of good closeouts, for example. All your resources should know that you're on the "available" list to be among the first notified about such closeouts.

Good closeouts can add thump to your clearance sales. They provide more merchandise to run bigger and more successful sales. And, very important, they can often cut your losses on markdowns of your own regular merchandise, often by half or more.

Much of the viability of your Sales Forecast depends upon the performance of your lines and also the performance of your resources.

Keep a record of sales performance, line by line. Don't be influenced by "names" or labels. Set a realistic level of sales performance for each line. If a line consistently falls below that level it's not contributing its due share to your overall sales targets. Reappraise it and, if necessary, consider shifting to another line. Don't be swayed by sentiment or a false sense of loyalty.

Keep a record of the performance of your resources—deliveries, service, dependability. Each of those, depending upon their quality, affects your sales, and can be either a drag or a healthy thrust toward reaching your Sales Forecast targets.

A common mistake among some retailers is failure to keep records of units sold. This can distort the Sales Forecast. Unit pairage is a much more reliable basis than dollar sales for a forecast. And especially if unit sales records are kept by major merchandise categories. Not only does it give you a sound basis for sales projections, but it tells you precisely where your sales are soft and need buttressing.

THE BUDGET

If you've used the right tools to make a realistic Sales Forecast, and prepared the right plans to reach the target, you're ready to prepare The Budget. The planned Outgo is dependent upon the anticipated Income. And The Budget, of course, is simply every item of cost or expense required for store operation.

All such items are obvious: cost of merchandise and sales, rent, advertising, utilities, etc. But not so obvious to many retailers is what can or should be done in budgeting such items.

Last year's figures are a starting base. But those figures aren't necessarily written in stone. Nor do you automatically add 5 percent or so for "inflation" and feel protected. Some of those items may contain fat which you've mistaken for muscle. In other instances you may have skimped too long and have penalized your sales and profits.

For example, you know what you selling costs (salespeople) are. But what is *each* of your salespeople costing you? You may be paying one more, but he or she is costing you less because of more productive sales performance. Conversely, the lower paid salesperson may be costing you more with much lower performance. You can remedy this, thus increasing sales while reducing selling cost. This justifies an adjustment of this item on The Budget.

You can take a closer look at such taken-for-granted costs as lighting, freight, insurance, etc. Often these aren't as "fixed" as you think. By closer checking, many retailers find they can save as much as 25 to 30 percent; or that they've been paying more than they should.

Keep in mind the dramatic arithmetic: for every 2 percent saved on expenses, you add 33 percent to net profit. Surely every store has at least 2 percent of fat on its expense budget.

It can work in reverse. For example, you may have been skimping on your advertising to "save" money (which is like stopping your watch to save time). Where you should be spending a minimum of 3 percent you've been spending 1 percent. This has probably cost you more in sales than you realize. Or, under your more ambitious promotion and selling program for the new season or year, you decide to raise your 3 percent ad budget to 5 percent. In either case, "last year's figures" have to be changed to fit to your more ambitious plans.

Every ship captain has a navigational plan before starting a journey. It consists of a pre-planned direction and speed to arrive at the destination, plus the right inventory of supplies to assure a safe and comfortable trip.

It's precisely the same format for a retailer: a pre-planned direction and pace, and the right inventory to reach the destination as planned. The combination of the right Sales Forecast and the right Budget will assure reaching the destination of the Projected Profit.

36

The Ten Most Common Selling Mistakes

*There are three things to remember
when selling: know your stuff;
know whom your stuffing; and then
stuff them elegantly.*

*Keep your words soft and sweet
just in case you have to eat them.*

Becoming an effective shoe salesperson is essentially a matter of avoiding the common mistakes of selling. The mistakes are just as often the fault of management as the fault of the salesperson. The quality of the sales performance reflects the quality of the teaching.

Here, in our view, are the 10 most common mistakes in shoe selling. And also suggestions for preventing or remedying them to achieve productive results for store and salespeople alike.

1) Lack of Stock Knowledge. Every sale begins with the stock—matching the right shoes in the right size with the customer's wants and needs. Lack of stock knowledge can slow the sale, annoy the customer, lose the customer's confidence, and even lose the sale itself. How can it be prevented?

    a) Make sure the stock is well organized, easily accessible, and the stockroom itself well-lighted.

    b) With new salespeople, use the buddy system—an experienced salesperson instructing in all details of stock location and selection.

    c) During lull or slow periods, have the salespeople, especially the newer ones, spend time in the stockroom learning the stock.

    d) Make sure box labels are easily visible, and some with special markers to identify things like PMs, outsizes, broken lots, etc.

2) Lack of Product Knowledge. The first law of all selling: know thy product. The majority of salespeople lack this knowledge. It diminishes their selling effectiveness—the ability to sell with more conviction, establish product credibility, build customer confidence in the store and salesperson.

It's all based on the principle: Give the product a reason for being and you give the customer a reason for buying. Here are suggestions for developing "product information selling":

a) Hold periodic in-store meetings for the sales personnel. Have a couple of them deal with the topic: What's in a shoe and how to sell it.

b) Product knowledge deals with the shoe's components like the counter, outsole, linings, upper materials, etc. Each contributes something to the shoe's wear performance, fit, comfort, look. Each has functional values and selling points that help the sale when cited to the customer.

c) Make the words "quality" and "value" come to life by showing how the different components and materials of the shoe translate into *customer benefits.* Customers don't buy shoes. They buy what the shoe will *do* for them.

3) Lack of Fitting Skill.   Much shoe fitting in stores is superficial and unskilled, due mostly to inadequate training or careless and uncorrected habits. Stores with superior fitting service have a competitive edge because customers are impressed and also because it results in more wear satisfaction. Here are ways to upgrade fitting skills and service:

a) Hold in-store meetings as training sessions. The objective: not merely adequate fit but excellence of fitting skills and service.

b) There are books and other literature on shoe fitting. Have the salespeople read and study them.

c) Have a store policy on fitting—excellence of fitting standards and service.

d) Use the buddy system—the experienced fitters teaching the less experienced.

e) Take extra care. Measure both feet and fit to the longest or widest. Test fit not just for length and ball width, but heel, toplines, throat and vamp, arch, waist, instep, heel-to-ball. Let the customer *know* what you're doing, and why. This is uncommon and the customer is impressed.

4) Lack of Fashion Knowledge.   Most customers aren't buying a shoe but a look to enhance personal appearance. Most salespeople skim the surface of fashion: "It's the latest fashion" . . . "It looks very nice on your foot" . . . "It's a pretty color." Customers become immune to this trite stuff. They want fashion guidance, constructive fashion comment that has a ring of authority.

a) Use the language of fashion. Don't limit yourself to the word "color." Speak of tone, shade, hue, tint, cast. Don't merely say "genuine leather," specify the kind of leather—calfskin, kidskin, cordovan, lizard, etc. Refer to the surface finish with terms like aniline, lustre or pearl, burnished, gloss, matte.

Don't use trite phrases like "an attractive style." Be more specific and speak, for example, of a D'Orsay pump, diamond-tip oxford, elegant sandal, a smart espadrille, ghillie tie. And use descriptive words like silhouette, profile, sculptured, slender lines, etc.

b) Keep pace with fashion trends by reading current fashion magazines, plus the trade papers. Become familiar with the fashion names.

c) In selling, relate the shoes to the clothing, the go-with or coordinated idea. And attuned to the end use—daytime, evening, casual, sport, tailored.

5) Weakness in Opening the Sale.   The first 90 seconds are vital to getting the sale off on the right foot, to establish rapport, to make that important first impression. A sale well started is half made.

a) In greeting, act as a host to a guest in your home—friendly, warm, congenial. Show a take-charge competence, also eagerness to help. While removing the customer's shoe and measuring for size, get a clear idea of the kind of shoe the customer has in mind. The more specifics the better. It not only will save back-and-forth time but informs the customer that you're trying to select exactly what she or he wants.

b) Bring out at least three styles similar to what the customer asks for. The customer appreciates a sense of choice.

c) Avoid time-consuming small talk. Keep the talk upbeat about the shoes—the fashion or look, the fit, the quality or value (product information). Let everything focus on customer benefits, the positive.

6) Weakness in Closing the Sale. A sale half finished is half dead. Customer indecision or vacillation can be both frustrating and sometimes fatal to the sale. The selling weakness is in letting it happen, or being inert when it does happen. To prevent or overcome this:

a) Avoid confusing the customer with too many surrounding shoes. Remove those in which the customer has shown little interest and concentrate only on the priority shoes.

b) Keep alert for clues. If the customer is leaning in favor of one shoe, then focus on extolling the merits and virtues of that shoe. Help the customer to feel more assured about making that selection. Customers want help.

c) If the customer makes a tentative decision ("Maybe the blue pump will be best for me"), quickly reinforce the customer's semi-final decision: "You've made an excellent choice—a handsome style and a perfect fit." Then the closing: "Would you like to wear them out now? Or shall I wrap them?"

7) Laxity in Multiple-pair Selling. It's estimated that 75 percent of potential multiple-pair sales are missed due to lack of followup effort. Much of this is the fault of management for failing to train or have a policy on multiple-pair selling. Here are suggestions for remedy:

a) Run a couple of in-store meetings focusing on the techniques of multiple-pair selling.

b) *Every* customer should be regarded as a multiple-pair prospect.

c) Recognize that multiple-pair selling is a customer service and not "pushing" unwanted merchandise on the customer. Customers appreciate being shown and asked.

d) If the customer is undecided between two pairs, sell the first pair, then focus on selling the second pair. "If you like both, then don't deny yourself this other pair."

e) If the customer doesn't have enough money for the second pair, suggest a deposit to hold the second pair. Or mention that the store takes credit cards.

f) Never ask the customer, "Will there be something else?" That's asking for a no.

g) While showing or suggesting a followup pair, get the second pair onto the customer's foot. A shoe on the foot is worth two in the hand.

h) Listen for clues while selling the first pair. The customer may mention a planned boat cruise. That can suggest colorful casuals or an evening shoe. A camp trip suggests moccasins, and so on.

8) Laxity on Accessory Sales. Some shoe stores do 20 percent or more of volume in accessories, others only 5 percent. The difference is in the store policy and the selling—with both management and the salespeople at fault. Here are a few suggestions for improving accessories sales:

    a) The store must have a selection of accessories to sell in the first place.

    b) The store should have a firm policy that accessories should be shown and suggested to every customer with every footwear sale.

    c) Once bought, all shoes have to be cared for. So every shoe sale is a natural for a followup shoe-care accessories sale.

    d) Handbags should be *shown,* not merely suggested, as a followup to every women's shoe purchase. And the right *kind* of bag to coordinate with the shoes. Salespeople should be trained in shoe/bag coordination.

    e) Hose is another natural followup accessory for men, women and children alike. And again, shown and not merely suggested. Remember, 80 percent of all purchases are made by the eye.

9) Customer Communications.   This area is frequently abused or neglected. It means things like attitude, courtesy, enthusiasm, patience. They play a powerful role in selling and in earning repeat business.

    a) The attitude should be friendly, warm, cordial.

    b) Courtesy is vital. Lack of it is a prime customer complaint.

    c) Enthusiasm indicates belief in the product and value being sold. It's contagious.

    d) *Patience* expresses empathy and understanding by the salesperson. Customers notice and appreciate it.

    e) Communications is more than talk. It's expressed mostly in the personal behavior of the salesperson in the selling process.

10) Extra-Mile Service.   Customers will say to a friend, "The salesperson went out of his way to help." It's the extra-mile idea. Customers remember because it's an unusual experience.

    a) Try to render some small extra service, something unexpected. For example, run the customer's old shoes under an electric buffer for a few seconds, returning them shined before they go back onto the foot. Or insert new laces to replace worn ones on the old shoes—free. Instead of saying, "Sorry, we don't carry that size," offer to order a special-size shoe from the factory (with the customer placing a deposit).

    In selling, a mistake is more than a fault. It's a cost against sales. Avoiding these 10 common mistakes can mean better earnings for the salesperson, more sales for the store, and better service for the customer. It's a package where everybody wins.

37

How to Conduct an In-Store Sales Training Program

The word "NO" was invented so sales people could prove their worth.

Selling is opening the door for the customer—not pushing him through it.

Next to the cost of merchandise, selling costs are the store's single highest expense. Selling costs continue to take an excessive bite out of profits. In fact, shoe store sales productivity or selling performance has been virtually static for at least a half century.

The chief reason is the lack of effective sales training. It's estimated that fewer than 20 percent of shoe stores and departments provide any kind of genuine sales training program. As a consequence, sales performance in most stores falls below potential—with an earnings loss to both the stores and the salespeople.

For every $40 shoe sale, about $5 is automatically sliced off the top for the salesperson's cost. In the average shoe store or department the average salesperson will serve 3,000 to 4,000 customers a year (though only about 75 percent will be sold). The salesperson will average between 10,000 and 15,000 separate try-ons or fittings a year.

That adds up to a lot of customers, try-ons and expense. And in the majority of instances it's all done with little or no training concerning the product, the service, the selling.

The truth is that most shoes are bought, few are really sold. To merely serve up to the customer what's asked for is service but not selling.

To fault the salespeople is one of management's most common mistakes. Whatever the quality of the sales performance, it's almost always a direct reflection of management performance. Salespeople are usually only as effective as they're trained or allowed to be.

Surveys show that most stores agree that sales training is important and valuable. Then why don't most stores have an in-store training program? The common reasons given: I don't have a plan, a format. The salespeople aren't interested. We can't find the time.

But those are excuses, not reasons. Proof: some stores have successful training

"Never mind, I'll wait until your boss gets back."

programs. They create the plan, make the time, and the salespeople respond with enthusiasm.

What's to be gained by an in-store sales training program?

1) Lower selling costs.
2) Improved customer service and selling performance.
3) Increased sales and higher sales productivity.
4) Fewer returns, mis-fits, complaints.
5) More repeat business.
6) Better morale and reduced personnel turnover.
7) Better store image and reputation.
8) More profit for the store, more earnings for the salespeople.

DEVELOPING A PROGRAM

How do you develop an effective in-store sales training program—a simple, workable plan or format? Here are guidelines culled from success-proven programs:

1) **Explain the Purpose.** Begin by letting the salespeople know the purpose of the program: to increase store sales. But state another obvious result: better earnings and upgraded skills for the salespeople leading to professional performance. So you appeal to both pocketbook and pride. It works.

2) **Hold Meetings Regularly.** Preferably weekly, but not less than twice a month. Regularity sustains interest. Make attendance compulsory.

3) **Select a Particular Time.** The usual time is before the store opens in the

morning. Serve coffee and doughnuts. And no interruptions—visitors, phone calls, etc.

4) **How Much Time?**   Not less than 45 minutes, but 60 is better. All of it working time. And begin promptly.

5) **Have a Precise Agenda.**   Program each meeting for topic content, format, timing, etc., so the job gets done within the allotted time.

6) **Come Prepared.**   No off-the-cuff, no rambling, no fumbling.

7) **Have a Topic Schedule.**   Pre-plan topics for several meetings in advance. Give the schedule to the salespeople. Stick rigidly to one topic per meeting, and no digressions.

8) **Use Visuals, Samples, Props.**   Make it show-how as well as tell-how. Use swatches, sketches, shoes, components, etc.

9) **Audience Participation.**   Get everyone involved in the discussions, brainstorming. Make the salespeople active participants and not just spectator-listeners. Motivate their input of ideas, views, suggestions.

10) **Use Demonstrations.**   For example, one salesperson in the role of customer, another as salesperson. Use a little theatrics. It's entertaining and heightens interest.

11) **Close the Meeting on Time.**   Sum up the highlights. Leave time for questions and answers. Announce the topic for the next meeting.

And now some *don'ts:*

a) Don't overwork the "lecture" approach.

b) Don't try to cover too much ground in one meeting.

c) Don't digress or get bogged down with small details, rambling.

d) Don't do all the talking. Listen, too.

e) Don't allow arguments to develop.

"Remember—if it doesn't fit, sell style. If it fits, sell comfort. If it's an atrocity, sell price."

INSTRUCTORS AND TOPICS

Who will serve as the instructor? This has a lot of elasticity. It can be the boss (owner) or store manager. But they're not necessarily the best. The key is to select the best *communicator,* as well as the person most knowledgeable about the topic.

The role of "instructor" can change with the meetings, varying with the owner, the manager, the buyer, the store's top salesperson, etc. Occasionally use a guest instructor, depending upon the topic. It may be a shoe traveler well versed in a particular footwear category. Or a neighboring clothing merchant speaking on apparel fashion.

Another common question: What topics do we select to discuss? And won't we soon run out of topics?

Topic possibilities are endless. Some examples: extra-pair selling; handling customer returns or complaints; opening and closing the sale; the leather story; facts about man-made materials; fitting—men's, women's, children's, infants'; handling price resistance; selling accessories; how to sell the quality story; stock knowledge; customer communications; how to sell comfort; etc.

Then there's the vast area of fashion. Examples: the new season's color story; how to use the language of fashion; the heel story; the fashion boot story; the materials story (finishes, textures, etc.); the role of shoes in fashion coordination; how to be a fashion counselor. Fashion is a constantly shifting story and hence is constantly open to fresh discussions to keep pace with trends.

Still another question: How do we get salespeople to attend meetings on their own time? This need be no problem at all if handled or presented properly. You're asking the salespeople to give up only 45 or 60 minutes of their time once a week or bi-weekly.

Most important, however, if they understand that the program is as much for their benefit as yours, they'll respond enthusiastically. For them it means becoming more skilled, more knowledgeable, more professional, more effective. This means a chance for better earnings, a better future. Contrary to some opinion, salespeople aren't disinterested. They're eager to learn.

Much also depends on how effective you make the meetings—how interesting, lively, informative, productive and motivational. It's management's challenge to keep the meetings animated and stimulating.

For store management to be neglectful or passive about in-store sales training can be one of its gravest and most costly mistakes. The salespeople actually control much of the store's power center. Stop and think about it. Most of the store's sales are made through the salespeople. They bear enormous influence on the store's volume, profits, growth, image, quality of service. They are largely responsible for missed or lost sales, and also for some share of the markdowns.

They are the customer's one direct and personal contact with the store—and thus their performance becomes the customer's impression of the store's merchandise, policies, integrity and reputation. They largely determine whether the customer does or doesn't return.

Therefore, to allow such a potent source of influence to function undirected and untrained can be a costly mistake. An in-store training program is the answer.

And as we've shown, a simple and practical format can prove effective and mutually productive.

THE LAST THREE FEET

Your store spends money to advertise and increase sales. It spends money to create attractive window and interior displays, and for fixtures and decor. It invests time and money to buy the right merchandise and offer good values. It spends years trying to build a sound store image and reputation.

And all for what? To bring in customers. Now, by virtue of all that investment of time and money the customer is in the store. Up to that point nothing has been sold; not a sound from the cash register.

Right here is the final moment of truth—the last three feet of a long journey now separating the customer from the salesperson. Who will now take command of this vital moment, this ultimate confrontation? Not the general (the boss). Not the colonels or captains (managers, buyers). The one person with the total responsibility in these frontline trenches is the foot soldier, the salesperson.

How the salesperson acts, how his or her abilities are used, will make the difference between win or lose, sale or no sale, satisfied or dissatisfied customer, repeat business or lost business.

Every dime and hour of investment you've spent, every strategy you've devised, to bring that customer into your store—all the power and control is suddenly taken out of your hands and the entire responsibility placed into the hands of the salesperson to make or break at the last three feet.

In a battle, the generals plan strategy and see that all required supplies are furnished. But the actual fighting is done by the foot soldier. The outcome of the battle depends entirely on his training and skills.

It's no different with the sales personnel in a store than with the military personnel in an army. It's the performance of the foot soldiers, based on the quality of their training and skills, that will determine whether the strategies of the generals will fail or succeed.

WHY GOOD SALESPEOPLE CHANGE JOBS

Better pay isn't always the reason why good salespeople change jobs. Surveys show there are 10 other important reasons why good salespeople leave.

1) *Better opportunities for advancement* in another store or job.
2) *Boredom* with the present store or job or management.
3) *Lack of appreciation* for work well done or work done beyond basic requirements.
4) *Lack of store or business growth,* hence stuck in a dead-end job.
5) *The boss expecting clones of himself.* "That isn't the way I did things when I was selling shoes." Or, "Young people today don't want to work hard anymore."
6) *Poor morale among employees.* A depressing work environment.
7) *Indifference* of store management to suggestions and ideas.

8) *Excessive pressure* applied by management, or unreasonable expectations.
9) *Uncompetitive management*—failure to keep pace with competition. Feelings of frustration in working for a "loser."
10) *Impersonal attitude* of management toward the personnel. Aloof and uncaring.

Good salespeople have pride and ambition, a winner attitude that wants to be associated with a store that also has pride, ambition and a winner attitude. Good salespeople have goals and want a sense of future. They want to work in an environment that is also goal-oriented.

38

Supervision of Salespeople— How Does Management Rate?

A leader has two important traits.
First, he is going somewhere;
second, he is able to persuade other
people to go with him.

Many of us forget when we finally
reach the top of the ladder of
success—it took a good many
people to hold the ladder.

In the best-selling book, *In Search of Excellence,* by management consultants Thomas R. Peters and Robert H. Waterman, Jr., the reasons for business success were precisely cited.

One thing that all successful businesses have in common is good employee relations and performance, and high employee motivation and morale.

Another important discovery: it's not so much a matter of "finding" the right people as developing them, or allowing them to self-develop, via the policies and motivations provided by management.

Since primitive times employers have experienced frustrations with employees, and employees have griped about management. The issue isn't which is right or wrong. What's really important is that both management and personnel performance are penalized via lowered operating results.

Now, management makes a habit of evaluating salespeople and performance of salespeople. This, of course, should be done. But why always a one-way street? It's equally important that management evaluates its own performance regarding supervision of sales personnel. Which raises the question:

Who is more responsible for the performance of sales personnel—the salespeople themselves, or store management?

MANAGEMENT RESPONSIBILITIES

There's no quibbling with the answer. Management has, by far, the major responsibility. It hires the personnel. It sets the policies and monitors the rules and standards by which the personnel must function.

It provides the merchandise for the salespeople to sell. It's responsible for the displays, advertising and other operations which draw the quantity of traffic to be sold. It's responsible for the salability of the stock, the availability of sizes, and various other factors which influence customer response and sales.

Just as a carpenter is only as efficient as his tools, so too the sales people are only as efficient as the merchandise, traffic, supervision and policies with which they must work.

This certainly doesn't relieve the salespeople of responsibilities of their own. If the store is expected to carry the ball at least to the 50-yard line, the salespeople, by their own skills and initiative, are expected to carry the ball across the goal line and score points.

But in this short chapter let's concentrate on management's role in the supervision of sales personnel for improved performance.

Now, before you can improve anything you must analyze and "rate" the performance of what you're trying to improve.

In this chapter is a rating chart for evaluating management's supervision and direction of sales personnel. However, to obtain the maximum effect from this "test" the ratings should be made separately by *both* management and the salespeople.

Granted, this is an unusual approach. But it can be enlightening and productive when the two ratings are compared. For example, management may give itself a "good" rating, while the salespeople might assign a "mediocre" rating. It may also work in reverse, with management giving itself a lower rating than that given by the salespeople.

Either way, it prevents the evaluation or rating of performance from being one-sided and losing perspective with reality.

Also important, the evaluation sheet on management should not be signed by

Tall gentleman: "You graduated from a shoe college?"
Short gentleman: "Oh yes. It's a little higher than Oxford."

the salespeople when turned in by them. This encourages a more honest appraisal by the salespeople.

The chart contains a list of 15 functions of management in the supervision of sales personnel—and also a simple method for scoring and rating. If management wishes, it can add or delete from this list (if so, it must adjust the rating scores accordingly).

Very important, the ratings must be on the basis of quality of performance for each item, as well as quantity.

WHAT EVALUATION ACCOMPLISHES

Well, what does the evaluation plan accomplish? First, it allows for a rating of management supervision of sales personnel by *both* management and salespeople—a process rarely used by stores. This results in a much more objective and realistic assessment of management performance.

Second, it pinpoints the exact areas or functions of management supervision that are weak, fair or strong. This enables management to apply remedial action precisely where it is most needed. Instead of effort toward "general" improvement, it zeros in where corrective action is most productive.

Third, the process raises the morale of the salespeople and their respect for management. It signals to the salespeople that management cares and that the salespeople are being given a voice in the supervision areas directly related to their jobs.

Now, let's take a closer look at a few items on the chart as examples for applying the ratings or evaluations.

1) **Conducting In-Store Sales Meetings.** First, it's either yes or no. If no, the rating here is zero. If such meetings are held less than monthly, the rating would be 4 or less. If more frequently, then a higher rating.

    There's also the matter of quality—regularity of attendance, format and content of the meetings, audience participation level, etc. In short, how interesting and productive the meetings are. This is a fair-judgment rating and can lift or lower the score. It is here, also, that rating input by the salespeople themselves is so important.

2) **Clear-cut Job Functions.** Some stores think these should be self-evident, which they aren't. That scores low. Some stores spell it out on paper. That scores well. The clearer and more precise the job functions, the less cause for misunderstandings, conflicts and foul-ups. Management and salespeople often have different views on this.

3) **Productive Use of Lull Time.** When there are lull periods with few or no customers, do your salespeople just kill time? Or are they preassigned productive things to do—like studying the stock, checking customer records, making calls or sending reminder cards to customers, studying the competition's ads, etc.?

4) **Employee Contests.** These are excellent incentives as well as sales builders, and salespeople like them. Yet most stores don't use them. How about your store? How many contests, and how frequently? What effects?

5) **Store Policies Spelled Out.** On such things as returns, greeting customers, handling waiting customers, multiple-pair and accessories sales, price bargaining,

handling customer complaints, preventing walkouts, etc. Is it all played by ear, or do the salespeople have clear store guidelines to follow?

6) **Listen to Grievances.**   Most store managements do, of course. But there are important differences in how it's done. The listening can be brusque and impatient, or expressing genuine interest and concern. Again, it's also a matter of how the grievances are handled. If this isn't done fairly and with reasonable promptness, then the salesperson's attitude is that management "doesn't listen."

You should now have a good idea of how to make a fair evaluation of the items on the chart list. Those items collectively comprise a viable program for management/salespeople relations, and also provide management with a good insight into its performance in these relations.

Management Self-Evaluation Scoresheet

Score on Rising Scale of 1 to 10

PERFORMANCE RATING CATEGORY	1–2	3–4	5–6	7–8	9–10
Conducts in-store sales meetings	☐	☐	☐	☐	☐
Provides selling/fitting training	☐	☐	☐	☐	☐
Defines job functions clearly	☐	☐	☐	☐	☐
Provides earnings incentives	☐	☐	☐	☐	☐
Has overtime schedule	☐	☐	☐	☐	☐
Delegates authority	☐	☐	☐	☐	☐
Provides employee benefits	☐	☐	☐	☐	☐
Uses lull time productively	☐	☐	☐	☐	☐
Runs employee contests	☐	☐	☐	☐	☐
Listens to grievances	☐	☐	☐	☐	☐
Displays fairness, not favoritism	☐	☐	☐	☐	☐
Instills good motivation	☐	☐	☐	☐	☐
Criticizes only in private	☐	☐	☐	☐	☐
Offers advancement opportunities	☐	☐	☐	☐	☐
Spells out store policies	☐	☐	☐	☐	☐
TOTALS	☐	☐	☐	☐	☐

Grand total (all columns):

Ratings:
0– 30—Poor
31– 60—Mediocre
61– 90—Fair
91–125—Good
126–150—Excellent

Supervision of Salespeople—How Does Management Rate? 187

SHORT COURSE IN EMPLOYEE RELATIONS

The six most important words are, "I admit I made a mistake."
The five most important words: "You did a good job."
The four most important words: "What is your opinion?"
The three most important words: "If you please."
The two most important words: "Thank you."
The one most important word: "We."

NOTICE TO SALESPEOPLE

The following rules were posted on the backroom bulletin board of a large Chicago shoe store in 1896, to be observed by the salespeople:

Salesmen, when disengaged, will take positions near the front door instead of the back. Customers do not come in at the rear.

Don't stand outside the front door when at leisure. It is excellent notice to competitors and customers that trade is dull.

Employees are requested to wear their coats in the store. It is not pleasant for a customer to be waited on by a salesman in shirtsleeves or with hat on.

Keep mum about our faults. Always have a good word to say about our business.

THE CONSULTANT

The centipede's feet were killing him. So the wise old owl suggested that he change himself into a man. The owl explained: because a man has only two feet, the discomfort of the centipede's feet would be reduced by 98 percent.

"A great idea," said the grateful centipede. "But how do I do that?"

Replied the owl, "That's your problem. I only set policy."

39

Dos and Don'ts of Training Sales Personnel

Dumb questions are easier to handle than dumb mistakes.

Most shoe stores and departments don't have a serious training program. One common excuse is that management "doesn't have the time."

That's ironic because much of the store's fate is in the hands of the salespeople. They determine the level of sales, productivity, selling costs, lost sales, quality of service, store image. So saying there's no time to train personnel is almost like saying there's no time to operate the business.

Many stores assume that new personnel will learn by "experience." While good performance comes from experience, experience comes from faulty performance. The latter can cost you plenty.

There are some fundamental Dos and Don'ts of training sales personnel. Here are some guidelines.

Training should be slanted for three categories of sales personnel: part-timers, new full-timers, and veteran or experienced personnel.

Part-timers usually don't require any extensive training because most will be only temporarily in your employ. But some will eventually become full-timers, or

"That's exactly what I'm looking for, but why did you have to bring it out so soon?"

will become long-term part-timers. So it's important that part-timers become reasonably well-versed in the fundamentals of fitting, selling and customer service. Customers don't distinguish between part-time and full-time employees. Hence the training of part-timers should include the following:

1) Essentials of fitting.
2) A good knowledge of the stock.
3) Basic approaches to selling such as greeting the customer, opening and closing the sale, multiple-pair selling, PMs, accessories selling, etc.
4) Store policies on customer service, prices, returns, salespersons' responsibilities, hours, etc.

There should be a few simple, concise instruction sheets spelling out all the details. Salespeople can't be expected to remember everything told to them. The written instruction guide sheets allows them to study the rules. It prevents mistakes and upgrades performance.

New full-timers require more in-depth instruction. Many stores use the "buddy" system, assigning the newcomers to an experienced salesperson who is responsible for the training of the newcomer.

While this is helpful, often it's not as effective or productive as it should be. The experienced salesperson may neglect the newcomer during busy periods; or he or she may lack the patience or interest or ability to train well.

By far the most effective way, in combination with the buddy system, is for management to prepare a simple sales training "manual" of perhaps 25–30 pages that becomes a standard format used by all personnel. It would be written in simple, concise language and include a few sketches. Many better shoe stores utilize such an instruction plan. It would contain brief sections on the following:

1) Basics of shoe fitting (sizes, lasts, fitting procedure, etc.)
2) Basics of product knowledge (parts of the shoe, information on materials and components, etc.)
3) Basics of footwear fashion (styles, colors, patterns, trim, heel heights and types, etc.)
4) Stock knowledge (arrangement of stock, PMs, size fillins, closeouts, accessories).
5) Selling knowledge (greeting customer, opening and closing sale, number of pairs to show, multiple-pair sales, avoiding walkouts, etc.)
6) Customer service (handling complaints and returns, courtesy and patience, etc.)

These sections can be developed to any extent desired. But keep it all relatively brief and simple so as not to confuse and overwhelm. More advanced training can be obtained later.

Finally, there should be a brief section on store policies and the salesperson's responsibilities. The following should be spelled out: pay scales, incentives and bonuses for particular performances, hours and overtime, housekeeping and other non-selling duties, quotas, commissions on PMs and multiple-pair sales, vacations, health insurance and other fringes, personal grooming and appearance.

Now the first thought of management is, "Who has the time to prepare such an instruction program?"

Well, let's look at the alternatives. When new salespeople flounder on the job because of lax or erratic training, they lose sales, sometimes alienate customers, lose morale and become discouraged, develop hostilities toward management, affect store image, among other negatives. So, failure to properly train can cost the store plenty.

Conversely, the short time it takes to prepare a simple, in-store training manual proves highly profitable. It results in more productive sales performance, better service, avoids costly mistakes, builds morale, lowers selling costs, reduces personnel turnover, improves store image.

A very important part of the training program—and this applies to all salespeople—is to establish and sustain motivation. The most counter-productive attitude for a salesperson is the feeling that one is in a deadend job.

It's important to instill the feeling that the work and the job have a future, a career outlook, opportunity for advancement and growth—something to work for besides a week's pay. This is especially important for younger people. There are opportunities ahead like buyer, manager, a partnership, etc., or one day owning one's own store. Meanwhile there are good earnings opportunities as salesperson, depending upon performance and ambition.

Never depend upon salespeople to be self-motivated. Some will be. But motivation is the job of management. This is often overlooked.

Conduct regular in-store sales meetings weekly or bi-weekly, but never less than monthly. A minimum of one hour, usually in the morning before the store opens. Attended by all sales personnel. Stick to one topic for each meeting.

In addition, special meetings can be held to discuss a new season's merchandise that has just come in. Explain why the store bought each shoe, its selling features, fashion timing, the ad program, etc. Such meetings are great for morale and motivation. They add momentum to the selling enthusiasm. And they help to cement the feeling of "team."

Utilize an employee evaluation system. Such evaluation should be done every six months, but not less than annually. There should be a "system" to this—meaning a checklist of job factors by which to measure performance. This might include things like sales and quota performance, walkouts, multiple-pair and accessories sales, courtesy and customer service, fitting skills, movement of PMs and closeouts, factors like attitude and personal grooming, etc.

The evaluation should be done by the store manager. Then there should be a personal meeting and discussion with the salesperson. This has multiple benefits. It's good for the salespeople's morale and motivation because it indicates that the store cares and is observing performance—and also rewarding it when deserved. This in turn benefits the store because it spots weaknesses and strengths in individual job performance, thus helping to maintain a high level of sales productivity.

Now, some Don'ts:

1) Don't show impatience. This can come from your own high expectations, or an ego that says, "When I was starting out . . ." But it can kill incentive and morale.

2) Don't criticize or reprimand in front of others. An old rule, but still commonly violated. It embarrasses everybody and accomplishes nothing constructive.
3) Don't take job performance for granted. What seems easy to you may not be for the newcomers trying to absorb a variety of rules and skills.
4) Don't assume a job with pay is enough. Not today. Especially for promising and ambitious young people—the kind you want in your employ.
5) Don't assume that learning by "experience" will do the job. A lot of costly mistakes can occur during the "experience" period.

Finally, there's an old but sound rule: before you instruct the trainees, instruct the trainers. The quality of the student's education reflects the quality of the teaching by the teacher.

Instead of griping about how difficult it is to find and hold good salespeople today, do something to change it. Many stores do it well and profit from it because they take the time and effort to properly train employees.

THE DOS

1) Use separate training plan for part-timers and full-timers.
2) Prepare a simple, concise guide manual.
3) Deal with specific subjects (fitting, selling, etc.)
4) Conduct in-store sales and training meetings.
5) Spell out job requirements.
6) Spell out store policies.
7) Provide motivation and incentives.
8) Have an employee evaluation plan.
9) Extend praise and recognition when due.

THE DON'TS

1) Don't show impatience.
2) Don't criticize or reprimand in front of others.
3) Don't take job performance for granted.
4) Don't assume that a job with pay is enough.
5) Don't assume that learning by "experience" is enough.

COST OF SALES SERVICE

1) Store does an annual volume of $350,000.
2) Selling cost is 11% or $38,500.
3) Average sale is $35—so 10,000 transactions a year.
4) Average service or selling cost is $3.85 per sale.
5) A daily average of 33 buying customers or $1150 a day—or service/selling cost of $127.00 a day.
6) That $127.00 service/selling cost is equivalent to your net profit (6%) on 60 pairs.

Moral: Service costs you more than you realize. So make sure you realize a full return on those costs.

The shoe store owner got motivation fever. He decided not to give orders or instructions to the personnel. He'd let them take the initiative, make their own decisions. So he gave them authority to act on their own.

A few days later the store manager approached the boss. "Shall I finish this project or go on to the next one?" he asked.

"Yes," said the boss and walked away.

A few minutes later the manager asked him, "Do you mean yes I should finish the old project, or yes I should begin the new one?"

"No," answered the boss, and walked away.

THE TEN COMMANDMENTS OF SALESMANSHIP

First Commandment. Thou shalt remember that only thy customer is entitled to free use of the mouth, and the salesperson is obligated to liberal use of the ears.

Second Commandment. Thou shalt always show and suggest additional merchandise after the first sale is completed, so that thy customer is not denied the right of further selection.

Third Commandment. Thou shalt treat thy customer as a guest in thy home so that he or she shalt wish to visit with thee again.

Fourth Commandment. Thou shalt remember that true selling begins when the customer says "no" or is indecisive.

Fifth Commandment. Thou shalt not argue with thy customer, for thee may win the battle only to lose the war.

Sixth Commandment. Thou shalt not fit wrong sizes if right ones are not available, for thy customer has put his faith and trust in thee, and thou shalt not disappoint or deceive him.

Seventh Commandment. Thou shalt serve with skill and knowledge and not with fakery, for it is to be remembered that a customer's hair can be cut many times, but he can be scalped only once.

Eighth Commandment. Thou shalt know thy stock in intimate detail so that thy customer is served quickly and well.

Ninth Commandment. Thou shalt know thy product in all details, for thy customer has placed his confidence in thy counsel and guidance.

Tenth Commandment. Thou shalt not forget thy role as salesperson, which is to sell to the maximum degree with the maximum skill and effort, to the maximum benefit of thy customer, thy store and thyself.

40

Evaluating Performance of Salespeople

It's not the cost of selling that's up, but the cost of not selling.

Good salespeople, like good cooks, create an appetite when the buyer doesn't seem hungry.

Management in most shoe stores or departments tends to use the loose gauge of personal judgment in evaluating salespeople or sales performance. Such a gauge is unreliable and often gives off misjudgments.

The most common and obvious measurement used is week-to-week dollar sales. This alone isn't enough. For example, there are aggressive, pushy salespeople who chalk up high sales. But often these hustlers also alienate customers, many of whom don't come back. The gauge of dollar sales alone can be deceptive.

"Where's the salesman who goes kitchy-kitchy-koo?"

To make an objective, complete and accurate judgment on sales performance you need a scorecard. And on the scorecard you need specific performance functions to score.

Nor can the salesperson be judged solely on any one or two performance functions. For example, he may rate high on sales but do a poor fitting job; he may rate high on stock knowledge but low on product knowledge; high on customer service but low on personal appearance.

Thus to make a fair appraisal in the best interests of both the store and the salesperson, the evaluation must embrace a variety of performance functions. Let's take a quick look at them.

Sales Volume. The average level of dollar sales delivered weekly. Obviously very important. But beware of this as a sole gauge. A bulldozer knocks over lots of trees but can leave carnage behind. Also, the merchandise and clientele of some stores are geared more for service excellence than high sales.

Multiple-Pair Sales. A real test of sales performance. For an average store, anything over 23 percent is excellent, 17 to 22 percent good. These averages depend upon the kind of merchandise and clientele. Fix your averages accordingly.

Accessories Sales. Four or more accessories sales for every 10 transactions is excellent; 2 to 3 in 10 is good. Below that is poor performance. However, much depends upon the selection of such merchandise offered by the store.

Fitting Skill. The more service-oriented the store, the more important this evaluation function. Fitting skill involves not only the know-how but the time-saving efficiency and customer satisfaction manner in which it is done.

Stock Knowledge. One of the very most important because it's so closely linked with quick-finding the right styles and sizes and speeding the service; and also important in being able to quickly spot PMs and other merchandise for follow-up sales.

Product Knowledge. Know thy product is the root of all sound selling. Many shoe salespeople fall short on this score. Product knowledge generates credibility and confidence in the customer, creates appreciation of product value received, and enhances the sale.

Fashion Knowledge. Particularly important where fashion merchandise is involved. Customers need and want fashion guidance. If they can lean with confidence on the salesperson for this help, not only is the first sale quickened, but it improves chances for follow-up sales.

Personal Appearance. This is an obvious asset. It's the important first-impression impact on the customer. It also reflects on the quality of the store and merchandise. And it begins with the salesperson's own shoes (would you buy hair-growing tonic from a bald-headed barber?).

Customer Counseling. This is a vital but often overlooked function of good salesmanship. It is an advisory role about shoe care, foot care, fashion guidance, product information, etc. It's not only a helpful and remembered customer service, but often leads to additional purchases.

Preventing Walks. Selling begins when the customer says no—and the no is converted into a yes. Also, it switches a "just looking" customer into a buying one. Preventing the walkout is a real test of the skill of salesmanship.

Courtesy. This one seems so obvious. Yet, as consumer surveys repeatedly show, it is commonly absent or violated. Indifference, insolence and smart-aleckism are examples.

Enthusiasm, Initiative.   These are intangibles, but as any merchant knows, they are invaluable assets in selling. They also are indicators of the salesperson's interest in the job or work.

We could add more to these. For example, customer service ability (beyond fitting), the skill of closing the sale, ability to serve two customers at the same time without offending either, ability to upgrade the sale, customer communications, how the salespeople use lull time, the movement of PMs, etc.

But what we've shown here provides you with a base for evaluating salespeople and sales performance. You can adjust it as you wish according to your kind of store or merchandise or clientele.

Included here is an *Evaluation Scorecard* with a suggested method of scoring and rating sales performance. It will help to give you a more precise fix on appraised performance.

This can be used in either of two ways: store management can make its own evaluation based on the scorecard items; or *both* the salesperson and management can each make their own evaluation, using the same scorecard. Then the two results can be compared.

This is followed by a personal discussion, item by item. Salespeople tend to either under- or over-score themselves on specific items. Nevertheless, it allows both management and the salespeople to deal in specifics when discussing improvement in performance. And it pinpoints exactly where the areas of improvement lie.

"*My feet are killing me.*"

Now, let's pose an old question: who is more responsible for the performance of sales personnel—the salespeople themselves or store management?

There's no quibbling with the answer. Management has, by far, the major responsibility. It hires the personnel. It sets the policies and monitors the rules by which the personnel must function.

It provides the merchandise for the salespeople to sell. It is responsible for the displays, advertising and other operations which draw the quantity of traffic to be sold. It is responsible for the salability and arrangement of the stock, the availability of sizes, and other similar factors with influence customer response.

Just as the carpenter is only as efficient as his tools, so too the salespeople are only as efficient as the merchandise, traffic and policies with which they must work.

This certainly doesn't relieve the salespeople of responsibilities of their own. If the store is expected to carry the ball at least to the 50-yard line, the salespeople, by their own skills and initiative, are expected to carry the ball across the goal line and score points.

Shoe salesmanship is not a single skill but a package of skills. When each part is functioning effectively, the whole becomes a productive performance that is gratifying for both the management and the salespeople.

Sample Evaluation Scorecard

Subject	Score
1) Sales volume	7
2) Extra-pair sales	5
3) Accessories sales	4
4) Fitting skill	8
5) Stock knowledge	7
6) Product knowledge	7
7) Fashion knowledge	4
8) Personal appearance	6
9) Customer counseling	5
10) Courtesy	8
11) Preventing walks	6
12) Enthusiasm, initiative, effort	5
Total	72

Scoring:	Excellent	9–10
	Good	6– 8
	Fair	3– 5
	Poor	1– 2

Ratings:	Excellent	108–120
	Good	72–96
	Fair	36–60
	Poor	12–24

Paid More, Costs Less

Good sales performance should be rewarded with higher wages, not only because it's deserved but because it reduces selling costs. An example:

Salesperson A

1) 8 prs. a day @ $40 each = $320 a day.
2) Pd. $4 an hour—8 hrs. = $32
3) Net sales = $288.
4) Selling cost to store = 10%.

Salesperson B

1) 14 prs. a day @ $40 each = $560 a day.
2) Pd. $6 an hour—8 hrs. = $48.
3) Net sales = $512.
4) Selling cost to store = 8½%

Salesperson B is paid 50% more but his sales are 81% higher, and his selling cost 15% lower.

SELLING BEGINS WHEN THE CUSTOMER SAYS NO

Most shoes are bought, few are sold. When the customer comes into the store, he or she is ready and willing to buy. The rest of the sale usually consists of serving up the wanted shoe in the needed size. Hence the shoe is more "bought" than "sold."

In this case (which is the usual case) the salesperson is more *service*-person than *sales*-person. There's a big difference between the two. Most sales require service. But the size of the sale, and often the sale itself, depends upon the quality or effectiveness of the selling involved. In short, genuine selling requires more than service—than serving up what the customer asks for. Here's what *real* selling consists of:

1) **Converting the Customer's "No" to "Yes."** This is where selling skill is put to the test, the ability to change a negative to a positive, a minus to a plus. That's selling.
2) **Making the Switch Sale.** When you don't have the requested style or the needed size—switching the customer to another style in the needed size and preventing loss of the sale. That's selling.
3) **Upgrading the Sale.** When the customer wants a better-price shoe but hesitates about spending the money. The salesperson shows the customer benefits of the better shoe (which means more profit on the shoe), and the customer buys it. That's selling.
4) **Selling Additional Merchandise.** Selling the second or followup pair, or selling go-with accessory items (handbag, hose, polishes, etc.). The customer has "bought" the first pair. Anything in addition is the result of salesmanship. That's selling.

Selling is the skill of persuasion, not pressure. It's not a matter of pushing but leading the customer. It's the technique of stimulating an appetite. That's selling.

USING LULL TIME PROFITABLY

There are some days, or some hours in almost every day, when business is quiet, when the salespeople find themselves with time hanging on their hands. Many salespeople use lull time to kill time—day-dreaming, cat-napping, small-talking with other salespeople, staring out the window, etc. This contributes to boredom and waste. This isn't the fault of the salespeople but of management. There are various ways for the salespeople to put that lull time to profitable use. Some examples:

1) *Study the stock.* New stock; regular stock; styles in broken size runs; PMs. This helps save both the salesperson and customer back-and-forth time. It also increases opportunities for PM sales.
2) *Check for missing or needed sizes.* This makes for a more disciplined sizeup system.
3) *Postcards, phone calls.* Contact customers to inform them of new merchandise in the store (not yet advertised); or buys or PMs or closeouts in their size. This is a customer service.
4) *Keep informed.* Have the salespeople study the fashion magazines, trade papers, women's pages of the newspapers—for fashion trends. This upgrades fashion counseling skills, creates more customer confidence, improves selling skills.
5) *Study newspaper ads.* Your own and the competitor's. This keeps the salespeople informed when customers ask questions or cite offerings by the competition.
6) *Help with the housekeeping chores.* Keep the displays neat, shoes clean; reduce the clutter look by getting shoes back to stock; etc.
7) *Study customer card records.* It's been a year since Mrs. Jones has bought her last pair? Why? A phone call may tell you—and may also bring in a sale.
8) *Think up ideas or suggestions*—for a promotion, an unusual ad, a better way to display, making use of an unused corner or wall, etc.
9) *Study for knowledge.* Books, articles, brochures, etc. to improve shoe product knowledge, fitting knowledge, foot knowledge, selling knowledge, etc.

THE STAGGERING WASTE OF SHOE-SELLING TIME

Each year some one billion people make footwear purchases in retail outlets. It's conservatively estimated that an average of 10 minutes of each customer's time during the shoe-buying process is wasted time. Time lost or wasted, for example, in unproductive or unrelated small talk by the customer or salesperson or both; or because of the salesperson's unfamiliarity with the stock room and time wasted looking for wanted shoes; or searching for missing sizes or styles; or trial-and-error fitting in the hands of an unskilled salesperson; or customer procrastination while the salesperson silently waits; and so on.

Ten minutes multiplied by one billion sales transactions comes to 170 million wasted hours, or 7 million wasted days, or 19,000 wasted *years*. Multiply those 170 wasted hours by an average hourly wage of, say, $7, and the total annual cost of that wasted selling time amounts to $1.2 billion.

Let's bring the numbers down to an individual store level. Take a store doing a modest volume of $350,000, selling 10,000 customers at an average $35 per sale. At a waste-time average of 10 minutes per customer, the total annual waste loss amounts to 1,667 hours. At a $7 hourly wage, the annual cost of the waste or unproductive time is $11,670.

Why so much wasted time? Mostly it's due to lack of sales training and selling skills—wholly the responsibility of management. This certainly doesn't mean that the customers or selling should be rushed. We're talking here of the *unnecessary* waste of time so common in the shoe-selling process.

Improved skills in fitting and selling procedures, along with a better knowledge of the stock, can cut this wasted time at least by half, to the benefit of customer and store alike.

IF I POSSESSED A STORE

If I possessed a shop or store
I'd drive the grouchers off my floor.
I'd never let some gloomy guy
Offend the folks who come to buy.

I'd never keep the sales help or clerk
With mental toothache at his work,
Nor let the person who draws my pay
Drive customers of mine away.

I'd treat the man who takes my time
And spends a dollar or a dime
With courtesy and make him feel
That I was glad to close the deal.

Because tomorrow (who can tell?)
He may want the shoes I have to sell,
And in that case how glad he'll be
To spend his dollars all with me.

The reason people pass one door
To patronize another store,
Is not because the busier place
Has better shoes, or gloves, or lace.

Or lower prices, but it lies
In pleasant words or smiling eyes.
The greatest difference, I believe,
Is in the treatment folks receive.

41

How to Recruit Part-Time Salespeople

Today's employer is yesterday's employee who found opportunity waiting for him at the end of the second mile.

There are approximately 300,000 people involved, directly or indirectly, in retail footwear selling. An estimated one-third of them are part-time employees.

Between 1975 and 1987, part-timers accounted for 40 percent of all the job growth in retailing, and in 1987 accounted for 38 percent of all retail employees. Part-timers will continue to represent an enlarging share of total retail employees. This will be especially pronounced in shoe stores and departments.

There are reasons for this. Experienced, full-time shoe salespeople are increasingly difficult to find because of competition from higher wage jobs, and because of the longer hours required. For example, with evening and Sunday openings now dominant, a store's week averages 60–65 hours.

Thus the competition for part-time salespeople continues to intensify. So the serious challenge: how to successfully recruit part-time help.

One opening question is important. Do you seek out or advertise for experienced or inexperienced salespeople? If you're looking for part-timers, experienced help will usually be difficult to find. Most are not only employed, but have the pick of the available jobs.

So start by settling for either of two things: (1) seek on the basis of "experience not necessary but helpful"; (2) or, "experience not essential, we will train." Either or both of these will attract more prospects.

Also, some stores prefer to train new salespeople to their own methods or policies, rather than change the habits of people whose experience isn't attuned to the store's policies.

Part-timers do offer certain advantages. They can be slotted precisely to the time periods most needed by the store. Because they work only short spans of a few hours, they tend to become less fatigued or bored on the job. And, in the case of many moonlighters working at part-time jobs, many have certain skills from their regular jobs that serve well as salespeople—such as being good communicators, working with other people, following rules and policies, responsibility, attitude, etc.

HOW TO RECRUIT

Where do you find your part-time prospects? Who are they? And what are the best means to attract them? Three very basic questions. And one thing to immediately recognize: there is no one simple answer to any of them.

The key to your approach depends upon your kind of store, clientele and merchandise. These will steer you toward certain personnel requirements, such as age or sex. Here, now, are some specific suggestions.

Advertising.   Classified newspaper ads are an obvious route and should be used. But success can vary, depending upon the job situation in your area. Also, a "part-time help wanted" sign should be used in your window.

If yours is a college town, try classifieds in the college newspapers. Same thing with high school papers (specifying seniors only). Bulletin boards are another exposure source—schools and colleges, YMCA/YWCA, church bulletins, etc.

Agencies.   Some employment agencies furnish part-time help. Their value is that they can do much of the initial screening for you, saving you much time. Call three or four local agencies and check. Sometimes they can be found in the Yellow Pages.

Try agencies that specialize in temporary employees—Manpower, Inc., Kelly Services, Strivers Temporary Personnel, Inc., National Association of Temporary Services, among others. They're listed in the Yellow Pages.

Local colleges usually have a job placement department especially for part-time work. A town or city school system may have an agency of Distributive Education for high school or vocational job placement. Student counselors often have access to prospects. Speak to school principals.

Other Resources.   Your own salespeople often can help. They are in a position to thoroughly explain the job to the prospect, and to select the best likely prospects. Further, they take a personal interest in the breaking-in process when the prospect is hired. As an incentive, offer a bonus for finding prospects.

Your own customers are another source. During a sale a customer may say something about looking for a job, or a son or daughter or in-law looking for part-time work. Or if you're impressed by the customer, you might tactfully suggest a part-time job. Even if she's not interested, she may know someone who is.

Try local chain stores on a selective basis, or even shoe chains. Young people in particular tend to go to chains on the assumption that job chances are greater. As a result, these stores may have more applicants than they can use. They may be willing to supply some prospect names.

The same applies to larger companies in your area. Not infrequently they are visited by people looking for part-time jobs. Contact the personnel managers or others who do the hiring.

WHO ARE YOUR PROSPECTS?

Your prospect resources consist of a variety of groups. You focus on those that best fit in with your needs or kind of store. For example:

Retirees. Many are active and energetic but have been forced into retirement at a particular age because of company rules. Many are eager for part-time work to supplement their reduced incomes, or just to keep busy. They're reliable, experienced in job skills, courteous, conscientious. Employees usually find these people highly productive on part-time jobs. If this group fits into your scheme of things, they provide an excellent part-time job pool.

Retirees in the 55-and-up age group are in the fastest-growing segment of the population and an expanding resource for part-time employees. Kelly Services, for example, now has a large special division called Encore for just such employees. Manpower, Inc., is job-placing more and more retirees in part-time work, many of them in sales.

Mothers with Children, or mothers with "empty nests," are another good source. Many aren't available for full-time jobs but need and want part-time jobs to supplement incomes. They're ideally suited for selling children's and women's footwear, plus the whole range of accessories. They bring maturity and experience to the job.

Moonlighters. These provide another prospect source. There are millions of them—teachers, municipal employees, postal workers, clerical workers, and numberous others seeking to supplement incomes.

Minorities. This is still another job pool being increasingly tapped by retailers. Many have the basic skills, plus the ambition and attitudes, to make good. Given the opportunity, they tend to try harder to prove their worth. Contact minority leaders. They'll help find people to meet your requirements.

It's a mistake to assume that part-timers come cheap simply because they're part-timers or lack experience. If you're expecting reasonably good quality and productive performance, the wages should match the expectations. This also reduces costly employee turnover. Further, cite some additional incentives such as merchandise discounts to employees, plus commissions or bonuses, etc. The extras are important to many.

THE FOLLOWUP

When you hire, be sure to spell out the duties in detail. A simple written sheet should supplement oral instructions. Part-timers need more precise directions than experienced salespeople, not only for satisfactory performance but for their own self-confidence.

It's also important to make them feel welcome and part of the family. They need a sense of acceptance. This should be conveyed to your regulars.

Before you hire part-timers, make sure your regulars know about it. Sometimes a full-time salesperson resents part-timers because they feel they're being denied opportunity to earn overtime wages. So clear the matter first with them to avoid conflict.

Be patient with part-timers. Some, such as mothers or housewives, may not have worked for a long time. Or, in the case of a high school or college student, it may be his or her first job.

Are part-timers productive and do they earn their keep? For the majority, definitely. In fact, it's one of the main reasons for the increase in part-time employment.

Training is obviously important, especially for those who have had no experience in fitting and selling shoes. A brief and simple guide list is very important. Items such as stock, fitting, store policies, extra-pair selling, accessories sales, selling techniques, etc. Any literature you can furnish for home study is of further help.

The buddy system works well with part-timers—a regular salesperson "in charge" of the instruction and breaking-in process. Learning the stock is vital and basic and should be the beginning point. Encourage questions. Be patient with beginner mistakes. Most part-timers are eager to make good.

Your objective is not only to obtain good part-time help but to keep them. Employee turnover can be costly, and it is higher among part-timers than regulars in shoe stores and departments. Some of this is unavoidable because of the transient or temporary nature of some of these employees. But some is due to faults of store management in the training and indocrination process, or lack of cooperation by regular salespeople, or other reasons—all of which are avoidable.

It's common for retailers to gripe. "It's hard to find good help nowadays." That's partly true, largely because the job market is becoming more competitive. But it's also true that many retailers don't train and groom them as they used to.

But the bottom line that must be faced is this. Part-time employment is steadily increasing as a consequence of the changing patterns of retailing itself, especially the 7-day weeks and evening openings. So if part-time employment is the new-day reality, then make the most of its opportunities for good results.

"Hotchkiss, go in for Tutwiller."

42

How to Buck Up Store Morale

A good boss is one who can step on your toes without messing up your shine.

You frequently hear words like "motivation," "enthusiasm," "attitude," "dedication," "determination." They're the vital stuff of selling and salesmanship. They're qualities eagerly sought in salespeople.

They're not the cause of high morale but the *consequence* of high morale. Importantly, however, high morale doesn't originate with the salesperson or other personnel. It's generated by store management.

It's a waste of time for management to gripe that "good salespeople are getting harder to find," or, "today they don't have the self-motivation like in the old days." That's passing the buck. Morale building is wholly a management responsibility, the result of inspiring and imaginative leadership, whether in an army, a football team or a sales staff.

What motivates morale? Employee studies reveal the following list of primary incentives: good earnings, opportunity for advancement, fair play, pride in both

"This is a perfect fit, but first show me all the others."

the work and company, self-esteem, recognition and appreciation for work performance, a feeling of belonging. Combined they create that vital attitude we call morale.

What specific actions can store management take to build personnel morale? Here are suggestions based on actual practices in stores noted for their strongly motivated salespeople.

In-store Sales Meetings.   This is a good starting point because it establishes several important values: a feeling of team, of belonging. It also advances skills and job knowledge and hence helps create a satisfying sense of job progress and upgrading.

Such meetings should have a fixed schedule, weekly or semi-monthly, and run for about an hour. Each meeting should have a topic and agenda. No "lecture" approach. Intermix the presentation with props, demonstrations, audience participation.

Lots of how-to. How to make multiple-pair sales, accessories sales, opening and closing the sale, fashion counseling, product knowledge, etc. Such meetings build morale because the salespeople feel they're learning, advancing, hence improving their own job worth.

Shoe Shows.   Each time you visit a shoe show, take one or two of the salespeople with you. Make sure all have a turn. Let them see and feel the exciting pulse of a show, how a show is shopped, the buys made. Introduce them to sales reps and fellow retailers as an "associate." Ask their opinion about certain buys and encourage them to ask questions.

This is excellent for morale. It upgrades their status, a feeling of being taken into the owner's or buyer's confidence, and of being part of the decision-making. It also gives them an insight into the complex buying process. When the salesperson returns to the store, it's with a fresh appreciation of the merchandise and a more intense interest in the selling.

Contests.   Run them frequently and keep them varied. You can run two or more of them at the same time for your salespeople. Contests stir the competitive spirit and upgrade performance not only for the material rewards but for the honors. Make sure the prizes provide sufficient incentive.

To make the contests fairer, divide the participants into two groups, experienced and less experienced. This prevents the prizes usually going to only the same few.

Operations Participation.   Give the salespeople an opportunity to contribute their ideas to store promotions, displays, advertising. For example, outline an upcoming promotion. Then hold a brainstorming session as to how the promotion may be handled. Many creative and productive ideas can emerge from such sessions. Most important, however, is that the salespeople are made to feel part of the total operation and not solely the direct selling. The same applies to the displays and ads. This is a definite boost to morale because it involves team spirit and a sense of gratification in the successful outcome of the projects.

Explain the Buys.   In most stores the salespeople are simply shown the new merchandise when it arrives in the store, then are expected to sell it. A minority of other stores do it better and with more productive results. They hold in-store meetings to introduce each new shoe for the new season.

Why was a particular shoe (or line) purchased? What justifies its place in the inventory? What are its particular selling features, its fashion rightness? How should the shoe be presented to the customers? It's all based on the axiom: Give the product a reason for being and you give the salesperson a reason for selling and the customer a reason for buying.

Otherwise, what do you have? The salespeople know little about the shoe other than it's new, and each salesperson, for better or worse, uses his or her own approach in selling the shoe. And sometimes, if the salesperson doesn't particularly like the shoe, he or she can hex it by neglecting it on the shelf, thus contributing to its sluggish sales and eventual markdown.

Explaining the buys in detail generates enthusiasm for the shoe and thus upgrades selling attitude and morale.

Performance. Most of us want an occasional reponse or evaluation to "how'm I doing?" The salesperson has his or her own personal appraisal. But it needs further outside reinforcement, especially from higher up.

Management should have a quarterly, one-on-one evelation session with each salesperson. It should always be friendly and constructive. Sales performance, based on records, should be discussed, plus suggestions, where necessary, for improvement. A salesperson may be chalking up good marks for sales, but also may have an irritating attitude that offends the other personnel, thus undermining morale. Both the minuses and pluses should be cited. And the salespeople should be encouraged to express their gripes. This friendly, mutual exchange clears the air and boosts morale.

Attitude is also a subject to analyze. Express praise and appreciation. Be tactful with criticism. The main point of the session is not only to upgrade performance

"I was a shoe salesman."

but to let the salespeople know that management is taking a personal interest in their progress and improvement.

Recognition and Appreciation. If a salesperson has worked hard to make a six-pair sale to a customer, do something spontaneous like a couple of tickets to the ball game or theatre. A token of performance recognition and appreciation. Or, if a salesperson is consistently outstanding in creating excellent customer rapport plus repeat sales (customers asking for the salesperson by name), award a small plaque citing him or her for "Excellence of Customer Service."

These don't have to be on any regular basis. Let them be unexpected surprises as recognition of achievement and management's appreciation.

Staff Dinners. At the end of each quarter or a busy season, take the salespeople and their spouses out to dinner at a nice restaurant. Maybe a couple of toasts but no speeches, no formalities, and minimum shop talk. Let it be festive. Again an expression of appreciation. But most of all it helps weld the team spirit. It also introduces the spouses to each other and to management to further cement the sense of family that strengthens morale.

Seminars. If there is a one-day or two-day seminar for salespeople in your area (a radius of, say, 100 miles), pay the expenses for a couple or more of the salespeople to attend. Then next time a couple or more of the others. This, too, is another uplift for morale because it shows management's interest in the educational advancement of its employees. If the seminars award a certificate, so much the better for morale.

Factory Tours. Is there a shoe factory or tannery or shoe supplier (makers of soles and heels, or lasts, etc.) within a 100-mile radius of your store? If so, arrange for a couple or more of your salespeople to make a plant tour for the day. This can be a productive experience that increases product know-how. It also pays back handsomely for the store via more knowledgeable salespeople and more effective selling. And, of course, it's an additional uplift for morale.

Advertising. Occasionally run a newspaper ad extolling your sales staff—its experience in fitting, fashion and product counseling, courtesy and excellence of service, training, etc. Run a small photo of each salesperson captioned with a few words about them. It's an expression of public recognition that raises self-esteem and morale.

Name Cards. Some stores have personal name cards made up for the salespeople to hand out to customers. The card is given to the customer after the purchase, with a comment such as, "I'll be at your service on your next visit." Many customers like this personalized touch because it enables them to deal with a particular individual rather than just a store. It also stimulates repeat business. But, importantly, the name card helps give the salesperson an identity, which is an uplift to morale.

Income. While man doesn't live by bread alone, we're not pigeons satisfied with crumbs. Within reason, be liberal with wages and earnings. It's a prime pillar of morale because earning level coincides with worth and self-esteem level. Low earnings result in high personnel turnover which can be costly to the store in recruiting costs, training, loss of sales through lower productivity, diminished customer service, etc.

Reward your good personnel with good earnings. This also stimulates less experienced salespeople to achieve better performance leading to better earnings.

Be fair with raises when deserved. Give year-end bonuses where warranted. Consider a profit-sharing plan. Each of these counteracts that stuck-in-a-rut feeling that undermines morale.

Pride in Store.   All of us are status-conscious. It's important to feel pride in the company or store we work for. And pride is an important part of morale. So do everything you can to make your store and business a prideful place to work for. That means its physical appearance, its reputation, the efficiency of its operation, its warmth for customers and employees alike.

Pride in Job.   The job of selling shoes hasn't had the most favorable public image over the years. It's the common butt of unkind jibes and is identified with menial work. That, of course, can depress pride and morale.

Instill the sales personnel with the importance of the required skills of their job. It requires technical knowledge of the product, fitting, the foot, fashion, psychology and human relations, selling skills, the techniques of service, etc. Even many salespeople themselves don't fully realize the scope of skills and experience required. Continue to get this point across and it will steadily build pride, self-esteem and morale.

The root of all morale lies in satisfactorily answering the eternal question of all employees: What's in it for me? We're all self-interest individuals. Hence the more self-satisfying benefits derived from the job and work, the more we enjoy it and the more enthusiastic and productive we are at it. It molds attitude, which in turn molds morale.

Providing the right incentives, benefits and leadership for building morale is the function of management. If accomplished, it pays handsome dividends.

MERCHANDISING YOUR SALESPEOPLE

Never take your salespeople for granted simply because they're being paid for their duties. Salespeople are as much of a salable commodity as your inventory. They should be merchandised to your customers in the same way. Here are some suggestions.

Advertising.   Occasionally run an institutional ad featuring your salespeople. In the ad show their pictures and a brief biographical caption of each highlighting their experience, skills and background. Or run a series of small ads focusing on one salesperson each time. Emphasize their customer service skills.

Windows.   Run an up-front window placard doing the same—photos, biographical sketch, skills, experience, etc.

Leaflets.   Prepare a small foldout as a stuffer with each purchase—again with photos and brief information about your salespeople. These can also be used as separate mailers or included with other direct mail material.

Business Cards.   Print up business cards for each salesperson as customer handouts after each sale. This further personalizes each sale and establishes an identity for the salesperson in the mind of the customer.

Publicity.   If your salespeople are active in community affairs—perhaps managing a little league team, hospital or other volunteer work, boy or girl scout leader, etc.—prepare a press release for the local newspaper about some special accomplishment by the salesperson.

Encourage Training. If there is a local seminar on selling, have your salespeople attend. Or perhaps a special correspondence course on shoe fitting. Or attending a fashion seminar at a shoe show. A press release citing such participation by your salespeople is of interest to the local press, especially in smaller communities. These help build prestige for both the salespeople and the store.

What's the return value for merchandising your salespeople? It builds their pride and morale and spurs improved performance. It's an important personnel motivator. It also strengthens store image in a favorable way, which converts into traffic and sales.

But make sure your salespeople live up to the promotional hype. If your promotions extol their skills and high quality of customer service, be sure that the store maintains the high standards of the personnel and service as advertised.

THE GOOD OLD DAYS

Back in 1872, a large department store, including its shoe department, had the following rules, typical of most stores of the day, permanently posted on the bulletin board for its salespeople:

1) Employees each day will fill lamps, clean chimneys and trim wicks.
2) Each clerk will bring in a bucket of water and a scuttle of coal for the day's business.
3) Make your pens carefully. You may whittle nibs to your individual taste.
4) Men employees will be given an evening off each week for courting purposes, or two evenings if they go to church regularly.
5) After 13 hours of labor in the store, the employees should spend the remainder of their time reading the bible or other good books.
6) Every employee should lay from each pay a goodly sum of his earnings for his declining years so that he will not become a burden on society.
7) The employee who has faithfully performed his labors and without fault for five years, will be rewarded with an increase of five cents a day in his pay, providing profits from the business permits.

Anybody still yearning for "the good old days"?

43

Opening and Closing the Sale

You never get a second chance to make a good first impression.

There is no such thing as "hard sell" or "soft sell." There is only smart sell and dumb sell.

It's a law of show business that for a play or musical to be a success the opening act must effectively capture the attention of the audience. The same with a good book—it's vital that the first chapter "grabs" the interest of the reader.

So too with shoe business. In selling, a good opening can often account for as much as 50 percent of the sale. The first minute or two sets the tone or attitude for the customer/salesperson relationship. A good start almost always assures a winning finish.

Here are suggestions for getting the sale off to a promising start:

1) When possible, greet the customer near the door, and promptly. An unnoticed or unattended customer grows uneasy, feels spurned, generates a negative mood.

2) Your personal appearance counts for more than you think. It influences the customer's first impression—of you, the store, the service, the merchandise. Be attentive about your grooming and clothes.

3) Smile. Introduce yourself. "My name is Mary Jones (or Paul Smith). Now, how may I be of help?" You've now begun to personalize the service by offering your name. And when you say "now, may I be of help?" it's a direct question requiring a direct answer. The sale is on its way.

4) Lead the customer to a seat. Never "sell" with the customer standing. If she has bundles, take them and place them on the next chair. If she has a coat, ask if she'd like to remove it. Act like a host.

5) If you or the other salespeople are busy waiting on customers, make it a store rule that the salesperson nearest the door (or the new customer) takes a few seconds away to greet the entering customer. The customer is led to a seat, handed an appropriate magazine (fashion magazine for women, sports magazine for men), then a brief comment, "Someone will be with you in a few moments." You've acknowledged the customer and have given them something to occupy their attention while waiting.

6) When waiting on a new customer, try to subtly learn his or her name.

For example, ask if the customer has bought shoes here before—so that the name and size information may be on record. It's much better to work with a name than the usual "madam" or "sir." It further personalizes the service. And if the customer is a woman, *never* address her as "lady" or "honey." That's sheer insolence.

7) When the customer is seated, don't start the sale without first getting the shoe off his or her foot. Handle the shoe with respect. You might even say, "it's a very attractive style and reflects good taste." That's a compliment and a plus in your favor.

8) Learn clearly what the customer wants. "Something in red in a medium heel" isn't very clear. Take a few moments to get something more specific. It will save both you and the customer the frustrations of back-and-forth time in selections.

9) Measure the foot for size. While doing so make some comment: "Your foot has a nice arch" (to a woman), or, "You've got a well-shaped foot" (to a man). Again a compliment and another plus for you.

10) Bring out about three pairs keyed to what the customer asked for. It gives the customer a sense of choice, of service, and for you it saves some back-and-forth time.

11) Be alert for early clues for what may become a follow-up or second-pair sale. The customer may mention she's going on a cruise soon. That will open the door for a later follow-up suggestion of leisure, casual or sport-type footwear.

CLOSING THE SALE

All right, the sale is under way. You've established good and friendly communications with the customer. But the sale is still not moving toward a conclusion. It's your move to close the sale. Here are suggestions:

1) Don't sit silent and dumb while waiting for the customer to make a decision. This only creates an awkward lull. Salesmanship is a process of helping the customer to buy, to decide. Customers want this help. They need backup support for their own decisions.

2) Ask affirmative questions. "This is a handsome color, isn't it?" Or, "I'd call that a perfect fit, wouldn't you?" These draw out "yes" answers which lead to a "yes" buying decisions.

3) Narrow the choices. The customer has seen or tried on several pairs; has shown preference for a couple, disinterest in others. Move the latter away out of sight. This allows the customer to concentrate on the "finals."

4) Prevent stalling. Don't allow the customer to get you involved in some off-track conversation. Smile or nod, but tactfully steer the conversation back to the shoe-buying decision.

5) Invite the customer to try on the shoes again. Watch or listen for clues. The customer may say, "I think this dark red will go well with my new suit." This is a hint of her preference. So move in with a comment such as, "You're selecting our newest shade of red and one of our best-selling

styles. It should make a handsome match." You're complimenting her taste. And by saying "you're selecting" you're helping to confirm her decision.

6) Sum up the special features of the shoe. One or two of these may strike a decision-making note.

7) If she's wavering between two pairs, suggest that she take both. If she does you've won a double-header, and if she doesn't she feels required on the spot to make a choice of one.

8) Don't over-sell in your impatience to close the sale. While all customers want to be guided, none wants to feel pressured or pushed.

9) At the first sign of a decision, even a semi-conclusive one, move in quickly with, "Shall I wrap them or would you like to wear them?" Or, "Will that be charge or cash?"

When the shoes are finally wrapped and payment made, don't merely say "thank you." Add a comment such as "You've made a very fine choice. I'm sure you'll receive nice compliments when you wear them." The customer now feels assured of her good taste and wise selection.

UNTANGLING THE SNAGS

Now, as any experienced salesperson knows, not all sales are neat, smooth open-and-close affairs. Suppose the customer, after all your time spent, decides not to buy (in the average shoe store or department, three out of every 10 customers walks out unsold, for any of various reasons). Here, now, is the crucial test.

Up to now you've simply "serviced" the customer by giving him or her choices of what to buy and trying to guide the customer to a decision. Now, however, you're challenged to convert a "no" into a "maybe" and the maybe into a "yes." This is the ultimate test of salesmanship because real selling begins when the customer says no. Here are some suggestions for this dilemma.

1) If the customer decides not to buy, try to quickly pinpoint the reason. Is it the price? The wanted style or size not available? Some other reason? By knowing the answer you can quickly adapt and tactfully try a fresh approach that zeros in on the problem.

2) If price is the obstacle (she wants the higher-priced pair but doesn't have enough to pay), suggest that she leave a deposit and pick up the shoes later.

3) Or, despite your conscientious efforts the customer isn't satisfied with the fit of any of the shoes you've tried. Don't feel that you've failed (after all, even God doesn't get everyone's approval). Say to the customer, "Let me call Mr. Grant, our manager. He's a noted expert in fitting." The customer is flattered that she's going to get the attention of management. The manager (or it may be another salesperson) takes over. Psychologically, a fresh start with a new salesperson will often change the customer's attitude and result in a sale that otherwise would be lost.

4) If it's a case of a wanted style or color not available, and the store has open-shelf displays, invite the ready-to-walk customer to browse. Say, as you point to the display, "We have some very interesting things in our

selection display. Perhaps you'll see something I may have missed." She may not find what she came in for, but she may see something else that strikes her fancy.

5) When the customer says "no" don't become more aggressive. That only makes the customer more resistant and resentful. Keep your cool, courtesy and pleasant manner. You may lose the sale but you'll keep the customer. He or she will remember your courteous manner under the no-sale conditions.

Each "no" situation has its own reason. The important thing is not to be discouraged by a no, or to accept it as final or unchangeable. As someone said, "Good salespeople, like good cooks, create an appetite when the customer doesn't seem hungry."

44

The High Cost of Walkouts

A diplomat is one who can tell you to go to hell so tactfully that you start packing for the trip.

It's useless to put your best foot forward—then drag the other.

One of the worst enemies of shoe retailers is walkouts. The losses from walkouts, most of which can be prevented, are staggering. A little quick arithmetic provides an example.

In the average shoe store or shoe department, three of every 10 customers are walks. Let's use a sample store with $350,000 volume, and with an average sale of $35. That means 10,000 sales or transactions.

This store starts with 14,285 wanting-to-buy customers. But it loses 4,285 (30 percent) through walks. At $35 per sale, those 4,285 walks amount to a loss of $149,975. That adds up to 43 percent of the store's total volume. If the store averages a net profit of 7 percent or $24,500, then the net profit loss from the walks amounts to $10,498, or 43 percent of actual net profit.

From the 42 wanting-to-buy customers a day, the store averages 29 sales per day (30 percent walks). Let's say three of those 13 walks daily just simply give up on the store and never return.

Figuring conservatively that each regular customer will buy an average of three pairs a year from the store, those three permanently lost customers daily amount to 921 a year—a permanent dollar loss of around $96,000 a year. So it's true, every customer *is* worth his or her weight in gold.

All right, enough arithmetic. You get the message. Walkouts are poison to sales, profits and growth.

Now, what can be done to cut those losses and automatically increase sales and profits? The first obvious step: Learn the specific reasons why the walks are happening in your store. Here is a list of causes, based on shoe store studies, of walkouts, listed in order of frequency or importance:

1) Missing size in wanted shoe.
2) Absence of wanted styles (or limited style selection).
3) Price.
4) Fussy customer (or "just looking").
5) Service negligence (waiting, etc.)

6) Salesperson's lack of stock knowledge.
7) Insufficient merchandise shown.
8) Salesperson's discourtesy.
9) Incompetent selling.
10) Wanting to buy but not enough money.
11) Other (hard-to-fit foot, etc.)

Now analyze them. Three of them (Nos. 1, 2, 3) are store shortcomings. Five of them (Nos. 5, 6, 7, 8, 9) are salespersons' faults. And three of them (Nos. 4, 10, 11) are nobody's fault. You can't do much about the latter. But in the case of the store and salespersons shortcomings—representing about 85 percent of all walks—you *can* do something to remedy the faults and reduce the walks.

Now, even the best and most efficient stores inevitably miss some sales. Nobody wins them all. So the target isn't perfection but improvement.

What can improvement do? Some more quick arithmetic, again using our $350,000 store as a model. By reducing walks from 30 to 20 percent, the walks are cut from 3,990 to 2,660, a gain of 1,330 in sales. At $35 per, sales rise from $46,550 for a total of $396,550. The dollar net rises from $24,500 to $38,470, up 57 percent. And the percentage of net profit increases from 7 percent to 9.7 percent, up 38.6 percent.

If the walks are cut to 10 percent, sales or transactions increase by 2,660. At $35 per, that's a gain of $93,100 in volume. Dollar profit rises to $51,470, up 26.6 percent. And percentage of net profit rises to 11.6 percent, a gain of 65.7 percent over the original net of 7 percent.

But actually your *percentage* of net profit increases appreciably more because of higher sales productivity, lower selling costs, fewer markdowns, lessened overhead, more sales per square foot, etc. The earlier 7 percent net thus can rise to 8 percent or 10 percent or more.

Now, back to the causes of the walkouts. Your first vital steps are (1) to determine what *your* walkout rate is (most stores don't know) by keeping a systematic count or check, and (2) to keep a record of the *cause* for every walkout. Only by knowing the causes can you devise a cure.

Let's cite some of the remedies you can apply for improvement. Start with store or management shortcomings. For example, missing sizes. If you frequently miss them, it clearly indicates a lax size-up discipline, or faulty size buying in accord with your customers' wants. Both obviously need closer attention, and both are curable.

If you have many walks because of missing styles, it indicates your style buys aren't properly turned in to your customers' wants or tastes. You'd better review your buying program and resources—plus a careful reevaluation of who your customers are and their style tastes or wants.

The same applies to prices. If they're accounting for above-average walks, take a hard look at your price brackets as they relate to your local market. Maybe a couple of lower-priced lines are needed.

Next, give a closer examination to your salespeople's performance—in specifics. For example, lack of stock knowledge results in many lost sales that could have been made, whether on regular merchandise or PMs. You can do something about that via more disciplined policies or training. Or possibly by making some changes in the stock room for easier access.

Walkout causes like service negligence, discourtesy, incompetent selling, and insufficient merchandise shown, are open to obvious improvements. This is clearly a store management responsibility. If such causes are common in your store, then certainly your need to set an in-store sales training program in motion. This means not only demonstrating the how-to but establishing clearer and firmer selling and conduct policies.

Sometimes simple "policies" do a lot to cut walks. For example, if the customer wants the shoes but doesn't have enough to pay, suggest a deposit to hold the shoes. Nothing new about that. Yet, many stores fail to do it.

The "customer turnover" practice is also effective, especially if handled tactfully. That is, if one salesperson isn't making progress with the customer, the salesperson calls in an "expert" on that type of footwear. The sale then lifts out of a rut and gets off to a fresh start. The turnover, however, requires tact so the customer doesn't feel he or she is being abandoned, but rather is being offered a more expert service.

Thus, reducing your costly walkout rate boils down to this:

1) First determine what your walkout rate is. Keep a record.

2) Find out the chief or most frequent causes of your walkouts. Keep a record.

3) Set up a strategy or policy for remedying each of these common causes.

Stores that have used this approach have succeeded in cutting their walks by half or more. The result becomes a rich load of new-found business.

Simple Record System For Tracking Walkouts In Your Store

Week of September 14

Reason For Walk	9/14	9/15	9/16	9/17	9/18	9/19	Week
Out of size	✓✓	✓✓✓	✓✓	✓✓	✓✓✓	✓✓	14
Wanted style missing	✓	✓		✓✓	✓✓✓	✓✓✓✓	11
Price	✓		✓			✓	3
Fussy or "looking"		✓				✓	2
Service negligence			✓		✓		2
Lax stock knowledge			✓	✓✓			3
Not enough shown	✓		✓		✓		3
Discourtesy		✓				✓	2
Incompetent selling			✓			✓	2
Not enough money		✓			✓		2
Other (specify)							
Total walks	5	7	7	6	9	10	44
Total sales	18	21	27	25	30	32	153

Example: Walkouts In Shoe Store With $350,000 Volume

	With 30% Walkouts (average store)	With 20% Walkouts (save 1 out of 3)	With 10% Walkouts (save 2 out of 3)
Number of customers shopping	14,285	14,285	14,285
Number of walkouts	4,285 (30%)	2,857 (20%)	1,429 (10%)
Number buying	10,000	11,428	12,856
Average sale	$35.00	$35.00	$35.00
Total sales	$350,000	$396,550	$443,100
Merchandise cost (55%)	$192,500	$218,100	$243,700
Operating expense (38%)	$133,000	$133,000	$133,000
Expense for extra sales*		$ 6,980*	$ 13,965*
Total expense	$133,000	$139,980	$146,965
Net profit ($)	$ 24,500	$ 38,470	$ 51,470
Net profit (%)	7.0%	9.7%	11.6%

* Allow 15% for extra expense for selling the "saved" walkouts.

WHAT IT COSTS TO LOSE JUST ONE CUSTOMER A DAY

1) One customer permanently lost per day amounts to 304 lost per year.
2) Figured at an average $35 sale per customer—the loss per year is $10,640.
3) Figuring the average regular customer buys three pairs a year from the store—hence a total annual loss of $95,760.
4) If the store's annual volume is $350,000, the lost customers amount to a sales loss equal to 27 percent ($95,760) of the store's volume.
5) If the store's net profit is 7 percent ($24,500)—then the profit from the lost sales ($95,760) amounts to $6,703, which is equal to 27 percent of the store's net profit.

All of this loss because of only one permanently lost customer per day, for whatever the reasons: missing size in the wanted style, discourteous or poor service, etc. The numbers boggle the mind—and they should.

THOSE SALES YOU DON'T MAKE

Baseball games are won on the basis of the number of runs scored. They're usually lost by the number of men left on base—the runs that *could* have scored and won the game, but didn't.

The performance of a business should be scored in the same way, by the number of men left on base—more precisely, the potential sales that *could* have been made but weren't. That's a serious oversight by many retailers. They count up their made sales but rarely count those that were missed but could or should have been made. That's lopsided arithmetic. The retailer sees only the actual and closes his eyes to the potential.

The missed sales referred to here aren't the walkouts due to missing sizes or styles or other reasons. Even more sales are missed because of failure to follow up on the made sales with *additional* sales to the same customer. So the question isn't whether the customer bought, but did he or she buy all they were willing to buy if more effective followup selling had been used?

Retailers constantly speak of their open-to-buy position. But they seldom speak or think of the *customer's* open-to-buy position. According to the National Retail Merchants Association, the average store could sell at least 30 percent more if it focused as much on followup sales as it does on the first purchase.

Many stores and especially salespeople have what's called a "spending block"— a mental block about customer spending. They *think* if the customer has bought the pair of shoes asked for, the selling mission is completed. They *think* the customer has limited funds to spend. They *think* selling the customer more than what he or she came in to buy is over-selling or pushy selling. They *think* all customers are one-pair buyers. They *think* the bird (actual sale) in the hand is worth two (additional merchandise) in the bush. So they mental-block themselves out of thousands of dollars in potential additional sales to all those open-to-buy customers.

So never be satisfied with the sales you make. Keep asking yourself, "How many sales *didn't* I make that could or should have been made? How many open-to-buy customers slipped through our fingers for lack of trying?" Then add 30 percent onto your store volume and you'll be close to the answer. If that doesn't stimulate your juices, you're in the wrong business.

45

Taking the "Ice" Out of Price

Always be prepared to answer price
objections; never belittle a serious
price objection; relate price to
customer benefits; never apologize
for a price.

There is always free cheese in the
mousetrap.

There is no business that doesn't occasionally meet with price resistance. A perennial problem in stores is how to overcome these objections to price which frequently results in lost sales.

In some shoe stores the attitude or policy is to shrug off these walkouts with comments such as "you can't win them all," or "these just aren't our kind of customers, so we suggest they try another store with cheaper merchandise and lower prices."

But other stores are smarter. They use a different attitude and strategies to win these customers over to the store's price. They not only succeed in eliminating the price resistance and making the sale, but they also win themselves new customers who become regulars.

The first step in the strategy is to view price objections from the *customer's* viewpoint instead of the store's. The store considers its price fair and therefore assumes that the customer's price objection is unfair and unjustified. These are the stores that gripe about such customers as "habitual price hagglers" or who take an adamant stand, "That's our price, take it or leave it."

The first intelligent step in meeting price objections is to ask the customer, "Why do you think the price is too high?" First, it shows you're willing to listen. Second, it automatically opens the door to tactfully overcoming the *reason* for the price objection. If the customer says, "I don't want to pay that much for a pair of shoes"—that's a quite different reason than if the customer says, "I don't think the shoes are worth that much," or, "I can buy the same shoes elsewhere for less."

In the first case you can try switching the customer to a similar style in another, lower-priced shoe. But if you try to convince that same customer that the higher priced shoe is worth the price, you've hit a stone wall. So, knowing *why* the customer is objecting to the price is the first important step in resolving the price problem. It indicates which strategy to use for overcoming *that* customer's reason for the price resistance. So don't assume the reason. Ask for the reason.

Every person who doesn't buy has two reasons for not buying: one that sounds good, and the *real* reason. Some customers use "the price is too high" as a reason because it sounds good and logical. But beneath the surface may lie the real reason. Among the most common:

1) The customer can't afford the price; or can afford it but doesn't have enough money in hand.
2) The customer really wants something else and is using "the price is too high" as an excuse to leave. For example, the customer may be dissatisfied with the selection available, or may dislike the service or the salesperson.
3) The customer believes that the product's value doesn't match the price asked.
4) The customer wants the shoe but is trying to push the price down to what he or she can or wants to pay.
5) Using price objection as a stall or feeler while trying to get more information or reasons from the salesperson to help in the buying decision. This is a common tactic with indecisive customers.
6) The natural price haggler in regard to almost anything he or she buys (a common and acceptable attitude found among many cultures throughout the world).

OVERCOMING RESISTANCE

There are several basic rules for overcoming price objections.

Never Argue. It's the old axiom of winning the battle but losing the war. For example: "Madam, it's clear you don't understand a good value." or, "Sir, you're mistaken if you think you can buy this shoe cheaper somewhere else." Such replies are insulting and sure sales-killers. Always keep in mind the rule of viewing a price objection from the customer's standpoint, and also learning why the customer thinks the price is too high.

Never Challenge the Customer. Example: "If you think you can buy it for less somewhere else, go right ahead." The customer is likely to do just that. You've lost the sale *and* the customer.

Never Belittle a Price Objection. It's disrespectful and an injury to the customer's self-esteem. Example: "How can you expect to get the shoe you want for the price you want to pay?" Or, "It's clear you don't understand quality when you see it." Again both the sale and customer are lost.

Never Apologize for a Price. Instead, for instance, say something like, "The price is very fair for the quality and value of this shoe. But let me show you something else you'll like, and more in line with the price you have in mind."

Never be Evasive. Evasion or excuse-making is a signal to the customer that the shoe may actually be over-priced. For example, saying to the customer, "Well, everything, you know, is higher priced today." That's evasion. It does nothing to justify the value received for the price asked.

Never Lose your Cool. Some retailers or salespeople quickly lose their composure when confronted by a price objection, especially by a tactless customer who blurts, "The shoe isn't worth the price." The salesperson, feeling that the store, the shoe and the salesperson have been insulted, will snap back with a snide or sarcastic remark. The two personalities, customer and salesperson, are now in collision. The sale is headed for limbo, and so is the customer.

It's rare that you can spot a price-resister at the beginning of the sale. But what you *can* do at the beginning is to prevent any potential price objections from surfacing during the course of the sale. This is done by building customer desire and appreciation for the shoe. When customer desire or want is strong enough, the importance of price rapidly fades.

During the selection and try-on process, highlight the shoe's key features. Depending upon the type of shoe, these features may relate to comfort, quality, wear performance, fit, easy maintenance, design or construction, esthetics or fashion, etc. This creates value appreciation. The customer now isn't buying just a shoe but a shoe of special quality and appeal.

There's a saying, "No shoe is over-priced unless it's under-desired." If the customer dislikes the shoe, he or she probably wouldn't take it free. But if the desire for the shoe is strong enough, then almost any reasonable price is a price the customer willingly pays. Therefore it's up to the salesperson to create this desire.

Never talk price at the beginning of a sale. At this point the customer hasn't had time or hasn't received enough information to evaluate the worth of the shoe. Spend those first few minutes building value appreciation (see "What's In A Shoe and How to Sell It" on page 236). Don't talk in generalities or use innocuous phrases like "It's a beautiful shoe," or "It looks nice on your foot," or "This shoe will give you a lot of wear," or "It's the latest fashion."

Deal in specifics. Within a couple of minutes you can put together an impressive package of features, each dealing with some particular selling point: fit, comfort, quality, fashion, wear performance, etc. That package quickly develops into a value story that upgrades the shoe, increases the customer's desire for the shoe, and helps lead to a buying decision without serious thought about price.

Sell Customer Benefits. While you're citing the shoe's features, translate each into customer benefits to build customer desire. For example, to say the leather is fine calfskin isn't enough. But if you follow up by saying, "Calfskin is the finest of all leathers. It molds beautifully to your foot because it's soft and supple, and it also keeps a polished, new-looking surface"—*then* the fine calfskin becomes something more than just another leather because you've cited what it will do for the fit, feel and look of the shoe.

If you're speaking of the shoe's style or look, then "it's a very pretty shoe" falls flat. But if you cite "the new subtle taper of the toe" and "the unusual low-cut sides of this D'Orsay pump" and "the elegant look of this sculptured heel"— these give the shoe distinctive fashion character and add to desirability. Because the shoe's specific fashion features, as you've pointed them out, will enhance the look of the foot, they become customer benefits.

Pride and status are two other benefits that customers respond to. Surveys show that a strong customer motive for buying new apparel and footwear is to enhance personal appearance that draws flattering response or admiration from friends and others. "Where did you buy those beautiful shoes?" or, "You have such excellent taste in shoes, like that unusual pair you're wearing."

Comments like that generate pride and status. Catering to these important buying motives is part of good salesmanship because they convert into customer benefits. Saying to the customer, for instance, "You'll receive a lot of nice compliments about this shoe from your friends;" or, "This X Brand is a shoe you can wear with pride." Such comments are not only reassurance of the customer's good taste and buying decision, but they also help to defuse any thought of price objections.

COUNTERPOINTS

The customer says, "I can buy the same shoe at another store for less money." Sometimes the customer may even name the store.

Don't argue. *Agree* with the customer, but with a quick followup. Examples:

"That's possible. But it's very likely they're offering out-dated shoes at lower prices because they have only a few broken sizes in stock. So you'd be taking the risk of not getting the right size or good fit. Is that worth the lower price?"

Or, "Yes, their prices may be lower but they give you no professional fitting service. If you get a faulty fit then the shoe isn't a bargain at all but a waste of your own money."

Or, "The price may be lower, but you don't get anywhere near the same full style selection."

Or, "We've been in business 15 years. We've stayed in business that long because we've given our customers excellent value, good service and fair prices— which is why they keep coming back."

You're basing these counterpoints on truths. In most instances where shoes are sold at below regular prices there are reasons for it: absence of fitting and other services; out-dated or cancellation or closeout merchandise; broken lots or missing sizes; aged merchandise; limited style selection; markdown sales to clear out unwanted merchandise. So in making your counterpoints you're not knocking or criticizing the competition but simply stating the facts of business. Most of all, you're diminishing or eliminating the customer's I-can-buy-it-cheaper-elsewhere argument.

Again, say a pair of men's shoes is priced at $60 and the customer objects that the price is too high. An effective reply: "If you use these shoes for six months the cost will be only 33 cents a day. And if you wear them a year they'll cost only 16 cents a day. For all the service, comfort and style this quality shoe will give you—would you call 33 or 16 cents a day a high price to pay?"

This strategy works very effectively. That's why we see so many ads for products or services that use this same idea of only a few cents a day cost. It's not a gimmick but factual arithmetic. When brought to the customer's attention in this manner, it takes the "ice" out of price.

A variation of this principle works with children's shoes where price objections tend to be more common. For centuries many parents have bemoaned the price when buying children's shoes: "Children's shoes are so expensive these days." Now, unknown to parents, the average active child will cover about 700 miles (an average of eight miles a day) of highly abusive shoe wear over a three-month period. Say your shoe's price is $30. Your reply to the price-resistant customer:

"Your active child will cover about 700 miles of shoe wear over only a three-month period. That makes the cost of the shoe hardly more than four cents a day. Considering all the protection and wear this shoe will give for healthy foot growth—certainly four cents a day can hardly be called expensive." That places the shoe's price and value in fresh perspective for the customer. The shoe is no longer high-priced but reasonably priced. You've translated price into customer benefits.

Let's try another, again with a man customer (though it can also be applied to women customers). The customer says the price should be lower. Your reply, "Yes, we could lower the price simply by lowering the quality. But the same thing could apply to your job. It probably could be filled by a lower salaried person. But the job wouldn't get done as well. The same with a shoe. The difference is in quality of performance."

That strikes home because it touches the customer's ego and sense of self-worth. He now fully appreciates the comparison you've made and has no choice but to agree with you.

Often the customer very much wants the shoe but doesn't have enough money to pay for it, or doesn't have a credit card. The solution is usually simple and practical. Ask the customer to place a deposit (for a pre-specified period), then come in to pick up the shoes when the money is available. While this may be an obvious solution, the customer usually doesn't think of it, or may be too embarrassed to ask. Your suggestion of a deposit quickly resolves the problem.

There is always the temptation to cut the price to meet the customer's objections and make the sale. While this may be acceptable on rare occasions, it is dangerous and counter-productive if allowed to happen frequently. Even if you cut the price the customer isn't always satisfied. The customer asks himself, "Could I have haggled more and gotten an even lower price? Have other customers done better than I? Are all the prices in this store started too high in the first place to allow for "bargaining room?" So you really haven't satisfied the customer even at his price. Further, it doesn't take long for word to get around that the customer can "deal" when buying at your store—that your prices are open to negotiation. Such a reputation can threaten your survival.

Shoe retailers constantly claim that, among all commodities, shoes are a "best buy" for a variety of justifiable reasons. But if you frequently buckle under to your customers' price resistance, then your convictions are more shadow than substance. Or as one wise philosopher said, "It's much easier to fight for your convictions than to live up to them."

One of the store's best weapons against price objections is to be prepared. This begins with a store policy. It's followed by training and meetings of sales personnel on techniques not only for meeting price objections, but making the sale and keeping the customer's business. To allow the salespeople to "play it by ear" can be damaging to sales and store reputation. Few stores, unfortunately, prepare their salespeople to handle these situations effectively.

An important law to remember: All prices are relative. They're relative to what the customer *thinks* is a right price, and to what the customer is willing to pay. If you have surrounded the shoe with a convincing value and benefits story, and have created enough customer desire for the shoe, the almost invariable result is elimination of price objections.

Some shoe retailers become paranoid about prices. That's usually because they've lost sight of or ignored the value story they have to tell. It's also because they often underestimate what their customers *really* want—the value justified, the benefits made attractive, and the desire made strong for the shoe. That is a powerful combination to disperse price objections. These self-doubting or vacillating retailers should ask themselves: "If price is so important, how come the low-priced stores don't get all or most of the business? How come that customers don't usually buy the cheapest available?"

There's a difference between price and value. Price is what you pay. Value is what you get for what you pay. The final decision on value belongs to the customer, not the store. But it's in the store's power, via the techniques used by the salespeople, to strongly influence the customer's appraisal of value and the customer's degree of desire.

When is the price right? When the customer thinks it is. The hula hoop in its heyday sold for $2 because it was in such demand. Two years later it was selling for 10 cents—and still at a profit. The same can be said of Cabbage Patch dolls, pet rocks or any other product. Market demand determines price and price acceptance.

The function of the merchant is not to supply demand but to *create* demand. That is the very essence of all selling—creating desire and value that in turn creates demand. That principle is also the prime and effective weapon for taking the "ice" out of price.

CUSTOMER PAYS FULL PRICE, THEN DEMANDS SALE PRICE

Occasionally it happens. The customer buys a pair of shoes in your store and pays full price. Three days later he or she sees the same shoe advertised by you at a markdown of 30 percent.

The customer comes in angry and demands a 30 percent refund or credit on the purchase. The customer argues that the salesperson or store should have told him or her that the same shoes would be available three days later at 30 percent less. The customer claims the store violated a moral obligation.

What to do? It becomes a sticky problem. To refuse satisfaction is to alienate the customer. The issue: Does or doesn't the store have a moral obligation to notify customers paying full price that the shoes will be sold a few days later at a markdown price? And does the customer have rightful claim to a refund or credit equal to the amount of markdown?

There is no easy answer. It's only the rare store that has a policy on this. Most stores simply play it by ear.

Some stores will make the refund of the markdown price difference. Some will set a fixed time limit, say three to ten days "eligibility" for a refund from the date of full-price purchase to the sale-price date. Others will offer a pro-rated discount. For example, refund or credit for full markdown difference if the original full price was paid three or fewer days before the sale; or half the markdown difference if the full price was paid four to seven days before. Still others are flexible, depending how indigant the customer, or how good a customer.

Some stores prevent it happening at all by a mail notice in advance to all their regular customers that a sale will take place on a given date.

SHOES BY THE INCH

In Colonial America, shoes were priced by the inch. The larger the foot the higher the price. This also applied to other articles of clothing.

The price-by-size method, of course, made sense. Larger sizes required more materials and more labor.

In fact, the shoe industry still uses the system today in juvenile footwear. A shoe of the same style and make costs less in children's, more in youth's, most in boys'. Price increases correspond with size increases.

Logically, the same principle should apply to adult shoes and apparel—coats, shirts, dresses, suits, etc. But this would result in a complex pricing system. So instead, prices are averaged out.

But from the standpoint of costs in the averaging-out system, the big-foot persons is still buying his or her shoes at the expense of the small-foot person. Maybe in a future computer-run world somebody will find a more equitable answer to the size-price matter.

PRICE

It's unwise to pay too much, but it's worse to pay too little.

When you pay too much, you lose a little money, that is all.

When you pay too little, you sometimes lose everything because the thing you bought was incapable of doing the thing it was expected to do.

The common law of business balance prohibits paying a little and getting a lot; it can't be done.

If you deal with the lowest bidder, it is well to add something for the risk you run.

And if you do that, you will have enough to pay for something better.

John Ruskin

46

Moving PMs Faster, More Profitably

Initiative is doing the right thing
without being told.

What you don't do is often more
important than what you do do.

PMs are a perennial problem for retailers. They're costly shelf-robbers that steal from profits. But they're unavoidable and you have to live with them. However, while they are pests they don't have to be a plague.

A PM can stand for any of several things: Premium Merchandise, Poor Merchandise, Post Mortems. In slang they are known as spiffs. But if you take the more positive view, PMs can also stand for Profit-Makers or Potential Moneymakers.

PMs should not be confused with markdowns. The latter can be sold off in a special clearance or closeout sale. But unlike a clearance sale, PMs don't create traffic. Instead, they have to be plucked from shelves and sold one by one.

The causes of PMs are well known: broken size lots; and sizes (small/large, wide/narrow); remnants of closeout colors and styles; the consequence of an overbuy or a poor buy; delayed clearances; etc. No store is without them.

But some stores do better than others in fast getting rid of PMs, and even show a reasonable profit from them. How do they do it? They have a system, a policy or plan, for unloading PMs before they become distress merchandise.

SUGGESTED METHODS

PMs are like a bridge hand. It can be played any of several ways. The experienced pro plays the hand the smartest way, using a combination or series of moves. Let's look at some of these approaches.

The first thing is timing. When does or should a shoe become a PM? Have a disciplined policy on this. A prospective PM will send out early warning signals based on pace of sales. Many retailers stall on this, hoping the shoe will show signs of life. It usually doesn't, then it gets costlier to unload. Slow-moving shoes tend to get neglected by salespeople, which further slows the movement of these shoes.

Stock should be checked at least every couple of weeks to spot the duds and slow-movers. If a fashion shoe is dragging after 30-45 days, put a PM on it even if it's in mid-season. Don't follow the habit of many retailers and wait until the season is over. Then the shoe becomes clearance merchandise at 50 percent off. If PM'd in mid-season it can often be sold at only 15 to 20 percent off. On a $40 shoe, the difference in pocket is $12–$14. Delay on assigning PMs is a costly sin.

There's also the opposite side of the coin—PMing shoes too soon. Like children, a few shoes are slow starters, then suddenly catch up. Timing is a judgment call. Between too late and too soon is just right. The important thing to recognize right timing in the first place.

All PM boxes should be clearly coded or tagged via a color marker to visually stand out from the full-price merchandise. The coding can be a bright sticker label that reads, "Thank you—Jones Shoe Store"—in case the customer takes the purchased shoes home in the box. Or a gummed label can be used, peeled off the box when the shoe is sold.

PMs in the stockroom should be very visible to the salespeople. This means bright lighting (why are so many stockrooms so dimly lighted?). Second, the question: should PMs be separated in a special PM section, or intermixed with the regular or full-price merchandise?

Experience shows that the most effective way is to mix the PMs with the regular merchandise, but on the condition that the PMs are clearly labeled and visible. This allows the PMs to be stocked by proper classification. For instance, if the customer asks for a navy blue pump in a medium heel, the PM pump may be a slightly lighter blue and slightly higher heel. But it's close enough to be brought out as an alternate choice in the customer's size. But if the shoe was assigned to a special PM section, it could be forgotten or overlooked by the salespeople.

SALESPEOPLE ARE KEY

Salespeople, of course, are the price movers of PMs. But only if management is the prime mover of the salespeople. And this is where the hole in the dike is often found—the failure of management to establish a policy and system to indoctrinate the movement of PMs as a *habit*.

Older salespeople usually do better with PMs because they've acquired both the habit and experience. They can be used both as teachers and motivators for younger salespeople via the buddy system. Once the younger ones make PM selling a habit, they too do better.

Most salespeople have some pride in job performance. If they're made to see PMs as a challenge or test of their selling ability, which it is, most will respond.

Also important: give the salespeople the first chance at moving PMs before this merchandise goes into advertised clearance sales. Let them know you are doing this. This will be an incentive for them to move the PMs faster because it's money in their pockets, whereas the clearance sales aren't.

Incentives for salespeople are vital for moving PMs. That means commissions. How much commission? Enough to make it worthwhile and to motivate action. Usually the best way is a percentage of the PM selling price, in the 7 to 12 percent range, with an average of 10 percent. If the PM price is $30, then $3 is the commission and $27 the net selling price. This is fair enough considering that if the shoe reaches clearance sale point it sells for $20. So both the salesperson and the store benefit. The salesperson moving 10 PMs a week at $3 per pair adds a nice $30 to his or her paycheck.

Contests are another incentive. These should be in addition to commissions on PMs. A couple of examples. Use a bingo card for each salesperson, with each square punched out with each PM sale. The first salesperson to have all the squares punched out receives a prize or bonus.

Another is the small horse race board. With each PM sale the salesperson's horse is moved forward a notch. The salesperson whose horse is ahead at the end of the week gets a prize or bonus. There might also be a prize for the second-place winner.

Contest prizes or bonuses must be enough to make it worthwhile. A dinner for two, or a couple of theatre tickets, or a money prize. Contests are good motivators not only for the prizes, but because of the pride of winning and recognition by peers and management alike as a top performer.

PMs don't get sold simply because they're shown or offered to customers. It's also a matter of technique, the how-to- of presentation. A PM should *never* be presented as a "bargain" because it's a castoff. It should be shown as fresh merchandise, a jewel. This upgrades its value without losing its appeal to the customer because of the special lower price.

Another caution on PMs. Sometimes an unscrupulous store manager will assign an easy-to-sell, still-alive shoe to a PM classification—then collect a portion of the PM commission on these good-moving shoes. It has been known to happen.

Salespeople aren't the only channel through which to move PMs. Hashing is another method. A special bin or counter or rack can contain a mix of PMs—hashed by sizes or styles or other groupings. These displays are well-lighted with signs like "Big and Small Sizes: 30% Off" (the same can be done with narrows and wides). This appeals to customers with outsizes, plus the extra appeal of the special price. The same hashing can be done with PMs in color or style or heel height groupings.

PMs can also move well through mailing lists. If your customer card records show customer sizes (which they should), then you can pinpoint your mailings to the customers on a size matchup basis. If your cards show 10 customers who wear 10AAA, and if you have 15 PMs in that size, then a personal postcard (or standard letter form) with a one-line description of the shoes, plus the attractive PM price, can sometimes bring in 25 to 30 percent of those customers. Salespeople can do this in their lull time. The cost is minimal, the response usually very good.

Summed up, PMs are a headache but they don't have to be a chronic disease. If you have a policy and a system for moving PMs, you'll move 50 percent more of them—and faster and more profitably than stores that have no PM policy or system.

47

Nineteen Ways to Build More Multiple-Pair Sales

Confucius says, "Salesperson who cover chair instead of opportunities, end up on bottom."

Ability without enthusiasm and you have a rifle without a bullet.

A few years ago a survey was taken among several hundred shoe retailers regarding multiple-pair selling. It was found that 52 percent had no store policy or program for this. And of the 48 percent who had a policy, over half admitted that it was more a policy "on paper" than really functional.

The survey further revealed that 60 percent of the retailers said that less than 10 percent of their sales involved multiple pairs, and only 14 percent averaged over 20 percent.

What comprises a good performance in multiple-pair sales? Here are national averages based on shoe store performance records:

Rating	Women's Footwear	Men's Footwear
Poor	Under 10%	Under 7%
Good	20%	15%
Excellent	30% or more	20% or more

Thus, according to survey findings, about 80 percent of shoe stores or departments fall below the "norm"—that is, realistic potential—in multiple-pair sales.

Several years ago the Gallup organization conducted a national study of consumer shoe buying habits for American Footwear Industries. The report, "Consumer Research on Footwear," revealed a surprising finding: 32 percent of consumers make multiple-pair purchases, and these amount to 54 percent of all footwear purchased.

The message is clear. There's a lot more multiple-pair business available than many retailers realize. The truth is that most customers are *under*-sold. In reality, most shoes are *bought,* and only a minority are *sold.* When the store simply provides what the customer asks for, that's merely servicing the customer. When the sale involves more than the customer asked for, *that's* selling.

Multiple-pair selling does more than increase volume. It reduces selling costs via higher productivity.

It's estimated that today it costs a shoe store about $12 to bring in one new customer via the cost of advertising, promotions, windows, direct mail, etc. Thus each 100 new customers costs the store $1,200. But if 60 regular customers result in multiple-pair sales it would be the equivalent of "finding" 100 new customers.

BUILDING THE PROGRAM

Well, how do you build a more productive multiple-pair sales program? First, there must be a clear *store policy,* plus targets. And it must be a firmly enforced policy and not merely a "paper" plan. Example: a firm store rule that a follow-up or multiple-pair effort must be made with *every* customer, *every* sale.

Second, there must be a *how-to-program* to achieve more multiple-pair sales. This begins with several in-store meetings or training sessions (an hour weekly) to show salespeople the techniques of multiple-pair selling. And, of course, incentives must be provided, such as extra commissions, bonuses for surpassing multiple-pair quotas, etc.

All right, let's get to the specific how-tos. Here are 19 ideas or ways to build multiple-pair sales:

1) Regard every customer as a prospect for additional purchases. Studies show the average customer is willing to buy 25 to 35 percent more—if buying interest is stimulated.

2) Makes salespeople realize that follow-up selling is a customer service and is not pushing unwanted merchandise onto customers. Customers appreciate being shown and asked.

3) Never sell the second pair as an "extra" pair. Extra suggests something unneeded, wasteful. Instead, sell it as a customer want or benefit. Give the merchandise a reason for being and you give the customer a reason for buying.

4) Run occasional in-store training sessions to show and demonstrate to the salespeople the successful techniques of multiple-pair selling.

5) Never ask customers if they'd like to see "something else." That's asking for a "no." Without asking, show and suggest. Seeing is believing. Ninety percent of purchases are made with the eye.

6) For suggested follow-up purchases, show something opposite to the first pair. If the first purchase is a dress shoe, show and suggest boots, casuals, slippers, etc.

7) Suggest a customer benefit for the follow-up pair—the suggested second pair is a just-in new style not yet advertised; or a specially priced closeout, luckily in the customer's size.

8) While showing and suggesting, get the second pair onto the customer's foot. Now it's *her* shoe, in *her* size, something she can see and admire in a personal sense. A shoe on the foot is worth two in the hand.

9) Listen for clues while selling the first pair. The customer may mention a pleasure cruise she's taking. That suggests colorful casuals or an evening sandal. Mention of a camping trip suggest moccasins. And so on.

10) Think a season ahead. If it's early spring and you've sold a pair of spring dress shoes, follow up by showing a pair of whites or summer sandals. Customers like the idea of being a step in advance—and also saving another shopping trip.

11) If the customer has come in in January or July to buy a clearance shoe, follow up by showing several new styles for forthcoming spring or fall. Present them as "advance fashion." Or, in reverse, if a new style is purchased, suggest a clearance or PM item as special-price purchase.

12) In most cases, wait to complete the first sale before starting the second. Avoid confusing the customer.

13) If the customer likes and wants the second pair but doesn't have enough money to pay for them, suggest a deposit to hold the shoes.

14) Upgrade the sale. If you've shown a $25 shoe but the customer is leaning toward the $40 pair, concentrate on the latter. It's like selling a second pair for $15.

15) Know the stock intimately. This enables you to mentally pinpoint just the right style or size or PM for a particular customer—and enhances the chance of the second-pair sale.

16) Have a good assortment or selection of merchandise. This is vital to provide the right offerings to make follow-up sales.

17) Never show just one pair of what the customer asks for. Bring out three pairs related to the requested style—plus two quite different styles. Concentrate on the first three, but allow the customer to keep eyeing the other two.

18) Sell the second pair on the basis of alternate wear, especially to men. The same shoes shouldn't be worn every day. For added shoe life and better foot and shoe hygiene, shoes need at least a day's rest. This creates a logical "reason for being" for the follow-up pair.

19) Give your merchandise lots on exposure via attractive interior displays. Impulse buying stems from seeing and contributes to second-pair sales.

Lastly, keep records. How many actual sale transactions were made last year? How many were multiple-pair sales? How many involved two pairs? Three or more pairs? You can't judge your performance without records. Also, keep separate records for men's and women's multiple-pair sales. You can't run a business successfully on an "educated guess" basis. Further, without records you can't determine whether your multiple-pair sales performance is improving or declining.

But back to the root issue. There's a lot more multiple-pair business out there than you may realize. The fact that some stores average 20 percent in multiple-pair sales while others average only 7 percent, clearly indicates that the only difference is a matter of having a policy and a program, plus making the effort.

PESSIMIST AND OPTIMIST

Two frogs fell into a deep bowl of cream. One was a pessimist and soon drowned. The other, an optimist, kept swimming around and around, for no reason he could logically explain. It was just his nature. But in the morning he found himself high and dry on a large pat of butter.

The Product

48

What's in a Shoe—and How to Sell It

Last year a million quarter-inch drills
were sold—not because people
wanted the drills but because they
wanted quarter-inch holes. People
don't buy things. They buy the
benefits of things.

Over the life span of the average American, he or she will buy between 300 and 450 pairs of footwear. They'll visit shoe stores or departments even more times for those purchases. With each visit they'll hear pretty much the same tired words and phrases from the salespeople: "It's a nice shoe" . . . "It looks very nice on your foot" . . . "It's a fine value" . . . "It seems to fit very well" . . . "It's one of our best-selling styles" . . . "It will give you a lot of comfort."

After a while the customers have heard it all, the same trite phrases repeated time after time. Soon many of the customers simply tune out to what the salespeople are saying. As a consequence, it's estimated that 80 percent of all footwear is

"These are ideal for you. They've got novocaine insoles, for women who wear shoes several sizes too small."

bought and only 20 percent sold. In short, the customers get to believe that they know as much about shoes as the salespeople (and usually they do). So what it boils down to is that the customer really knows little about the product he or she is buying, and the salesperson often knows little about the product he or she is selling.

The bottom line is this. There's a lot more to a shoe than what the eye sees. A shoe is made up of a lot of parts and features, each of which contributes to either the look or the performance and value of the shoe. Each of these parts translates into a *customer benefit*. And right there is the key to it all: knowing what's in a shoe and how to translate them into customer benefits. When that's done you then have the very foundation of effective professional selling. You then have customers who will be hearing *fresh* words and ideas that give them—often for the first time—an understanding and appreciation of what they're buying and the benefits and satisfactions they can expect from their purchase. The term "value received" takes on new meaning.

On-the-floor selling of footwear usually focuses on three things: look, fit and price. Most stores and salespeople assume that if these three things are delivered to the customer's satisfaction, that's all the customer expects and wants and hence the service obligation has been fulfilled. Wrong. The only reason the "selling" stops there is because the store and salespeople usually have little more to add. This is why the large majority of the public knows so little about footwear, or why so many myths and misconceptions about footwear have developed in the minds of consumers over the many years.

As a result, shoe retailers bemoan that consumers "don't appreciate the full value they get in a pair of shoes." And it's true. It's also true that the fault lies not with the consumers but with the stores and salespeople who fail to use "informational selling."

The remedy is obvious. The more you know about the product, the more you know how to show, tell and sell, and the more appreciation the customer has for what is being purchased. The objective is simple and clear: the more you know, the better you sell. So let's take an inside look at a shoe and view its selling points part by part.

POINTS TO FEATURE

The Shoe's Crafting. When selling to a woman use terms like "finely crafted" or "quality detailing." When selling to a man use terms like "shoe engineering" or "construction." Men and women respond differently to terms related to how a shoe is structured. In either case *don't* get overly technical.

You might mention that it takes about 130 separate operations to make the shoe, plus about 25 different parts or components to put the shoe together. Then cite what this precise and skilled crafting means in terms of customer benefits: a shoe that holds its shape well with wear, that delivers good performance and wear satisfaction. Mention that this is what assures the shoe of its built-in quality. It's like buying a car. You buy it for its style and color and brand reputation. But you also want assurance of its safety, its operating economy and good performance.

That's where "construction" comes in. A few words about it, along with pointing out a detail or two, gives the customer assurance of a sound product.

Upper Materials. Don't generalize. Be specific. Mention the *kind* of leather or other material. Speak of *texture* (soft, mellow, supple, firm). Have the customer touch the material, which brings your words to life. Refer to the *surface finish* (matte, aniline, pearl, napped, burnished, metallic, etc.). Mention the *grain* (pebbled, boarded, smooth, crushed), and have the customer touch the surface. Speak of the shoe's *breathability* that keeps the foot cool, dry, fresh feeling, comfortable. Speak of *conformability*—the material's ability to adapt easily to the shape and movements of the foot like the skin on the hand. Mention *easy maintenance,* such as easy wipe with a damp cloth (man-made materials), or a fine shine with polish (leathers). If the shoe's upper materials are in color, speak of the *color fastness* of the dyes.

The upper materials are one of the most visible things about a shoe and a prime consideration in buying. When you mention a few highlights about the materials it gives the customer a greater appreciation beyond what the customer can see. The shoe takes on added esthetics and value.

The Sole. Don't leave this up to the customer's eye. There are several specific things you can highlight about the sole. Its *design,* such as on an athletic or work or casual shoe. Relate it to good *traction* for easier, more secure walking. The sole's *material.* Try to be specific here—leather, rubber, man-mades (urethane, vinyl), etc. Translate it into good wear, even tread; or in the case of a resilient sole material, speak of its underfoot cushioning for added comfort. Speak of the sole's *flexibility* and relate it to walking ease. And while citing these features, *show* them to the customer, or even have the customer touch the sole such as for its resilience or traction design or type of material.

The Heel. Depending upon the kind of heel, there are four specific things that can be pointed out: (1) the *design* (shape, style, height) of the heel as part of the shoe's fashion character. In this case use terms like "elegant" or "sculptured"; (2) the *materials.* A woman's heel is usually strong plastic, so relate it to strength and security. In the case of a stacked heel refer to "layers of leather." (3) The *covering.* Some heels are covered with a contrasting material such as a fabric, or with a contrasting color. These are there as fashion highlights; (4) the *toplift.* Here the customer's prime interest is in its durability to prevent the runover look or the need for frequent replacement. Today's toplifts are long-wearing. This should be cited for added assurance.

The Counter. Don't let this be taken for granted. A firm counter means two primary things: security for the foot's heel inside the shoe, and helping to keep the backpart shape of the shoe with wear. Don't assume that the customer knows this. Have the customer feel the firmness of the counter—then mention what the counter does for the shoe, the foot, the customer. It's part of the quality story.

Box Toe. This is rarely mentioned in shoe stores. A firm box toe (as most of them are) does two things: it keeps the shoe's toe shape intact for the life of the shoe, and it protects the toes. Have the customer feel the firm box toe, then cite this as another important detail in the shoe's fine crafting. Few customers have ever had this mentioned to them.

The Linings. These are in the shoe for four purposes: (1) to serve as a protective buffer zone between the foot and outside upper; (2) to help hold the shape of the shoe; (3) to absorb foot moisture and prevent staining through onto the outside upper; (4) to give the inside of the shoe a finished look.

Linings are used in different places. You can speak of the forepart (vamp) lining, the rearpart (quarter) lining, and underfoot (sock) lining. If the shoe is lined in all three places, mention it and also show it. Also cite *why* the linings are there—and translate these into customer benefits (protection, holding shoe shape, absorbing moisture, etc.)

Linings come in different materials: leather, fabrics, vinyl, etc. and also different colors and textures. Each of these contributes to the shoe's esthetics, and hence can be cited as an added fashion feature in the same way a fine lining of a suit or coat is an important styling and quality feature in a garment. If the shoe is fully leather lined, it's the mark of a top quality shoe. Some shoes have padded or quilted linings. These should be pointed out as an added comfort feature against the foot.

Stitching.   On many shoes this is used as a decorative feature on one or more parts of the upper. Highlight it as a special styling touch, and also as a mark of quality—in the same way as fine stitching is cited or sought as a quality mark on a garment. Don't let it pass unseen or unmentioned.

The Last.   This is an important part of the shoe's arsenal of selling features. In selling men's shoes you speak of the last, but in selling women's shoes you use the term "shape" which is more fashion-oriented. The last is the plastic mold over which the shoe is made and determines much about the shoe's size, fit, shape, look and wear performance.

The shoe's fit is influenced as much by its shape as by its size. Whereas fit is so important in the selling process, the role of the last should be given attention. Refer to the last as contoured to the foot's shape for good fit and wear comfort, and also helping the shoe hold its shape with wear. Lasts come in different style shapes. So depending upon the particular last (or shoe shape), use terms like slender, sculptured, contoured, molded, tailored, silhouette. In short, give the last a descriptive identity of its own that relates to the customer's foot.

Weight.   The shoe's weight depends upon the type of shoe being sold. If you're selling a fashion or dress or casual shoe, for instance, emphasize *lightness* of weight. Have the customer hold the shoe in the palm when you cite the shoe's light weight. If you're selling a men's work or outdoor boot, or a men's wingtip brogue, then *heft* is important because men associate it with sturdy support and rugged wear. And again, have the customer feel the shoe's heft in the hand while you're speaking of the shoe's solid structure and sturdy character.

Ornamentation.   These are important finishing style touches to the shoe—a buckle, bow, buttons, collar or trim, overlays, decorative ornaments, etc. Say something about it: "an unusual brass buckle" . . . "mother-of-pearl buttons" . . . "a grosgrain bow" . . . "a distinctive ornament." Speak of these as subtle eye-catching touches that give the shoe added visual appeal.

Special Features.   If the shoe has special features like a cushion insole, or an arch cookie, or a cushion midsole, or a padded collar, or air vents under the arch, etc.—point them out and translate them into customer benefits for extra comfort and wear satisfaction.

Parts and construction of a man's Goodyear Welt Process.

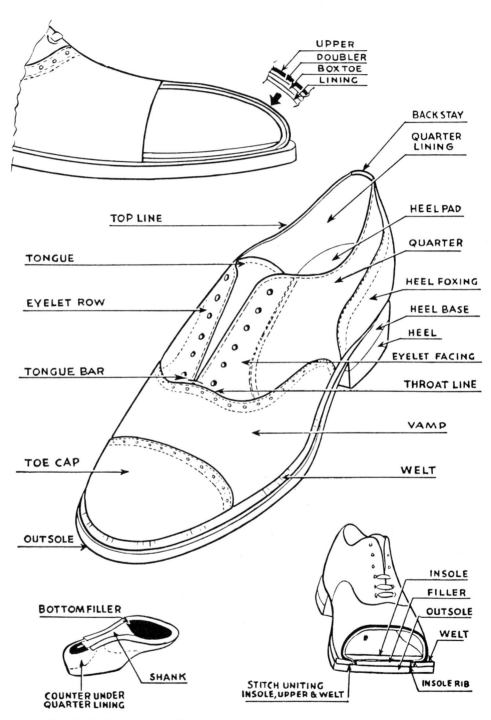

UPPER
DOUBLER
BOX TOE
LINING

BACK STAY

QUARTER
LINING

TOP LINE

HEEL PAD

TONGUE

QUARTER

EYELET ROW

HEEL FOXING

HEEL BASE

HEEL

TONGUE BAR

EYELET FACING

THROAT LINE

VAMP

TOE CAP

WELT

OUTSOLE

BOTTOM FILLER

SHANK

COUNTER UNDER
QUARTER LINING

INSOLE

FILLER

OUTSOLE

WELT

STITCH UNITING
INSOLE, UPPER & WELT

INSOLE RIB

240 *Profitable Footwear Retailing*

Parts and construction of a woman's Goodyear Welt Process.

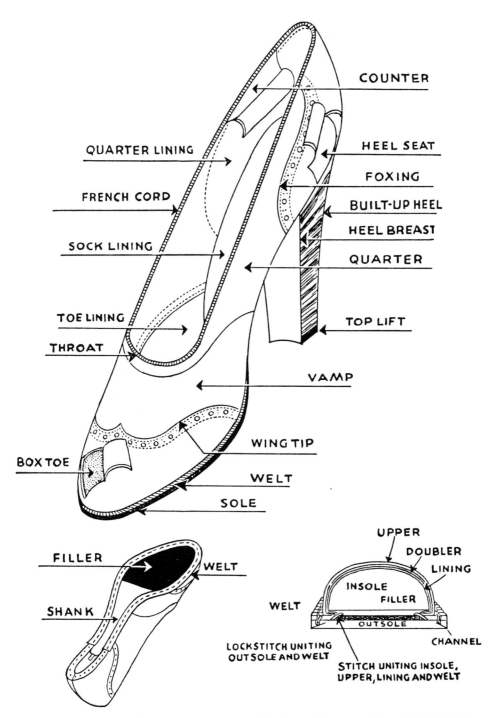

COUNTER

QUARTER LINING

HEEL SEAT

FOXING

FRENCH CORD

BUILT-UP HEEL

HEEL BREAST

SOCK LINING

QUARTER

TOE LINING

THROAT

TOP LIFT

VAMP

WING TIP

BOX TOE

WELT

SOLE

FILLER

WELT

SHANK

UPPER

DOUBLER

LINING

INSOLE

FILLER

WELT

OUTSOLE

CHANNEL

LOCKSTITCH UNITING
OUTSOLE AND WELT

STITCH UNITING INSOLE,
UPPER, LINING AND WELT

What's in a Shoe—and How to Sell It 241

Keep in mind that *everything* in a shoe is there for a purpose, as a customer benefit to contribute to the look, fit, comfort and wear satisfaction of the shoe. As you've seen, there are a lot of specific features about a shoe beyond simply the shoe's fit and style. So it's the old axiom: don't keep the light hidden under the bushel.

No, you *don't* have to give a "lecture" about the shoe. In fact, any lengthy discussion about the shoe's details should be avoided. Keep it brief, concise, a few words here and there about the shoe's features. Also, don't cite each of these features one after another. Drop your comments in at intervals during the fitting/selling process. Each feature of the shoe that you highlight and translate into customer benefits creates a steady buildup of value being received by the customer. It also helps to reduce or eliminate price resistance or questions about value received for price paid.

One successful shoe store emphasizes to its salespeople: An informed customer is your best customer. The more the customer understands about the product being purchased—especially about its benefits to the customer—the greater the customer's appreciation for both the product and the service. This store has an exceptional record for customer loyalty and repeat business.

There's a difference between need buying and want buying. If consumers bought only the shoes they needed, they'd buy little more than a pair a year. But average per capita footwear consumption in the U.S. is over five pairs annually. Those "extra" pairs are the result of want buying.

Retailers and salespeople are not in the business of supplying demand but of *creating* demand. A good share of created demand is the result of "informational selling" that makes customers *want* to buy because of so many customer benefits that have been cited to them when buying their footwear.

49

The Meaning of Quality and How to Sell It

When you buy something for a song, watch out for the accompaniment.

The bitterness of poor quality lingers long after the sweetness of cheap price is forgotten.

Quality is perhaps the most used—and abused—word in shoe business. In fact, it's so overused that many consumers have developed an immunity to it. That's unfortunate because most consumers respect the idea of quality. But when it comes to *explaining* quality or translating it into understandable terms, they rarely get any help from shoe business, whether on the selling floor or in the ads.

The word "quality" is from the Latin *qualitas,* meaning "what is it worth?" Well, how many times have you seen or heard a shoe salesperson (or owner or manager) explain or demonstrate *why* the shoe is worth its asking price? What you usually hear is, "It's a good value," or "It's a quality shoe."

All right, let's see if we can make the word or idea of "quality" come alive with tangible meaning. The first significant fact: quality in the customer's mind is related to two things: the product, and the services surrounding the product.

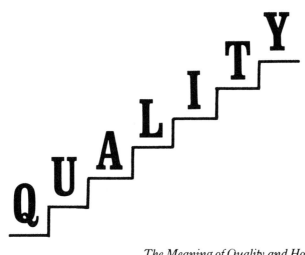

THE PRODUCT

The quality of a shoe is determined by the quality of its materials and components and how they are put together. When you speak of quality you must deal with specifics about the product, then translate those specifics into customer benefits. Selling quality involves three senses: sight, hearing and touch.

It's often very effective to have the customer hold one shoe in his or her hand while you're trying on the other. This allows the senses of sight and touch to play a role while you're telling your quality story. Now let's cite some examples:

Upper Materials.   Never use innocuous terms like "fine leather" or "genuine leather." Be specific. Speak of fine calfskin, soft kidskin, genuine cordovan, tropical lizard, fine-napped suede. Calling the material by name gives it distinction, adds character and class. Cite customer benefits: quality leathers mean more comfort, easier care, stay new-looking longer, express style elegance.

The Linings.   If the shoe has a leather lining, call it by name—lambskin, kidskin. Cite that a leather-lined shoe is automatically a mark of quality. Speak of its breathability qualities for a dry, cool, fresh feeling against the foot. If it's a quilted or cushioned lining, speak of "pillowed comfort."

The Counter.   Cite its "cupped contour" for maximum heel security and comfort. Have the customer feel the counter. Show its pear shape in profile—sculptured for perfect heel fit.

Styling.   This is an important mark of quality, class. Hold the shoe in profile on your fingertips. Now speak of its sleek silhouette, its toe expression, its arch-hugging contour, its elegant lines. Use "the language of fashion." It upgrades the shoe's inherent style character.

Crafting.   Don't speak of "construction." Speak instead of crafting. Then cite crafting details. For example, the upper stitching (the finer the stitching the better the quality); the ornaments or trim; the foot-hugging toplines, the puckered seam (if a moc), etc. Mention that it takes 150 operations, many of them hand-crafted, to make such a quality shoe. Don't let the shoe's crafting details go unnoticed or be taken for granted.

The Outsole.   If it's a leather sole, mention it. It instantly expresses quality. But other soles also have special features to relate to quality. A traction sole for sureness of step. A foam or crepe sole for soft resilience and comfort. Each sole has its own performance mission. Each deserves special mention translated into customer benefits.

The Insole.   It may be cushioned, or contoured, or have an arch cookie. Cite them as extras used to upgrade comfort and quality. Not only show them, but have the customer touch them.

The Box Toe.   It rarely gets mentioned. It serves two purposes: to maintain the style shape of the toe for the life of the shoe, and to allow for toe-room freedom inside the shoe. A quality box toe does both. This should be cited.

The Finish.   All shoes are given a special finish—aniline, matte, burnished, lustre, metallic, etc. Relate the finish (call it by name) to the distinctive style character of the shoe.

Texture.   Each material has its own distinctive textural character. Calfskin, glove leather, patent, grains, fabrics—each has a special surface appearance to contribute to the shoe's fashion character. Mention this and also have the customer touch the surface.

Flexibility.   If it's a flexible shoe, demonstrate it. Then translate it into walking ease and comfort.

Shoe Weight.   If the shoe is especially lightweight, it's a selling point. Give the customer two shoes, one lightweight, the other heavier. The weight differences make a dramatic contrast. Relate it to comfort. For example, a difference of only four ounces in a pair of shoes makes a difference of one *ton* of extra foot-lift load a day for the wearer. Lighter shoes reduce foot fatigue.

Comfort.   Don't just say comfort. Demonstrate it by touch and talk. The suppleness of the leathers, the cushion insole or resilient outsole, the shoe's flexibility or its light weight, the foot-contoured last, the heel security of the counter, the moisture-absorbant linings, etc.

SERVICES

The customer judges quality as much by the store's services as by its merchandise. A high-quality product can be seriously downgraded by poor service while a shoe of moderate quality can be appreciably upgraded by excellent service. Many stores have yet to discover this basic truth.

Service is what creates an "aura of quality" around a product. What kind of services?

Appearance of Salespeople.   The general appearance and demeanor of the salespeople is the customer's first impression. It reflects on the quality image of the store and the merchandise. Ironically, many stores have no rules or policy on this.

Fitting Service.   Most stores offer fitting service. But often there are wide differences in the quality, the professionalism, of the fitting service. Interestingly, only about 20 percent of shoe salespeople receive any formal instruction on shoe fitting. For most, it's on-the-job training at the expense of quality performance.

Size Selection.   This is definitely an important customer service and the responsibility of management. Limited size selection sharply diminishes quality image.

Style Selection.   Like size selection, a good range of style selection is essential for a good quality impression. And the salespeople must *present* a selection. If the store has both size and style selection, most customers are willing to pay something extra because the quality level of the merchandise is upgraded.

Fashion Counseling.   Here again, few stores train their salespeople in fashion counseling. Qualified counseling makes an important impression and upgrades the quality status of both the merchandise and the store.

Shoe Care Counseling.   In most stores it's a case of sell and run. With every sale a few moments should be taken to counsel the customer on the care of the shoes just purchased. This is not only a quality service but invariably leads to accessories sales.

Little Extras.   In the average store, the old soiled shoes are returned to the foot in the original soiled condition. It takes only a few seconds to run them under a buffer and return them polished. Again, worn socklinings on the old shoes should be replaced with new ones. A fresh feeling on the foot and the customer is impressed.

Customer Communications. To say "thank you" to the departing customer is expected. But for the customer to receive a thank-you note or card a few days later isn't expected—but is remembered. Or an occasional notice of a special promotion, or some clearance shoes in the customer's size. Customers are flattered with the thought that they're on the store's "preferred" list.

Needless to say, with each customer you don't present the whole gamut of quality selling points as cited above. You're selective. And you alter the quality story in accord with the type of customer or type of merchandise.

What's quality? It's a process of upgrading the whole presentation. It's a process of providing information and counseling, of adding some vital extras that makes the difference between the ordinary and the extraordinary, the mediocre and the superior.

What difference does it all make? It's the old adage: Business goes where it's treated best. The touches of class become the real touch of quality.

50

Selling Craftsmanship in a Shoe

Give the product a reason for being and you give the salesperson a reason for selling and the customer a reason for buying.

Enthusiasm without knowledge is like haste in the dark.

Many shoe retailers and salespeople shy from talking about "shoe construction" either because they know little about it, or because they think the customer doesn't particularly care.

They're wrong. How a shoe is constructed or crafted has a lot to do with how it wears, looks and feels, its price and quality, its performance and value. These certainly are important to the customer.

The first law of all selling: Know thy product. So if you're selling shoes, or if you profess to be a professional at your job, then you should know at least a little

of how a shoe is put together. This doesn't mean you have to be an expert on shoemaking. Nor does it mean that you should get involved with "technical" talk or explanations when selling shoes.

It's like buying a man's suit. A good salesman will point out certain features that make a difference in the quality and fit of the suit. He'll cite important details liking the lining, the buttonholes, the stitching and seams, the materials, the tailoring. This increases the customer's appreciation for the value he's getting, and also respect for the salesman's knowledge.

The same thing with shoes. It takes only a few moments to cite a few informative points about the shoe's construction without getting "heavy" about it. The result: better customer appreciation of the product, the value and the store and salesperson, and more momentum given to the sale itself.

WHAT'S A CONSTRUCTION?

First, except in a small minority of cases, don't talk "construction" to the customer. The term is too utilitarian and heavy. Instead, speak of *craftsmanship* or "crafting." Customers tune in better to those terms. For our own practical uses in this chapter, however, we'll speak of construction.

It takes between 100 and 150 spearate operations to make a shoe. Essentially, a shoe's "construction" simply means the particular method used to attach the sole to the upper—though, of course, shoemaking involves many other operations. The sole can be attached to the upper by stitching, cementing, heat-sealing (vulcanizing or injection molding), nailing, stappling, etc. There are many variations or versions for each of these, and each is its own kind of construction. In fact, there are some 800 known ways of making or "constructing" a shoe. However, only about a half dozen are used to make virtually all our shoes.

Some 60 percent of all shoes use the cement process by which the sole is attached to the upper by adhesives for a permanent bond. About 20 percent are heat-molded, and another 13 percent use the Goodyear welt construction. The remainder consists of other constructions with such names as stitchdown, McKay, Littleway, silhouwelt, California, etc.

Why so many different kinds of constructions? Why not make it simple and use just one or two for all? There's good reason for the variety. Each kind of construction gives the shoe its own particular look and performance. Hence each construction has its own fashion and performance reason.

Let's take a quick look at the principal types of construction.

Goodyear Welt. This dates back more than a century and is known as the king of constructions because of its sturdy structure. Here the sole is attached to the upper by stitching. Two important parts of this process are the special insole and the welting (a flat strip of leather or other material around the upper rim of the outsole).

This construction is used for better-grade men's and boys' dress shoes. But it tends to produce a heavier, less flexible shoe. While it's fine for a men's wing-tip brogue, it's too much for a women's fragile fashion shoe.

Cement Construction. This came into its own with the introduction of the Compo process in 1928, becoming the first reliable method of sole bonding by adhesives. This process has many variations—for example, the slip-lasted or California constructions. Cement constructions result in much lighter, dressier, more flexible shoes and are used for the large majority of women's and girls' shoes, along with some men's casuals and lighter dress shoes.

Heat Sealing. (vulcanized and injection molded constructions). This means heat-molding the sole to the upper without use of stitching, cementing, nails, staples, etc. The soles are always rubber types or plastics such as PVC or urethane that soften for easy molding to the last, then allowed to harden. The soft material is poured into a sole mold, then pressed and sealed under the upper on the last. The result is a tight, secure sole bond.

These molded constructions are used for certain types of footwear such as all sneakers, most athletic footwear, many work and outdoor boots, some casual shoes and some children's footwear.

Stitchdown. This is a sewn shoe, a very old and simple method of stitch-attaching the sole to the upper. It can have a single or double sole. It's used for certain types of lower-priced footwear such as sturdy sandals, some utility-type shoes or boots, some children's shoes, and sometimes for a different look on men's casuals. Today, relatively few shoes are made on this process.

Moccasin. There are two types: the genuine or handsewn, and the machine-made. The original handsewn moccasin is the oldest known shoe construction, dating back some 15,000 years. The original was simply a large piece of leather wrapped under and around the foot and secured with rawhide thongs. The same principle applies to the modern genuine moccasin construction.

This was the way the American Indians made their moccasins. But they added something new—a decorative "plug" or small, flat piece of leather over the top of the forefoot which they ornamented with colored beads. When the plug was sewn to the rest of the upper it created a puckered seam around the top rim of the shoe, the distinctive mark of a genuine handsewn moccasin.

Today, many moccasins have the moc look but are machine-sewn rather than handsewn and lack the handsewn look. Also, the leather doesn't wrap around from under the foot to give the cradled effect of the genuine moccasin. This also applies to the loafer, which is an offspring of the moccasin.

OTHER PARTS OF THE CONSTRUCTION

There are other parts and steps involved in putting the shoe together. Let's briefly cite the important ones.

Upper. This doesn't start as a single unit. It consists of several pieces called patterns. When these are sewn together they form the single-unit upper that fits over the last, and then attached to the outsole.

Insole. This is the layer of material (leather, cellulose, composition, etc.) between the outsole and sole of the foot. It's actually the structural heart of the shoe because just about every component in the shoe is anchored to it. Some shoes have cushioned insoles for added comfort.

Counter. This is the backpart stiffener that holds the shape of the shoe's backpart. It also secures the heel of the foot inside the shoe and hence is important to fit. A few shoes such as some loafers, or open-back shoes, have no counter.

Box Toe. This is the stiffener or "roof" over the toe of the shoe. It can be hard, medium or soft. Its purpose is to retain the dome-like shape over the toe for toe-room allowance and also to retain fashion shape.

Shankpiece. This is a flat, finger-like slab of material (wood, metal, plastic, fiberglass) sandwiched between outsole and insole at the shank or arch area. It's a reinforcement for the bridge of space between heel and ball. It's not an "arch support."

Linings. They're in the shoe to help hold the shoe's shape, and also as a buffer layer to protect the shoe's outside upper from staining by perspiration. Linings are made in a variety of materials: leather, vinyls, fabrics. There are three main types of linings: *quarter lining* (around the shoe's backpart); *vamp lining* (under the shoe's forepart); *sock lining* (over the insole). There are also others like tongue and strap linings. Some shoes, such as some mocs, loafers and casuals, are unlined.

Lasting. This is perhaps the single most important operation in the shoemaking process. It consists of "pulling" the upper tightly over the last before the outsole is attached. This is done by machines with ingenious finger-like pincers that pull the upper at the toe, sides and heel to assure that the upper conforms to every contour of the last. Precise lasting is vital to the proper fit and look of the shoe.

HOW TO SELL CRAFTSMANSHIP

Never sell on the premise that what the customer sees is what the customer gets. Customers are interested in the quality and value of what they're buying. And knowing something about the craftsmanship in a shoe gives more credibility to its value. It also gives the customer more pride in the shoe he or she has purchased.

Here are some tips or guidelines in selling craftsmanship in a shoe.

1) Avoid getting technical or the use of heavy terms. Use your words selectively. Use "craftsmanship" or "crafting" instead of "construction." Speak of a sole being "bonded" rather than "cemented" to the upper.

2) Mention that it takes about 125 separate operations, plus about 20 different parts or components, to make a shoe. The numbers are impressive. Don't let the customer think the shoe is made with a cookie cutter.

3) If you mention a type of construction, cite some of the construction's particular features. For example:

   Goodyear welt: solidly stitched, long-wearing, sturdy, holds its shape with wear, excellent support.
   Cement (bonded): Light weight, flexible, comfortable, trim lines.
   Heat-sealed (vulcanized or injection molded): Weather-tight bond of sole to upper, sturdy, long-wearing, good underfoot support.
   Moccasin (including loafers): Cradled support, hand-sewn, maximum comfort.

4) Make sure to *demonstrate* your selling points. Most buying is done with the eye.

5) When selling men's shoes, speak of the shoe's *engineering* and how all the shoe's parts are precisely fitted together. When selling women's shoes refer to *design crafting* for the shoe's look, fit and comfort.
6) Relate craftsmanship to *quality.* In *any* product, nothing reflects quality more than the product's craftsmanship.

7) Relate the craftsmanship to shoe performance and wear satisfaction.

Avoid trying to give a show-off lecture about the shoe's craftsmanship. Don't try to give the customer an A-to-Z course on shoemaking. Select three or four highlights about the shoe's structure and concentrate on those. Combining words with simple demonstration requires only two or three minutes to get some effective selling points across. This will give an added dimension to the much-used word "quality" in selling. This kind of "informational selling" builds credibility in the product, the store, the salesperson.

Fashion and Footwear

51

The Psychology of Footwear Fashion

Prince Charming fitted the glass slipper to Cinderella's foot, leaned back and exclaimed, "Ah, the perfect fit!" Cinderella replied, "Yes, I know. But do you have it in a higher heel and a smaller size?"

"The clothes you wear reveal what you want people to think of you." (Dr. Joyce Brothers)

"Marcia, I wish you wouldn't wear those ridiculous shoes—they're causing everyone to stare."

Fashion can neither be created nor effectively sold unless it's understood. Fashion doesn't simply burst onto the contemporary scene from inspiration or by quirky accident. Fashion is bought and worn by people. Hence there is a *psychology* behind fashion, a *reason* for its existence, its constant change, its constant appeal. Once this is understood, fashion can be presented to customers with more effective results.

In this brief chapter we will discuss two very important aspects of fashion: the psychology or nature of fashion, and how popular footwear fashion was born in America.

THE ELITIST NATURE OF FASHION

Fashion is a snob. It always has been and will be because elitism is an inherent part of fashion's nature.

Status is one of the two prime functions of all fashion (sex attraction is the other). Though fashion is found in every culture from the most primitive to the most sophisticated, the status motive is the same everywhere. Fashion is designed primarily to set people or "classes" apart as an insignia of rank, wealth or social strata.

Fashion was never intended for the mass population, the commoners. It was never designed as a democratic or egalitarian institution. Up until only about 1920 everywhere throughout the world it was confined to only the very few—the nobility and aristocracy, the gentry, the small segments of wealth or upper social class. And it still is in many parts of the world today. Because the many accoutrements of fashion are so visible, fashion itself is one of the most important of status symbols that signify class distinctions.

For example, in the footwear and apparel business we traditionally speak of "high" fashion to distinguish it from middle or low fashion which we more tactfully call "volume" or "popular" fashion. These are clearly elitist distinctions related to both the product and the clientele. Similarly we refer to "haute couture" for the world of high fashion in apparel, or "haut monde" in referring to high society.

Thus fashion has always been used to separate and distinguish classes. It's no different today than in centuries past. Nowhere in the world is there such a thing as a true classless society. And fashion has always been used as the clearest mark of class distinctions.

Throughout history footwear fashion has always played an elitist role. In ancient Greece only warriors were permitted to wear red boots, a proud symbol of courage. In ancient Rome only the emperors and their families were allowed to wear shoes or clothing of purple—which gave rise to the expression "born to the purple" or royalty (a tradition that continued for centuries in the church).

In the Middle Ages of Europe, persons below certain rank were prohibited from wearing leather shoes or boots. In 16th century England no commoner could wear high-heel shoes, which by law were reserved for the aristocracy and affluent (from which came our expression "well-heeled"). In Colonial America persons of farmer or shopkeeper class were not permitted to wear shoes "of bright riband or cloth." Even the moccasins of the American Indians were specially decorated with certain arrangements of colored beads denoting rank.

The Psychology of Footwear Fashion 255

In 1639, in Massachusetts, Connecticut and Virginia, laws prohibited shoemakers and tailors from making shoes and garments for commoners or servants that were as costly or lavish as those made for the gentry class (similar laws prevailed in England, France and Spain).

Traditionally, we speak of "looking up" to an admired person or one of higher rank; and conversely of "looking down" on one of more humble station. From this ancient custom of status by stature emerged the platform shoe dating back 2,500 years ago to ancient Greece, and the high-heel shoe dating back 450 years to medieval Italy.

Elitist society easily retained their exclusivity of fashion simply by pricing it out of the reach of the common classes. It is no different today. In centuries past a pair of fashionable shoes could cost the average family several months wages. And a pair of jeweled shoe buckles, popular with the aristocracy, could cost more than 10 years of income for the average wage earner.

But it went beyond sheer economics. When or where would a shop worker or peasant ever be able to wear the fragile footwear of fashion? So almost all footwear was strictly utilitarian in design and construction to meet the utilitarian lifestyles of the commoners.

The elitist folk had a very good reason for keeping fashion out of the possession of the general population, whether by laws or prohibitive cost. Fashion was a vital status insignia, a visible mark of rank or class or wealth. To attempt to penetrate that barrier was the ultimate presumption, subject to severe penalty.

For example, in the 15th and 16th centuries a popular fashion was called the "startup." It consisted of an elegant shoe below and a separate, legging-like laced top of different color. When some socially ambitious commoners began to copy the fashion, they were charged as contemptible imposters and were fined in court for "usurping the rights of rank." From this we got our word "upstart," a bold, presumptuous, arrogant person.

Nevertheless, while elitist society kept a tight rein on the exclusivity of fashions because of their status value, they and their artisan shoemakers were responsible for introducing many of the fashion footwear ideas common today. These included platform shoes, high heels, pointed toes, the use of exotic leathers and other luxury materials, ornate trims and ornaments, such basic styles as the oxford, D'Orsay pump, balmoral, the heeled mule, shoe goring, clothtop shoes, and many others.

Pointed toe shoes, for example, date back 3,000 years and were originally designed as a status shoe to demonstrate that the wearer was of high birth with a long, narrow and "aristocratic" foot that could wear such a slender, elegant shoe. Even today, women speak of having an "aristocratic" arch—significant in times past because a nicely contoured arch indicated that the owner was not a common laborer whose arch had been flattened by toil.

Have times changed? Are we less elitist today about fashion, and is fashion any less a status symbol now than in the past? Not a bit. The wealthy, the prominent, the celebrities, the upper social strata—they continue to use footwear and apparel fashion to set them apart from the mass, and also a fashion stride ahead of it. They patronize elitist shops, buy elitist designer names and brands, pay elitist prices.

Sociologist Neil J. Smelser, in his book, *Theory of Collective Behavior,* says,

"It is important to style leaders to be among the first in order to reap the psychological rewards of being in the forefront of fashion and remaining above and apart from the crowd. It is almost as important to flee from a new style or fashion when it is adopted by the masses. Further back in the procession among the followers, the motivation of fashion is more purely sociable—the feeling of belonging to the crowd rather than being conspicuously original."

This is why the prestigious European and American designers of footwear and apparel find their original creations victim of piracy by volume manufacturers. As soon as their new, exclusive, high-priced footwear and apparel appear in the elitist stores, they are copied and rushed into mass production to soon reappear in chain and other volume stores. The "upstart" masses want to look like the fashion leaders. But as soon as this starts, the fashion leaders switch to a new fashion to remain a step ahead and apart. So fashion is a game of chasing and copying the leaders in order to upgrade one's status by looking "fashionable."

Says psychologist Dr. Joyce Brothers, "The clothes you wear usually reveal what you want people to think you are." The more status impression we make, the greater our acceptance. Charles Darwin noted that the female zebra would not mate with the male jackass. But when the jackass was painted with zebra-like stripes, the female zebra readily received him.

Fashion is essentially a masquerade, a game of imagery that we all play to establish a status identity. There is a touch of the elitist in all of us, and this is one of the main driving forces of fashion's perennial popularity. Footwear fashion has always been in the forefront of this illusion. The universal expression of "putting one's best foot forward" indicates the important status role of footwear in fashion to enable the whole fashion illusion to "get off on the right foot."

These facts about the psychology of fashion are important to understand and remember because they are among the customers' main motives for buying fashion.

HOW VOLUME FOOTWEAR FASHION BEGAN IN AMERICA

Perhaps as much as 85 percent or more of all fashion-type footwear falls into a category known as volume or popular fashion. The term means precisely what it says—fashion designed and priced for the mass market and mass consumption. Volume fashion differs distinctly from what we call "high fashion" or haute couture in terms of design, quality, price, marketing, retailing, clientele.

We think that fashion available for everyone in America has always been with us. It hasn't. What we today call volume fashion is a relative newcomer on the fashion scene, first appearing only about 1920. Prior to then there was only "fashion." It didn't have to be labeled "high" fashion because only a tiny, upper-strata segment of the population could afford it or lived a lifestyle where fashion could be put to everyday use. Footwear styling was largely utilitarian or a poor-cousin imitation of full-fledged fashion. Fashion not only served mainly an elitist clientele but had its own elitist character. In fact, the terms "ladies'" and "gentlemen's" shoes, commonly used up through the early part of this century, had nothing to do with sex gender but as upper class labels.

Thus fashion in both footwear and apparel, from the beginning of civilization into the early 20th century, was the private domain of the few, off limits to the

EVOLUTION OF THE SHOE

majority. Then suddenly, about 1920, fashion exploded, breaking loose from it centuries-old elitist chains. Almost overnight "volume fashion" became available to all—sought, bought and worn by all.

What caused this sudden upheaval? History now records this event as one of the major social revolutions of the 20th century. It began in America and spread like a happy contagion around the globe.

The footwear and apparel industries were in no way responsible for this social revolution. In fact, they were totally unprepared, taken completely by surprise. Around 1920 there was no such thing as a "fashion industry" in existence. There were private dressmakers and tailors who catered to a small, affluent clientele. There were exclusive custom shoemakers and bootiers and a few high-priced fashion shoe shops. Most American shoe stores sold what were pretty much "basic" shoes with very limited style selection. Elitist-level women bought gowns and elegant footwear from Paris, and men bought suits and fine shoes from London.

The Great Mass Fashion Catalyst was the post-World War I period which brought two significant events that were to create a tidal wave of change. In 1919, the Volstead Act (prohibition of liquor) became law; and in 1920 the 19th Amendment, giving women the right to vote. Both were to have cataclysmic effects politically, culturally, socially, economically.

Jazz, a frenetic new kind of popular music, swept the nation like a hurricane. A postwar prosperity burst onto the economy. Real estate prices, along with the stock market, went on a binge. Henry Ford startled the nation by paying an unprecedented wage of $5 a day. Bootlegging became a major industry, as did such social innovations as speakeasies, road houses and night clubs. The restraints of propriety were being snapped in all directions.

It was now that the real revolution, the sudden emancipation of fashion, occurred.

Suddenly women's skirts, for centuries held to ankle length or lower, abruptly rose calf high, then scandalously knee high. Other sacrileges appeared: women cut or "bobbed" their hair, rolled their stockings, smoked in public, drank out of flasks and romanced in the "rumble seats" of roadster cars, wildly danced the frenetic Charleston, Varsity Drag and Black Bottom. Society's traditional rules of behavior and manners of dress appeared to be on a roller coaster to hell.

With women's legs finally emerging from behind their centuries-old curtains, the foot and ankle came into prominence. They had to be dressed in a dramatic and glamourized manner. There was now a mass demand for "fashion" at popular, affordable prices.

The fashion-inexperienced shoe manufacturers were confused and unprepared. There were few genuine or creative shoe designers. The same applied to the last designers because last shapes seldom changed. For example, a women's pointed-toe last used in 1898 was still in use in 1918. So suddenly everyone desperately put their hand to "styling," much of which consisted of copying the styles or design ideas seen in the windows of the elitist stores who catered to the carriage trade.

A new class of footwear called "novelty shoes" emerged—lots of high heels, ankle and instep straps, baby doll toes, big bows and buckles and novelty trims, combinations of leathers. And all available at moderate or popular prices.

Men's shoe styles quickly followed with their own novelty looks, a break from the traditional "gentlemen's shoes." Young college men took the lead, followed by others. It was the Roaring Twenties and the Flapper Age. The uproarious footwear and apparel styles suited the frenetic new lifestyles.

Thus the 1920s was the Great Experiment for the footwear industry. It was its first experience with "volume fashion," with mass-produced fashion churned by frequent turnover. Almost overnight it changed the structure of the footwear industry, including shoe retailing. The new pace of seasonal and yearly fashion turnover quickened the pace of merchandising and markdowns, and also sharpened the buying skills of retailers. The new era of fashion gave rise to a new breed born of demand, the shoe designer. Other segments of the industry were pushed to put their creative talent into service—tanners, lastmakers, producers of fabrics, ornaments, components.

And so was born volume footwear fashion in America. It rapidly spread to Europe and elsewhere as fashion, once the private domain of the few, opened its arms to the general public. Volume fashion's inaugural period in the 1920s will remain a historic landmark in the footwear industry—and a social milestone for the nation as a whole. For it was the true birth date of egalitarian or popular-price fashion. And the very nature of the footwear industry today is the child of that memorable era.

ART'S VIEW OF FASHION

For centuries fashion has been the target for comment not only by those who create or wear it, but by poets, artists, historians and others, too. If we sometimes wonder why fashion is in a constant flux of change, here are some viewpoints by some famous people:

Shakespeare. "The fashion wears out more apparel than the man."

Oscar Wilde. "Fashion is a form of ugliness so intolerable that we have to alter it every six months."

Thoreau. "Every generation laughs at the old fashions but religiously follows the new."

Jean Cocteau. "Art produces ugly things which frequently become beautiful with time. Fashion produces beautiful things which always become ugly with time."

Ambrose Bierce. "Fashion is a despot whom the wise ridicule—and obey."

James Laver (British historian). "Fashion has only a fugitive's lease on life. It is always like ice cream melting on a hot tin roof."

Mark Twain. "No woman can look as well out of fashion as in it."

52

The Five Basic Elements of Footwear Fashion—and How to Present and Sell Them

To those who don't understand it,
fashion is an elusive mystique.
To those who do, fashion is a clear
science.

We refer to fashion as a "mystique." It has a subtle, volatile quality, an intangible character often hard to grasp or define. As a result, while shoe retailers and salespeople sell fashion, many have difficulty really understanding it. That's usually because they view the shoe as a single, total unit rather than seeing its separate fashion

"The thing to do is get right back up on them again before you lose your nerve!"

The Five Basic Elements of Footwear Fashion 261

parts. It's like viewing a painting. The average person will see it in its totality, then comment that it's beautiful or unusual. But the art connoisseur will view the painting differently, appraising its parts—color, proportion, texture, form, perspective, lines, etc. He sees more and hence understands more.

While fashion transmits a mystique, fashion itself isn't mysterious. It has an "anatomy" that can be quickly dissected, examined and understood by everyone. That's very important for shoe retailers and salespeople, because the more they understand and appreciate the elements of fashion, the more effectively they can present and sell it to customers.

The anatomy of fashion consists of five basic elements, as follows:

Shape. This is the basic architecture of all fashion, the underlying framework upon which fashion's other parts rest. In the case of footwear, shape is determined by the last. From this emerges the full profile and illusion, the lines and contours, the silhouette or form. All fashion, whether footwear, apparel or anything else, begins with shape.

Key elements of shoe shape are the toe, the vamp or upper forepart, heel height, side shape, edge slant, among others. For example, the toe shape may be pointed, round, square, snipped, bump, recede. The sides may be tapered or walled. The vamp may be long or short; both the height and style of the heel are part of the shape illusion.

Design. This is determined by the covering of the last or how the last is "dressed." It is the design that establishes the shoe's basic style. For example, an oxford and a pump are two distinct styles, two different ways of dressing the last. While an oxford and pump may have essentially the same basic shape or shell, the two consist of different designs. The design is composed of the upper patterns (like the patterns of a dress), and the patterns can take any of limitless forms. It is largely here that the designer's creative talent is applied and where the shoe's "look" becomes so vividly visible to give it its own distinctive character.

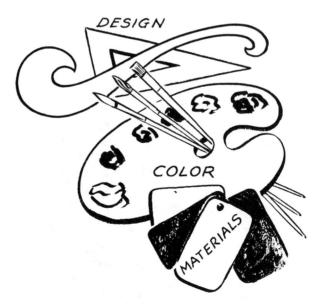

Materials. A given shape and design assumes further distinctive character in accord with the materials used. Shoes of identical shape and design will look different with the use of different materials—say patent or suede or linen or glove leather. Materials introduce a third dimension to fashion. Suede, for instance, not only looks but feels differently than patent. That combination of touch and sight gives materials an important role in fashion.

Materials involve qualities like texture, weight, surface grain, finish. *Texture* is the feel of the material. Snakeskin, pigskin, fabrics, kidskin, suede, etc.—each has its own unique feel or texture which gives it its fashion character. *Weight* is the thickness or "body" of the material. Glove leather, for instance, is thicker, plumper and heavier than kidskin, which is why each is used in different types of footwear for a different fashion effect. *Surface grain* reflects the nature or type of material. For example, genuine snakeskin, pigskin, lizard, ostrich, alligator, calfskin—each has its own distinctive surface grain that distinguishes it from other leathers. Finally, *finish* is the finishing touch to the surface. The finish may be aniline (polished), matte (dull or flat), burnished or antiqued (dual-toned), lustre or pearl (eggshell), gloss (patent), glazed (subdued polished), and so on.

Color. Color illuminates the whole illusion of fashion's shape, design and materials. It will surprise you to know that there are 17,000 officially listed colors. Almost all, of course, are variations of a few basic colors. But it gives you an appreciation of the enormous range of shades and the limitless subtleties of color in fashion.

Further, there are different reflections of color, which is why we use color terms like bright, pastels, flat or soft, dual-toned, etc. For example, an identical red in a bright and a pastel will look different because they reflect light differently. This is why designers are so meticulous not only in the selection of colors but their reflective tones. And finally there's the use of combination colors in footwear for contrasting effects.

Because color preferences or requirements are so personalized for the customer, fashion itself, by virtue of color selection, enlists that subtle quality called taste. The selection of color also reflects moods and personality itself. Customers buy and wear certain colors in footwear to convey a particular image or mood, or to coordinate with apparel or costume, or to fit with particular occasions. It is these things that give color a "rightness" to fit in with the total look of fashion.

Ornamentation and Treatment. This is the fifth and final dimension of fashion, those subtle touches or effects that cohese the other four elements into a complete, final unit. The bow or buckle, the trim or tassel, the button or ornament, the sequins, the pinking or perfs or scalloping. They are the final decorative effects, the candles on the cake that symbolize the finishing garnish of fashion's completed mission.

That, essentially, is the entire structure of footwear fashion, of all fashion. If you have a grasp of those five basic elements you have the full grasp of fashion itself. Fashion is now de-mystified. It becomes tangible and easily understandable. You now know the vital parts that make fashion tick.

But let's take it a point further to make it even easier to visualize and understand. Let's say you're building a house. You start by laying in the foundation and erecting the framework. That represents the *shape* of the house. You are now going to give it a particular style—say a Cape or Tudor or Colonial or ranch. That becomes the *design*. You then cover it with a particular substance: wood or brick or stone or shingle or stucco. You now have the *materials*. You then paint it a particular *color*, and perhaps a contrasting color for the trim. Finally you apply the finishing touches: a lawn, shrubbery, fountain, garden or rose bushes, etc. This becomes the *ornamentation* or treatment.

In building your house you've used exactly the same five basic elements as used by the fashion designer in designing shoes or apparel. If you take each of those five basic elements separately, each has countless variations. And if you put all five together, then the possible combinations are infinite. This is why we see so many variations of fashions, and such a constant turnover of fashion. That's why it's almost impossible for fashion to stand still.

The customer, like the designer, also sees and judges those same five basic elements when buying shoes. He or she views the shape, style or design, materials, color and ornamentation. The customer's eye quickly puts those five elements together and sees the combination as "the shoe" or "the fashion."

And right here we come to the nub of it all. If the designer consciously uses those five basic elements to create the shoe, and the customer uses the same elements to make the buying decision—then why doesn't the *salesperson* also use those five fashion elements in *selling* the shoe? Yes, a minority does. But the majority doesn't, and in failing to do this they forfeit much of the sell-power of fashion.

Let's see if we can change that.

SELLING FASHION MORE EFFECTIVELY

The shoe is on the customer's foot. The salesperson says, "It's a very pretty shoe. It's the latest fashion. Selling like hotcakes, too. It's a nice color, don't you think? And real genuine leather. You'll get a lot of compliments from your friends when you wear it."

What has the salesperson really said about the shoe? Actually very little. A pretty shoe? That's up to the customer to judge. The latest fashion? The customer usually knows whether it is or isn't. A nice color? For what or when or whom? Genuine leather? That's like saying something is genuine fabric or genuine wood. Meaningless.

Yet, ironically, that's the way a lot of salespeople sell fashion in footwear. No real fashion information about the shoe. No helpful guidance. No dealing with fashion specifics, only loose generalities. That's *not* the way to sell fashion. In fact, it's not the way to sell anything.

So the first law: Talk about fashion specifics. Think in terms of those five basic fashion elements. Not only are they specifics, but exactly the specifics the customer is interested in and understands.

Let's start with *shape*. Unless you're selling a comfort or orthopedic shoe, avoid the term "last." Instead, speak of shape or silhouette or profile or lines or contours or sculptured form. These are esthetic terms, and fashion *is* esthetics.

Focus first on toe shape because usually that is the focal point of the shoe. Shape or form is something you *show*. Touch the toe of the shoe and describe its fashion form as sleekly tapered or clean lines or having a fashion profile; or if round or oblique or square, give a *reason* for those shapes, such as a "natural look" now important as a fashion statement in footwear. Never let toe shape be taken for granted simply because the customer can see it.

If the shoe has a walled last, cite its importance both as an interesting fashion feature and for added comfort. If the sides at the ball slant, speak of the graceful grading to match the same downslant of the side of the foot for a custom look.

Hold the shoe sideways on your fingertips at the customer's eye level, then speak of the shoe's nice profile or silhouette, its sculptured character, its clean lines. Then say, "It creates the same elegant look for your foot."

Move to the heel, again holding the shoe sideways in profile. First, in women's shoes give the heel its proper name: cuban, Louis, stiletto, museum, dutchboy, etc. It now has an identity which adds something to the shoe's fashion character.

Relate shoe shape to fashion, fit and comfort. That's the ideal combination customers seek. And the key to it is shape. Speak of the shoe's shape matching the conformity of the foot.

Design offers many possibilities in selling because design or "style" is the most visible part of the shoe. Every shoe has its own design character. A shoe begins as a type of style—pump, oxford, ghillie, boot (demi, calf, etc.), clog, mule, moccasin, sandal, espadrille, etc. So refer to the shoe by its name, not simply as a "shoe."

Depending upon the type of shoe, highlight its details. If it has straps, call the strap design by name: instep, T-strap, sling, cross. Cite a hugging *topline* for its good fit and look, and also to the *throatline* in the same way. If there is something unusual about the shoe's *pattern*—an overlay or underlay, for instance—point it out. If a man's shoe has only one or two *eyelets* instead of the usual five or six, cite it as a fashion feature that helps to make the style distinctive.

In highlighting the design specifics you avoid the tired cliches like "a nice looking shoe" or "a pretty style." When you point out specifics you are showing *why* the shoe is unusual and attractive.

Materials have almost endless possibilities for enhancing the shoe's fashion appeal in selling. Think in terms of the four features of materials: texture, weight, surface grain, and finish. Each contains its own fashion story. Texture responds to touch, so let the customer *feel* the material while you're talking about it. If it's a soft leather, refer to its rich, mellow, pillow-soft texture. If, as on a man's shoe, the leather is firm, relate it to good foot-hugging fit. If it's glove leather, speak of its soft plumpness and conformability.

Do the same thing with *weight*. Materials of different weights are used on different types of footwear for a fashion reason. For example, heavier materials are used on many casuals or service-type shoes to give the shoe a sturdier look (which is also the reason for their heavier soles). In reverse, lighter materials such as kidskin or calfskin or fabrics are usually used on dress shoes for a more elegant look. So relate materials weight to the type of shoe and what the customer wants from such a shoe.

Surface grain responds to both the customer's eye and touch, so enlist both in selling fashion. If the surface grain is distinctive such as snakeskin or lizard or pigskin, etc., have the customer feel the grain and refer to its unique character.

Sometimes the grain is fine, such as a boarded grain on calfskin, or a scotch or pinseal grain. Mention it as a mark of quality. Or sometimes the top surface is perfectly smooth, such as on smooth calfskin or cordovan or patent. Refer to its ability to take a good polish for a clean look.

Finishes of materials are there to give the material a special finished look. Don't sell on the principle that what the customer sees is what the customer gets. The finish is applied for a fashion purpose, to enhance the shoe's esthetics. So call the finish by name: aniline, matte, lustre or pearl, antiqued or burnished, gloss, napped, glazed. For example, if the shoe has a burnished finish, refer to its subtle dual-toned look like fine, polished wood. Such comments enrich the value of the shoe.

More than any other factor, materials reflect the quality of a shoe. The customer relates fashion with quality. So the more the selling gives a quality image to the materials, the more the shoe's fashion image is strengthened (see the chapter, How To Sell Quality).

Color should never be taken for granted because the customer can see it. Color has an almost infinite number of shadings, and exactly the right shade is important to the customer, especially when the shoe is being costume-coordinated. Therefore, call the colors by given names, even if you have to invent them. Brown, for example, is too general and dull. It takes on more class and identity when a more precise name is assigned—like russet, mahogany, maroon, hazel, cinnamon, chestnut, ginger, cocoa, chocolate, umber, coffee, etc.

Colors have tones, like bright, pastel, dual, subdued, deep, reflective. These are subtle effects that add fashion dimension to color. So don't say something trite like "it's a nice color" or "a pretty color." When you specify a tone—pastel or cast or depth, for instance—the shoe's color value is enriched.

The *ornamentation* or trim effects on a shoe should not be taken for granted. These important fashion details should be highlighted by precise description. A button isn't just a button. It's a mother-of-pearl or jeweled or ceramic or copper button. A bow isn't just a bow but a grosgrain or satin or leather bow. A buckle isn't just a buckle but a silver, brass or copper buckle; and it has a shape: square, round, oval, triangle. If the upper of the shoe has fine, decorative stitching, cite it to the customer. If the shoe has a topline trim or collar of contrasting material, say something about it. If the shoe has pinking or scalloping or perfs or cutouts, mention these as subtle fashion touches.

Finally, a word about handling the shoe when selling fashion. Because salespeople are constantly handling shoes, many get into the faulty habit of holding them like a hammer or a fistful or sausages. This deglamourizes the shoe and, like Cinderella's broken fantasy, converts the elegant carriage into a pumpkin.

A fashion shoe is a work of art and should be presented as such. You don't sell diamonds out of a brown paper bag. You show them as you would the crown jewels. So too with a fashion shoe. Hold the shoe in profile on the tips of your fingers, or grasp it lightly with your fingertips and move it slowly around so the customer can view it from all angles. Handle it delicately as you would a small, expensive vase. It then becomes an object of beauty to be admired. It's a touch of show business, which is what fashion shoe business really is.

STYLES, FASHIONS AND FADS

Styles, fashions and fads. We commonly use these terms interchangeably. But they have quite different meanings and should be used in their proper context.

Style. It's from the Latin *stilus,* a sharp, pointed instrument used by ancients for writing on wax tablets; a kind of etching needle to make a tracing of a design or object. And that's precisely what a style is—a particular design or shape or form; a basic profile with a character of its own.

In footwear, for example, a pump is a style with its own distinctive character or profile. There can be thousands of different versions or design "treatments" of a pump, but there is only one pump style. Thus a style is a genus, a one-of-a-kind original that may give off countless variations or sprouts, but always from the one immutable root. Throughout all history there have been only seven basic footwear styles: the oxford, pump, boot, sandal, mule, clog and moccasin.

Fashion. This is any particular version or treatment of a basic style that appeals to contemporary or popular taste. While the pump style of today and a century ago are essentially the same, the pump *fashions* of today and yesterday are quite different because the contemporary lifestyles and tastes are different. Fashion's "reason" is that it is a reflection of its time and the public mood.

Any given fashion, no matter how popular, has a relatively short life, a marked time span, simply because there are limits to the public's fashion tolerance span. Also, fashion is strongly influenced by political, social and economic forces which move in cycles. These in turn cause shifts in public moods and lifestyles, which in turn alter the direction of fashions and generate new fashion cycles.

Thus style has permanence, while fashions evolve and change.

Fads. A fad is a toylike fetish characterized by some whim whose novelty captures overnight popularity and also meets with an overnight demise. A fad's audience is almost always the young, enamoured with novelty. A fad can spring up at any time, from any source, and hence is wholly unpredictable. Like a firefly, a fad has its moment of brilliant flash, then instantly fades and disappears. Styles and fashions have reasons, fads do not. Footwear fads remain one of human nature's unresolvable mysteries—perhaps never to be understood, yet a reality we learn to live with.

53

Footwear Fashion and the Seven Basic Styles

On the surface is complexity. Deeper down at the center is simplicity.

Each year an estimated 200,000 new footwear "styles" are introduced to buyers in the U.S.—new shapes, patterns, treatments, shoes with new heel or sole designs, color and materials combinations, etc. Over a five-year period a million new styling or design effects.

Perhaps only a quarter of them go into actual production, and of these perhaps less than half prove profitable. It's an indication of the constant and tremendous inflow of innovative footwear styling.

But now an astonishing fact surfaces. Of the millions of new fashion and styling treatments, all stem from only seven basic shoe styles: the boot, oxford, pump, mule, moccasin, sandal and clog.

Further, the "newest" of these, the oxford, is over 300 years old, and the oldest, the moccasin, about 14,000 years old.

At this starting point, however, we should make a brief but important distinction between a style and a fashion.

Style is from the Latin "stylus," meaning an instrument for drawing an outline or profile of something. Hence a style is the basic shell, a design profile or concept. A boot, for example, is a style representing a basic concept in footwear.

A fashion is any version or variation of a style that is contemporary or currently popular. Thus we can have a demi-boot or knee-high boot, loose-fitting or leg-hugging, or any material or color treatment. Each is a boot fashion, but all are variations of the basic boot style.

The important distinction: styles are permanent, fashions are not.

Now, the idea that all footwear fashions stem from only seven basic designs at first usually stuns most shoemen. Their first reaction: "Impossible. I can name at least several other basic styles outside of those seven."

But when put to the test, they soon realize that their "other" basic styles are simply offshoot versions of the original seven. For example:

Slingbacks are merely open-back pumps or mules with backstraps. All strap shoes are pumps with straps attached. A ghillie is simply a unique treatment of an oxford. A monk strap is a pump with a wide instep strap and high tongue.

The seven basic shoe styles.

MONK

PUMP

MOCCASIN

SANDAL

OXFORD

MULE

BOOT

Most slippers are some version of a mule or pump. Platforms are variations of the clog. The loafer is an offshoot of the moccasin. Most sneakers or athletic shoes are oxfords made with leather or non-leather materials. And so on.

Now, another surprise. Not one of those original seven basic shoe styles was ever designed by or for a woman. All were designed exclusively by and for men.

That's not as chauvinistic as it may appear. All the seven basic shoe styles were designed originally not for any fashion value but for their utilitarian use. The oxford, for example, was designed as a more practical way to hold the shoe onto the foot. The boot was designed for leg protection for horse riders and hunters.

However, from many centuries back women have "adopted" those utilitarian men's styles, applying their esthetic talents and ingenuity to alter these styles into works of art and creative fashion.

HOW THEY ORIGINATED

How and when did these seven basic shoe styles originate? How did they get their names? Here, briefly, is how they all started.

Oxford. The name is derived from Oxford, England. When the laced shoe was introduced there in 1640 it became popular with the university students, and from there both the name and style spread. (Later, Thomas Jefferson was to be called a "foppish follower of Parisian fads" by his peers when he was among the first in America to switch from the traditional buckle shoes to laced oxfords).

Boot. Originally this was a two-piece unit: shoe below, legging above. When they were joined as a single unit it became a boot. Centuries ago the popular cavalier boots were high and widely flared at the top. They resembled a bucket, so the French called them "butt" for water bucket, and the word slowly evolved into "boute." When the Normans crossed the Channel to England in 1066, the English adopted the style and called it "boot."

Pump. In the Elizabethan era a thin-soled slipon shoe was worn by the carriage footmen who were called "pumps" (they pumped the carriage pedals). When similar shoes were adopted as a fashion by the gentry, they retained the name pumps.

Clog. From an old English word meaning a lump of wood. The clog originally was a platform-like piece of wood on which the shoe rested to protect the shoe from mud and rain. Later, leather uppers were attached to the wood bottom to become the clog.

Mule. This is from the ancient Sumerian term "mulu," meaning an indoor shoe or a slipon scuff. It was the original slipper. Many centuries later when a heel was put under the mule, it became a backless fashion shoe—but also still used as a slipper.

Sandal. The style dates back over 9,000 years and is the most universal of all shoe styles. The name is derived from the Latin "sanis," meaning a board. The sandal was originally a board-like slab of leather sole held onto the foot with rawhide thongs.

Moccasin. The oldest known shoe construction, dating back about 14,000 years, perhaps earlier. It was adopted by the American Indians who added the innovation of the moccasin "plug" on the vamp, which was ornately decorated with colored beads. The word "moccasin" is American Indian and means a foot covering.

Thus the creative part of footwear fashion isn't the innovation of new *basic* designs, but rather of adapting those few basic styles, the seven originals, to fresh interpretations.

The fact that over the centuries there have been many millions of those "adaptations" is a tribute to the creative abilities and imagination of the shoe designers.

When we realize that all footwear fashions emerge from only seven basic styles, it helps to uncomplicate the "mysteries" of footwear fashion for the average shoeman. It means that deep at the root of fashion are a few perennial styles, and what blooms above is merely a floral forest of creative versions stemming from those few roots.

54

Using "The Language of Fashion" in Selling

Fashion is the native tongue of all women, and universally understood by all men.

Fashion is the native tongue of all women. And also of all style-aware men. They don't buy shoes. They buy a look. They buy a shoe for what its look will do for them. The shoe has meaning and value for them when it translates into fashion. That's why it's so important to speak "the language of fashion" when selling fashion footwear.

Many stores and salespeople fall seriously short here. Hence much of the sales-appeal and value of the shoe is lost in the selling process. The use of hackneyed terms like "a nice shoe" or a "pretty color" or "real leather" reach deaf ears.

"This is the very latest—open toe, strapless, backless; but we don't have it in your size."

272 Profitable Footwear Retailing

Those are utilitarian, shopworn terms and do nothing for the shoe, the customer or the sale. But when you use the language of fashion you do the unusual. This upgrades the product and adds class to the selling, and also helps move the sale.

Here are some guidelines for using the language of fashion:

Color. Never say it's "a nice color" or a "pretty color." Be specific. Give the color a name (often on the shoe box label): Burgundy, Pastel Pink, Navy, Rust Brown, Chestnut Tan, Berry Red, Emerald, Pewter, Bark, Powder Blue, etc. Or if in the metallic family: Goldtone, Silvertone, Coppertone. The customer instantly relates such terms to his or her apparel. Once you specify the color by name, then you can speak of it being "one of today's leading fashion colors."

Also refine the color by using such terms as shade, tint, tone, cast, hue. This gives an added dimension to the simple word "color." Further, speak of the color having a "deep tone" or "soft hue." Romance it.

The color dictionary lists over 17,000 different colors—most of them, of course, variations of the basic colors. But that gives you an idea of the subleties of color that are important to the fashion-conscious customer. There is also a Color Association of the United States which in advance of each season issues the "official" apparel and leather colors which are adopted by the footwear, apparel and accessories industries. It's not only important for shoes retailers and salespeople to be aware of these colors, but to make their names part of "the language of fashion" in each season's selling.

Materials. Never use innocuous terms like "real leather" or "a nice fabric" in selling. They're meaningless and actually downgrade the shoe, especially for the fashion-minded customer who wants a little glamour in the product.

Specify the material. If it's leather, then speak of kidskin or calfskin or pigskin or cordovan or lizard, etc. If it's a fabric shoe, again specify: linen, satin, gabardine, shantung, etc.

Speak of the material's *texture*. For example, glove leather, or buttery soft, or mellow, or firm. This gives the leather descriptive character. Also, when speaking of texture, have the customer feel the leather as you speak. This makes your words come alive.

Speak of the leather's *surface grain,* which is an important part of the leather's (and shoe's) esthetics. Refer to "top grain," which means natural or undoctored and is the highest quality. Some leathers have very distinctive grains, such as alligator, pigskin, ostrich, lizard, snakeskin. Or embossed grains like pebbled or scotch or marbled or boarded. Or the surface can be just "polished smooth." Point these surface characters out to the customer as something visually distinctive.

The shoe's *surface finish* is another important esthetic feature, and manufacturers and tanners spend considerable money to apply special finish effects. These finishes have different names like aniline (polished), matte (eggshell flat), burnished or antiqued (hand-rubbed or dual-toned effect), pearl or lustre (transluscent like a pearl), gloss (patent), glazed (a faint sheen), waxy (as in glove leather), napped (fine nap as in suede, or coarse nap as in brushed). Associate these terms with words like opaque, lustre, frosty, radiant, luminous, burnished—much as you would with a fine gem.

Shape. This refers to the last. But if you're selling a fashion shoe, don't use the word "last." Instead, speak of shape or profile or silhouette. These are more fashion-oriented. Cite the toe shape particularly because it's the most fashion-important part of the last. Specify the toe shape by name: tapered, snipped, oval, needle, recede, walled, etc. This lends character to the shape.

Shape also involves the rest of the shoe, such as its length-look profile (hold the shoe near eye level in your hand to show its profile). Refer to the silhouette, the sculptured character, the lean, elegant lines, the sleek contours. Use words like slender and slim. Speak of the clean or graceful lines of the shoe's arch and waist area.

Style and Design. Avoid using hackneyed terms like "a nice-looking shoe." Show *why* it's an attractive style. For example, cite the throatline shape (at the rim of the vamp). This can be square, round, peaked, V-cut, off-sided, etc. If the shoe has ornamentation, point it out—bow, buckle, tassel, buttons, ornament—and cite it as a nice finishing touch.

Don't refer to the shoe as a shoe. Give it its precise name: pump, sandal, oxford, boot, clog, moccasin. Or refine it further, such as a ghille tie, a blucher oxford, monk strap, slingback pump, espadrille, Swedish clog, demiboot, D'Orsay pump, three-eyelet tie, slipon. If a woman's shoe has a strap, call the strap by its fashion name: T-strap, instep strap, halter strap, cross strap, side strap, etc.

Fashion Details. There are other fashion features to the shoe that should be highlighted. Among them:

The *heel* should never be taken for granted, especially on women's shoes, simply because it's visible to the customer. Heels have names like Cuban, Louis, baby Louis, stacked, continental, stiletto, wedge, museum, dutchboy, hooded, and so on. Call the heel by its name. Heels also come in different shapes: curved, squareback, setback, flared. Speak of the heel being sculptured, contoured, chiseled. These citations give the heel an identity of its own and becomes part of the shoe's fashion story.

Modern *soles* are often an important fashion feature of the shoe. This can relate to the sole's material (leather, crepe, rubber, man-made). Or its color or contrasting color, such as a red cushion sole on a grey buck upper. Or the sole's surface design. Or the cover material as on a platform shoe. The emphasis should not be on the functional features (durability, traction), but on the fashion features that enhance the look of the shoe.

Detailing is often overlooked as a selling feature in fashion footwear. For example, fancy or decorative stitching on the upper ("note the fine, tailored stitching"). Or it can be a collar or trim of contrasting material around the shoe's topline. Or an overlay or puckered plug on the vamp; or an attractive lining; or decorative touches like perfs, pinking, cutouts, pleating. Don't let the customer (or yourself) take these touches for granted. They add fashion character and should be highlighted in the selling.

FASHION SELLING POINTS

When selling fashion, the customer regards you as a fashion counselor or guide. So talk and act like one—but not in a show-offy manner.

Don't hold the shoe in your hand like a club or dead fish. It's a jewel. Treat it as such and the customer will respect and admire it more.

Make touch a selling tool. Have the customer touch the leather, the lining—and at the same time speak of the tactile esthetics of these features.

Sell the "inside story" as part of the fashion story—the lining, the cushion insole, the craftsmanship, the contrasting colors.

Use fashion coordination. Footwear is an accessory. It's bought to be worn with certain apparel or for certain occasions. So *never* say "this shoe can be worn with anything or anywhere." No shoe can.

When selling to women use the word "fashion." When selling to men use the word "style."

Keep abreast of fashion and the language of fashion. Read the men's or women's fashion magazines, or the fashion pages of the newspaper or the trade publications. This will not only keep you informed of current and upcoming fashion trends, but will keep you tuned in to the current fashion terms.

Don't assume that because the customer looks when buying they automatically see. They often overlook many of the shoe's subtle fashion details. It's up to the seller to highlight them.

Fashion is the song of romance and the language of fashion is its lyrics.

55

Fashion Cycles and How They Work

"Those who explore the past to find the future are chasing ghosts. In all fashion the past is dead and we cannot revive it." (Design consultant Robert Riley)

When something stylish quits looking queer, they change it.

Everyone knows that footwear and apparel fashions move in cycles. But do these cycles have any predictable regularity or rhythm to them? How long do these cycles last? And what causes the shift from one cycle to the next?

Shoemen spend a lot of time and effort trying to forecast fashion trends. Understanding the forces of fashion cycles can help in determining both short and long range forecasts—and especially to distinguish between a ripple and a wave in the fashion cycles.

First, something fundamental. Fashions change, but basic styles never. For example, a pump is a basic style. No matter the cycle, the pump is forever. But the fashion character of the pump changes periodically—open or closed, pointed or round toe, low or high heels, etc. So too with other basic styles like sandals, oxford, boots, etc. Cycles apply to fashions, never to basic styles.

"New" fashions are introduced season to season, year to year. These are not cycles but merely ripples of change within the same cycle. Boot fashions, for example, had a peak cycle of popularity for several years. But within that cycle, boots varied a bit year to year.

However, when a cycle has run its full course, then the year-to-year ripples crest to wave size and a complete new cycle—a major and sustained fashion shift—occurs. The ripples aren't cycles, but the waves are. Good fashion forecasting is the ability to distinguish between a ripple and a wave.

A major fashion change or cycle involves a radical shift in direction. For example, from broad to narrow toes; from squat heels to high, slim heels; from thick to thin soles; from heavy looks to light, elegant looks.

Such major changes NEVER occur on a year-to-year basis. If they did they would create financial and inventory chaos for manufacturers and retailers alike—as well as for consumer shoe wardrobes.

HOW LONG IS A CYCLE?

Footwear fashion cycles in America began only about 65 years ago. That's when mass or volume fashion made its bow. Prior to then fashion was "elitist," available or affordable only to the well-to-do. Thus it was in the early 1920s that the process of fashion cycles really began.

We know, of course, that apparel and footwear fashion cycles move in tandem because they are naturally mated. But how often do major fashion cycles occur? And is there any dependable regularity to them?

The visible records over the past 65 years show that a major fashion cycle occurs about every 9 years. Not precisely but closely approximate.

A major new cycle goes into the ascendency for about two years, peaks for approximately five years, then moves toward a descendency over the next two years as the new cycle starts its move upward. Nothing happens abruptly.

True, a hot item may burst onto the scene. But this is merely a coincidental ripple. It doesn't make waves nor affect the course of the cycle. The same applies to fads. Most have the fragile life span of a moth.

Now, let's illustrate a somewhat recent cycle. About 1966–1967, narrow toes, slim heels and dressy looks were in demise. The cycle moved toward the opposite extreme (cycles usually do)—thick or platform soles, low-chunky heels, broad or bump toes, heavy-look shoes, boots, etc.

The cycle grew to maturity, but by 1975–1976 had run its course. The new cycle started gradually toward dressier, more elegant looks, narrower toes, lighter soles, higher and slimmer heels, a decline in the long dominance of boots.

Similar or parallel changes appeared in all apparel—the movement toward dressier, more traditional and classic clothing.

Now, an intriguing question: Why do major fashion cycles occur on this approximate 9-year pattern? The answer is unknown. However, clothing psychologists and sociologists believe that the public has a limited "mood span," just as a child or adult has a limited attention or concentration span. When the mood span can no longer be sustained, a major shift in public mood and lifestyle is set in motion. Fashion change is one of its inevitable consequences.

WHAT CAUSES FASHION CYCLE CHANGES?

There is a persistent and popular myth that manufacturers or designers are the instigators of major fashion changes. Many also believe that manufacturers and designers deliberately generate major fashion changes to create obsolescence and thereby stimulate more sales by "forcing" people to buy the new fashions.

Both views are absurd. No manufacturer or designer, no matter how large or influential, has the power to buck or alter the main cycle. As the record shows, many have tried and failed.

The movement of major fashion cycles is beyond their control. Manufacturers and designers do not make the fashion weather. They only forecast it and dress their products accordingly.

Fashion cycle changes occur almost wholly as a result of a combination of political, social and economic forces which establish new lifestyles. These are the result of a mass shift in public mood and attitude. New fashions move in to adapt to these changes. Fashion change is a consequence and not a cause by itself.

For example, the 1966–1967 period saw a burst and dominance of the youth culture accompanied by free-wheeling, almost rebellious and uninhibited lifestyles. It was matched by much social and political unrest—campus and urban riots, the war protests, the communes, the drug culture, ethnic "rights" movements, protest marches, etc. Defiance was the mood.

The contemporary "fashions" matched the mood, scene and lifestyle: mini-skirts, jeans, uncut hair, slovenly attire, ethnic fashion fads, boutiques, grubby sneakers, monster shoes, heavy boots, village sandals, platforms, gaudy colors, heavy trimmings, etc.

The cycle ran its predictable course and the turnabout occurred in the mid-1970s as the public mood turned strongly conservative. So did lifestyles. And so did apparel and footwear fashion—the mass return to more traditional attire, classic dress-up looks, more conservative and even some semblance of elegance.

No manufacturers or designers or industries dictated any of these forces of change. As always, they went about fulfilling their fashion function of "adapting."

We have long assumed that a "fashion leader"—a manufacturer or designer, for example—is one who consistently initiates new fashion trends. It's not so. The leaders are simply those who can spot or sense a shift in a major cycle and get in on the ground floor of the new direction. As the inevitable new cycle starts its ascendency we then assume that the "fashion leader" was responsible for it when actually he or she was just smart or intuitive enough to get onto the bandwagon before the others.

The failure to understand fashion cycles has traditionally been costly to manufacturers and retailers alike. For example, the failure to recognize that a major cycle is terminating its course leads to over-laden inventories of "old cycle" merchandise. This happened with pointed toes and high heels after the mid-1960s, and again with the monster-type shoes in the mid-1970s. They became distress merchandise.

Thus, one key to sounder inventory control and protection against inventory losses is often not so much a matter of trend-watching but cycle-watching.

56

In-Store Fashion Sales Training

*Tell me, I'll forget. Show me, I may
remember. But involve me and I'll
understand.*

It doesn't make sense. Over 80 percent of all footwear is bought primarily with "look" in mind. And look means fashion, style-appeal. Yet perhaps not more than 10 percent of the nation's approximately 300,000 retail shoe salespeople get any in-store training on the principles of footwear fashion and how to sell fashion.

What difference does it make? Probably tens of millions of dollars in additional sales that *could* be made but *don't* get made.

But the benefits of in-store fashion training go further. Among the proven results: it can increase traffic and sales; builds multiple-pair sales; lowers selling costs by raising sales productivity; reduces markdowns; upgrades store image; improves the morale of salespeople and reduces personnel turnover; boosts earnings for salespeople and profits for the store.

What's the objective of an in-store fashion training program? First, to indoctrinate the personnel about the basics of fashion, especially footwear fashion. Second, to develop the techniques of fashion selling and fashion counseling. Third, to keep personnel attuned to *current* fashion developments to tie in with their selling functions.

THE GROUND RULES

Launching and conducting an effective program costs nothing and involves little time. But first, let's get to the ground rules for conducting these meetings.

1) Set up a pre-planned "course"—a minimum of ten meetings held once a week, but not less than twice monthly.
2) Meeting length, one hour. Best time, 8 to 9 AM. Same day each meeting. Exclude all interruptions. No cheating on time.
3) Each meeting should concentrate on *one* topic. Have a precise agenda and stick to it.
4) Use props, samples, visuals, demonstrations. Involve audience participation. Avoid too much "lecturing." Encourage salespeople to take notes.
5) Avoid time-wasting on petty details, digressions.
6) Make attendance compulsory. That includes *all* store personnel. Fashion should involve and excite the *whole* store.
7) Close the meeting promptly at the appointed time.

A common dilemma of store management: What do we present and discuss? The topic potentials are actually limitless. But first start by removing the confusing "mystery" about fashion. Begin by discussing the five basics of *all* fashion: shape, design (patterns), materials, color, and treatment (ornaments, trims). This establishes a foundation. It allows salespeople to translate fashion into tangible realities.

Next, *each* of these is a topic for single meetings. Shape means lasts, toe expressions, silhouettes, line, profile.

Design means the styles and patterns. There are only seven basic styles from which *all* footwear fashions stem: the sandal, boot, oxford, pump, mule, clog, and moccasin. Fashions are simply contemporary versions of each of these.

Materials involve the leathers, fabrics, man-mades. Certain materials find their way into certain types of footwear. Why and how?

Color has countless possibilities for discussion. Treatment consists of the final decorative touches—ornaments, stitching, perfs, cutouts, pinking, collars, etc.

Other meetings can focus on single fashion components such as heel shapes and heights and types, or soles (materials, bottom designs, etc.) as related to the shoe's look and fashion character.

A meeting can center on "the language of fashion" and how to use it in selling. For example, instead of merely saying a color, use more subtle terms like shade, hue, cast, tint. A touch of class. Instead of saying "fine leather" speak in specifics— fine calfskin or kidskin or pigskin or lizard. It adds fashion enrichment.

Discuss fashion subtleties like surface textures and finishes. Don't say suede but fine napped or brushed. Speak of top grain or pebbled grain or crushed leather. Specify the kind of surface finish—lustre, pearl, waxed or glove, aniline, glazed, matte, metallic, antique or burnished. Such terms add character and value to the shoe, and each contributes its own fashion look.

Don't speak of "construction" but of craftsmanship or crafted detailing.

Each season the store buys new shoes. The buyer selects each for a reason, mostly a fashion reason. But seldom are the salespeople informed *why* the shoes were selected. So hold one or more meetings, going over each shoe and the fashion rationale behind it. Thus the store's "reason for buying" becomes the salesperson's "reason for selling" and the customer's "reason for buying."

The same applies to your local advertising of these shoes. Let the salespeople know in advance. Show them pre-prints.

THE TEACHERS

Who does the "teaching" at the meetings? It can be divided among several: the owner, the buyer, an experienced or effective salesperson, a guest speaker. It should not be repeatedly the same person.

A couple of times a year invite the buyer from one of the local fashion clothing stores to be a guest speaker (with samples). The objective: to discuss incoming apparel fashions and hence enable the shoe salespeople to coordinate the shoes with the clothes and also be conversant with current trends.

Sometimes you can invite one of the more knowledgeable and articulate shoe travelers to talk about incoming trends in his fashion category—boots, casuals, dress shoes, etc. Not his product or brand or line, but the broader scope of his category.

Use demonstrations. Let the salespeople take turns before the others at selling fashion based on lessons learned—with another salesperson acting as customer. Let there be audience critique, suggestions, participation. Let it be a "floor show."

Use a meeting to discuss customer counseling on fashion—the use of the techniques and the language of fashion.

Another meeting can discuss tie-in sales of fashion accessories: handbags, hosiery, clipon ornaments, shoe care items, etc.

As you can see, the range of topics is as broad and varied as you wish to make it. But never lose sight of the objective—to give the salespeople more confidence and effectiveness in selling fashion by developing more fashion know-how.

Once the training program has developed momentum and the salespeople are applying the learning on the selling floor, take the next step and *merchandise* your salespeople.

In your ads, even your windows and displays, plus an occasional mailing piece—talk about your "experienced fashion counselors." Show pictures, mention names. It's great for morale and stimulates personnel enthusiasm and confidence. It builds team pride and also enhances store image.

Most customers need and want fashion counseling and guidance from the salespeople. When they receive it they have more confidence in the salesperson, the store, the product. And they're more open-to-buy. Credibility is one of the most effective sales tools.

Tests repeatedly show that fashion-trained and fashion-oriented salespeople sell more, earn more. So if the rewards are shared by both the store and salespeople, the next step is obvious. Start your own in-store fashion training program.

Customer
Relations

57

What Makes a Satisfied Customer?

Consumers are statistics; customers are people.

Tact is the ability to give a person a shot in the arm without letting him feel the needle.

Retailers constantly speak of "satisfied customers." But when asked what makes a satisfied customer, they tend to get a little tongue-tied or they give some simplistic answer.

Retailers constantly speak of providing for the "needs and wants" of the customer. But again, when asked to specify those needs and wants, much gets left out.

Now, the first law in retailing for satisfying customers is this: *make yourself necessary.* That means the merchandise, the store, the services, the customer treatment. When you become necessary to the customer's needs and wants, you automatically have a satisfied customer.

Satisfied customers become loyal customers, and customer loyalty is the foundation of all repeat business. A store pays an enormous penalty for dissatisfied customers. For example:

A dissatisfied customer usually becomes a permanently lost customer. If you permanently lose just one such customer a day, the loss is about $150 a year per customer (three pairs of shoes a year with an average of $40 per pair, plus accessories). Multiply times 320 such customers over a year and the sales loss is a staggering $51,000 a year.

If the dissatisfied customers withdraw their family's business from your store, the annual loss in sales can reach a shocking $150,000 or more a year.

Astounding? Of course. But nevertheless true.

Well, what are the prime elements that result in a satisfied customer and customer loyalty? They are as follows:

1) Merchandise selection.   4) Quality of services.
2) Store atmosphere.   5) Product performance.
3) Treatment by personnel.   6) Store followup.

Merchandise Selection. This is a prime reason why customers patronize a shoe store—a good selection of styles and the availability of needed sizes and widths. Obvious as this is, it's a negative factor in some stores ("They never seem to have my size. . ." or "They don't have much to choose from.") Merchandise selection is the starting point for attracting customers.

Store Atmosphere. Many customers consider shopping an exciting and pleasurable adventure. The store atmosphere—the lighting, decor, fixtures, displays, layout, etc.—should be conducive to this. It's part of the "shopping satisfaction."

Treatment by Personnel. Every customer wants to feel appreciated and respected. You're not selling a "buyer" or "consumer" but a person. Personalized treatment is reflected by store policy and the actions of the sales personnel.

It means a warm welcome, courtesy, patience, visible desire to be helpful. The best model: treating the customer as you would a welcome guest in your own home. An important part of the satisfied-customer syndrome.

Quality of Services. Service is the divine right of customers. If, as retailers say, the customer is king, then he or she should be treated as royalty.

It begins with the quality of the fitting service. It's not enough to merely fit the shoe. It's the way it's done—superficially and carelessly, or with professional skill, care, a touch of class. Ask yourself: in what way is my fitting service superior to the competition's? If you can't answer in specifics and with conviction, you're falling short of customer-satisfaction potential.

Customer counseling contributes significantly to customer satisfaction because it increases the customer's believability in the store, the product, the salesperson. It can be fashion counseling in the selection of a style, color, material, heel height, etc. Or shoe counseling in the upkeep of the shoe to help it stay new-looking longer. Customers shouldn't have to ask for this guidance. It should be volunteered as part of store service.

Surprise the customer with simple "extra" services. Never put an old shoe back onto the foot without a quick brushing or buffing. Insert new laces (free) for worn or frayed ones. A free shoe horn (your store name imprinted) with every purchase. A new socklining to replace old, worn or wrinkled ones.

If you're selling bettergrade shoes, how about monograming the customer's initials on the inside counter or under the shank—the same as done on men's hatbands? It's unusual, a touch of class, and it enhances the pride of ownership.

The customer card record further personalizes the service. Show the customer the record. It further strengthens the customer's loyalty attachment to the store.

In the case of children, the customer record is very important, especially where reminder cards are sent. But carry it further. Keep a footgrowth record. Then about once a year send the parent the child's "foot growth progress report." For example, "Over the past year Johnny's foot has grown two-thirds of an inch, or two full shoe sizes." Not only does this make the parent more aware of the importance of shoe size changes, but the information makes a family conversation piece. Further, customers tend to stay more attached to stores where their records are kept on file.

If an infant is being fitted to its first pair of shoes, take a Poloroid shot of it and give it to the parent. It's a memorable event for the parent, and a similar idea as bronzing those first infant shoes.

Translate your mailing list as your "preferred customer" list and designate it as such. You use this list to send out mailings of upcoming clearance sales, or new merchandise just in the store. And the customers are told they're getting this information before it's advertised because they are on the store's "preferred customer" list. They're flattered by this and it further cements loyalty to the store. It also builds sales.

Almost everyone has access to a credit card. But a charge account specifically with *your* store often steers the customer's buying to your store rather than elsewhere. The charge account translates into something personal—"my store."

The followup selling—the accessories, the extra pair, etc—add further to the service effort. Customers like the attention of being shown more and having additional choices, even if no extra purchase is made. The customer views this as extra service.

Product Performance. This is obviously an important part of the satisfied customer package. Have the shoes worn well? Been comfortable? Kept their shape well with wear? Responded well to maintenance?

Much of the product's performance will depend upon how well the shoe was fitted in the first place. And also on the shoe care counseling.

Product counseling contributes to customer satisfaction. This information should be volunteered by the salesperson, not offered only if asked for. It can be information about the materials. And not just saying "real" leather but specifying what kind of leather or other material. A few words about the shoe's crafting. Or special styling features such as the fine stitching or the pattern or silhouette. Perhaps a few comments about the sole or heel, or the shoe's flexibility or breathability.

This kind of volunteered product information adds appreciation of value received by the customer. And it also upgrades the salesperson's credibility for his or her knowledge and skill and service efforts.

Store Followup. Much retail selling, unfortunately, is a sell-and-run or kiss-and-goodbye proposition. This is curable. Simply send a followup postcard to the customer with a thank-you for having made his or her purchase in your store. Customers are surprised by this nice touch. They appreciate and remember it.

Then there are those customers who haven't visited your store in a year or more. Why not? A simple "we've missed you" note can often work wonders in retrieving many of these customers. It's ironic. Stores spend a lot of money and effort to attract new customers, yet little or nothing to retrieve lost or missing ones.

What makes a satisfied customer? As you've seen, there's no one thing, no single magic button. You can have good service but limited selection of styles and sizes, or vice versa. You can have good product performance but a dull, drab store that discourages shopping.

Customer satisfaction is a combination of elements which together become a highly effective format for winning customer loyalty and repeat business which is the foundation for success and growth.

You can give a man a haircut many times, but you can scalp him only once. So, too, making the sale doesn't necessarily mean winning the loyalty and repeat business of the customer. Every sale should be approached with the attitude that everything you do is designed to fulfill the mission of a "satisfied customer" that will ensure his or her repeat purchases—again and again.

WHAT IS A CUSTOMER?

A customer is royalty and we are his servants.

A customer isn't dependent on us, but we on him.

A customer isn't an interruption of our work—he is the purpose of it. We aren't doing him a favor by serving him. He is doing us a favor by giving us the opportunity to do so.

A customer isn't an outsider to our business—he is a vital part of it.

A customer isn't a cold statistic. He is a human being with feelings, attitudes and thoughts like our own, and also with prejudices and gripes, just like us.

A customer isn't someone to argue or match wits with. Nobody ever won an argument with a customer.

A customer is a person who brings us his wants and needs. When we do justice to them we satisfy him—and we profit by it.

Without the customer there is no business, no job, no income, no profit. There is nothing.

58

Why Customers Get Lost—and How to Prevent It

You can cut a man's hair many times, but you can scalp him only once.

It takes less effort to keep an old customer satisfied than to get a new customer interested.

Retailers constantly talk about inventory control, budget control and expense control. But never about customer control.

You say you can't "control" customers. Wrong. Retailers do it every day, or try to. They simply express it in other ways like "repeat business" or "customer loyalty."

But the average retailer today has much less control of his customers than he realizes. And many of those retailers who boast, "I know my customers," may be deluding themselves.

Let's look at some numbers and see the consumer realities retailers must live with today—realities of "lost customers" that may be costing the average retailer up to 50 percent of his potential annual volume.

According to the Census Bureau, each year 17 percent of the population moves, mostly to another state or town or trading area. That means that the retailer needs another 17 percent in *new* customers each year just to stay even, and 25 percent to 30 percent to show growth.

That's just for starters. In addition, according to the National Retail Merchants Association, the average retailer will lose over 20 percent of the customers for a variety of other reasons, as follows:

- 4 percent attracted to competitive stores, promotions.
- 3 percent to missing sizes.
- 3 percent because of discourteous or incompetent services.
- 2 percent due to prices.
- 2 percent because of product dissatisfaction.
- 1 percent due to unsatisfactory handling of complaints.
- 1 percent deceased.
- 1 percent due to inconvenient location.

So over one-third of the average shoe store's customers are "mobile" customers, not regular or loyal repeaters. Does that mean that the other two-thirds are your "steady" customers? Not quite, as we'll see later.

Keep in mind that we're not talking here about the missed sales or walkouts, the customers who will usually return for a later visit. We're talking about the *permanently* lost customers.

This becomes a serious matter of customer turnover. And it receives very little attention by the average retailer. If the customer loss amounts to 25 percent a year, then the retailer has an almost 100 percent customer turnover about every four to five years.

You may be tempted to question or argue with those numbers. But unless you keep active customer records (and only an estimated 20 to 25 percent of retailers do), your hands would be tied. Do you know, for example:

What percentage of your customers buy just one pair of shoes a year from you?

How many have bought only one pair and never returned?

What percentage buy an average of two pairs a year from you? Three pairs? Four or more pairs?

What percentage of your customers account for 35 percent of your business—or 60 percent?

Without having the answers to such questions, how can you claim (1) "I know my customers"? (2) to know how many customers, or what percentage, you're losing each year—and how many new ones you're gaining? (3) to know what share of your customers is reliable regulars, and what share transients?

Without such information you actually know a lot less about your business and customers than you think you do.

REMEDIES AND PREVENTIONS

How can the lost-customers situation be remedied or minimized? Three strategies are involved:

1) Use ways to replace the 17 percent of customers who move away each year.
2) Find ways to prevent the drainage or loss of customers because of store shortcomings or competition.
3) Find ways to attract business away from the competition.

For every 17 percent who move away, another 17 percent or more of newcomers will move in. All will be looking for new stores to patronize. All stores will be competing for them. To attract them you need:

1) A strong, consistent ad program that identifies your store—the merchandise, prices, services, etc. You're vying for new customers as well as regular ones. Make sure the advertising takes in the full sweep of your trading area, not just the core. Consumers have more mobility today.
2) A strong store image is very important to stand above the crowd. It must lure newcomers via windows, interiors, lighting; an attractive place to shop.
3) Frequent and imaginative promotions that catch the eye and ear of newcomers and convey the impression of an "alive" store.
4) Brands. Nationally known brands follow customers everywhere. They also reflect the reliability and quality image of your store.
5) Frequent window changes. Newcomers do a lot of comparison shopping. Frequent window changes give the impression of constantly fresh merchandise and good selections.
6) Exceptional service, not just good service. The aim is to make a lasting first impression on the new customer.
7) Customer records. Get the new customer "on record." Let him or her *know* that a record is kept on file, and why (to send advance notices of special sales, or new merchandise; or a record of the customer's size and preferences, etc.) This helps attach the customer to the store.
8) After each purchase, and using the customer record card, send a follow-up thank-you note. A small thing that makes a big impression.

Next, how can you prevent or reduce drainoff of your regular customers to competitive stores? When you lose these customers—ordinarily an average of about 15 percent a year—it tells you one of two things: (1) what you're doing or offering isn't fully satisfying the customer; (2) one or more of your competitors is offering something better or more attractive.

So you start with two soul-searching questions: Where did the customers go? And why did they leave?

Unfortunately, most retailers can't answer either of those two questions. However, the surveys, as cited earlier, give a good indication of why most of them leave or are lost—usually out of sizes, limited selections, faulty services, product dissatisfaction, etc. These are things you can do something about.

Your remedial action is obvious: closely analyze the "fault" areas of your operation, and correct the faults one by one.

Services, for example. They become habits and are taken for granted, faults and all. Or the price brackets haven't changed much while the trading area's inflow of new customers lean toward different price brackets than yours. Or you haven't made any improvements in your size-up habits in years; or haven't made any important changes in your lines or merchandise selections.

Habits and complacency are the enemy of retailing. Everything in your operation should be given a good reappraisal every year, based on the questions: "Is everything I'm doing the best that can be done? Am I losing customers, and if so, why?"

Here again is where customer records are invaluable. A periodic runthrough will tell you how many you haven't seen in a year, and who they are. The missing element is why you've lost them. See how one store in Salt Lake City handles this.

Each year the store goes through its card records and selects all customers it hasn't seen in a year. Salespeople then make phone calls to these customers. The calls are friendly, no sell involved. "We've been going through our customer records and find you haven't visited our store over the past year. Is there a reason? We've missed you."

Or a personally addressed short note is sent. The message is the same: "We've missed you. Why haven't you visited our store lately?"

The response is excellent. About 75 percent of the phone calls will provide information as to why the customers haven't been in the store. They reveal any dissatisfactions (which the store notes and tried to correct). In many cases where there's no special reason, the customers will often visit the store for a purchase. These "recovered" customers return because they were flattered by the store's attention.

In the case of the short notes, two things happen: (1) the store, via the undelivered and returned mail, is able to keep a check on deceased or moved-away customers, and hence keep the customer record files up to date; (2) many of the customers return, usually saying the same thing, "The store showed it cared enough about my business, so I'm back again."

About 35 percent of the "lost" customers are recovered each year simply because the store shows that it cares about them.

The third leakage point is loss of customers to competition. The cause is usually the same. Either what you're doing or offering isn't enough, or the competition is offering more or doing it better. The remedy isn't always a case of copying the competition. For example, you can match the competition's cut prices and end up with more volume but no profit.

Famous golfer Sam Snead once said, "Forget the competition. Always play against par."

Have your own standards of excellence whether in fashion, merchandise selections, sizes and fitting, brands, services, store image, etc. If you maintain a par of excellence for your type of operation, the worry shifts to your competition because he, not you, must match par.

Getting to the new residents in the trading area early is important. Here are a couple of suggestions.

If there is a Welcome Wagon service in your community, join it. Many shoe retailers have had success with it. Welcome Wagon offers an "official" and personalized welcome to new residents in a trading area. It provides new families with a list of local stores and services with details about what these businesses offer. There is usually a special introductory, get-acquainted offer—purchase discount, special premium or gift, etc.

To be included in the Welcome Wagon program the store, of course, must enlist in the plan. Welcome Wagon keeps close touch with the names and addresses of new residents, and hence enables the participating stores to make early contact with them.

Direct mail is another effective avenue. Once a month go to the local town halls within your trading area. You can obtain names and addresses of new residents (homes, condos, etc.)

Send the household head a "welcome to Jonesville" letter. This can be a form letter, but it's important that it be personally addressed (avoid addressing to "Resident"). The letter starts out with a cordial welcome to the community, then offers information about your store, merchandise, personnel, brands, services, accessories, etc. It can include inserts of any current promotional literature (a promotion, sale, etc.).

It should include a purchase discount coupon as an introductory, get-acquainted offer, such as a 15 percent or 10 percent discount on the initial purchase.

Shoe clubs provide another way of creating and sustaining a flow of new customers. Many stores have operated these successfully for years. The principle is simple. Selected customers are enlisted. Or a sign can be posted at the checkout counter: "Earn Cash Or Free Merchandise. Ask About Joining Our Shoe Club."

There are various ways to work the plan. For example, for every six new customers sent to the store by a shoe club member, a commission or bonus is paid in the form of merchandise or cash or purchase credits. Each new customer is identified by a slip or coupon given to him or her by a club member.

Some shoe club members are very enthusiastic and productive participants. If enough such members are enlisted the program can become very successful not only in sales but in creating a steady flow of new customers. Many stores have scores, some even hundreds, of shoe club working members who earn nice rewards for their efforts.

Retailers usually place all their focus on things like inventory control, budgets, buying and selling. They're all vital, of course. But every business enterprise rests on one foundation: customers. And if you don't maintain reasonable control of your customers, all the rest stands on quicksand.

THE STORE SHOWED THAT IT CARED—AND THE CUSTOMERS CAME BACK

A family shoe store in Salt Lake City randomly selected customers from its files who hadn't made a purchase in the past 18 months. The customers were phoned and asked why they hadn't been in the store. The replies or findings were as follows:

- 11 said they weren't satisfied with the service on their last visit.
- 20 complained that "it wasn't the first time you were out of stock in my size."
- 12 replied that either their favorite brand was missing, or the style selection had become more limited.
- 17 said the prices had gotten too high and now they were shopping around more.
- 9 were shopping where the traffic was easier and the location more convenient.
- 24 had moved or were deceased.
- 117 had no special reason.

But within the next month, 42 of those 117 "no reason" customers were back in the store to buy. Their total purchases amounted to $1,645. Many of them made similar comments: "I figured if you called and showed you cared enough about my business, I owed you a visit."

But the store also obtained valuable feedback information from the other replies—about the service, the out of stock, limited size selection, etc. It took steps to improve each. The result was fewer walks, more repeat business.

The moral: When customers know that you really care, they'll care enough about coming back.

59

Handling Returns and Complaints

Handling customer complaints requires the tact and skill of handling porcupines without disturbing the quills.

Keep your bristles down. A porcupine gets no petting.

Merchandise returns and customer complaints have always been an ailment of retailing—and perhaps more than average in shoe retailing.

For example, a survey conducted by the National Family Opinion Institute showed that among 44 different product lines, footwear ranked 11th from the bottom in the consumer's view of satisfaction and value received. In this respect, while 11 percent of consumers gave shoes a good rating and 51 percent a fair rating, 39 percent assigned a poor rating. Thus footwear seems to be vulnerable to returns and complaints.

It's estimated that between 2 percent and 3 percent of purchased shoes are returned to stores by customers for any of various reasons. If all those returned were debited as a "loss," that adds up to about 25 million pairs a year, or some $800 million at retail and $400 million wholesale. That's a frightening sum because it amounts to almost 3 percent of the total estimated net profits of retailing.

But if 2 to 3 percent of shoes are returned with complaints, how many are *not* returned by dissatisfied customers who simply never patronize the same store again or buy the same brand?

For example, studies show that women more frequently return shoes—their own or their children's. But far fewer men do so. The latter simply don't buy again from the same store. Thus the 2 to 3 percent figure may, in terms of product or other dissatisfaction, be appreciably higher than that level.

Today, some retailers believe that returns and complaints are on the increase. Among the reasons they think are responsible are less experienced or inadequately trained sales personnel (such as more part-timers), lower standards of quality controls in factories, increased use of imports with more limited size selections and quality standards, higher consumer expectations when paying higher prices, more aggressive consumer demands on product performance, etc.

What are the chief reasons for returned shoes? They vary by product category. Studies show the following:

For children's shoes: sole wear, broken seams, general shoe wear performance. For men's shoes, wear performance, fit and comfort, miscellaneous (squeaks, cracked insoles, etc.). For women's shoes: fit and comfort complaints, miscellaneous damages (straps, ornaments, heel breakage, etc.), shoe-related foot problems (shoes making the feet burn or perspire, etc.).

The issue of "justifiable" shoe returns has long been debatable. But according to studies of shoe returns by SATRA, the British shoe research organization, 50 to 75 percent of all returns are due to shoemaking faults. They estimate that the figures are about the same for Britain and the U.S.

It's well known, of course, that there is some abuse of privileges on returns by consumers and retailers alike. But what share of returns are justifiable? According to surveys, manufacturers and retailers are pretty much in agreement. About two-thirds of each group think that more than 50 percent of all shoe returns are justified.

HANDLING RETURNS

We now have an overview of the seriousness of the return problem. How should stores handle returns?

The first rule: have a store policy and make sure all personnel are familiar with it. Yet, surveys show that while 48 percent of stores say they have a policy, 52 percent don't. Many of the latter claim that each return problem is different and each has to be "played by ear." That's partly true, partly not.

For example, some stores have a policy of no cash refunds on returns, though they offer a merchandise credit. This is done to prevent customer abuses (for instances, shoes have been shoplifted, then returned for a cash refund). Where this policy is used, make sure signs are posted in the store and at the checkout counter.

Beware the "Satisfaction Guaranteed" policy used in ads, counter cards, etc. It can be taken too literally by some customers with unjustified returns, and the store is in a bind with its guarantee policy. Spell out what the guarantee is for.

Again, some salespeople in their zeal to make the sale will "guarantee" such things as long wear, perfect comfort or fit, etc. But each of these becomes a customer's judgment. If the customer hasn't been satisfied with the wear or comfort or fit, the store can be obliged to make good. Hence, salespeople should be cautious about expressing any guarantees.

Then comes the dilemma of deciding whether a return claim is justified or not—and if it is, what kind of make-good should be used.

It boils down to the store's policy on leniency. The dilemma: how lenient? One recent study showed that while 59 percent of shoe retailers think they are "fair" with customers, another 41 percent think they're too lenient. Some of the independents think that department stores have "spoiled" the returns situation with excessive leniency, forcing the independents to match them.

The store's decisions must be flexible—a full money refund, a new pair, a merchandise credit, a compromise of part credit based on amount of time of wear—or a complete turndown.

Sometimes the decision gets sticky. No store wants to be unfair or lose the customer. Some stores go to extreme and accept all returns on a no-questions-asked basis. That can be costly, especially for smaller stores which have minimal assurance on borderline cases that the manufacturer will give them a compensating credit.

On a compromise adjustment where a part credit is given on worn shoes, some stores let the customer decide on the amount of the adjustment. They say to the customer, "You've gotten a fair amount of use from these shoes. What is that worth to you—and we'll allow you the difference." Usually the customer's suggestion will be fair, and sometimes appreciably less than what the store is ready to offer. This method satisfies both the customer and the store.

In many instances, such as a broken seam, loose buckle, loosened sole, etc., an offer to have the shoe repaired at the store's expense is sufficient. It also saves a hassle with the manufacturer.

The question of "ethics" is often involved. There are consumers who are chronic abusers of return privileges, or who make unreasonable demands. For example, customers can wear the shoes for a considerable time, then return them claiming that the shoes make their feet burn or perspire; or are uncomfortable; or weren't fitted properly in the first place; or have gone out of shape; etc. They want a new pair or a refund or an "adjustment."

There are no pat solutions here. Certain factors must be considered. Is it a regular customer and a one-time complaint? If so, then a full credit is automatic—even if the complaint isn't fully justified. Also, for the smaller retailer especially, he must often consider whether the manufacturer will give credit for a return, or whether he himself will have to absorb the loss.

It's not unusual for consumers to abuse shoes, then return them for a new pair or a refund. For example, placing the wet shoes of their children over a radiator to dry (or even in an oven), causing the leather to crack or the seams to break. Here again the "adjustment" is a matter of store policy on leniency, or whether the customer is a regular.

This raises an important matter when the original purchase is made—the matter of shoe care counseling by the store. In the case cited above, parents should be advised never to dry wet shoes over a radiator, plus other advice. Such information can help prevent or reduce returns, especially those from wearer abuses.

It's not unusual for some retailers themselves to use unfair or unethical tactics on returns to manufacturers. One study showed that 65 percent of manufacturers think retailers are too lenient with consumers on returns, and that about 30 percent of the retailers' returns are unreasonable or unjustified.

Then again, there are the outright violations of ethics. For example, the retailer giving a partial refund to the customer, then collecting a full credit from the manufacturer.

Nevertheless, most manufacturers (domestic more so than importers, according to retailers) tend to be fairly lenient with retailers on returns—and the larger the account the more leniency shown. In fact, one survey reveals that 65 percent of manufacturers think they are too lenient, and 72 percent of retailers think that manufacturers in general have a fair policy on returns.

The retailer should know the return policy (most are spelled out) of each resource with whom he does business. Further, the retailer should obtain a copy of "Suggested Guidelines For A Shoe Returns Policy," issued by the National Shoe Retailers Association. (9861 Broken Land Parkway, Columbia, Maryland 21046).

REDUCING RETURNS

By taking certain precautions, returns can be reduced and some prevented. For example, carelessness in fitting can be controlled, thus cutting later returns on this score. Customers deliberately insisting on a faulty size or fit should be forewarned that the store can't be held responsible.

But the error may not always be the fitter's. Occasionally a new lot of shoes will be found to be "poor fitters," such as some fault with the patterns. These can spell trouble and should be returned to the manufacturer as quickly as possible.

As new shoes come into the store, they should be examined for defects— color mismatches, lost buckles or ornaments, nicks or scratches, defective stitching, etc. Yes, it's time-consuming but it will save headaches later.

Store management and sales personnel should be cautioned against making "guarantees" to the customers about wear, fit, comfort. Or over-zealous expressions such as "if you're dissatisfied in any way, don't hesitate to bring the shoes back." For some customers that's an open invitation to bring the shoes back.

There should be a policy as to who personally handles the return and confrontation with the customer—the boss or manager, or the salesperson. If the latter, they should be trained in handling returns. For example, never arguing with a customer. This may win the battle but lose the war—meaning the customer.

Lastly, the store should keep a careful record of its returns—their number, reasons for returns, manufacturers or lines involved, justified versus other, action taken, losses, etc. This information will not only help reduce returns but also reduce the number of dissatisfied customers or resources associated with returns.

HANDLING GENERAL COMPLAINTS

Not all customer complaints involve returned shoes. Any complaint can be a negative mark against the store.

Surveys conducted by the National Retail Merchants Association have found the following customer complaints to be the most common: salespeople discourtesy, waiting for service, high pressure, waiting on two or more customers at the same time, not showing sufficient merchandise, lack of product knowledge, rushing the sale, confusing labels, indifference or incompetence of salespeople.

All, of course, are remediable or preventable. But if any of them occur habitually it demonstrates negligence on the part of management in training, policies or monitoring.

Also, never begrudge a customer complaint. Be grateful. It gives you a second chance to satisfy the customer and also an opportunity to learn by your mistakes. What to worry about is the legion of customers who never complain but also who never return to the stores to buy.

Who should handle complaints? When possible, the owner or manager. Customers prefer to have their complaints heard at top level because this is where the final decisions are made, and beyond which there is no buck passing.

Common sense psychology is vital in handling complaints or customer gripes. Never allow the customer to "lose face" by trying to prove him or her wrong. Listen sympathetically. Let the customer say everything he or she has to say. It's a kind of emotional purge. And being listened to is often enough to satisfy the customer and sometimes even results in an on-the-spot sale.

Your personal demeanor while listening to the complaint is equally important. The right use of tact, courtesy, patience, a smile and soft voice, empathy and expression of sincerity—these can disarm the customer and defuse the situation. And when the customer feels that he or she has, via your attitude, "received satisfaction," you then have a satisfied customer.

Don't hesitate to apologize. An apology isn't an admission of guilt, only a common courtesy.

Lastly, when you're in the right you can afford to keep your dignity. When you're in the wrong you can't afford to lose it.

60

Keeping Waiting Customers Contented While Waiting

Nothing interests a customer so much as himself.

In the average shoe store or department, three of every 10 customers walk out unsold. Of the various reasons, one is having to wait for service, or being ignored while waiting during busy periods. Many customers lose patience and walk.

Not only is the sale lost, but often the customer is permanently lost—especially when he or she feels they're a victim to the store's don't-care attitude.

So the common problem: how to keep waiting customers satisfied while waiting?

It starts with store policy, passed down to the salespeople, about ways to handle the waiting-customer problem. So the first rule: have a policy, and also a method.

Keeping Waiting Customers Contented While Waiting 299

Let's say the store is busy and all the salespeople are occupied. There may even be a couple of additional customers waiting to be served.

In comes a new customer. She quickly views the scene. She has a choice: Decide not to wait and walk out, or slowly wend her way to a seat and wait.

This is a vital moment. If he or she is allowed to walk, you've lost the customer and the sale. If he or she finds a seat and just waits, impatience can rapidly set in and what you have is a delayed walkout.

Those few moments are tremendously important because they determine whether the customer has taken control, or whether the store has assumed control of the customer and the prospective sale.

It's at this point of customer entry into the store where store policy begins. The rule: the salesperson closest to the door excuses himself from the customer he's waiting on and moves to greet the new customer. The salesperson is not "deserting" the current customer because what the salesperson will now do will take little more than a minute or so.

The new customer is greeted with a smile and words like, "Good morning. Let me help you find a seat." The customer is escorted to a seat.

This instantly does two things: (1) it acknowledges the presence of the customer; (2) being guided to a seat is an act of courtesy. The two together immediately tells the customer his or her business is wanted and appreciated.

The other customer whom the salesperson left momentarily (the salesperson has already said "excuse me for a moment") doesn't feel abandoned or neglected. That customer is already occupied looking at the shoes he or she had been shown or fitted to.

Now, back to our new customer. The salesperson says in a reassuring way, "We're busy right at the moment, but someone will be with you very shortly."

Psychologically, this is an important moment. Nobody likes to feel ignored, or regarded as just another body coming into the store. The customer is bringing money into the store to spend. The customer wants to be respected as a valued buyer.

The store should not only care about that but show that it cares. Therefore, acknowledging the new customer's presence, no matter how busy the store, is a vital first step in holding the customer and making the sale to follow.

If the customer is wearing a coat, offer to remove it. This gives the customer a more relaxed, at-home feeling. It also reduces the possibility of a walkout if he or she becomes impatient with waiting.

Remove one shoe, look inside and say, "I'm curious about your shoe size. Does this say 7B"? Then place the shoe under the seat. This tactic is not to learn the size but to get the shoe off the foot, which further discourages a walkout while waiting.

Where do you seat the new customer? Not just anyplace. Two of the best seating sites are (1) facing a window looking outside where there is pedestrian or other traffic, or (2) facing other customers who are being shown or fitted to shoes.

In both instances the customer is viewing *action*. Nothing is more boring or patience-trying to a waiting customer than facing a blank wall or rows of shoes in boxes. The idea is to keep the customer's eyes and mind occupied.

Another important gesture is to give the waiting customer one or two magazines to scan or read. For a woman, perhaps a copy of *Vogue* or *Woman's Day;* for a man, *Esquire* or *Gentleman's Quarterly* or *Sports Illustrated.* Make sure the magazines are clean and current. Handing the customer a tattered, year-old magazine is like passing on a pair of hand-me-down shoes.

When you offer the magazines, say, "You might like to look at these until one of our people is able to serve you shortly."

If the customer has one or two small children with her, offer something to occupy the child: a couple of balloons, a comic book, etc. Nothing can be more devastating to a store or other customers than a couple of yowling kids running up and down aisles or pushing shoe cartons into the wall. Not all mothers are disciplinarians to keep this kind of mischievous behavior under control.

It's now time for the salesperson to return to the customer he or she was waiting on. Keep in mind that the acknowledging and seating of the new customer, along with the amenities, hasn't taken more than a minute or so.

When taking leave from the new customer, smile and say, "Please excuse me. Someone will be with you shortly." It's further assurance to the customer that he or she won't be forgotten. Further, the customer now has the means to remain occupied and prevent impatience from setting in.

If the waiting period extends longer than expected, it's important to return to the waiting customer about every five minutes to express further assurance. This doesn't have to be done by the same salesperson but by any of the store personnel who happens to be nearby. This, too, should be store policy.

One of the worst sins is to allow a waiting customer to lose his or her turn to another waiting customer who has entered later. This can draw an angry response like "I was here first!"—or a walkout in a huff. So keep them in right order.

There is still another way to keep a waiting customer pleasantly occupied while waiting. If the store has open displays, or shoes exposed on shelves or special bargain bins, suggest that the customer do a little browsing while waiting.

The salesperson's comment might be, "Perhaps you'd like to look around at some of our displays until someone has a chance to wait on you. We have a lot of interesting things to see." The salesperson should then lead the customer to the display or browsing area. This can sometimes result in a multiple-pair sale because of the customer finding something additional he or she hadn't planned to buy.

Here again it's important not to forget the customer once he or she has been allowed to browse. Salespeople should be on the alert and once in a while inform the browsing customer that service will be available shortly. This further helps to prevent a customer walkout.

Finally, when the waiting customer is served, the salesperson should start with the comment, "I'm sorry you had to wait longer than we expected."

After the sale is made and the shoes wrapped, a further comment, "Thank you for waiting. I'm sure you're new shoes will make it all worthwhile."

Now, a few rules to remember:

1) No customer wants to be ignored while waiting.
2) Accord new customers personal recognition or acknowledgment when entering the store—no matter how busy the store at the moment.
3) Get the customer seated; or, if the store offers browsing opportunities, direct the customer accordingly.

Keeping Waiting Customers Contented While Waiting 301

4) Give waiting customers personal assurance that service will be forthcoming shortly.

5) Keep waiting customers occupied, visually and/or mentally, while waiting.

Some stores have a policy of waiting on two or more customers at the same time. This policy is arbitrary. While it provides dual service, it certainly diminishes the quality of the service. Though the old adage speaks of killing two birds with one stone, in the case of customer service it can sometimes mean killing two sales with one salesperson.

Studies show that most customers prefer the exclusive attention and service time of the salesperson, even if they have to wait for it—but *only* provided they are accorded the courteous treatment, as outlined here, while waiting.

The proper treatment of a waiting customer will not only prevent a walk and lead to a sale, but the good impression of the treatment will win the store the customer's repeat business and valuable word-of-mouth advertising.

61

Are You Really a Service Store?

Business is like a tennis game. The player who doesn't serve well is usually the loser.

A customer talks about good service—but she talks even more about bad service.

A few years ago a survey was taken among several hundred shoe retailers. The question: You say you're a service operation. What services do you offer?

Over half of the answers were limited to only one service: fitting. Another 30 percent listed up to three services. Only 12 percent could list more than five different store or customer services.

The majority of shoe stores and departments consider themselves service operation or even "full-service" stores. Yet many fail to make full use of the service concept, even though this is one of the strongest competitive weapons a store can have. Further, sales service, next to the merchandise itself, is the single highest operating cost, ranging between 10 percent and 13 percent of sales. Yet, perhaps the majority of stores fail to get full return on what it costs them.

Sales personnel have two primary functions: service and selling. They're separate, yet each is an important part of the other. Merely "waiting on customers" isn't enough. Every salesperson does that. The question that needs to be asked is: what is the quality and effectiveness of the services provided by the salespeople.

But services are by no means the sole responsibility of the salespeople. There are many additional services that are the responsibility of store management. So when examining the quantity, variety and quality of the store's services, the focus must be on the service performance of both management and the sales personnel.

What is service? It can be defined simply as a benefit, help or convenience for the customer. Whereas that cost is built into the price of the shoes, it's important that the customer feels that he or she is getting what they're paying for. Failure to deliver it in full quantity and quality is short-changing the customer. The store is also short-changing itself by not getting full return on the services it's paying for.

All right, what kind of services can you offer that will help create more customer satisfaction and repeat business, build sales and profits, and lower selling costs?

Here's a list of basic services you can develop:

Fitting. All service stores offer fitting service. Is yours just average, or is it different, superior and rememberable? How well trained is your sales personnel in fitting? If they're experts at this function, do you exploit their skills in your advertising or via other channels?

Fashion Counseling. Most customers need and want fashion guidance when buying footwear. Do you provide such a service, or do your salespeople simply use the tired phrase, "This is the newest fashion." Do you hold in-store fashion training meetings? Do the salespeople know the "fashion reason" behind each new shoe that comes into the store? Are they adept, via training, in using "the language of fashion" when selling? These are among the tools of fashion counseling that convert into an important customer service.

Product Information. This is one of the most neglected areas in shoe store customer service. Customers want to know what they're buying and what they're getting for what they're paying. The idea of "quality" has no meaning unless it's demonstrated and made visible. It's management's responsibility to train salespeople to provide this service. The more the customer is informed, the more he or she appreciates the value received.

Charge Accounts. If you have them, do all your customers known about this convenience service? It can often result in extra sales.

Credit Cards. Do you have signs posted around the store, in your windows or ads? Do you offer the most popular cards (for example, MasterCard and Visa alone account for almost a third of all credit card business)?

Dyeing and Coloring. If you provide this service, do you wait to be asked, or

do you give it wide exposure? If you're in the women's fashion business and don't provide this service, why not?

Wide Assortment.   A very positive customer service, but too many stores that provide it take it for granted. It's a very promotable service and should be exploited.

Showing a Variety.   It's one thing to have a broad selection, but quite another to show the customer more than what he or she asks for. Customers like additional choice and consider this a store service of trying to please customers.

Full Size-width Selection.   A very important customer service. If you have it, don't hide your light under a bushel. Promote it in your ads and windows. Relate proper size not only to comfort but good shoe performance, shape retention and other benefits.

Out-sizes.   There are many people searching for out-sizes and widths. For such customers it's a service that wins both their patronage and gratitude.

Hard-to-fit Feet.   Do you specialize in this, or at least provide some prescription shoe service? Don't keep it a secret between you and the local doctors. Stores that provide this service are often as much as a hard-to-find problem as the hard-to-fit feet in search of them.

Gift Wrapping.   Free or for a nominal charge—for Christmas, Mother's Day, Father's Day, birthdays, etc. It's appreciated and remembered. Promote it with your holiday ads.

Thank-you Notes.   A followup thank-you postcard or note to the customer after the purchase is a nice personalized touch and enhances the store's service image. The customer appreciates recognition that his or her business is appreciated—and remembers.

Gift Certificates.   Don't make them available just for the Christmas season. Gifts are given year round for many occasions, so make them available on a year-round basis. And very important: let your customers know about them.

Free Parking.   If you're in a hard-to-park location, this is a definite plus factor to bring customers in—provided you let them know such a service is available.

Repair Service.   Do you have facilities for major or minor repairs, and are such repairs for customers made on the spot? Do you have an arrangement with a local repair shop to handle such work as a convenience service for customers? Repair shops are dwindling in number, harder to find. Such a service is appreciated—and can also be a source of added income.

Customer Records.   This reflects genuine personalized customer service and an important factor in building repeat business—provided your customers know that their foot/shoe record is "on file."

Accessories.   Presenting accessories items as a followup to the shoe sale belongs in the service category. The suggestions are presented as customer benefits.

Shoe-care Counseling.   Do you sell and run—or do you give customers shoe-care guidance for their followup use? Advice about the use of cleaners and polishes, shoe trees, waterproofing, etc. The customer appreciates these suggestions—suggestions which also can result in accessories sales.

Advance Notices to Customers.   About upcoming clearance sales, or new merchandise just in, or a special closeout or PM in just their size. These can be even more effective when the mailers mention that these advance notices are limited to the store's "preferred customers" list.

THERE'S STILL MORE

There's more beyond the "basic" services listed in the foregoing. There are a number of simple extras or pluses that can further strengthen the service image. For example:

1) Don't put the soiled old shoes back onto the customer's foot after the purchase. Run them under a shine buffer for a few seconds, and presto! New, fresh-looking shoes.
2) Old shoes often have soiled sock linings. It takes only a few seconds to remove the old lining and insert a new one to make the shoe look and feel fresh again. If needed, also insert new laces in old shoes. Show the customer what you've done. And mention no charge involved.
3) Does the customer have an unwieldly number of small packages? Insert them in a convenient shopping bag with your store imprint on it.
4) For the kids, a free balloon, or a small crayon box or coloring book—with the store's imprint.
5) For waiting customers during busy periods—a fashion magazine for the women, a sports magazine for the men. This keeps them occupied and lets them know they're not being ignored.
6) Wherever possible, address the customer by name and avoid "sir" and "madam" (and *never* a woman as "lady"). The world's sweetest sound is a person's own name.

We won't mention the obvious elements of good service: courtesy, smiles, patience, quick and efficient service, etc. They should be automatic.

We've now listed some 26 different services your store can provide to make it a full-fledged service store. But quantity and variety isn't the whole story. To make the concept of customer service come alive with excitement, the quality of the services must have excellence. That's how a service reputation is built.

Finally, your services should be merchandised with the same aggressiveness as with the merchandise in your store. Promote them via your windows and advertising, plus counter cards. For example, a window poster citing such services as credit cards, or dyeing and coloring, minor repairs, gift certificates and gift wrapping, etc. Run an occasional ad citing some particular service offered by your store, such as fashion counseling, or a broad range of size-width selections. Or consider printing a simple leaflet or folder listing all of your services, with one-line descriptive comment beside each. Insert one in the package with each purchase, or use them as an additional insert when you do a promotional mailing.

Service is a highly salable commodity—yet, ironically, one of the least merchandised by shoe stores. Service doesn't mean giving a lot of extra time when making a sale. Every sale has an opening, middle and closing. Efficient service can actually make these three steps a smoother, faster process.

What are the values of providing a good quantity and quality of services—to the customers, to you and the store?

1) Helps build a strong service image for the store and salespeople.
2) Helps achieve the mission of all businesses: satisfied customers.
3) Ensures more repeat business and customer loyalty.
4) Develops more customer appreciation of value received.
5) Develops more customer confidence in the store and salespeople.
6) Makes your store a preferred place to shop and buy.
7) Strengthens competitive position against stores depending primarily on low or cut prices.

So when you or your salespeople greet the customers with, "May I be of service"—make sure you offer the services to live up to the greeting. If you're going to abide by the axiom that the customer is king, then make sure that your customers are treated like royalty.

THE COST OF SALES SERVICE

1) A store does an annual volume of $350,000.
2) Cost of sales personnel is 11 percent or $38,500.
3) Average sale is $35.
4) Average sales/service cost is $3.85 per sale.
5) A daily average of 33 buying customers for average daily total sales of $1,150.
6) Total sales/service cost of $127.
7) Average daily gross margin is 44 percent ($506), and average daily net is 6 percent ($69).
8) Thus the daily $127 sales/service cost is equal to 25 percent of the daily gross margin, or
9) The average daily sales/service cost ($127) is equal to the net profit on 60 pairs (60 prs. at $35 = $2,100; at 6 percent net = $126).

62

How to Take a Customer Survey

The only way the customer tells the
store and salesperson what she
thinks of them is through the cash
register.

Many store owners boast, "I know my customers. I know what they think and want." But that may be more bluster than fact.

Taking your customers' wants and needs for granted can be risky. That's why market testing and consumer surveys have become an important and valuable tool of modern business.

You, too, can do the same, and at very minimal cost. You'll learn a lot about your store—about your customers, your merchandise, your services, etc.—that may surprise you. And if you put the information to use you can upgrade the whole operation to your profit and growth.

How do you conduct a customer survey? The first step: What do you need or want to know from your customers? So you start by preparing a questionnaire.

The questionnaire should be brief and simple, yet contain all the essential questions you want answered. The accompanying questionnaire in this article can serve as a guide. It can be altered as you wish. All of it can fit on one side of a 4 × 6 stamped, self-addressed postcard for convenient return.

Make the questions short and concise to fit on one line. Present them for simple yes or no checkoff answers. The easier you make it for the customer, the better the response.

In the brief introduction you can offer a "free gift" for those who sign their name and address. You send them a store-imprinted shoe horn or a pair of laces. The gift followup gives you chance for another followup "thank you." The names can also supplement your mailing list.

If yours is a family store, have a place to check off Male or Female. These cards can later be separated to help you evaluate two categories of customer response. (You may find your store fares better with men than women, or vice versa).

You might now be saying, "Isn't it better and simpler to ask the customers while they're in the store?"

Definitely, no. It takes too much time that can't be afforded, especially during busy periods, and also may annoy customers in a hurry to leave. Further, most customers will be reluctant to give honest or negative replies when face-to-face with the store questioner.

The best way is to insert the questionnaire card into the package or carton with the purchase. Then *mention* that the card has been inserted and request that the customer fill it out and return it within the next few days. That saves time all around.

Allow the cards to accumulate for two to three months, then tabulate the replies. This will give you a clear, objective view of the customers' attitudes about your store, merchandise, services, etc. You are now faced with the realities from the other side of the fence.

Three months later do another tabulation with another sample group of customers. Usually they will pretty much confirm the findings from the first batch.

You now have a reasonably good cross-section of replies and a survey "report." What do you do with the information? You *act* upon it. Those replies are the equivalent of instructions from your customers.

Pay especial attention to the negatives. Any collective score averaging above 25 percent equates with a problem. If, for example, the replies on the quality of your services average 37 percent "no," that clearly signals a problem with your salespeople as well as the management.

If the score shows 32 percent dissatisfaction with your style selections, it indicates faults with the store's buying. If 35 percent question your prices and values, it calls for a serious reappraisal of your price brackets and lines.

Never question the customers' judgments in the replies. You may think some of them wrong or biased or uninformed, but the customer holds the gun—the power to buy or not buy from your store.

Pay particular attention to the volunteered comments. They can contain very helpful suggestions and direction. Don't just find them "interesting." Some will merit action on your part.

If your survey has uncovered one or more serious problems, and you have taken firm steps to correct the problem, consider sending out a small mailing piece to your customers.

For example, if there was a 32 percent negative response on your style selections, and you have changed and broadened your inventory, tell your customers about it—that you've added three new lines or brands, a new line of fashion casuals, more colors, more selections in styles and heel heights, etc.

Consider something else. Prepare a special 4 × 5 leaflet, the front page titled, "The Jones Shoe Store—Some Interesting Things You Should Know About Us." The other three pages briefly cite highlights about your store. For example:

- How long you've been in business at the present location.
- How well-trained your salespeople are, and the store's policy on courtesy and service.
- The brands you carry, plus all the footwear categories—men's, women's, children's, work and outdoor, athletic, slippers, boots, duty shoes, etc.
- Your inventory—the broad selection of sizes and widths, styles.
- The excellence of your fitting service.
- The credit cards you honor.
- List your types of accessories. Suggest them as ideal gifts for birthdays, holidays, etc.

How to Take a Customer Survey 309

• Your honest prices, excellent values, fair dealings, fair treatment on returns, etc.

The leaflet can be included in every package with each purchase. It can also be used as a mailing piece to customers and prospects.

But this is done *after* you've taken your survey, and *after* you've corrected any shortcomings revealed in the survey. The survey will keep you "honest" when you list all your store's attractive features in your leaflet.

Is it all worthwhile? Absolutely. Each year, American business and industry spends hundreds of millions of dollars on consumer surveys and the market testing of products. The prime objective: to learn what the customer thinks or about consumer attitudes. The findings determine the course to be taken.

That, essentially, is what your own customer survey is—the findings serving as a compass to steer your ship away from the rocks and onto a safe course toward successful operation.

SAMPLE CUSTOMER QUESTIONNAIRE

Your views and comments are important in helping us to serve you better. Please complete and mail this postage-paid card questionnaire. If you sign your name and address, we'll send you a small gift free. Thank you for your cooperation.

1) Was the service prompt and courteous? ☐ Yes ☐ No
2) Was the fitting service efficient? ☐ Yes ☐ No
3) Was the general service satisfactory? ☐ Yes ☐ No
4) Were you satisfied with our selection of styles? ☐ Yes ☐ No
5) Did we have the size you needed? ☐ Yes ☐ No
6) Were you satisfied with the price and value? ☐ Yes ☐ No
7) Was the quality of our merchandise satisfactory? ☐ Yes ☐ No
8) Do you find our location convenient? ☐ Yes ☐ No
9) Would you recommend our store to others? ☐ Yes ☐ No
10) Do you find our store and merchandise reliable? ☐ Yes ☐ No

I am ☐ Male ☐ Female. Your first visit to our store? ☐ Yes ☐ No

Additional comments are appreciated _____

_____

Name _____ Address _____

_____

Note: Postage-paid postcard is included with the wrapup package, which saves initial mailing cost. Survey card does two important things: (1) provides helpful feedback information; (2) serves as excellent customer relations first by thanking the customer for making the purchase, and also by showing that the store is interested in the customer's view of value and service received.

THE BETTER MOUSE TRAP THAT FAILED

The maker of the little wooden snap trap, successful since 1848, decided to improve the product. So the company made an in-depth study of mice—their sleeping, feeding, mating and other living habits. Having learned everything they could about mice, they then built a space-age mousetrap, a fancy plastic device like a tiny bathtub into which the mouse would be lured to meet his doom. In effect, the mouse packaged himself in plastic and suffocated.

It was a dismal flop. Before, the housewives—those who usually had to contend with the dead mouse, usually before breakfast—thought nothing of throwing away the ten-cent trap, mouse and all. But the new $5 trap, even though more efficient, was a different story. The housewives didn't like the idea of extracting the dead mouse, then cleaning the trap for reuse.

The company overlooked one marketing reality. It should have spent less time researching mice and more time researching customers.

Vendor
Relations

63

Improving Buyer/Vendor Relations

Cooperation resolves most problems. Freckles would make a nice coat of tan if only they could get together.

If you don't believe in cooperation, consider what happens to the wagon when one wheel comes off.

You're hopelessly lost driving in a foreign country. You stop and ask a stranger for directions. He listens, shrugs, throws up his hands. You keep trying. He keeps shrugging and shaking his head. You think he's stupid, he thinks you're mad.

The result: mutual frustration. The cause: communications failure.

It happens every day in shoe business between buyers and vendors. But the irony here is that both speak the same language, are in the same business, have mutual problems.

Nevertheless, they experience frustrations due to communications failure. And each thinks the other unfair, unreasonable.

So common did these problems become that some 20 years ago the National Shoe Manufacturers Association (now FIA) and the National Shoe Retailers Association established a Vendor/Buyer Committee. Like most good intentions, nothing ever came of it. The same problems prevail today.

Is there any hope for solutions to these perennial problems between buyer and vendor. We're not sure. But airing them out might help alleviate some of them. Let's take a look at some of the findings of our modest survey of retailers and vendors.

RETAILERS' COMMON GRIPES

Here are the most common complaints we've found among retailers:

Deliveries. The Number One complaint. Late deliveries, incomplete deliveries, substitution of sizes or styles. Seldom with advance notice on the delivery situation; a simple communications failure.

One retailer told us, "The vendors spend money to advertise, promote and sell their shoes, then foul up deliveries. It's waste for them, expense and lost sales for us. It's just dumb business."

An independent retailer told us, "The resource said there were production delays on a hot-seller we ordered. But two weeks later a big store in a nearby shopping center was running a heavy promotion on the shoe. That's deception. We cancelled the order and the resource, as well."

Returns.   In most instances vendors are reasonably liberal about credit on returns. Still, in many instances retailers have a hassle getting a credit.

"What irks me," said one merchant, "is the many firms that have no guidelines or policy on returns. It becomes a matter of the vender's day-to-day judgment. If they're confused, why make us the victims?"

Credits.   Failure to be credited on returns, cancellations or changed orders is another gripe. Often enough to make retailers careful in examining billings or invoices "to keep 'em honest." It's rarely dishonesty. But paperwork mistakes in the credit department or elsewhere aren't unusual.

Quality Control.   "We occasionally get shipments with some shoes having nicks or scratches, or mismatched colors, an open seam, and so on," complained a midwestern retailer. "This costs us in time and money to examine every pair, or the hassle of returns and credits. We're seeing a definite decline in quality control. Maybe the flood of imports has something to do with it."

Freight Charges.   Sometimes it's a case of overcharge, but mostly it's a careless use of shipping routes by some vendors. We were told by several retailers, "These overcharges can add up to hundreds of dollars a year, unnecessarily. The shipping department is slipshod—doesn't make the effort to ship the fastest and least expensive way."

Canceled Stock Numbers.   The failure of many vendors to notify stores about canceled stock numbers. Says one buyer, "I prepared a promotion on two shoes that were moving well with us, only to learn the vendor had closed them out a month earlier. It cost us in time and expense."

Out-sizes.   Added charges (50 cents to $2 a pair) for women's sizes 10½ and over, or EE widths, for example, is a common irritant. Griped one merchant, "When will the manufacturers learn that feet are getting bigger, or ethnics with unusual sizes are in the market? Many of yesterday's out-sizes are in-sizes today and shouldn't be premium-priced."

Closeouts.   Smaller retailers complain about "favoritism" on venders' closeouts. "The bigger accounts get first shot, we get the leftovers, if any. That's discrimination."

Mats and Aids.   This is an old story—mediocre quality of ad mats and many of the dealer aids. "With most vendors," said one New England store, "this is an area that sorely needs upgrading. Much of it is waste for them and us."

Poor Communications.   Letters that don't get answered, phone calls not returned, requests ignored. Also, no initiative by the vendor "to just call us once in a while to say hello or thanks. We need to be stroked occasionally."

Pressure for Early Orders.   This appears to be increasing. One store echoed the view of many: "We're trying to buy closer to season while the vendors are pressuring us to buy ridiculously ahead. We're moving in opposite directions. The question is: who's giving who the business?"

Lack of Vendor Guidance. Many retailers cite this. Said one, "Years ago many manufacturers had fashion coordinators who issued fashion trend reports, and sales managers who issued 'what's selling' bulletins. Today we rarely see either."

MANUFACTURERS' GRIPES

Abuse of Co-op Advertising. This has always been common, especially with large accounts who, say the vendors, use their buying leverage to take advantage with such abuses.

Abuse of Returns. "We don't mind closing our eyes occasionally to an unjustified abuse on returns," said one producer. "But we keep a lookout for habitual offenders. They scream the loudest when we say no."

Unjustified Cancellations. The retailers who overbuy, or think they've made a wrong buy, then want to cancel after they've received the merchandise. Worse still, they make unjustified complaints, like saying the shoes are poor fitters.

Slow Pay. Every vendor has his share of habitual slow payers, always in arrears. There's the story of the manufacturer who sent one such retailer a wire. "After checking our records we note we've done more for you than your mother. We've been carrying you for 20 months."

In another instance a manufacturer wired a retailer who had placed a large order, "Cannot ship until you pay for last consignment." The retailer wired back, "Cannot wait that long. Cancel the order."

In-stock Bankers. In-stock firms resent being used as "interest-free bankers" by retailers who habitually buy in small-pair lots while the manufacturer carries the cost of the inventory load. They say that's abuse of services.

Exaggerated Expectations. Retailers who buy very little from the vendor and then complain about low-priority treatment. Should they be given the same service priorities as major customers? Most manufacturers think not.

Lack of Feedback Information. "The retailers want market and trend information from us, but they feed back little or no information to help us," complains one resource, echoing others. "This should be an information sharing business, a two-way street."

Concessions. Many major retail accounts expect exaggerated concessions like post-dating on invoices, extras on coop advertising, priority choice on closeouts, discounted prices, purchase discounts beyond date limitations.

Late Buying. This is becoming increasingly common. But the problem is last-minute buying and expectation of early delivery. "You can't enter late and expect the best seat in the house," remarked one vendor.

Failure to Attend Shoe Shows. Both national and regional shows are reporting declining buyer attendance, or shorter stays by buyers, or visits that conclude with "see me back at the store." Producers complain about the heavy expense of such shows, with diminishing returns for their efforts.

WHAT CAN BE DONE?

Those are the team lineups for the shoe business Superbowl game, Buyers versus Vendors. The gripes are pretty equal so the game usually ends up in a tie. What can each team do to minimize the complaints of the other?

The relationship between buyer and vendor must be one of collaboration, not confrontation. They are natural partners, not adversaries. Neither can survive nor prosper without the other.

Communications breakdowns are the root of many of the problems. One retailer offers an intriguing suggestion:

"Suppose the company sales manager or even the president makes just four personal phone calls a day to customers—a total of about 20 minutes a day. That's 100 calls a month, 1,200 a year. If two company executives do it, that's 2,400 personal calls. Friendly-talk, Keep-in-touch calls. The retailers are flattered, feeling the vendor cares. And the vendors get enormous feedback information about trends, market conditions, retailers moods and problems, etc. Now *that's* communication."

Delivery problems are perennial but not incurable. Some vendors have excellent records on deliveries (below 2 percent), others deplorable (above 3 percent). Delivery problems are factory management problems. Retailers who put up with it contribute to the problem. The same applies to shortcomings on quality control.

Vendors can also upgrade their mat and dealer aid services. Retailers are rarely surveyed to learn their wants and needs.

Vendors should take a second look at premium charges for what they've too long called "out-sizes." As one retailer friend said, many of those sizes today are more in than out.

There appears to be much need and want for fashion and market guidance services once so common. Revival of this can improve communications.

Retailers also have some clean-up work to do, though the cures for some ills are yet to be found—like abuses on co-op advertising, returns and cancellations, or poor credit. These are ills of human nature.

But retailers can help remedy other problems. For example, providing more sales and trend feedback to resources. One retailer sends copies of his weekly "what's selling" (and what isn't) computer data sheets to each of his vendors. As a result, he's prized by each vendor and is on the "priority treatment" list of each. The old story of one hand washing the other.

Retailers should face the reality that if you buy little from a vendor you can't expect to receive "equal" treatment with the larger accounts. You can't feed like a pigeon and roar like a lion.

When should a retailer sever relations with a vendor? When the faults become major, habitual and intolerable, regardless of what "stake" they've built up in the brand or line.

The vendor's primary obligations are sound value and excellence of service. The retailer's primary obligation is to meet his ethical and contractual commitments to the vendor.

The problems of buyer/vendor relations are age-old and probably started when Eve sold the apple to Adam. The buyer/vendor connection isn't a love relationship in that one is expected to be blind to the faults of the other. It's a hard-nosed contract with mutual obligations for mutual benefits. It's rarely perfect, but realistically workable if the obligations are met.

COOPERATION

If two goats meet each other on a very narrow hanging bridge high above a torrential river, what do they do? They can't turn back, and they can't pass each other, for the path hasn't an inch of spare room. They know that if they get into a butting match, both will tumble into the raging water below and drown. What do they do?

In silent mutual agreement, one goat lies down so that the other can gently step over its body. As a result, each goat arrives at its destination safe and sound.

How come this common sense works with goats but not with people?

64

Profiting from Vendor Support Systems

The door of opportunity is opened by pushing.

Some people expect the door of opportunity to be opened with an electric eye.

Many vendors offer or provide a variety of dealer-help materials, some free, some at modest cost. Unfortunately, the majority of retailers fail to take advantage or make use of them, to their own loss in knowledge, skills, sales and profits.

Let's take a closer look at some of these dealer support systems and the opportunities they offer for alert retailers.

Cooperative Advertising. Shoe retailers spend an estimated $700 million a year on advertising. While many manufacturers and other resources provide a cooperative ad program, only about 25 percent of retailers make use of it, even though it can cut their ad costs by as much as half or more.

If a store does a $350,000 volume and spends 3 percent for advertising, the ad budget amounts to $10,500. If co-op advertising contributes $5,000, the retailer is either saving $5,000 or can increase his ad budget by a third to $15,500 without additional cost to himself.

True, all co-op ad programs, such as some of the ad mats, don't meet the wants or needs of many retailers. But many do or can, yet continue to be bypassed. Ironically, it's the larger or more successful retailers who make the most consistent use of co-op advertising. It accomplishes two things: it substantially reduces the retailer's ad costs, and it allows him to increase his ad budget for greater promotional impact without adding to his normal ad budget.

Ask *all* your resources about their co-op ad program, and to send you all co-op ad material such as ad mats. You can then select the best for your needs. Most important: make more use of co-op advertising.

Point-of-purchase Materials. Vendors make heavy investments in point-of-purchase materials, some of which are free, others at modest cost. These include items like window and counter cards, price tickets, display fixtures, electric signs, turntables, etc. All are designed to move merchandise.

If you invest in the merchandise of the resource, it makes sense to utilize point-of-purchase and other aids that help move the merchandise. Ask each of your vendor sales reps to show and explain *everything* available in point-of-purchase materials (many don't show or explain unless asked).

Fashion Information. Some resources prepare and issue periodic advance fashion reports. Ask your resources (or sales reps) if they issue such reports, and request to be placed on the mailing list. Do the same with resources you *don't* buy from. They'll be glad to place you on the list as a customer prospect. The combination of these fashion reports can be helpful guidance for your buying plans and also as trend indicators.

Catalogs. You receive seasonal catalogs from your own vendors. But ask to be placed on the mailing list of selected vendors you *don't* buy from. This provides you with a broader view of trends, plus aiding your own buying plans. Most vendors will respond to such requests. The catalogs also frequently offer a selection of point-of-purchase and promotional materials.

Informational Literature. Some vendors prepare and provide educational and dealer-help materials. These may deal with topics like foot health, infants' or children's shoes, athletic shoes, work boots, etc. They differ from catalogs and are designed as instructional brochures. They're excellent for in-store training use for sales personnel by upgrading knowledge and skills.

Notices of such literature usually appear in the trade press, or you can sometimes learn it from other sources. No matter the source or vendor, write for a copy. There's an abundance of such literature available, most of it free.

Special Promotions. Many vendors, especially brand houses, occasionally run large-scale national promotions dealing with a new line, or new groups of styles. They prepare elaborate national ad campaigns, sometimes involving consumer contests or sweepstakes with big prizes. They try to get as many of their dealers as possible to participate with backup local advertising, window cards and banners, and other materials linked to the promotion.

But only a minority of dealers usually participate, missing out on a free promotional ride and potential extra sales and new customers. Alert retailers get involved with these traffic and sales builders, and so should you.

Sometimes a store will create its own special promotion woven around one or several brands. If that happens, the store should ask the vendors to share in the cost proportionately, which most will do.

Store Operation Helps. Some vendors have special departments to provide a variety of store operation aids ranging from inventory control, advertising and merchandising to displays and store remodeling. Other vendors, while not having such departments, will offer some help here on a selective basis. Ask your vendor sales reps if their companies can provide such services—or what dealer-help services they will provide.

Giveaways. Giveaway or premium items are provided by some vendors. Items like ballpoint pens, balloons or comic books for kids, emery boards for women, shoe horns, shoe bags, etc. Some are used as free giveaways to retailers' customers, others as free premiums such as with a multiple-pair purchase, and still others for special promotions. These are usually purchased from the vendor at nominal cost. Ask your sales reps for a list or samples of all such items available from their companies.

Suppliers. Some of the major suppliers to shoe manufacturers sometimes prepare and issue some excellent educational materials available to retailers who write for them. For example, Sterling Last Corporation has two outstanding educational brochures: *The True Story of Shoe Sizes,* and *Historical Highlights of American Lastmaking and American Shoemaking.* The Poron Division of Rogers Corporation has a splendid brochure: *Shoe and Foot Comfort—the Facts Versus the Myths,* plus a special market report on *Walking and Walking Shoes.* All are free for the writing.

Some tanners, suppliers of soles and heels, linings, man-made shoe materials and other components occasionally prepare special information brochures that contain much educational material of value to retailers. They are ideal for in-store sales or training meetings. Notices of these appear in the trade press, and most are free on request.

Vendors of handbags and hose, especially the manufacturers, prepare occasional educational or promotional materials available for the asking. Some of the shoe polish firms issue informational leaflets or booklets on shoe care, for shoe care counseling of the retailers' customers.

Swatches.   Tanners and suppliers of man-made materials prepare seasonal swatch cards or pads showing the new colors and textures. Some are free on request or are available at modest cost. These are ideal for advance guidance on shoe buying and also for in-store sales meetings.

Trade Shows.   Most retailers think they "shop a show." But most miss a lot more than they see. *Every* booth or room should be visited to see what's being offered in dealer-help materials or promotional literature. Carry a shopping bag and pick up all the free literature you can. Take it home and study it. It will prove an enlightening and profitable venture.

This applies to more than just shoe shows. It also includes the supplier shows exhibiting leathers and other materials, shoe components, services, etc. Check their dates and locations in the trade press show calendars. If the locations are reasonably close (say 100 miles), a visit will prove worthwhile. Most exhibitors offer free literature on new products, or educational materials. Some of this can give you advance information and a competitive advantage. Few retailers take advantage of these shows.

Trade Associations.   While these are not vendors they sometimes provide similar dealer-help literature or materials. The National Shoe Retailers Association has an extensive list of publications, plus dealer-aid items, available at nominal cost. The National Retail Workshops provides sales training video cassettes for shoe retailers.

The New England Tanners Club has an excellent educational booklet, *Leather Facts.* Leather Industries of America, as well as the Sole Leather Council and the Pigskin Council of America also have educational materials available on these specialty leathers. The Footwear Industries of America has booklets on shoe constructions and shoemaking. A short letter of inquiry will bring you a list of available literature and their cost, usually small.

In-store Sales Meetings.   Many stores either conduct regular in-store sales or training meetings, or want to. Their perennial and common problem: where do we get the instructional materials, or samples or props, or where do we find the qualified instructors?

As to the educational materials, we've already cited a variety of prospective sources and types. But what about the "experts" on given products or topics to conduct a training session? These, too, are often available, usually without cost, or in some instances only for travel expenses.

Start with your sales reps. The experienced and articulate ones can serve well as experts on their given category, and without commercial plugs for their own products. For example, a sales rep for a casual shoe line can talk informatively about fashion trends in casual footwear, while another rep for a men's dress shoe line can do the same for men's style trends.

If your in-store topic is on something more technical—for instance, how a shoe is made—one of your resources will gladly send a technician to conduct the meeting with props and samples, and usually at no cost. The same applies to a tanner for a session on leathers, or a producer of manmade materials, or linings or cushion insoles or other components—especially if the company is within reasonable distance of your store (say 100–150 miles). And at no charge.

You may be familiar with the fable of the two mules who starved to death while standing near a bale of hay. They starved because neither would move. Same thing with many retailers who remain inert and do nothing about the abundance of dealer-help materials or literature all around them from vendors and other sources eager to help, if only asked.

The trade press frequently carries notices of new educational or dealer-help materials, some free, some at modest cost. Follow up by writing for them. And remember, you don't have to be a customer of the vendor to receive such materials.

Inquire of your vendor sales reps what promotional or dealer-help materials their companies have to offer. Ask to see everything.

The average shoe retailer actually sees less than one percent of the promotional and educational material available relative to his business—much of it free for the asking. The majority of these materials can help in some way to improve traffic, sales, knowledge and skills, operations and profits.

There's a gold mine right under your feet. Start digging.

SECOND TIME IS BETTER

A shoe retailer received a "Second Notice" billing from one of his manufacturer resources. This bothered the retailer who was always prompt about paying his bills to maintain a good credit standing.

He immediately sent a check to the manufacturer, and also called the company president to explain, "I would have paid sooner," said the retailer, "but I never received your first invoice."

Said the manufacturer, "Yes, I know. It's a new company policy. We stopped sending out first invoices. We've found that second notices get much faster response."